Sam Richards's CIVIL WAR DIARY

Sam Richards's CIVIL WAR DIARY

A Chronicle of the Atlanta Home Front

Edited by WENDY HAMAND VENET

The University of Georgia Press
Athens and London

Paperback edition, 2025
Publication of this book was supported
in part by the Kenneth Coleman Series in Georgia History and Culture.

© 2009 by the University of Georgia Press
Athens, Georgia 30602
www.ugapress.org
All rights reserved
Set in Sabon by Graphic Composition, Inc.

Most University of Georgia Press titles are
available from popular e-book vendors.

Printed digitally

Library of Congress Cataloging-in-Publication Data

Richards, Samuel P.
  Sam Richards's Civil War diary : a chronicle of
the Atlanta home front / edited by Wendy Hamand
Venet.
       p. cm.
  Includes bibliographical references and index.
  ISBN-13: 978-0-8203-2999-4 (cloth : alk. paper)
  ISBN-10: 0-8203-2999-1 (cloth : alk. paper)
  1. Richards, Samuel P.—Diaries. 2. Merchants—
Georgia—Atlanta—Diaries. 3. Atlanta (Ga.)—Social
life and customs—19th century. 4. Atlanta (Ga.)—
Social conditions—19th century. 5. Georgia—
History—Civil War, 1861–1865—Social aspects.
6. United States—History—Civil War, 1861–1865—
Social aspects. 7. Merchants—Georgia—Atlanta—
Biography. I. Venet, Wendy Hamand. II. Title.
  F294.A853R53 2009
  975.8'23103092—dc22
                                    2008052959

British Library Cataloging-in-Publication
Data available

In memory of my father,
Lavern M. Hamand

Contents

Acknowledgments · ix
Editorial Policy · xi
List of Abbreviations · xiii
Introduction · 1

ONE · October 1860 to September 1861 · *29*

TWO · October 1861 to April 1862 · *70*

THREE · May 1862 to December 1862 · *104*

FOUR · January 1863 to June 1863 · *153*

FIVE · July 1863 to December 1863 · *183*

SIX · January 1864 to October 1864 · *209*

SEVEN · November 1864 to August 1865 · *244*

Afterword · 293
Appendix: Richards/Van Valkenburg Family Tree · 299
Index · 301

Acknowledgments

Many people have assisted me in editing the Richards diary. The staff of the Atlanta History Center supported this project from the beginning. My sincere thanks go to Mike Brubaker, who helped me countless times in the reading room, and to Paul Crater, Gordon Jones, Betsy Rix, Michael Rose, and Sue VerHoef. John Roma, librarian at Second–Ponce de Leon Baptist Church, shared with me archived materials relating to Sam Richards's Baptist congregation. At the Washington Memorial Library in Macon, Georgia, Christopher Stokes provided assistance in locating sources and in helping me to understand prewar and wartime Macon. Carl Van Valkenburg and Chase Van Valkenburg Jr., descendants of Sallie Richards's older brother, shared information about their family. The Cannonball House Museum in Macon allowed me to see a portrait of Lieutenant Colonel James Dunbar Van Valkenburg. Thomas Dyer and Bruce Eelman read the manuscript for the University of Georgia Press, sharing with me the benefits of their expertise. Derek Krissoff has been a patient and understanding editor, Ellen Goldlust-Gingrich has been a skilled and meticulous copyeditor, and Jon Davies shepherded this manuscript through the production process with great care. I also thank my husband and sons, who are always willing to pitch in when I need them to help. I know that I can always count on them. I dedicate this book to the memory of my father, Lavern M. Hamand, whose love for the study of history inspired my lifelong interest in this field.

Editorial Policy

Chapter 1 focuses on the period in which Richards lived in Macon. In this chapter, I have omitted sections of mundane text, signified by dates without text and by ellipses within entries. Chapter 2 begins with the Richards family's move to Atlanta in October 1861; from this point forward, the diary is presented in its entirety. For the most part, I have left Sam's writing as it appears in the diary, although I have occasionally added bracketed material for purposes of clarity. I have regularized quotation marks and moved terminal punctuation to precede closing quotation marks. I have used brackets to indicate the complete date of each entry. Whenever possible, I have added footnotes to identify people and events, relying on both contemporary accounts and scholarly interpretations. Each chapter begins with an introduction framing the material in that chapter and suggesting its major themes. A brief afterword follows the Richards family's life after the Civil War and characterizes the postwar diary.

Abbreviations

The following abbreviations are used in the notes.

ADI	*Atlanta Daily Intelligencer*
AHC	Atlanta History Center, Atlanta
ASC	*Atlanta Southern Confederacy*
JJR	Jabez Judson Richards
MT	*Macon Telegraph*
NYT	*New York Times*
SPR	Samuel Pearce Richards
SPR diary	Diary of Samuel Pearce Richards, Atlanta History Center, Atlanta
SVVR	Sarah Van Valkenburg Richards
SVVR diary	Diary of Sarah Van Valkenburg Richards, Atlanta History Center, Atlanta

Sam Richards's CIVIL WAR DIARY

Introduction

Samuel Pearce Richards liked to write. In 1842 at age eighteen, he started keeping a diary. Week after week, month after month, year after year, for a total of sixty-seven years, he wrote about what he observed, what he read, and how he felt. He wrote in a neat hand in small clothbound volumes, fifteen in all. There is no indication that Sam Richards ever intended his diary to become public. He regarded his older brothers, Will and Addison, as the writers of the family. They, along with their wives and one of the Richards sisters, wrote and published stories, novels, poetry, reviews, and even song lyrics. Sam wrote for himself. He began the first volume of his diary by suggesting that the "keeping of a journal will prove a source of pleasure, and of improvement, [and] will afford gratification in after days, to recall the incidents and scenes, through which it shall be my lot to pass, and which would otherwise be forgotten." Following his death in 1910, the S. P. Richards Company first loaned and then donated the diary to the Atlanta History Center. The collection also includes a small number of letters, newspaper clippings, and personal papers, along with a family Bible and the diary that Sam's wife, Sarah Van Valkenburg Richards, kept in the 1850s.[1]

I have chosen to edit and publish Sam Richards's account of the Civil War years. During that time, Richards and his brother, Jabez Judson Richards, co-owned and operated a bookstore in the central business district of Atlanta, the second-most-important city in the Confederacy during the latter half of the Civil War. Sam's diary represents the best surviving individual chronicle of wartime Atlanta. The portion excerpted here begins in October 1860, shortly before Abraham Lincoln's election to the U.S. presidency, when Richards, his wife, and their children resided in Macon, Georgia. It carries the Richards family to Atlanta through the war years and into their period of forced exile in New York after William T. Sherman ordered the evacuation of Confederate civilians from Atlanta. It ends with their return to Atlanta in August 1865.

Sam Richards never thought of himself as a talented writer, and, indeed, his sentences are sometimes long and his spelling and grammar are inconsistent, but he was a very good diarist. He was intelligent and well read, and he was an astute observer of the world around him. Many qualities make this diary special. The first is its completeness. Richards did not write on a daily basis but nevertheless wrote regularly. A second feature is the range of topics about which Richards wrote, beginning with why he supported Southern independence. A staunch Unionist during the tumultuous 1850s, he became a fierce proponent of Confederate nationalism during the following decade while doing everything in his power to avoid military service. Unlike fiction's Rhett Butler or Richards's middle-aged brother-in-law in South Georgia, Richards steadfastly refused to aid the Confederacy militarily even in its most critical hour. His diary traces the evolution of Confederate conscription policy and represents one of the most candid and detailed accounts by a Confederate draft dodger.

Richards's diary offers a variety of insights into the era's business dealings. A middle-class merchant who was not part of the city's elite, he found himself in the midst of Atlanta's economic boom. He rode the crest of wartime prosperity, making immense profits and investing in city lots, country acreage, and slaves. Like many Confederate civilians, he applauded the Richmond government's efforts to promote independence until those decisions impinged on his personal sense of freedom. In addition to the draft, he decried taxes and impressment of goods and animals needed by the army.

His diary tells us much about wartime city life, which included theatricals, military benefit concerts, and civic celebrations on the one hand and military setbacks, crowded hospitals, and apprehension about the spread of infectious diseases on the other. His writing traces the spiraling effects of inflation and the accompanying soaring costs, food shortages, and poverty for some of the city's disadvantaged residents. As one of the small number of residents who refused to evacuate as the Union Army drew near in the summer of 1864, Richards chronicled life in a city under siege. Expelled by General Sherman's army after Atlanta's fall, he was forced to abandon his home and business.

S. P. Richards was a deeply religious man whose diary reveals a wealth of insights into wartime spiritual practices. A member of Atlanta's Second Baptist Church, Richards dutifully recorded the topics of sermons he heard there and days of fasting and prayer that he and others observed. Showing a robust ecumenical spirit, he attended services at a host of other Protestant churches in Atlanta and New York while a refugee there, although his ecumenicalism did not extend to Roman Catholicism. Richards often speculated about the religious meaning of the war and its significance for the region's white and black people. As a stalwart of his church choir, Richards wrote about the importance of music to his and others' lives.

The Richards diary also offers a window onto race relations in the wartime South. A prewar renter of domestic slaves, he became the proud owner of several bondspeople during the war. Because his diary was intended for his own edification and never made public during his lifetime, he spoke with a level of candor—and racism—that modern readers might find startling. Mary Gay, who lived in nearby Decatur, Georgia, and published a wartime memoir in 1897, spoke of slavery's benign qualities and her pride in her allegedly loyal slaves, whom she called "Ebony Confederates." Richards's diary presents a very different picture. He wrote of white people's unease about slavery's future and acts of "impudence" by bondspeople emboldened by wartime upheaval and advancing Union armies. He recorded instances when he whipped slaves and felt himself victimized by a system that he believed should have produced compliant and grateful servants but clearly did not do so. When Sherman's men entered Atlanta in September 1864, Richards noted the obvious: his slave property "vanished into air."[2]

Perhaps more than anything else, this diary offers glimpses into family life in nineteenth-century America. Following a rocky courtship, Sam Richards became the happily married father of ten children. His devotion to them is apparent in the many small acts of kindness recorded in the diary. In the midst of a particularly stressful time, he gave his wife a birthday gift of a framed picture depicting English life in olden times—a loving husband's effort to cheer up his wife in the midst of wartime strain. But if the diary reveals a close-knit family, it also presents the portrait of a family facing intense pressures, of a wife who reared children while volunteering at a local hospital, of two parents who feared for their children's health and buried one of them, of a couple who saw siblings wounded and killed in Confederate service. Finally, Richards tells us about an extended family divided in wartime: two of his brothers resided in the North, and one of them was an outspoken Unionist whose public comments appalled Sam. The process of wartime division and reconciliation thus plays out in the diary's pages.[3]

Sam Richards came from a family of writers, clergymen, and artists. He was born in England in 1824, the fourth of eight children born to Baptist minister William Richards and his wife, Ann. The two eldest children, William Carey and Thomas Addison, were born in London in 1818 and

1820, respectively. The family subsequently moved to the Oxfordshire village of Hook Norton, where Ann Richards tended to the needs of her growing family and her husband earned a "meager salary" by preaching the gospel and teaching at a boys' boarding school. Ann gave birth to Jabez Judson in 1821 and to Samuel Pearce three years later. Three daughters followed: Katherine Ann in 1826, Ellen Jane (Nell) in 1829, and Amelia S. (Amie or Mollie) in 1831. Hoping for brighter prospects in a nation where the Baptist denomination was gaining in popularity, the family departed for America in 1831 on a three-masted sailing ship bound from Liverpool to New York. One last son, Henry, was born in 1833 after the family's arrival in America.[4]

William Richards's new life in America combined preaching with efforts to achieve business success. For three years, he served as minister to a Baptist congregation in Hudson, New York, before leaving the ministry to move to Baltimore as an agent of the Brattleboro Typographic Association, a business that printed religious books. He also served as the unpaid preacher to the Calvert Street Baptist Church. The family did not remain in Baltimore for long before William decided to try his luck in Georgia, where the South's larger population of Baptists would afford him more opportunities. After being appointed general agent responsible for selling the six-volume "Comprehensive Commentary" in Georgia, he moved the family first to Forsyth and a year later to Penfield.[5]

In 1833, Georgia Baptists created Mercer Institute (which later became Mercer University), a manual labor school located in Penfield and designed in part to train young men for the ministry. This institution and an affiliated female seminary enrolled one hundred students, and the town, carved out of central Georgia's Greene County on land donated by a religious benefactor, grew to become a community of five hundred inhabitants that boasted two newspapers and a variety of boardinghouses and shops. In the 1830s, Penfield seemed like a town with a bright future, a center for Baptist religious and cultural life. William and Ann Richards built a house, and along with two of their children, Sam and Kate, became charter members of Penfield Baptist Church, formed in 1839.[6]

The Baptist church was the spiritual, intellectual, and social center of the Richards family's world. Family members attended church at least once and often twice on Sundays, and their friends were congregation members. By the time they moved to the South, the Baptist church had been a growing presence in the region for more than one hundred years. By the 1830s, the denomination's numbers were exploding, fueled by rapid settlement of the region and the revivals that swept the South during the Second Great Awakening. Pro-mission Baptists such as the Richards family believed in a benevolent and just God, Jesus's death as atonement for the sins of humanity, and eternal rewards for all those who were devoted to Christ and who opened their hearts and minds to God's love. Members of this branch of the Baptist denomination were at odds with those known as "anti-mission" Baptists, also called Hard Shell or Primitive Baptists, who were Calvinists of the old school. William Richards proclaimed his pro-mission views by naming several of his sons, including Sam, after famous missionaries.[7]

With a large family to support, William Richards tried his hand at a variety of pursuits. He spent a year as principal of Mercer's female seminary, and he served as Penfield's postmaster for several years. He raised crops. He also remained active in Baptist affairs, traveling frequently to attend meetings and preaching when asked to fill in for a vacationing or ailing colleague. Although Richards provided at least a minimal level of private schooling for his sons and daughters, money was always tight. At age twenty-one, Sam decried his family's economic travails by confiding to his diary, "Oh! this *poverty*! What a deal of trouble and vexation it gives."[8]

The Richards children were bright, creative, and ambitious. A biographical sketch of Kate Richards DuBose written in 1860 characterized them as "remarkable for aesthetic proclivities."[9] Although Kate became a short-story writer and poet of some note, the eldest, Will, was considered the family's brightest star. He was the only one to graduate from college, receiving a degree from Hamilton College in 1840.[10] Will Richards's professional ambitions were far-reaching: he tried his hand at public speaking, teaching, writing, editing, and eventually preaching.

Sam greatly admired his oldest brother, whose talents far exceeded Sam's. As a teenager, Sam accompanied Will on lecture tours of the South designed to "enlighten the villagers" on a variety of scientific topics, including astronomy, chemistry, and pneumatics. Sam sold tickets at fifty cents each, set up the experiments, and sometimes performed them. One of Will's most popular lectures focused on electromagnetism. In Pendleton, South Carolina, in September 1842, the brothers demonstrated a magnet's ability to lift up to fifty pounds, and Sam noted proudly in his diary that "the house was full, and every thing went off *well*." In Apalachicola, Florida, in April 1845, Sam delighted an audience by breathing hydrogen and counting to forty. Another of their lecture trips, this one in 1843, took Sam through Marthasville, Georgia, "a small new village at the terminus of the 'Western Atlanta R Road.'"[11] Renamed Atlanta in later years, it became Sam's home in 1861.

Sam enjoyed working with his brother and presumably shared in the proceeds. In addition to opportunities for travel, their lectures brought him the attention of female audience members, some of whom presented the brothers with bouquets of flowers. In his diary, he often commented on the appearance of the women they met—some were "*pretty*," others merely "*passable.*"[12]

William Carey Richards also had literary ambitions and a passion to bring his own cultural values to a region that lacked urban centers and an adequate number of schools. In 1842 he published *Georgia Illustrated*, a book that he hoped would instill in residents of the state an appreciation for their "natural scenery and public edifices." "The scenery of Georgia is not less beautiful and attractive than that of other sections of the Union," Richards wrote. Chapters focused on the history of Pulaski Monument in Savannah; the Medical College of Georgia in Augusta; the city of Columbus; and Tallulah Falls, including an illustration by Thomas Addison "Add" Richards. A talented artist and illustrator, Addison also worked with Will on his next project, a literary magazine that Will hoped would rival those of New York, Boston, and Philadelphia.[13]

Will named his publication *Orion* after the brightest constellation in the Southern Hemisphere. Richards sought to woo readers who patronized Northern literary magazines such as New York's *Knickerbocker*. "The establishment of an elevated literary Magazine in Georgia, would be a glorious monument to the literary credit of our people," he wrote in the September 1843 issue. *Orion* included articles designed to stimulate interest in and travel to the state's monuments and natural wonders, editorials on a wide range of topics, including phrenology and female education, and fiction, poetry, and literary criticism. *Orion*'s contributors included well-known Southern writers such as William Gilmore Simms. The magazine was also very much a family project. In addition to Addison's illustrations, Will's wife, Cornelia Holroyd Bradley Richards, wrote stories. While traveling around the region lecturing, Will and Sam sold subscriptions. The rest of the family helped mail copies to subscribers. In spite of their efforts, Will Richards struggled to keep the magazine going, and in an effort to find a more welcoming home, he moved the magazine from Penfield to Charleston, South Carolina, in 1844. *Orion* failed to shine, however, and folded after just two years.[14]

Unwilling to give up his dreams, Richards tried again in 1848 with the *Southern Literary Gazette*, published in Athens, Georgia. This time, Will paid attention to issues of financing, lining up one thousand subscribers before he began printing. Like *Orion*, the new journal combined fiction, poetry, and reviews. Changing its name to *Richards's Weekly Gazette* in the second year, he tried to make it family oriented, offering prizes for favorably reviewed submissions of stories and poems. Even with his family's help—Sam and Jabe dutifully peddled subscriptions and Kate wrote articles under the pseudonym Leila Cameron—the publication struggled. Will Richards first sold a partial interest and then relinquished control to Joseph Walker of Charleston, South Carolina, before giving up on the South altogether. He moved first to New York and later to Providence, Rhode Island. Although Richards continued to practice the evangelical religion that dominated the South, he ultimately condemned the slave labor system that sustained the region's economy. Richards found the North a more comfortable home for an intellectual. He finally achieved both literary and financial success with *Schoolfellow: A Magazine for Girls and Boys*, which contained fictional stories designed to build character, articles on science and history, and a puzzle section, "The Sphinx." The magazine found a market, with an estimated subscription list of ten thousand by the end of its first year, 1849. It continued to publish until 1857.[15]

Like most Americans of his era, Sam Richards idealized the family unit. He was close to his parents and all of his siblings. When he was not traveling with Will, he enjoyed spending time with his parents in Penfield and with Will and Cornelia Richards at their home in the university town of Athens, Georgia, not far away. The family retained its English identity to a point, once singing "God Save the Queen" from the porch of their home on July 3 as a prelude to Penfield's annual Independence Day celebration. On another occasion, Sam wrote of enjoying a pipe and conversation with his uncle, Robert Richards, about the imperious "Queen Vic," who had ascended the throne of England several years earlier. He sometimes waxed eloquent about the delectable mince pies he recalled eating during the Christmas season in England: "Oh! for the good old times of 'Merrie England' . . . especially at Mince Pie time."[16] Over time, Sam spoke less often about his British heritage. Although he never lost his affinity for mince pies, he identified strongly with the American South and its geography, culture, and institutions.

The Richardses were musically gifted. Sam and his brother Jabe had fine voices and enjoyed singing in church and at evening gatherings of family and friends. Both men played the flute, and they often performed duets. His sisters played the piano; Kate also played the guitar. When Addison Richards painted a portrait of her with the instrument, Sam pronounced it a good likeness and "a beautiful picture."[17]

By the 1840s, Addison Richards had begun to earn a name for himself regionally as an artist. When the family had lived in Hudson, New York, Addison had been inspired by the scenic wonders of the nearby river and

Catskill Mountains, and he became a painter in the tradition of the Hudson River school. Those artists focused on landscape and paid particular attention to the use of light and shadow. After the Richards family moved to Georgia, Addison traveled widely with a sketchbook, drawing pictures of mountains and waterfalls. Sometimes Sam accompanied him. In June 1842, Add sketched Table Rock mountain for *Orion*, and Sam described his brother as "a right clever sort of fellow." Two years later, Addison left Georgia and moved to New York City, where he began to build a national reputation. He resided in New York for the rest of his life. While studying at the National Academy of Design, he supported himself by giving art lessons. He became the institution's corresponding secretary in 1852 and held the post for the next forty years. In addition to contributing illustrations to leading journals of opinion such as *Harper's* and *Knickerbocker*, Addison wrote and illustrated books on travel, including *Tallulah and Jocasse*, a book of short stories focused on two North Georgia waterfalls, and *The Romance of the American Landscape*, which took its readers to more far-flung destinations, including Cave-in-Rock on the Ohio River and Lake George in Upstate New York. Sam and his brother remained close through correspondence.[18]

By 1846, Sam had begun to feel dissatisfied with the lack of direction in his life. The tight-knit family unit that had once centered around Penfield had begun to break up as the Richards siblings found jobs away from Greene County. Jabez moved to Athens and opened a store in 1844. Kate, Ellen, and Amelia finished their education and took jobs as teachers or governesses in places at some distance from their family. On New Year's Day 1846, Sam considered the prospect of another year on the lecture circuit and confided to his diary, "Will and I are to be wanderers to and from the earth [again] I pressume. I am getting tired of traveling." After seven years, the wandering life had lost its allure. The brothers did not make as much money as they had in earlier years, and on occasion they reduced their ticket price to twenty-five cents to bolster the number of patrons. They were incensed when, on several occasions, audiences equated their scientific experiments with mere hucksterism. Forced by lack of interest to cancel a lecture in Eatonton, Georgia, Sam wrote, "This *lecturing* is too uncertain business for any comfort. . . . I've a great mind to run off to Texas and fight Mexicans for $10 a month."[19] In actuality, however, Sam had no interest in joining America's volunteer army in the Mexican-American War.

Sam also disliked his wandering life because he yearned to find a wife and settle down. Now twenty-two years old, he had neither the income nor the prospect of a wife to inspire him. That changed in the spring of 1846, when he began courting Elizabeth "Libbie" Hathaway. Libbie was one of three sisters who had known the Richards family in Hudson during the early 1830s. After the deaths of their parents, the three moved to Georgia, and two of them found jobs as schoolteachers at Pleasant Grove Seminary near Athens. While Sam wooed Libbie, Jabez courted her sister, Sarah. On one occasion in March 1846, the brothers serenaded the sisters on the flute, accompanied by a friend playing the guitar. The following month, Sam wrote coyly in his diary that he had "robbed [Libbie's] bosom of a rose, but I trust left no *thorne* in her." By the summer of 1846, he had invited her to read his diary and wrote of long walks and evenings of conversation.[20]

Despite his affection for Libbie, Sam decided to begin a course of study at Mercer University, hoping to find a professional future on which to anchor his life. He passed his qualifying exams during the summer of 1846 and began classes on August 31. Three days later, Libbie was gravely ill with what was feared to be a fatal illness, and she died on September 7. Dumbfounded by the news, Sam poured out his sorrow into his diary. On September 10, he wrote, "I can hardly realize that I shall never see her again, on Earth!" For many years after her death, he marked the date in his diary and often played her favorite song, "Love Not! The One You Love May Die!" on his flute. Wearing mourning clothes, a bereaved Sarah Hathaway married Jabez Richards on December 26, 1846. The third sister, Mary, resided with the couple in Athens.[21] Both Sam and Jabe regarded Mary as a member of their family, and she lived with one or the other of the brothers for the next two decades.

Sam Richards did not enjoy being a college student. Libbie's death and his isolation from the rest of the Richards siblings only made him more restless. He spoke of the monotony of study and recitations. For his first college speech, he was assigned the topic, "Should *Women* be raised to *political equality* with Men?" For Richards, the issue was settled by Scripture, which to his mind decreed woman's place as man's helpmeet, not his political rival. The subject was not worth debating, in his view, and he also did not relish public speaking. With characteristic bluntness, he recorded, "I did not make a very lengthy speech or very eloquent. I have long since come to the conclusion that I never was intended for an orator, not possessing enough of that indispensable thing, *gab*." While he made satisfactory progress at Mercer, Richards ultimately decided to pursue a career in the book trade, a choice that did not require a college education. Sam dropped out of Mercer without receiving a degree.[22]

Introduction 9

By early 1848, he had resumed the wandering life, this time as a peddler of books. Unhappy with this profession and unhappy that he had failed to find a romantic partner in the time since Libbie's death, Richards was again at loose ends. The summer wedding of his younger sister, Kate, to the scion of a prominent family from the Middle Georgia town of Sparta only accentuated his lack of direction. When Jabez approached Sam about forming a business partnership as co-owners of a Macon bookstore, Sam jumped at the chance.[23]

Sam and Jabe had always been close. Two and a half years apart in age, the brothers had shared many experiences in youth and adolescence. Together they had dammed a creek near the family home in Penfield to make a pond for bathing and swimming. It became a favorite with the entire family. They performed militia duty together, attended lectures and concerts, sang and played the flute, and courted the Hathaway sisters.[24] They made an effective team as business partners. With four years of experience running shops in Athens and Penfield, Jabe played the role of senior partner, proposing changes, expansions, and updates. Sam found that he had an aptitude for bookkeeping and proved himself adept at organizational and administrative duties. The J. J. & S. P. Richards Book, Music, and Fancy Store opened in the fall of 1848 on Cotton Avenue, with a large sign advertising the business.

The brothers had come to Macon at a good time. The city was a prosperous and bustling community that became the sort of regional center for Middle and South Georgia that William Richards had hoped Penfield would be when he moved his family there in the 1830s. Between 1845 and 1859, Macon's population swelled from 4,189 to almost 10,000. Hard hit by the Panic of 1837, the city's economy had subsequently rebounded, fueled by industry and railroads in addition to its traditional base in the cotton trade.[25]

Sam's social life began to improve. He boarded in a room above the store but ate his meals at the house Jabe had rented so that Jabe and Sarah, pregnant with their first child, might "go to housekeeping." She gave birth to a stillborn son in January 1849, before the couple moved to Macon, casting a pall over what should have been a happy home life in the couple's first abode independent of relatives. Unlike Penfield, where the town's social life was anchored by Mercer alone, Macon attracted a wide variety of public speakers and performers, and Sam took advantage of the cultural opportunities afforded by his new home. He heard lectures on politics, phrenology, and literature; attended the circus; and listened to operatic singers and minstrel shows. He was especially captivated when British author William Makepeace Thackeray lectured in Macon and hoped that Charles Dickens might one day speak as well.[26]

The Baptist church always provided Sam Richards with a source of inspiration and guidance, and he joined the local congregation soon after arriving in Macon. At the Sunday evening service on October 22, 1848, he met James Van Valkenburg, a deacon of the church who also directed the choir and welcomed the Richards brothers as singers. Also present were two of Van Valkenburg's daughters, eighteen-year-old Harriet and Sarah, who had just turned sixteen. Sarah accompanied the choir by playing the seraphine, a keyboard instrument in which foot pedals are used to force air through bellows. Harriet made a greater first impression on Sam Richards because she was older, more outgoing, and sang loudly. The girlish Sarah, nine years younger than Sam and known to her family as Sallie, kept her eyes on her keyboard.[27]

Over time, Sam became better acquainted with the Van Valkenburgs. Like the Richards family, they were a large tribe—nine children in all—who were musically inclined. James Van Valkenburg had moved his family to Macon from New York City in 1847, motivated by the desire to pursue business opportunities and find a home in a more salubrious climate for his wife, Mary Church Van Valkenburg, whose health was delicate. James Van Valkenburg built a steam-powered mill on Mulberry Street that visitors and customers regarded as a marvel of modern technology. The mill ground up to 150 bushels of wheat or corn in a day, and its inauguration earned praise from the editor of the *Macon Telegraph*, who congratulated Van Valkenburg for "the success of his enterprise in establishing a mill of this kind in Macon." James Van Valkenburg was also a major presence in the local Baptist church, and Sam admired him. "Deacon Van V. led the exercises and acquitted himself very well in his calm, simple, yet earnest manner," Sam confided to his diary on January 14, 1849. "He is quite an addition to this church as it was not until he and his family came to Macon about a year ago that they had any choir of regular singing in the church." Five days later, Van Valkenburg held a choir practice in his home and formally introduced Sam to Harriet and Sallie. Sam was pleased to have "done something toward making acquaintances," and he was even more pleased when, two days later, the "Deacon's daughters honored me with a bow of recognition in consequence of our introduction the other night. . . . [I]t was quite a treat to have some token of acquaintance from the fair sex in my solitary condition."[28]

Jabe and Sam slowly but surely began to make money. To increase their profits, the brothers took turns making sales trips to rural Georgia,

Introduction 11

disliking the days of lonely travel but recognizing that such trips could be remunerative. Then, on February 19, 1850, disaster struck. Sam was awakened in the night by bright lights flooding his room and voices calling from below. The building next to their store was enveloped in flames. Uttering a quick prayer, Sam carried out some of their most valuable stock, including pens, cutlery, and books, but within fifteen minutes, the store had burned to the ground. He must have salvaged his diaries as well because all of his other personal possessions perished in the fire. In writing about the conflagration three days later, Sam was uncharacteristically philosophical: "I have thought when viewing such a scene in past times that there was something grand and awful in a large fire sweeping away tho' it may the property of fellow beings but on this occasion I could only regard it as a remorseless tyrant." The fire destroyed an entire city block, causing an estimated thirty thousand dollars in damage.[29]

The Richards brothers had no choice but to start over. They were still beholden to their landlord, who offered them retail space in a building he owned on Cherry Street. Insurance covered a thousand dollars of their losses—about half the total, Sam estimated. The brothers sent letters to their creditors in New York and Philadelphia asking for extensions on their loans and received positive responses. By February 28, eleven days after the fire, they were back in business; on their first day, they sold a total of ten cents worth of goods—twice their opening day sales in the fall of 1848. The wife of the Baptist minister gave Sam some of her old bed linens to replace the ones he had lost, and a friend presented him with a hand-me-down coat. He paid five dollars for a pair of replacement boots.[30]

With his business back on track, Sam focused his attention on matters of the heart. On Valentine's Day 1851, he decided to send secret missives to two young women from the Baptist church, hoping that at least one of them would respond. Sallie Van Valkenburg did. Sam sent her a "very loving" message written backward, a clever and romantic trick, he thought: she would have to use a mirror to read the words. To his delight, she responded by sending him a poem written in red ink that began,

> I think of thee when eve's last blush
> Falls mournfully on heart and eye
> Of thee, when Moon's first glorious gush
> In gold and crimson o'er the sky.

Sam confided to his diary that Sallie's poem was "so sweet that it allmost took away my breath to read it." When a blushing Sallie admitted authorship, Sam was smitten. To the end of his life, he believed in the power of Valentines and always stocked them in significant quantity in his bookstore.[31]

Courting Sallie was not an easy proposition. A short time after the couple declared their interest in one another, the Van Valkenburgs moved two miles outside town, meaning that Sam had to make a lengthy walk just to see Sallie. In May 1851, Sallie's mother died suddenly. Her obituary, written by the Reverend Sylvanus Landrum, indicated that her "sufferings were indescribable." Sallie's bereaved brothers and sisters took comfort in their mother having been brave to the end, singing the hymn, "Jesus My All to Heaven Has You," within an hour of her death. Donning mourning clothes, the family returned to church services in early June. Sam wrote that Sallie, while "serious and thoughtful . . . looked better and prettier in her garb of sadness than ever." Sallie now had new responsibilities. While twenty-year-old Harriet bore the greatest domestic burden, Sallie was expected to help out with the household and the younger children.[32]

Once he had set his heart on courting Sallie, nothing would dissuade Sam Richards. He gave her a diary and urged her to write in it. As a reader of his brother's literary magazines, Sam knew that a middle-class man of the 1850s should seek a wife who combined attractiveness, compatibility, virtue, and a "cultivated mind." Sam greatly admired his brother Will's wife, Cornelia, who was both a literary woman and a devoted wife and mother. At Sam's behest, Sallie dutifully commenced writing in her diary on April 28, 1852. She promised to write regularly to improve "both my composition and handwriting"—and to please "a *very particular friend* of mine, who has been urging me to do so for a long time." Sam and Sallie shared a similar religious outlook, an interest in literature and music, and a strong physical attraction. At five feet, six inches tall and 133 pounds, Sam was average size for a mid-nineteenth-century man. An avid walker and gardener, he was trim and fit, had a full head of brown hair that he wore stylishly long, and sometimes sported a mustache. Sallie was also of average size for a woman of her time, standing five feet, one inch tall and weighing 116 pounds. Sam admired her curvaceous figure and her dimples when she smiled. In July 1851, he helped her into the family carriage for the first time and was pleased by the touch of her hand. He wondered when he might have the nerve to kiss her.[33]

Despite their mutual attraction, the courtship of Sam Richards and Sallie Van Valkenburg was anything but placid. While their interests were compatible, their personalities often clashed. Both were strong minded, sometimes impatient, and often quick to anger. They quarreled frequently. In their war of wills, Sam had gender, age, religious teachings, and Georgia law on his side, and they both knew it. Sallie subsequently struggled with her emotions as she tried to be obedient to Sam while remaining true to herself. "He is *all* my heart desires," she admitted to her diary on May 2, 1852, adding that she would never marry a man who was not the dominant partner. But she also wrote that Sam was too quick to find fault with everything she did, including her writing and composition. Sam often used the word *naughty* to describe her behavior, an indication that he sometimes treated her as a child, and she resented it. By May 1852, she found that she had "yielded too much already" in quarrels with Sam, and she would "have to give him a piece of my mind even at the risk of displeasing him. . . . [I]f he should ever read this—remember Sam, this my journal is to contain my feelings, independent of what you or any one else may think—I would not keep one if I could not write them freely." On July 18, Sallie wrote, "[H]e thinks I am the most disobliging creature he ever saw. I think I am very submissive." In another case she wrote in despair, "I am not under his control yet."[34]

The couple seemed determined to put aside their differences. Sam asked Sallie to marry him, and she agreed. With her father's permission, they became formally betrothed. Sam finally realized "the long cherished thought and desire of years . . . and I had some one to call *my own*, to love, and be loved by!" In a symbolic gesture, Sam gave Sallie the mementos he had received from Libbie Hathaway six years earlier. Sam and Sallie's arguments did not end, however, and he told her that after they married, he might feel justified in whipping her if she disobeyed him. Sallie took the comment seriously and threatened to back out of the marriage, undoubtedly aware that Georgia law allowed a husband to beat his wife. Sam wrote, "I told her I expected to have to whip her when we were married, but I coaxed her over and made her believe I was only *in fun*." Several months later, recalling their conversation and knowing that Sallie sometimes read his diary, just as he read hers, Sam wrote, "I have no doubt that there are some wives who *ought* to be whipped and whom whipping would do good. . . . I don't think such a course would do with *Sallie*." For his part, Sam believed that Sallie intentionally provoked him. "Why *will* the naughty girl persist in doing what she knows will vex and grieve me, and yet profess a desire to please and gratify me?" The couple's prewedding jitters were partly fueled by the knowledge that their marriage would create an irrevocable bond. Divorce was legal though hard to obtain in Georgia. Among the members of their religious and social group, however, it was not tolerated. As a practical matter, Sam and Sallie could not leave the marriage even if it proved unhappy.[35]

As if there were not drama enough in their courtship, several events in the spring and summer of 1852 threatened to derail the wedding. Sallie's father, once a revered member of the Baptist congregation, ran afoul of some church elders, who accused him of fraud. An investigation by five church members led to Van Valkenburg's exoneration, but the minister, Rev. Landrum, who had written a glowing obituary for Sallie's mother the previous year, suspected that Van Valkenburg was being let off too easily. Sam never wrote in his diary about the specifics of the charges, but he noted that James Van Valkenburg had experienced financial "difficulties and straits." Years later, Van Valkenburg wrote a letter to the *Macon Telegraph* in which he complained about the challenges of being a manufacturer in a plantation society: a "cotton buyer without a dollar of his own" might easily get a bank loan, he explained, while "every new enterprise . . . by mechanics generally met with opposition and discouragement." Sam sympathized with Sallie's father and believed that Landrum had been "poisoned" against Van Valkenburg by a small group of church members. Angered at James's ill treatment, the Van Valkenburgs ceased to attend the Baptist church, and Sallie's father expected her to avoid its services even after she married Sam. A dedicated Baptist, Sam thought his wife should attend church with her husband, but the more immediate issue was who would perform the wedding. Because he wanted to be married by a Baptist clergyman, Sam implored his father to make time in a busy schedule to come to Macon before the end of the year.[36]

In July 1852, Sallie's older brother, James Dunbar Van Valkenburg, then in his mid-twenties, scandalized the community by eloping with fifteen-year-old Mary "Mollie" Morgan. Morgan's widowed mother had strongly opposed their courtship, banning Van Valkenburg from seeing Mary and forging a letter from Mary telling James she did not want to see him again. Fearing that the couple might elope, Mary's mother positioned a relative to stand guard in the girl's room at night and had another relative stationed on the piazza with a gun. The young couple would not be dissuaded. Under the guise of visiting her sister, Mary slipped away in the middle of the night, and the couple rode fifteen miles on horseback in the rain, finding a preacher somewhere along the way to marry them. At daybreak, they arrived at the Van Valkenburg home, where a surprised Sallie was introduced to her wet and bedraggled sister-in-law. Rumors persisted that James had wed Mary Morgan for her money, which Sallie believed included a twenty-thousand-dollar inheritance from her father. Since married women lacked property rights in Georgia, Mary's new husband could control her money if he chose to do so.[37]

Sam and Sallie found the elopement story untoward and believed that Mary was an unsophisticated cracker despite her wealth. Sallie wrote cattily that the girl "has been raised on *Bacon, greens, and cornbread*, what a description of a bride. I hope none of my northern relations will set eyes on her." Over time, however, Sallie came to like her sister-in-law, and James and Mary's obvious devotion to one another allayed some of Sallie's fears about marriage. Sam was less forgiving. James had trouble finding a profession, and while he served as a volunteer firefighter and marched with the militia, Sam thought he needed to settle down more.[38] James Van Valkenburg did not come into his own until the Civil War, when, as a Confederate officer, he demonstrated maturity, leadership, and ultimately valor.

Sam Richards and Sallie Van Valkenburg wed on December 9, 1852, in the bride's home, surrounded by their friends and family. Sam's father officiated. In one small last act of defiance, Sallie ignored Sam's request that she wear a white dress and instead chose an off-white silk fabric from which to stitch her bridal gown. She believed that too many brides wore white swiss and wanted her dress to be different and special. Sam thought it was.[39]

Given the tumultuous nature of their courtship, the Richards marriage was surprisingly tranquil from the beginning. Traveling on business before their nuptials, Sam had warned Sallie that when he returned she should "wear a good strong dress [and] a high necked one too!" Once married, Sam's physical desire had an outlet. "I think I have the sweetest wife in Georgia and she says she is perfectly satisfied with her husband," he wrote proudly one week after the wedding. Sallie no longer feared that Sam would be a tyrant. In her diary, she wrote appreciatively of the many times Sam brought her books from his shop, and she expressed gratitude when he tended to her in times of illness. Sam no longer worried that Sallie might decide she did not love him. He wrote often in his diary of Sallie's kind and loving nature. They nevertheless had their moments. While returning from a trip to Sparta to visit his sister, Kate, and her husband, Charlie DuBose, Sam and Sallie took turns driving their buggy. Once, when Sallie held the reins, she nearly drove into a ditch, angering her husband, who refused to let her drive again. The couple lapsed into uneasy silence. That night, anxious to make up with Sallie, Sam read aloud to her, as he often did in the evenings. But Sallie fell asleep, angering Sam. In a fit of pique, he threw the book to the floor. This time Sallie took the initiative to make amends. "*She* concluded not to be *grumpy* all night as we had been all day and so came and put herself in my lap and of course I had to give in and be *good*," Sam wrote in his diary. "[W]e were 'mighty good' friends after that!"[40]

Unlike most brides in nineteenth-century America, Sallie Richards did not conceive a child in the first year of marriage. Friends told the couple to travel while they had the chance before the babies came, but the bookstore kept Sam anchored to Macon most of the time. To save money, they spent their first two years of marriage boarding with Jabez and Sarah, an arrangement that left Sallie with few domestic responsibilities. Insecure about her abilities as a housekeeper but eager to please Sam, she tried to learn how to bake. In one diary entry, he noted her success in making "some *nice* muffins" but added, "I wont mention the *cake*." Sallie had greater success as a seamstress, already having considerable experience making and mending her own clothes and those of her younger siblings. She began to make Sam's pants, shirts, vests, and coats, viewing the task as both a challenge and a creative outlet. Sam was impressed by the quality of her work and by the money she saved, noting with special praise a vest she made at a cost of 87½¢. To keep the peace in their families, the couple alternated between attending Baptist services and those of the Episcopal church, where the Van Valkenburgs now worshiped. By the end of the first year of marriage, Sam and Sallie felt secure in their mutual love but had begun to worry that childlessness might be their long-term fate. When his youngest sister, Amelia, gave birth to a baby, Sam noted, "Every body is having a baby except *us!* . . . [I]t will never do!" Sallie worried, too, though a friend assured her that she "need not despair—there is time enough yet." And indeed there was. By early 1854, Sallie was pregnant, and on September 8, 1854, she gave birth to a healthy baby girl, whom they named Dora. Nine more children would follow over the next twenty-two years.[41]

The partnership between J. J. and S. P. Richards underwent significant changes during the second half of the 1850s. In 1855, with Sam's consent, Jabe moved to Griffin, Georgia, northwest of Macon, and opened a new branch of their business. By July of that year, Sam wrote proudly that they had accumulated stock worth six thousand dollars in the Macon store and three thousand dollars in Griffin. But Jabe had even bigger plans. Taking a partner to run the Griffin store, he moved again, this time to Atlanta, which he saw as an opportunity for better long-term profits. "I don't like several features of the plan," Sam wrote in September 1855 without elaborating, "but I expect I shall have to let Jabez try it, he is so set upon it."

Visiting Jabe in 1858, Sam was favorably impressed with the life that Jabe and his wife had created in Atlanta, especially with their congregation at Second Baptist Church, which appeared free from the kind of discord that characterized the Macon congregation. Sam made another trip to Atlanta in 1859 when a telegram from Jabez brought the sad tidings that Sarah Hathaway Richards had died of consumption at the age of thirty-five. The disease had plagued her for a decade, and the advice of a variety of doctors around the state, coupled with annual trips to Florida, had failed to effect a cure. Mary Hathaway continued to reside in Jabe's household to care for his daughter, Annie.[42]

While Jabez planned for their future, Sam worried about the present. In 1857, the U.S. economy plunged into depression. Sam noted the suspension of specie payments at banks around the South. Even more worrisome, several publishing houses were in trouble, including Harper's, with which the brothers did business. "I trust that we shall be able to get safely through if the present tightness does not last too long," Sam wrote on October 19, 1857. The Atlanta store experienced difficulties, including fires in 1859 and 1860 that created losses beyond what insurance covered. Business was more stable in the Macon store, which Sam ran with help from his brother, Henry, and later, when Henry left to pursue other opportunities, a clerk named Asa Sherwood. In 1857, Sam moved into a new retail space with lower rent and a better roof to protect their books from rain damage.[43]

If the business world provided him with headaches, Sam's personal life provided him with great steadiness. In 1856, Sallie gave birth to a second daughter, Irene ("Renie"), and two years later a son, William Arthur (known by his middle name), joined their family. Another son died shortly after birth in 1859. Following Dora's birth, the couple had rented a house for themselves on Second Street in Macon, surrounded by attractive shrubbery and a garden in the back where Sam could grow vegetables. To Sam's delight, Sallie learned to make mince pies, his favorite culinary treat from childhood in England. Preoccupied by children, mince pies, and myriad other domestic responsibilities, Sallie stopped writing in her diary.[44] During the Civil War, a severe shortage in available paper stock led her husband to use its unfilled pages for his own journal writing.

When they "went to housekeeping" in 1855, Sam and Sallie hired servants for the first time. In the urban South, those who did not own slaves often rented them as domestic servants, negotiating annual financial contracts with their owners. During the 1850s, the practice of renting slaves was on the rise regionally, as their high prices at auction made ownership prohibitive for most Southerners. An estimated 5 to 15 percent of American slaves were hirelings, making couples such as Sam and Sallie Richards indirect beneficiaries of the slavery system. The Richardses usually rented two slaves, a young teenager to help with the children and an adult woman to assist with cooking, cleaning, and laundry. Rarely satisfied with their domestic help, they often chose not to renew their servants' contracts for a second year. The pages of Sam's diary reveal his ongoing frustration with the chore of finding acceptable domestics.[45]

Sam and Sallie Richards held views about slavery that typified their social class and the times in which they lived. As readers of the Old Testament, they knew that slavery had existed since ancient times. The minister of their Baptist church once wrote that the "world never has, and never can, exist without slavery in some form." The Richardses knew that the South's economy rested on slavery's profits and that their ability to live free from the burdens of household drudgery depended on their ability to rent slaves for modest prices. They also shared the racist assumptions of their generation. Sam and Sallie regarded African Americans as "poor ignorant creatures," as Sallie once put it, at best educable as servants, at worst intractable and rebellious. As avid readers who stayed abreast of literary trends, both mentioned reading Harriet Beecher Stowe's *Uncle Tom's Cabin*, but Sam recorded no specific reaction to the tale. Sallie did comment, albeit indirectly. When her aunt, Huldah Van Valkenburg, a New Yorker who had come South to help raise Sallie's younger siblings, read the novel, Sallie told Sam that "she is so much interested in it that she cannot let it alone," despite the fact that it was Sunday and the family disapproved of reading novels on the Sabbath. Moreover, Sallie added, "Aunt H is crying over the wrongs and hardships of the poor negroes. They have easier lives than *we* poor white folks—don't they?"[46]

The rented slaves who worked for Sallie and Sam did not have easier lives than the white folks. Sent off to work in a strange household, cut off mostly if not entirely from family and friends, they lived isolated lives of drudgery, utterly at the whim of their owners and those who hired their services. Renters had even less incentive than owners to treat slaves well, and abuse of rental slaves occurred frequently. As society's most vulnerable members, slaves, including hirelings, had few ways to rebel. At times, despite the consequences, they talked back, messed up on the job, or in extreme cases ran and hid. Sam Richards believed that his role as head of the household included keeping all of its members in line. He regarded it as not only a burden but also a duty to whip slaves who disobeyed his rules.[47]

Slaves were most vulnerable at times of high stress within the families for whom they worked. Such was the case in the spring of 1857, a year during which Sam had an especially difficult time finding acceptable servants. He negotiated a contract for Juliana, but her owner revoked it, and he then hired Sallie from a different owner. However, she was "such a dirty ignorant thing" that Richards paid ten dollars to back out of the contract. After his wife spent a month without help, Sam advertised at the post office and hired Dicey, a twenty-two-year-old who he thought would be acceptable.[48]

Dicey entered the household at a particularly tense time. The Richards children were sick, and Sam was especially worried about Renie, whose ailments required the administration of medicine he called "sugar of lead" and the application of blood-sucking leeches. Although the children seemed to improve, they came down with diarrhea, a condition that could be serious. Other events added to Sam's stress. His beloved vegetable garden was seriously damaged in a terrific storm. Sallie sent for him one day at work because his brother, Henry, ill for some time and convalescing in their home, suffered a "fit" requiring immediate help. Dicey, who apparently had a habit of running away, did so again after being scolded by Sallie for "ill behavior." She remained at large for a period of days, probably sheltered by sympathizers, before being caught and returned to the Richards household. Enraged by her impudence, Sam Richards, with the consent of Dicey's owner, had her taken to the guard house and whipped. Still angry, at least in part because he had to pay for her flogging, Sam recorded in his diary, "It cost me 2.50 to get that much *satisfaction*."[49]

Dicey remained in the Richards household through the end of the year. That summer, Sallie took the children to visit relatives, leaving Sam in Macon with her unmarried younger sisters, Mary and Martha, to act as housekeepers. Sam complained about the tendency of the young Van Valkenburg women to sleep late, missing breakfast. He suggested to Dicey that she awaken them, but she "would not wake them because they scolded her for doing so before."[50] Like most enslaved people, Dicey learned how to avoid provoking the white folks.

Although he upheld the institution of slavery, Sam Richards did not support those Southern fire-eaters who advocated secession from the Union as the only way for the South to protect slavery against growing calls in the North for its containment if not its complete elimination. Long after many men in Georgia had ceased to argue for Unionism, Richards still believed that his state might somehow manage to protect its peculiar institution while remaining part of the United States.

In the 1840s, Richards had enthusiastically supported the Whig Party. Founded the previous decade, the Whigs advocated a strong national government and support for economic development, ideas that appealed to Richards as an educated man of the business class. Shortly before the 1844 presidential election, Sam and Jabe put aside their temperance proclivities and drank a toast in support of Henry Clay, the party's founder and standard-bearer. Sam regretted that he was too young to give Clay his vote but wrote on his twenty-first birthday that he looked forward to the next presidential contest: "Wont I elect Harry Clay next election? Oh yes—by all means!" But the Whigs, anxious to reprise their electoral success from 1840, when the nomination of a military hero helped them win the election, nominated General Zachary Taylor of Mexican War fame. Shortly after his move to Macon, Richards attended a campaign speech in support of Taylor's candidacy delivered by Savannah's John Macpherson Berrien, whose long career in public life included service as a judge, Georgia state senator, U.S. senator, and attorney general under Andrew Jackson. Richards voted for Taylor on November 7 and wrote about the "grand *jubilee*" in Macon honoring the general's election. "Hurraa!!!!— the Whig houses were illuminated, but the poor defeated *demos* 'kept dark.'" Whig jubilation turned to sorrow the following year when Taylor died suddenly. Richards recorded the news in his diary, adding that he and others feared the future with Millard Fillmore, believed to have abolitionist tendencies, ascending to the presidency. That fall, Richards attended a memorial service held in Taylor's honor that included a speech by Eugenius Nisbet, who served one term in the U.S. Congress as a Whig and later became one of the founding justices of Georgia's Supreme Court.[51]

By the mid-1850s, the Whig Party had gone into decline in Georgia and nationally, hopelessly split over slavery. Its demise left southern Unionists without a political party at the national level. But Georgia's politicians included some strong Unionists, including Congressman Alexander Stephens, whom Sam met in 1849 when Stephens was vacationing and Richards was peddling books in Warm Springs, Georgia. Seeing Stephens for the first time, Sam was struck by the congressman's undistinguished appearance, calling him "a little, thin, sallow country cracker sort of a looking man that no one would take for a *great* man certainly." But Richards found Stephens's logic very persuasive. When he appeared in Macon in September 1851, Sam wrote, "He arose like an awkward sort of a schoolboy with his hands in his pockets and began in the smallest kind of a voice, and if I had not known he *could speak* I should not have thought so, but he spoke for an hour and a half, and the way he gave it to the, so called 'Southern Rights' party, was a caution." Stephens invited its adherents to "get upon the Union Platform before it was too late." That year, Sam supported Howell Cobb for governor as well as "the entire Union ticket." Cobb won the election with support from both Democratic and Whig Unionists. Richards did not cast a ballot in the presidential election of 1852. Like other Georgia Whigs, he was unimpressed by the party's last presidential candidate, Winfield Scott.[52]

During the mid-1850s, a number of Southern moderates supported the Know-Nothings (renamed the American Party in 1855), whose Northern wing took a strong anti-immigrant and nativist position. Its Southern wing focused more on ways to preserve slavery within the context of the Union.[53]

Richards voted for American Party candidates several times during the 1850s. In October 1854, he attended a Know-Nothing meeting at the home of a fellow Macon Baptist, and the following year voted for the American candidate for governor, Garnett Andrews. "There is no chance for his election," he acknowledged, yet, "I still felt it my duty to vote for him." Andrews lost to Democrat Herschel Johnson 53,478 to 43,222. In 1856, the American Party fielded a presidential ticket with Millard Fillmore in the top slot and Andrew Jackson Donelson as his running mate. That October, Richards attended a debate between the Democratic and American Parties attended by both men and women. Sallie and her sister Martha came but left after concluding that the proceedings were too "rowdy" for respectable women to witness. Sam did not record whether he voted in the presidential contest but noted that local Democrats "had an illumination and procession . . . to celebrate the triumph" of Democrats James Buchanan and John Breckinridge over "the Abolition candidates," Republicans John C. Frémont and William L. Dayton. He continued, "Sallie and I spent a couple of hours at the Schwabs also tonight. Their house was illuminated."[54]

In 1857, Richards voted for American candidate Ben Hill for the Georgia governorship. Continuing voting patterns from previous elections, the American Party carried the city of Macon but not Bibb County, and Hill lost by eleven thousand votes statewide to Democrat Joseph E. Brown. Although the American Party controlled a sizable number of seats in the Georgia legislature and dominated in two congressional districts, the party had peaked and begun to fade. Stephens remained an outspoken voice for Unionism, giving those who admired his perspective a forceful advocate, but a growing number of Georgians now turned toward advocates of Southern independence. In his diary, Sam Richards was silent on the issue of politics in 1858 and 1859.[55]

By 1860, Richards was thirty-six years old, middle-aged by the standards of his era—"the wintry side of thirty," as he put it. He had achieved moderate standing in his church and community and a modicum of financial security. He did not yet own a home, and he continued to rent but not own slaves. Nonetheless, he could now afford to purchase small luxury items for his family, including wicker chairs for the children, silver teaspoons, and a cameo pin for Sallie. More importantly, he could now buy his wife the one expensive item she had long coveted: a piano. Richards also felt secure enough in his business interests to leave Macon for an extended period. In August 1860, with his store in Sherwood's capable hands, Sam took Sallie and Dora to New York to visit family. They were gone for a month. Sallie had not seen many of her relatives since her family had moved to Georgia a dozen years earlier. Sam enjoyed the opportunity to visit with Addison and his wife, Mary Anthony Richards, who had married in 1857. Sam and Sallie Richards made a side trip to Providence, Rhode Island, where Will and Cornelia had settled after Will became pastor to a Baptist congregation there. Sam and Sallie did not see Aunt Huldah, who had surprised the entire family by marrying while in her late thirties and moving to Montrose, Pennsylvania. Sam wrote, "If she wasn't such a confounded abolitionist I should like to see Aunt H."[56]

Sam Richards's diary does not mention whether he discussed politics with his Yankee brothers during the trip, but the entire family knew that political storm clouds were brewing nationally. A few weeks after he and his wife and daughter returned, Sam wrote that the recent election results in Pennsylvania had led to "Black Republicans" winning the state "by a large majority," "a sure sign that the President elected will be Abe Lincoln the Abolition candidate and there are prophecies of dire disunion and distress." He added, "No one but God knows what the end will be."[57]

Notes

1. SPR diary, June 13, 1842; Ella Mae Thornton, "Mr. S. P. Richards," *Atlanta Historical Society Bulletin*, Dec. 1937, 73–79, indicates that the society

had been "given access" to the diaries at that point. They were donated formally in 1968.

2. SPR diary, Sept. 9, 1864; Mary A. H. Gay, *Life in Dixie during the War* (1897; repr., Atlanta: Darby, 1979), 68.

3. SPR diary, Oct. 9, 1862.

4. William Carey Richards, obituary of William Richards, Franklin Garrett Necrology database, AHC; unidentified article about Sam Richards, 1909, in Irene Richards lesson book, box 4, folder 5, Samuel P. Richards Papers, AHC.

5. William Carey Richards, obituary of William Richards, Franklin Garrett Necrology database, AHC; unidentified article about Sam Richards, 1909, in Irene Richards lesson book, box 4, folder 5, Richards Papers.

6. Jonathan M. Bryant, *How Curious a Land: Conflict and Change in Greene County, Georgia, 1850–1885* (Chapel Hill: University of North Carolina Press, 1996), 21–22; Thaddeus Brockett Rice and Carolyn White Williams, *History of Greene County, Georgia* (Macon, Ga.: Burke, 1961), 240, 248, 251, 257, 261; Spright Dowell, *A History of Mercer University, 1833–1953* (Macon, Ga.: Mercer University, 1958), 40–56.

7. John B. Boles, *The Great Revival: Beginnings of the Bible Belt* (Lexington: University Press of Kentucky, 1996), 3, 129, 133, 186; Christine Leigh Heyrman, *Southern Cross: The Beginnings of the Bible Belt* (New York: Knopf, 1997), 19, 112; Samuel S. Hill, *One Name but Several Faces: Variety in Popular Christian Denominations in Southern History* (Athens: University of Georgia Press, 1996), 26.

8. Rice and Williams, *History of Greene County*, 259; SPR diary, Jan. 29, 1846. According to Mary Levin Koch, "The Romance of American Landscape: The Art of Thomas Addison Richards," *Georgia Museum of Art Bulletin* 8 (Winter 1983): 27 n.6, William Richards owned 130 acres of land in Penfield.

9. Julia Deane Freeman, *Women of the South Distinguished by Literature* (New York: Derby and Jackson, 1860), 408.

10. James Grant Wilson and John Fiske, eds., *Appleton's Encyclopaedia of American Biography*, 6 vols. (New York: Appleton, 1900), 5:240.

11. SPR diary, Sept. 7, 1842 (Pendleton), Apr. 3, 1845 (Apalachicola), July 11, 1843 (Marthasville); see also Aug. 22, 1842, Aug. 21, 1843, Jan. 24, 1845.

12. Ibid., Aug. 21, 1843.

13. William C. Richards, *Georgia Illustrated* (Penfield, Ga.: Richards, 1842), 1; Drew Gilpin Faust, *A Sacred Circle: The Dilemma of the Intellectual in the Old South, 1840–1860* (Baltimore: Johns Hopkins University Press, 1977), 7–8.

14. *Orion*, Sept. 1843. Bertram Holland Flanders, *Early Georgia Magazines: Literary Periodicals to 1865* (Athens: University of Georgia Press, 1944), 70, 80, 87.

15. *Schoolfellow*, Jan. 1849. Flanders, *Early Georgia Magazines*, 95–98, 101, 103–7; John McCardell, *The Idea of a Southern Nation: Southern National-*

ists and Southern Nationalism, 1830–1860 (New York: Norton, 1979), 141–76; Faust, *Sacred Circle*, 147–48.

16. SPR diary, July 3, 1843, Jan. 29, 1844, July 4, 1844.

17. Ibid., Aug. 26, 1844.

18. Ibid., June 13, 1842; T. Addison Richards, *Tallulah and Jocasse; or, Romances of Southern Landscape* (Charleston, S.C.: Walker, Richards, 1852); T. Addison Richards, *The Romance of the American Landscape* (New York: Leavitt and Allen, 1854); Koch, "Romance of American Landscape," 5–14; Mary Levin Koch, "Thomas Addison Richards," in *New Georgia Encyclopedia*, available online at http://www.georgiaencyclopedia.org (accessed 24 September 2008). Today, top auction houses sell paintings by Addison Richards for thousands of dollars.

19. SPR diary, Jan. 1, 1846, May 2, 1846, Apr. 30, 1846 (reduced ticket price), June 12, 1846 (hucksterism), May 20, 1846 (Mexico).

20. Ibid., Mar. 30, 1846, Apr. 4, 1846, July 12, 18, 1846.

21. Ibid., Aug. 31, 1846, Sept. 3, 10, 1846, Sept. 7, 1847.

22. Ibid., Sept. 19, 1846; "History of the S. P. Richards Company," *Christian Index*, May 15, 1919.

23. SPR diary, Mar. 3, 1848, June 20, 1848.

24. Ibid., May 5, 1844, Aug. 24, 1844.

25. Ibid., Sept. 16, 1848, Oct. 22, 1848; Ida Young, *History of Macon, Georgia* (Macon, Ga.: Lyon, Marshall, and Brooks, 1950), 110.

26. SPR diary, Jan. 25, 1849, Apr. 1, 1850, Feb. 23, 1856.

27. Ibid., Oct. 22, 1848.

28. Ibid., Jan. 14, 19, 21, 1849; *MT*, Feb. 1, 1848; Young, *History of Macon*, 135; Mary Church Van Valkenburg obituary, box 3, folder 8, Richards Papers.

29. SPR diary, Feb. 19, 1850; Young, *History of Macon*, 146.

30. SPR diary, Feb. 19, 24, 28, 1850.

31. Ibid., Feb. 14, 19, 20, 1851, Oct. 9, 1852. Antebellum courtship practices are discussed in Bertram Wyatt-Brown, *Southern Honor: Ethics and Behavior in the Old South* (New York: Oxford University Press, 1982), 199–225.

32. SPR diary, May 21, 1851, June 1, 1851; Mary Church Van Valkenburg obituary, box 3, folder 8, Richards Papers.

33. SVVR diary, Apr. 28, 1852; SPR diary, July 6, 12, 27, 1851; Jonathan Daniel Wells, *The Origins of the Southern Middle Class, 1800–1861* (Chapel Hill: University of North Carolina Press, 2004), 77–78. Cornelia Holroyd Bradley Richards was a prolific writer. Among her most popular books was *At Home and Abroad; or, How to Behave* (New York: Evans and Brittan, 1853), which she wrote under the pseudonym "Mrs. Manners."

34. SVVR diary, May 2, 1852 (heart desires), May 9, 1852 (fault finding), May 21, 1852 (yielded too much, not under his control), May 26, 1852 (dominant partner), July 18, 1852 (submissive); SPR diary, Apr. 9, 1852 (naughty).

35. SPR diary, Apr. 1, 1852 (betrothal), Apr. 20, 1852 (mementoes of Libbie), May 7, 1852, Oct. 4, 1852 (whipping), July 6, 1852 (naughty girl); Eleanor Miot Boatwright, *Status of Women in Georgia, 1783–1860* (Brooklyn, N.Y.: Carlson, 1994), 25, 61.

36. SPR diary, Mar. 12, 1852, Apr. 6, 1852. See also SVVR diary, May 2, 1852; MT, Feb. 8, 1862.

37. SVVR diary, July 17, 19, 1852. The marriage was listed in the *Macon Weekly Telegraph*, Aug. 24, 1852. Although Mary's inheritance was sizable, Sallie may have overestimated it. The 1860 Census shows Mary Morgan Van Valkenburg with three thousand dollars in real estate and eighty-four hundred dollars in personal property, including six slaves. Because this property is listed in her name, it is possible that her inheritance was protected under the terms of her father's will or that of her mother, who died in 1859. See Eighth Census of the United States (1860), microcopy 653, Bibb County and Georgia Slave Schedules; *Monroe County, Georgia: A History* (Forsyth, Ga.: Monroe County Historical Society, 1979), 460. The state of Georgia changed the law to allow married women control over their inheritances in 1866. See Sandra R. Zagier Zayac and Robert A. Zayac Jr., "Georgia Married Women's Property Act: An Effective Challenge to Coverture," *Texas Journal of Women and the Law* 15 (Fall 2005): 1.

38. SVVR diary, July 17, 19, 1852, Oct. 7, 1852; SPR diary, Apr. 24, 1860; Young, *History of Macon*, 182; *Macon Directory for 1860* (Macon, Ga.: Andrews, 1860), 75, 98.

39. SVVR diary, Nov. 18, 1852, Dec. 13, 1852; SPR diary, Dec. 9, 1852.

40. SPR to SVVR, Aug. 8, 1852, box 3, folder 6, Richards Papers; SVVR diary, July 14, 1853, Sept. 13, 1853 (books), Aug. 22, 1853 (Sparta incident), Nov. 11, 1853 (illness); SPR diary, Dec. 16, 1852 (sweetest wife), Aug. 9, 1853 (happy marriage), Aug. 23, 1853 (Sparta incident).

41. SPR to SVVR, Aug. 8, 1852 (advice about travel), box 3, folder 6, Richards Papers; SVVR diary, Mar. 6, 1853, Apr. 3, 1853 (church), May 13, 1853 (sewing), Nov. 5, 1853 (childlessness); SPR diary, July 2, 1853 (sewing), Sept. 16, 1853 (baking), Nov. 10, 1853 (Amelia's baby), Sept. 8, 11, 1854 (Dora's birth). Sallie G. McMillen has discussed how Southern women had higher fertility rates than their Northern counterparts in *Southern Women Black and White in the Old South* (Arlington Heights, Ill.: Harlan Davidson, 1992), 48–50.

42. SPR diary, Jan. 4, 1855, July 20, 1855 (Griffin store), Sept. 26, 1855 (Atlanta plans), Sept. 6, 1858 (Atlanta Baptists), Dec. 14, 1857, Apr. 30, 1859, July 18, 1859 (Sarah Hathaway Richards). In addition to the stillborn son in 1849, JJR and Sarah also had a daughter, Blanche, who died at age three in 1853, the same year that her sister, Annie, was born. SPR and SVVR were very fond of Blanche. See SPR diary, June 5, 1853, SVVR diary, June 5, 1853.

43. SPR diary, Oct. 19, 1857 (Panic), Nov. 18, 1859, July 12, 1860 (Atlanta fires), May 23, 1857, Sept. 1, 1857 (Macon store).

44. Ibid., July 18, 1856 (Irene), May 23, 1858 (Arthur), Dec. 14, 1859 (stillborn son), Dec. 1, 1855 (pies); SVVR diary, Mar. 1, 1857.

45. See, for example, SPR diary, Jan. 29, 1857; Thomas D. Morris, *Southern Slavery and the Law, 1619–1860* (Chapel Hill: University of North Carolina Press, 1996), 132–33.

46. Macon pastor E. W. Warren quoted in Elizabeth Fox-Genovese and Eugene D. Genovese, *The Mind of the Master Class: History and Faith in the Southern Slaveholders' Worldview* (New York: Cambridge University Press, 2005), 202; SVVR diary, July 30, 1852 ("poor, ignorant," describing an African American church service), Nov. 13, 1852 (*Uncle Tom's Cabin*); SPR diary, Nov. 4, 1852 (*Uncle Tom's Cabin*); SVVR to SPR, Nov. 21, 1852 (Aunt Huldah), box 6, folder 3, Richards Papers. The scholarly literature on Southerners' defense of slavery is vast. Eugene D. Genovese has discussed slave owners' belief in a lightly tasked work force in *Roll, Jordan, Roll: The World the Slaves Made* (New York: Vintage, 1974), 58. According to James Oakes, in the South, "[r]acism and the gospel of prosperity fused to form the prevailing ideology" (*The Ruling Race: A History of American Slaveholders* [New York: Norton, 1998], 138).

47. Ira Berlin, *Generations of Captivity: A History of African-American Slaves* (Cambridge: Harvard University Press, 2003), 221–24. For an example of a slave whipping, see SPR diary, May 5, 1862, when Ellen used some of her mistress's toiletries without permission.

48. SPR diary, Jan. 31, 1857, Mar. 3, 1857.

49. Ibid., Mar. 1, 2, 1857, Apr. 17, 1857 (children's illnesses), Apr. 13, 1857 (Henry), Apr. 19, 1857 (garden), Apr. 25, 1857, May 7, 1857 (Dicey). Dicey's owner, a Mr. Grier, was probably Ebenezer C. Grier, an attorney whose family owned eight slaves, one of them listed as age twenty-six in 1860 (Eighth Census of the United States [1860], microcopy 653, Georgia Slave Schedules). Southern courts debated to what degree a slave's hirer had authority to whip a slave (Morris, *Southern Slavery and the Law*, 137–39), but SPR took no chances and involved Dicey's owner.

50. SPR to SVVR, Aug. 2, 1857, box 3, folder 7, Richards Papers.

51. SPR diary, Nov. 1, 1844, Mar. 3, 1845 (Clay), Oct. 14, 1848, Nov. 7, 17, 1848, July 11, 1850, Oct. 1, 1850 (Taylor and Fillmore); Charles J. Johnson Jr., "John Macpherson Berrien," and Stewart D. Bratcher, "Eugenius A. Nisbet," both in *New Georgia Encyclopedia*. SPR also voted for George W. Crawford, the sole Whig to serve as governor of Georgia (SPR diary, Oct. 6, 1845). When Fillmore visited Macon in 1854, SPR described him as "a mild, kindly looking old gentleman" (SPR diary, Apr. 2, 1854).

52. SPR diary, Aug. 3, 1849, Oct. 22, 1851 (Stephens), Oct. 1, 7, 1851 (Cobb), Nov. 1, 1852 (1852 presidential election); W. Darrell Overdyke, *The Know-Nothing Party in the South* (Baton Rouge: Louisiana State University Press, 1950), 46.

53. Tyler Anbinder, *Nativism and Slavery: The Northern Know Nothings and the Politics of the 1850s* (New York: Oxford University Press, 1992), 103–6, 167–68; Overdyke, *Know-Nothing Party*, 45–46, 62.

54. SPR diary, Oct. 9, 1854 (Know-Nothing meeting), Oct. 1, 1855 (Andrews), Oct. 29, 1856, Nov. 12, 1856 (1856 presidential election); Overdyke, *Know-Nothing Party*, 96–98.

55. SPR diary, Oct. 9, 1857 (Hill); Overdyke, *Know-Nothing Party*, 263.

56. SPR diary, Feb. 7, 1859 (piano), Feb. 13, 1857 (Addison's marriage), Jan. 2, 1856 (Will's move to Rhode Island), Aug. 19, 27, 1860, Sept. 22, 1860 (trip), Oct. 24, 1858 (Aunt Huldah).

57. Ibid., Oct. 13, 1860.

ONE

October 1860 to September 1861

"I WAS A STRONG UNION MAN UNTIL LATELY"

One month after the fall of Fort Sumter, Sam Richards wrote with apparent resignation, "I was a strong Union man until lately." Like many white Southerners, Richards believed the election of Abraham Lincoln signaled the triumph of radical abolitionism over moderation and reason. Nonetheless, as his diary reveals, until Georgia left the Union, he held out hope that "wiser counsels will prevail" and civil war might be averted. Such would not be the case.[1]

Like other voters, Richards was caught up in the excitement of the 1860 election. Senator Stephen A. Douglas, the Democratic Party's candidate for president, spoke in both Macon and Atlanta in late October 1860. On both occasions, he was introduced by his friend, Senator Alexander Stephens of Georgia. Richards had long admired Stephens, and both Stephens and Douglas opposed secession. Sam Richards attended the Macon speech, among a crowd the *Macon Telegraph* estimated at twelve thousand, but could hear little of what Stephens and Douglas said in the midst of such a throng.[2]

Despite the presence of these prominent Unionists and despite Richards's condemnation of secessionists as "young *squirts*" and "*politicians* who aspire to office in a Southern Confederacy," he ultimately supported Confederate independence, a cause that had increasing support in his community and family. Judge Eugenius Nisbet, a fellow Macon Baptist whose support for the Whig Party and eulogy of President Zachary Taylor had impressed Richards, now played a leading role in Georgia secession. Richards heard Nisbet speak in favor of secession on December 1, 1860, and noted his previous support for Unionism. Nisbet later introduced the resolution that led Georgia to leave the Union.[3]

Members of the Van Valkenburg and Richards families lined up to support the Confederacy. On December 14, 1860, Sallie's brother, James, active in the militia and a fervent secessionist, signed his name to a call for Georgia's "immediate secession." Both James, married and the father of four children, and his brother, George, also married, joined the army a few weeks after the fall of Fort Sumter. Several months later, James was elected captain of Company I, 61st Georgia Volunteer Infantry, Army of Northern Virginia, also known as the Thompson Guards. The 61st saw action early in the war, including the Seven Days' Battles in 1862. James Van Valkenburg won promotion to major in 1863 and to lieutenant colonel in 1864.[4]

Sallie's beloved older sister, Harriet, had married into the planter class, the group with the largest stake in Confederate nationalism. After sitting out her prime courtship years to care for her motherless younger siblings, Harriet had taken a series of one-year jobs as schoolteacher to the children of wealthy planters in rural Georgia. In 1858, she married forty-four-year old Seth K. Taylor of Americus, the twice widowed father of seven children. Sam Richards believed that Harriet had made a marriage of convenience because she feared "Old Maidism," so he was pleasantly surprised to meet Taylor and find him convivial and "not ill looking." Harriet's marriage was financially advantageous. Richards reported that she was now the mistress of a fine home in Americus, a plantation outside town, and many slaves. Her stepson, Thomas Taylor, joined the Confederate Army.[5]

The only members of the Van Valkenburg family to express Unionist sentiments were Sallie's father and aunt, Huldah Van Valkenburg. Sam described James Van Valkenburg as "such a tory that it is no pleasure to hear from him." But Richards had little to do with his father-in-law during the 1860s. In 1854, Van Valkenburg married Mary Bradley of Texas, Georgia, a western Georgia community where he had opened a mill. The children of his first marriage disliked their stepmother and saw little of her as the couple spent an increasing amount of their time in Texas. James Van Valkenburg had negligible influence on Sam. Huldah Van Valkenburg married William J. Turrell, a Pennsylvania attorney and politician who supported the Union and the Lincoln administration, and moved north. The Richards family did not see her again until the final months of the war.[6]

While no members of the Richards family joined the military, they showed their devotion to Confederate nationalism in other ways. Kate Richards DuBose, Sam's younger sister, resided in Sparta, Georgia, with her husband, Charles, a politically well-connected lawyer who served as clerk of the Georgia Supreme Court beginning in 1860 and was a member of the Georgia legislature during and after the war. In the 1840s and 1850s, Kate DuBose published poems and stories, first in William Carey Richards's literary magazines and later in her own right. *The Pastor's Household*, a morality tale designed for the benefit of children, was perhaps her best-known work. This book, along with her poem, "Wachulla," won her a place in *Women of the South Distinguished by Literature* (1860) alongside better-known writers such as Augusta Jane Evans and Louisa McCord.[7]

When Hancock County mustered in a company of soldiers to fight for Southern independence in May 1861, community leaders turned to their local poet for appropriate words of inspiration. Representing the women of the county, Kate DuBose presented a flag to the assembled soldiers and spoke words she had written for the occasion. Her poem began: "Onward brave spirits with patriot devotion / Shrink not from duty though death be your meed." Kate's patriotism also led her to write lyrics for at least one Confederate anthem, "God Defendeth the Right." Her rhetoric presented a familiar picture:

> Long have we yielded to Northern Aggression,
> Yield we no more; as bold freemen we stand!
> Same to submit to a tyrant's oppression
> Rally for truth and our dear native land.
> Up, in the name of God! Wait we no longer,
> Now is the moment to do or to die;
> Fighting for freedom, each heart shall grow stronger,
> None be so craven, to tremble or fly![8]

Sam's sisters, Ellen and Amelia, married men they met while teaching school near Savannah, and their husbands, like those of Kate DuBose and Harriet Van Valkenburg, had ties to the planter class. Nell married Stephen Whitehead, who joined the Confederate Army, while Amie's husband was Henry R. Williams. The sisters lived in St. Peters Parish, just over the state line in South Carolina. In 1849, William and Ann Richards had decided to sell their land and home in Penfield, and they moved to St. Helena Island, near Nell and Amie. According to the 1860 Census, the Richardses had modest holdings of two thousand dollars in real estate and personal property, including two slaves.[9]

The two eldest Richards brothers continued to reside in the North. Although Addison and Mary appear to have been either sympathetic with the South or apolitical, William Carey Richards appalled his siblings by taking a stance of unwavering Unionism. Although Will had resided in Penfield, Athens, and Charleston for a decade and traveled extensively throughout the region as a lecturer, he came to regard the South as economically, socially, and intellectually backward and blamed slavery for the region's failure to modernize—and perhaps its failure to appreciate his efforts to bring literary enlightenment to its people. Because of slavery, Will Richards wrote, "Agriculture, Industrial Arts and Education were all dwarfed and stunted" in the South. Richards was no radical; he argued that white children were "degraded, intellectually, by association with the slave children." Nonetheless, Sam rejected his brother's view that secession had led Georgia down a "suicidal path." Labeling his brother a "fanatic," he decried Will's adherence to "the despotic government that is doing their utmost to destroy us and make slaves of freemen."[10]

Such strident language might seem surprising given Sam Richards's earlier support for Unionism. During the secession winter and spring of 1860–61, he shared many Americans' unease regarding political and economic issues. However, Georgia's vote to leave the Union, the "invasion" of the South by Federals (whom Richards insisted on calling "Hessians"), and early Confederate military victories erased any doubts in his mind about the righteousness of the Confederate cause. Georgia "resumed her sovereignty" by leaving the Union, he wrote on January 19, 1861. Confederates, he believed, represented "true republicans," in contrast to Northern despots.[11]

Religious references infused the rhetoric of Sam Richards and both his Confederate and Unionist siblings. Will Richards charged his congregation in Pittsfield, Massachusetts, to hear "in the intervals of the sullen boom of the cannon, the sweet tone of Divine promise [and to have] renewed confidence in the final success of our cause." Sam's writings about Georgia secession combined racism, anger toward the North, and the belief in "a just God" who would honor Southern claims of moral superiority. Like many white Southerners, he attributed Confederate victory at the First Battle of Manassas to divine intervention. Throughout the war, Sam's writing invoked sermons, scriptural references, and his personal religious beliefs. He frequently observed the days of fasting and prayer declared by Confederate president Jefferson Davis or by Georgia governor Joseph Emerson Brown. These fast days were designed to give religious meaning to the war through acts of individual and collective sacrifice and worship. In the South, fast days also represented an effort to build a national identity. Before the Civil War, fast days had been a Northern phenomenon, a legacy of the Puritans. During the war, Davis called a total of ten fast days, beginning on June 13, 1861, while Lincoln called only three.[12]

Jabez Richards's home in Atlanta became a gathering place for the Richards siblings who resided in the South, for it was centrally located to accommodate branches of the family in Macon, Sparta, and the Savannah area. In 1860, the widowed Jabez married Stella Wheeler, a young woman from Marietta, Georgia. With his usual bluntness, Sam described his new sister-in-law as "not very pretty, either in form or features but ... intelligent and amiable." Her youth and apparent good health no doubt appealed to Jabe, who had spent a decade caring for his consumptive first wife. The family hoped that Stella would be a good stepmother to seven-year-old Annie. As he had for several years, Jabe wrote to Sam praising Atlanta as a place to live and work, and by March 1860, Jabe had begun trying to convince his brother to give up the Macon store and relocate to Atlanta. Sam resisted, believing that business in Macon was too profitable. Wartime conditions soon forced him to reconsider.[13]

Notes

1. SPR diary, Jan. 6, 1861, May 10, 1861.

2. Ibid., Oct. 22, 1851 (earlier Stephens speech), Nov. 1, 1860; *MT*, Nov. 1, 1860.

3. SPR diary, Oct. 1, 1850, Dec. 1, 8, 1860.

4. Ida Young, *History of Macon, Georgia* (Macon, Ga.: Lyon, Marshall, and Brooks, 1950), 204, 246; Jack G. Thomas and Katherine Moore Thomas, *Confederate Burials, Rose Hill Cemetery, Macon, Georgia* (Macon, Ga.: privately published, 2003), 112; James D. Van Valkenburg record, Compiled Military Service Records, National Archives, Microfilm 266, 561; Stewart Sifakis, *Compendium of the Confederate Armies: South Carolina and Georgia* (New York: Facts on File, 1995), 275–76.

5. SPR diary, Oct. 19, 1857, Dec. 19, 1857, Jan. 12, 1858, June 13, 1858, July 28, 1861 (Thomas Taylor); *Macon Weekly Telegraph*, Jan. 19, 1858; William Bailey Williford, *Americus through the Years: The Story of a Georgia Town and Its People, 1832–1875* (Atlanta: Cherokee, 1975), 249.

6. SPR diary, Feb. 19, 1854, Oct. 31, 1863; SVVR diary, June 19, 1854.

7. Mrs. C. W. DuBose, *The Pastor's Household; or, Lessons on the Eleventh Commandment* (New York: Sheldon, 1858). "Wachulla" described a fountain in Florida. See Julia Deane Freeman, *Women of the South Distinguished by Literature* (New York: Derby and Jackson, 1860), 407–15; Susan J. Harrington, *Cemeteries of Hancock County, Georgia* (Milledgeville, Ga.: Friends of Hancock

Cemeteries, 2004), 506. SPR wrote about Charlie DuBose's appointment as clerk and reported his salary as five thousand dollars (SPR diary, Dec. 31, 1859; see also Apr. 5, 1860).

8. Forrest Shivers, *The Land Between: A Story of Hancock County, Georgia, to 1940* (Spartanburg, S.C.: Reprint Company, 1990), 154, 328; Mrs. C. W. DuBose and Hermann Schreiner, "God Defendeth the Right" (Macon, Ga.: Schreiner, 1861). In 1885, Charles DuBose played a role in a sensational legal case when he served as co-executor for the will of David Dixon, a wealthy Hancock County landowner who left his sizable estate to his biracial daughter, Amanda America Dixon, the product of his union with a slave woman. Amanda Dixon hired DuBose to fight white relatives who sought to claim her inheritance. She won in court. See Kent Anderson Leslie, *Woman of Color, Daughter of Privilege: Amanda America Dixon* (Athens: University of Georgia Press, 1995), 78–79, 83–85, 92, 104, 128.

9. SPR diary, June 9, 1860; Mary Levin Koch, "The Romance of American Landscape: The Art of Thomas Addison Richards," *Georgia Museum of Art Bulletin* 8 (Winter 1983): 27 n.6, citing *Richards Weekly Gazette*, Aug. 25, 1849, when William Richards offered his home and 130 acres for sale. See also Eighth Census of the United States (1860), microcopy 653, Beaufort, S.C.

10. SPR diary, Jan. 19, 1861, Aug. 31, 1861. For Will's views on slavery, see William C. Richards, *Thanksgiving for Peace: A Sermon Preached in the First Congregational Church at Pittsfield, Mass., on the Occasion of the National and State Thanksgiving, December 7, 1865* (New York: Sheldon, 1866), 32.

11. SPR diary, Jan. 19, 1861, June 24, 1861, Sept. 7, 1861. Anne Sarah Rubin has written that Southerners, including former Unionists, "seemed willing, if not eager, to turn their back on the Union in favor of this new nation, and to do so with nary a backward glance" (*A Shattered Nation: The Rise and Fall of the Confederacy, 1861–1868* [Chapel Hill: University of North Carolina Press, 2005], 11).

12. DuBose and Schreiner, "God Defendeth the Right"; William C. Richards, *Thanksgiving for Peace*, 9–10; SPR diary, Jan. 19, 1861 (secession), June 13, 1861 (fast day), July 27, 1861 (Manassas); Harry S. Stout, *Upon the Altar of the Nation: A Moral History of the American Civil War* (New York: Viking, 2006), 47–49.

13. SPR diary, Mar. 10, 1860 (Atlanta), Apr. 5, 1860 (marriage), July 16, 1860 (Stella).

Wed' 24. [October 24, 1860]

I have had "the blues" badly this week on account of dull times and no money to pay notes falling due, but as heretofore we have found relief from present distress and raised nearly $600 from sources that we did not look to until the last day. Mr. Craig has let me have $350 that he had deposited in bank and it appears that Mr Craig's brother in Atlanta has let Jabez have $220 that *he* had in bank, which Jabe has sent me.* And the two houses to whom I wrote asking extension in notes have replied very kindly so that if trade revives soon we shall get along but the prospect for business is not at all cheering.—We have been to [religious] meetings every night this week and have had very pleasant ones and several persons seem to be concerned about their souls.

Sunday 28. [October 28, 1860]

It rained this morning from 7 until 10 and we had but a small school tho' my three scholars were all there. They are good boys and get their lessons well, especially Leroy and Willie who seem to understand their lessons and do not merely learn them by rote.—Bro Warren preached from the text "And the book shall be opened" and called on any who desired prayer made for them to go forward, and several went up.† Tonight, four are to be baptized, who have joined since last Sabbath. I have not been able to enjoy the services of the day for thinking of "hard times" and fearing for the future which I ought not to do, I know, for I ought to have faith enough to believe that the same Providence that has directed and sustained for so many years, will continue to do so in the time to come.—

Tuesday 30. [October 30, 1860]

Business continues terribly dull and the political sky is dark. . . . The "Little Giant" Stephen A. Douglas was tonight welcomed to our city with 21 Guns and he *speaks* here tomorrow. A letter from Mary Hathaway to Sally tells us the good news that Sister Ellen is recovering strength slowly and I feel that our Heavenly Father has restored her in answer to prayer.

Thursday 1. [November 1, 1860]

Today is a comparatively quiet one in our city, yesterday thronged with human beings as it was to see and hear "the Douglas[.]" "Little Aleck" too as Hon. A H Stephens is called, was Here and preceded Douglas in speaking. I went to the Depot and saw the "Little Giant" and heard him

---

* David Craig worked at Schofield's Foundry and lived with SPR and his family, paying twenty dollars per month room and board. The entire family liked Craig, who was generous about giving gifts to the children (SPR diary, Sept. 2, 1859, Dec. 25, 1859).

† Rev. Ebenezer W. Warren of First Baptist Church was the Richards family's pastor beginning in 1859. SPR taught Sunday school (SPR diary, Dec. 25, 1859; H. Lewis Batts, *History of First Baptist Church of Christ at Macon, 1826–1968* [Macon, Ga.: Southern, 1969], 45).

speaking but could not distinguish much that he said.* Business was tolerably good yesterday. Henry R. Jackson spoke last night on the Secession side of the question.—

Sunday 4. [November 4, 1860]

Sat. 10. [November 10, 1860]

This has been a week of excitement and interest politically but a very dull one in *business*, and the result of the Presidential Election of the 6th inst[ant] has been that the Republican party—has succeeded in forcing upon the South Abraham Lincoln as president, with the expectation that we would submit to the imposition when we found it accomplished and all would go on calmly and quietly as ever.† But it is not so[;] the whole country is in a ferment and we are probably upon the eve of a revolution that shall dissolve the ties that connect the North and the South and the *Union* will cease to exist! It is a serious and momentous crisis and I fear will bring distress and ruin upon us. Several of the Southern States will probably secede either peaceably or otherwise. God grant it *may* be the former if at all. Several meetings of our citizens have been held this week and a company of "Minute Men" has been organized for defense and safety.‡

---

* Although presidential candidates in the nineteenth century generally did not campaign, instead leaving such politicking to their minions, Stephen A. Douglas campaigned extensively in 1860, fearing that the Union might splinter if his rival, Abraham Lincoln, won the election. Douglas and Stephens were known as the Little Giant and Little Aleck, respectively, because of their short stature (Thomas E. Schott, *Alexander Stephens of Georgia: A Biography* [Baton Rouge: Louisiana State University Press, 1988], 191–322). *MT*, Nov. 1, 1860, said that Douglas offered "nothing new. . . . It was a plain, forcible speech—thoroughly national in its spirit—and received with a good deal of enthusiasm." See also ADI, Oct. 31, 1860.

† Lincoln won the election with 39 percent of the popular vote nationally. In Georgia, John Breckinridge, the prosecession candidate, won 51,893 votes; John Bell, the border state Unionist candidate, won 42,855 votes; and Stephen A. Douglas, the Democratic candidate, won 11,580 votes. The city of Atlanta gave a plurality to Bell. See ADI, Nov. 8, 1860; Ralph Benjamin Singer Jr., "Confederate Atlanta" (Ph.D. diss., University of Georgia, 1973), 40–41.

‡ Both Macon and Atlanta created militia groups called Minute Men. Macon's Minute Men met in the city's concert hall immediately following Lincoln's election, quickly renaming themselves Minute Men Company no. 1 and enlisting five hundred members (*MT*, Nov. 10, 1860; Richard W. Iobst, *Civil War Macon: The History of a Confederate City* [Macon, Ga.: Mercer University Press, 1999], 35–

We hear that there has been a great fight in New York since the election, between the Union men and the Republicans.*

Sunday 11. [November 11, 1860]
A beautiful day and as quiet as tho' no trouble was impending. . . .

Sat. 17. [November 17, 1860]
It has been a dull week; people are too much engrossed in political matters to think of buying books. . . .

Sunday 18. [November 18, 1860]

Monday 19. [November 19, 1860]
. . . A *Georgia* flag has been flying today over our city—!

Friday 23. [November 23, 1860]
Today sales were pretty good for the times. . . .

Saturday 24. [November 24, 1860]

Sunday 25. [November 25, 1860]
. . . I had but *one* scholar this morning. Bro Warren preached about "Sheep" Sallie says and so he did and about Christ as the Shepherd, but my mind wandered much to other matters, as is too often the case nowadays.—Thoughts of "tomorrow" will obtrude themselves and the future looks dark and uncertain. "Disunion" seems imminent and that I fear will prove ruinous to *our* business. How strange it is that the fanaticism of the North should be so encouraged by the mass of the people at the price of the peace and Union of the whole country! Why cant they mind their own business and let us take care of ours? They will regret it when it is too late, I guess.—

Monday 26. [November 26, 1860]
One of our banks, "The Manufacturers," has "caved in," but promises to pay up after awhile and the money *passes* in trade somewhat yet but most persons are rather shy of it unless they are indebted to the bank in some way

---

36). Atlanta's Minute Men, anticipating the election's outcome, held a preliminary meeting before the election (*ADI*, Nov. 2, 1860).

* At midnight on the night of Lincoln's election, a group of his supporters known as the Wide-Awakes were parading around New York City in celebration when they were attacked by rowdies. In the ensuing fight, several people sustained injuries before the Wide-Awakes overwhelmed and dispersed their opponents (*NYT*, Nov. 7, 1860).

which a good many indeed are. Tonight I read aloud the first instalment of "Great Expectations" a new novel by Dickens in Harpers Weekly.—*

Wed 28. [November 28, 1860]

Today was the day appointed by the Governor for Fasting & Prayer and most of the stores were closed and as the weather was wet and unpleasant very little business would have been done anyhow. We had a prayer meeting at our church between nine and eleven o'clock and prayers were offered for our country and the Union, but Dick Branham made a *Secession* prayer.†

Sat. December 1. [December 1, 1860]

Last night was our Conference and the motion to change the hour of Communion from afternoon to the close of morning service was lost. After meeting I went to Concert Hall to hear Judge Nisbet address the Minute Men. He has until lately opposed Secession but now says it is the only remedy for the evils that threaten us and indeed the only way possible even to save the Union if that is desirable.‡ The future looks very dark and uncertain.

Sunday 2. [December 2, 1860]

Saturday 8. [December 8, 1860]

We have had right cold weather for several days until today; yest morning the thermometer said 32°[;] this morning 52° a difference of 20° in 24 hours.—It has been a discouraging week no business doing, no money coming in and nothing heard but "Secession," "Secession" until I am tired and sick of the word. At the election for City Council today several good men were stricken off the ticket by some men because they were "Submissionists" as they choose to style all who do not advocate *immediate Secession.* And I find that the Secessionists are chiefly *professional* men and young

---

* Charles Dickens's *Great Expectations* was serialized in *Harper's Weekly* between Dec. 1860 and Aug. 1861.

† Joel R. Branham graduated from Emory College, in Oxford, Georgia, and was ordained a Baptist minister in 1866. In Aug. 1860, Branham, who was choir director for the First Baptist Church, acquired an organ for the church. See Batts, *History of the First Baptist Church,* 34; William Cathcart, *The Baptist Encyclopedia: A Dictionary* (Philadelphia: Everts, 1881), 126–27. SPR discussed the organ (SPR diary, Dec. 13, 1860).

‡ Judge Eugenius A. Nisbet and Washington Poe were the featured speakers at this meeting. The *Macon Daily Telegraph,* Nov. 30, 1860, characterized the two as "able and experienced men [who] take strong secession ground" (quoted in Iobst, *Civil War Macon,* 37).

squirts who have but little or nothing to lose in any event, or *politicians* who aspire to office in a Southern Confederacy despairing of attaining to it under the present condition of things. T. R. R. Cobb of Athens made a speech *four hours* long last night at Concert Hall to a crowd, on "Secession."*

Sunday 9. [December 9, 1860]
Our former boarder Mr. Boardman dropped in upon us just after breakfast today; he has left the place at which he has been since he left us for lack of work [in] these tight times.—This is the 8th anniversary of our Wedding day, and we still "go in" for the "The Union!"

Thursday 13. [December 13, 1860]
Last Monday night I went to Bro Boykins to practise with others in preparation for a Concert that Dick Branham was to give for the purpose of paying for our Church Organ which is expected very soon; and again on last night we met there and this afternoon again at the Concert Hall for a final rehearsal. And tonight the Concert *came off* as announced! The performance was decidedly better than "the house" as the latter was quite *thin* not more than about 150 persons being there.—Sallie has a letter from Mary Add who says the times there are quite hard upon the *painters* publishers &c.—Kate Rogers has come South to Charleston in spite of Secession and Disunion.—†

Sunday 16. [December 16, 1860]
Rev Hornady preached for us this morning and Mr Branham being absent I had to be choirister.‡ . . .

---

* Thomas R. R. Cobb, an ardent secessionist, was the younger brother of Howell Cobb, a distinguished congressman and former speaker of the U.S. House of Representatives. T. R. R. Cobb gave many speeches advocating secession during this time, including addresses in Atlanta and Milledgeville. *MT*, Dec. 10, 1860, clocked this speech at four and a half hours and claimed that Cobb "succeeded in riveting the attention of the audience to its close." He became a brigadier general in the Confederate Army (William B. McCash, *Thomas R. R. Cobb: The Making of a Southern Nationalist* [Macon, Ga.: Mercer University Press, 1983], 196, 316–17).

| *MT*, Dec. 13, 1860, urged Macon residents to turn out for the concert "and give them a crowded house." Family members sometimes referred to Addison Richards's wife as "Mary Add." During his August 1860, trip to New York, SPR referred to meeting Kate Rogers and identified her as half-sister to his sister-in-law, Cornelia Richards (SPR diary, Aug. 27, 1860, Sept. 13, 1860).

‡ H. C. Hornady was pastor of Atlanta's First Baptist Church, located on Forsyth Street between Walton and Poplar, from 1861 to 1867. He also helped edit the *Baptist Banner* (*One Hundred Years of the First Baptist Church Atlanta, Georgia, Centennial Celebration, 1848–1948* [Atlanta: Ray, 1948], 16–20).

Sat. 22. [December 22, 1860]

This closing week of our "World's Fair" has been one of more business with us than for some time previous, and one of great political excitement[.]* Speeches *Immediate* Secession—and Anti-Immediate, tho' more of the former by a good many. South Carolina has declared herself *out of* the Union and yesterday at noon our Church bells were rung and one hundred guns fired in her honor. I think they had better have *tolled* the bells for the death of the Union. A letter from Amelia shows that even quiet *she* has caught the "So[uth]. Ca[rolina]. fever" and talks as hot secession doctrine as anyone and Charlie DuBose tells me that Father is the same say. For my part I think South Carolina has got what is vulgarly termed the "Swell head" *bad* or she would have waited for company a little while at least. I fear she will get us into a fight yet by her indecent haste.

Sunday 23. [December 23, 1860]

"Paul" our cook's husband died on our lot this morning after a weeks illness and I greatly fear utterly unfit for judgment. Ann is greatly distressed for she seemed to think much of him although he being given to drink sometimes ill treated her it is said.—Bro Warren preached twice today but Sallie did not go tonight as Irene and Arthur are "croupy" with colds.—Dora and I had a long walk and talk this afternoon by ourselves.—

Tuesday 25. [December 25, 1860]

Christmas Day—The weather is brighter than it usually is at this season but trade is *otherwise*. . . . We made our little folks happy this morning in finding that good old Santa Claus had not passed them by. Poor children—they ought to enjoy life now—the days of trouble and care will come soon enough probably. . . .

Sunday 30. [December 30, 1860]

Monday 31. [December 31, 1860]

But little hope of preserving the Union from present indications. The Abolitionists and Fire-Eaters are determined to destroy it. The year is closing in darkness and gloom; the natural sky seems to be in sympathy with a political sky—dark and portentous. God keep us from harm.

---

* Macon held a Belgian Fair, Dec. 11–12, 1860, along with its annual Cotton Planters' Convention, Dec. 3–22, to showcase products from Belgium and the American South (Young, *History of Macon*, 192–94).

Sunday 6. [January 6, 1861]

First Sabbath of the year.—Today and yesterday have been the only bright and pleasant days this year so far and tonight it is again dark and cloudy betokening more rain. We have been out three times today to church morning and night to preaching and in the aft to our Communion service at which there was a better attendance than I have seen for a good while. Bro Warren told us somewhat of the progress of the church during the past year and what he himself had done in the way of preaching, visiting, marrying and burying. He then exhorted us all to be more active earnest and faithful during this year than we had been during the past. . . . Nothing cheering as regards the state of our—Nation—there really appears to be some prospect of War but I hope wiser counsels will prevail.

Friday 11. [January 11, 1861]

Our annual Conference was held tonight and the Church Officers elected for the year. Political affairs continue to grow dark and yet more dark; *War*—actual war, seems to be impending over us—U.S. troops have been fired upon by the So' Carolinians and prevented from landing at Fort Sumpter which will probably soon be followed by more fatal action.*

Sunday 13. [January 13, 1861]

Monday 14. [January 14, 1861]

Sat. 19. [January 19, 1861]

This is an important day in the history of this State for Georgia has today "resumed her sovereignty" and the Ordinance for Secession has passed the Convention by a vote of 210 to 90 we hear!† Booming guns

---

* Fort Sumter, a federal installation in the Charleston, S.C., harbor, became the subject of intense interest during the early months of 1861. South Carolina had seceded from the Union shortly after Lincoln's election, and Charleston was the state's center of secessionist activism. Outgoing U.S. president James Buchanan decided to send an unarmed ship to reinforce the fort. On Jan. 10, 1861, the NYT reported that the ship *Star of the West* had attempted to reach Sumter the preceding morning and was shelled by a garrison of South Carolinians on nearby Morris Island. The ship then "put about, and went to sea."

†The Georgia convention's first vote on secession was 166 to 130 on a resolution introduced by Nisbet. Additional debate led to fading strength for moderates, known as "cooperationists," and a final vote of 208 to 89 (Michael P. Johnson, *Toward a Patriarchal Republic: The Secession of Georgia* [Baton Rouge: Louisiana State University Press, 1977], 114–17).

and pealing bells have announced the "joyful news!" I cannot sympathize in such demonstrations although I have lately been obliged to think that Secession was a stern necessity for us in the present crisis, for if Georgia had faltered it would have given aid and comfort to the Abolitionists in their fell designs of making war upon the South, to *coerce* her into *the Union* again! For two nights I have met a crowd of singers at Dr Emersons splendid rooms in order to practise a Southern Marseilles Hymn to be sung in open air upon the night of a great demonstration by the Minute Men, probably next Monday night. I received a letter from bro William today depricating the measures that we are taking as suicidal in the extreme as well as unjust to the North. I wonder that Will with his knowledge of our institutions and his views of slavery cannot see that we need desperate remedies and sympathize with us in the dire necessity. S. Carolina—Florida—Mississippi—Alabama and Georgia are now no longer connected with the United States of America but are preparing to form a Southern Republic[,] a "*White* Man's Republic" as one of our papers has it, and leave niggerism and "free dirt" proclivities to the North and the Abolitionists upon whom surely the curse of a just God must rest for *they have destroyed our Country.**. . .

Sunday 27. [January 27, 1861]

Until today we have had dark and rainy weather for more than a week and we gladly hail the return of sunshine. It has been bad weather all this month. Our preacher gave us this morning his views upon the subject of Slavery as of divine appointment and in accordance with the will of God and the teachings of the bible. Mr Stone our best tenor singer has "gone to the wars" he left last week with 84 others as a company of Artillery to defend if necessary our sea coast at Brunswick Geo. Charlie DuBose came in this afternoon as Supreme Court sits here tomorrow of which august body he is clerk. . . . Louisiana has joined the Secession ranks and Texas will probably come out this week.

Thursday 31. [January 31, 1861]

We have had some fine weather this week which has been very grateful to our senses after the previous darkness. Trade has been much better than I expected it would this month. Tonight Sallie and I went to Covenant meeting and there were so few there to *talk* that after praying by Bro

---

* The Republican Party of president-elect Abraham Lincoln had taken as its political credo "Free Soil," the notion of gradually ending slavery by preventing its spread into territories such as those acquired in the Mexican-American War of 1846–48.

Warren's request I felt constrained to say a word or two for the first time at these meetings.

Feb. 11. [February 11, 1861]

Nothing of much interest has transpired in our political world this month except the meeting of the Convention at Montgomery Ala which has elected Jefferson Davis of Miss. & Alex H. Stephens of Geo President and Vice President of the Southern United States. Seven States have seceded and are joined now in a southern Republic. There appears to be very little prospect now of Saving the Old Union. Our prayer now is that the new Union may *go in* without civil war and fraternal bloodshed. . . .

Thursday 14. [February 14, 1861]

St Valentines Day—The weather has been quite favorable for birds to mate and *Valentines to sell* for several days previous to this but this morning was wet and dark. It cleared up however at noon. But the Val' trade has not been as brisk as it was last year tho' yesterday was a very busy and fatigueing day to us. . . . Our Southern Congress is getting on harmoniously.—

Sunday 17. [February 17, 1861]

Bro Warren was not able to preach today and Samuel Boykin officiated and discoursed upon Election from the text "whom he did foreknow &c." . . .

Sunday 24. [February 24, 1861]

Monday 25. [February 25, 1861]

I began gardening by planting some corn peas, onions radishes and Eggplants as my orders are all off for the present and I have not much to require attention at the Store.

Thursday 28. [February 28, 1861]

I have brought about $50 worth of goods at the Belgian Sale this week tho' most of the things bring fair prices and some *more* than fair. I wish I had bought more *paper* as I understand the *duty* on that article will be 24% under the new tariff operation. Upon *Books* it is only 8 and but 4 per cent on Music in sheets.—The duties at present are in accordance with the old US. Tariff of 1857!*

---

* On Feb. 9, 1861, the Confederate Congress, meeting in Montgomery, Alabama, voted to enforce terms of the U.S. tariff of 1857 until the legislature had time to debate terms for a new tariff (Douglas B. Ball, *Financial Failure and Confederate Defeat* [Urbana: University of Illinois Press, 1991], 203).

Sunday 3. [March 3, 1861]

This my 37th *birthday annivy* has been a beautiful spring day bright and balmy which we have improved as much as possible as far as going out is concerned as we have been to S. School once church twice and Communion in the afternoon and between two and four oclock we walked down to the river. . . . Our singing went well tonight and we have at last heard from our Organ that it is to be shipped.

Sunday 10. [March 10, 1861]

I have been troubled with a swelled face for several days the ailment having the appearance of the Mumps but I do not think it is that. Yesterday I brought a new clock home; our old one not being as satisfactory as I could wish. I am going to send it to Auction. . . .

Tuesday 12. [March 12, 1861]

. . . Abe Lincoln has been safely put in power but we are not yet able to tell whether he means to fight or not!*

Sunday 17. [March 17, 1861]

Tuesday 19. [March 19, 1861]

When we got up we were quite surprised to find the earth covered with a white mantle of snow wh' had fallen while we slept. It was about two inches deep.

Sunday 24. [March 24, 1861]

Sat 30. [March 30, 1861]

We have had some very cool frosty nights this week which have nipped the springing vegetation badly. My beans and corn and cucumbers of which I had a few peeping up have been killed, but not much damage done. I have this week sown Okra, Butter Beans and more corn, beans and cucumbers, also Egg Plants and Tomatoes as my first sowing of Egg Plants had not succeeded well and tomato plants are not so plentiful as in former years, tho' I see a good many coming up in my radish bed. We have had several messes of radishes this week. . . . This has been a pretty busy day with me as trade has been pretty good and then I had several orders to make up and send off.

---

* Abraham Lincoln was inaugurated as the nation's sixteenth president on Mar. 4, 1861. His inaugural address used conciliatory language to reach out to citizens in the seceding states, but most white Southerners were not persuaded.

Sunday 31. [March 31, 1861]

Mr. Haygood tried to preach from the *large* "tax-t" "Trust ye in the Lord forever &c" but he made a very lame discourse and said some foolish things, which certainly did not edify *me*.* Verily, a good preacher is a great advantage and much to be prized. I should like brother Will to come and give us a preach, I liked the sermon I heard him preach at Dr. Haynes Church on Madison Avenue last fall very much.—At night, as our church was closed Sallie and I went to hear Dr. Mann at the Meth Church. His subject was "The Christians hope an anchor to the soul" and the discourse moderately good. The singing was quite an improvement upon the last I heard there as they have got up a choir again.—

Sunday 7. [April 7, 1861]

Monday 8. [April 8, 1861]

I set out four rows of tomatoes this morning and a good rain has since fallen to make them grow. Mr. Jardine has come to put up our Organ and I have spent most of th day at the church trying to assist. . . .

Tuesday 9. [April 9, 1861]

Our town is quiet again after the fuss of last week with so many companies of Volunteers coming and going[.] The last left this morning for Pensacola Fla. The peace indications have been disturbed lately and there seems to be considerable ground to expect a speedy collision between the North and the South. The telegraph today states that seven War Steamers are near Charleston and that an attempt will probably be made to reinforce Fort Sumter by them!—

Friday 12. [April 12, 1861]

The startling news came by telegraph this afternoon that the Charleston Batteries had been firing upon fort Sumter ever since 4½ Oclock in the morning, at which time the fight began, Major Anderson having refused

* Methodist minister and later bishop Atticus Haygood, a graduate of Emory College in Oxford, Georgia, served as an army chaplain during the Civil War and preached at Trinity Methodist Church in Atlanta. After the war, he advocated New South business development and African American educational opportunities. In the 1870s, he served as president of Emory College, and in the 1880s, he edited the *Wesleyan Christian Advocate*. See Frederick V. Mills Sr., "Atticus G. Haygood," in *New Georgia Encyclopedia*, available online at http://www.georgiaencyclopedia.org (accessed 24 September 2008); Harold W. Mann, *Atticus Greene Haygood, Methodist Bishop, Editor, and Educator* (Athens: University of Georgia Press, 1965).

to surrender when demanded by Gen Beauregard.* Great excitement in town.—I have been employed all my spare time this week at the Church assisting Mr. Jardine in putting up the organ in readiness for a public exhibition of it tomorrow night as advertised in the paper.

Saturday 13. [April 13, 1861]

No mails from the North for two days and we suppose Old Abe has stopped our mails.—*Victory!!*—At 2 P.M. today the news came that Our Flag was flying over Sumter the garrison having surrendered unconditionally. It is stated that *no one was hurt* on either side but that seems impossible and other accounts are more probable that Anderson's men at least have suffered considerably.† Great enthusiasm prevails and many of our citizens are preparing to go into service to fight the fanatical aggressors upon our rights and liberties.—After a hard day's work we finished the organ just as a hundred College girls arrived at night to hear the music.‡ We ran home to tea and returned at 8 o'clock and Mr Jardine and Mr Matthews played for about two hours and tried the utmost capacity of the new organ which fully realized our anticipation and gave general satisfaction. There are a few old fogies in our Church who are opposed to the organ and threaten to leave us. Alas!

Sunday 14. [April 14, 1861]

Our choir met in full force this morning and our organ, "with full voiced choir resounding" to assist made a greater display than our church has ever before seen or heard in the musical line.§ The Anthem "Sanctus & Hosanna" was our opening piece and Stamfield, North Danvers and Bridgeton the other tunes and the last went splendidly.‖ Mr. Jardine played the congregation out. Bro Warren gave us a good sermon from the

---

* Major Robert Anderson commanded the U.S. garrison at Fort Sumter. Brigadier General P. G. T. Beauregard commanded the Confederates.

† No soldiers on either side died during the shelling of the fort, although two U.S. soldiers were killed by exploding shells during a ceremonial salute before the Federal army's departure.

‡ Georgia Female College, later renamed Wesleyan College, was chartered in the 1830s as the nation's first women's college to grant degrees. It became a center for Macon's cultural and intellectual life (Richard W. Griffin, "Wesleyan College: Its Genesis, 1835–1840," *Georgia Historical Quarterly* 50 [March 1966]: 54–73).

§ "With Full Voiced Choir Resounding" was the title of a popular church anthem by Mozart.

‖ "Sanctus and Hosanna" was part of Mozart's final, unfinished composition, the Requiem Mass.

text "Ye must be born again." It is a beautiful spring day and it is sad to think that our country is actually at war brother against brother and all brought on by the fanatical ideas of the abolitionists of the north and their determination to do away with Slavery by any and every means.—Irene is troubled today with a similar ailment to that I mentioned March 10th as troubling me and Arthur had it also about two weeks ago and we have concluded that it must be Mumps tho' a light attack in my case at least. Dora will probably take it from Renie in about two wks, as the others have done....

Sat. 20. [April 20, 1861]

This has been a day of much excitement in Macon. Yesterday we heard that "Old Virginny" had at last *seceded* indignant at the determination of the of the U S Govt to *coerce* the Cotton States back. It appears that the attack on Fort Sumter and its result has aroused the whole North to the resolve to sustain the Government in its War Policy towards us and Lincoln has made a proclamation calling upon the North and also the Border Slave States for 75000 troops to fight the cotton states and all are responding to the call except the Border States which utterly refuse and now Virginia has seceded they will probably follow soon. We heard of a row in Balto [Baltimore] last night between the citizens and the famous 7th Regiment of N.Y. and a Massachusetts Regiment who were going to Washington to guard it against invasion!* Our two oldest companies leave tonight for Norfolk Va. George Van goes with the "Volunteers" and Mr. Craig leaves us to accompany the "Rifles" and as they will doubtless have fighting it is a sad and serious time here with them and friends left behind[.]† May our merciful God protect and preserve them. I expect we

---

* Maryland was a slave state with a deeply divided population. Although Maryland ultimately stayed in the Union, sporadic violence occurred there throughout the war. According to the *NYT*, Apr. 20, 1861, pro-Confederate citizens in Baltimore attacked members of the 7th Pennsylvania and the 7th Massachusetts as they marched through the city. Several soldiers were killed, as were several rioters. Martial law was declared.

† George S. Van Valkenburg enlisted as a private in Company B, 2nd Battalion, Georgia Volunteer Infantry, Bibb County, Georgia Volunteers, while David Craig enlisted as a private in Company C of the same battalion, known as the Floyd Rifles (Lillian Henderson, ed., *Roster of Confederate Soldiers of Georgia, 1861–1865*, 6 vols. [Hapeville, Ga.: Longino and Porter, 1959], 6:782, 794, 798). The Macon Volunteers and the Floyd Rifles, a total of 146 men, departed the city by rail, receiving a rousing sendoff from several thousand of the town's citizens (Iobst, *Civil War Macon*, 67).

are going to have a severe and bloody struggle for our independence[;] the vaunted Republican Government of the US has undertaken the role of a despot and *freemen* are to be beaten into submission to her behests and are expected to kiss the rod that smites them. I feel that our cause is a righteous one and expect the God of Battles will fight for us.—I have given my name today to form one of a new Military Co for *home* protection to be called "the Silver Grays" being mostly composed of men whose locks are turning gray with age, as *myself*!

Sunday 21. [April 21, 1861]

The weather today has been bright and pleasant but every one seemed sad and a gloom seemed to rest upon all in thinking of the friends who have left us perhaps never to return.

Thursday 25. [April 25, 1861]

In obedience to the call of Capt Ross of the "Silver Grays" I went to the Concert Hall tonight and Mr Saulisbury appeared arrayed in our proposed uniform! But upon motion of E. J. Johnston the company was disbanded by a majority vote as the "Volunteers" and "Rifles" who did not go to the war are desirous of keeping up their companies for home protection and will need their *arms* which we were expecting to get. So I am again free.

Sat 27. [April 27, 1861]

At midnight last we were aroused by the Fire Bells and going out I found Capt. Ross' house in flames and I helped pull up No. 3 to the scene of action.—

Sunday 28. [April 28, 1861]

Bro Warren is absent today and our Church is closed so we went to hear Mr. Wells at the Pres Church. The singing was quite indifferent and I did not think much of the sermon tho' Sallie liked it. . . . Not much news for several days from the Seat of War tho' yesterday a despatch stated that Propositions for *Peace* had been sent from Washington through *third parties* but what these parties were I know not. I fear that peace is not attainable yet. I wish it may be. . . . Dora took the Mumps as I expected soon after Irene.

Friday 3. [May 3, 1861]

Yesterday evening great guns were let off in honor of *Tennessee* who had just *seceded* by a large majority of the Convention.—"Come along-boys—'to Dixie[.]'" This morning I met a number of the best singers and performers of our city at Dick Branham's house to arrange for a Concert to be given in aid of our soldiers who have gone to war. Our conference met tonight but very few were present. A prayer meeting has been appointed for three afternoons in the week in behalf of our country and our church.—

Sat 4. [May 4, 1861]

Sunday 5. [May 5, 1861]

Monday 6. [May 6, 1861]

Tuesday 7. [May 7, 1861]
We had a bright and pleasant day and at the evening hour *ten guns* announced the fact that *Arkansas* had *seceded* unanimously!—We had a rehearsal today at noon and the "Soldier's Concert" came off at night to a full house and all appeared highly delighted and satisfied. . . .

Wed. 8. [May 8, 1861]
At 5 oclock this afternoon I went to a prayer meeting at our church, appointed as before said for the object of praying for our country and our soldiers, triweekly. This meeting began on Monday but it being wet there were but three present Bro Warren, bro Shakespere and myself but we had a prayer meeting as "two or three in Christs name." There was a soldier at meeting tonight which I learned was James Eels (or Ells as he now styles himself) a young man who once made considerable profession of attachment to the cause of Christ here but was run off about ten years ago for forgery and other evil conduct.*—I learn that we made $160 at our concert.—

Friday 10. [May 10, 1861]
I went to the "Camp" at 4½ oclock this aft' to see the troops reviewed by Gov Brown but he did not do it.† The 5th Georgia Regiment is now here[;] among the companies is the Clinch Rifles from Augusta a fine and well drilled body. Almost all the Northern papers are out against the

---

* James N. Ells edited a Macon magazine, *Southern Field and Fireside*, before moving to Atlanta, where he became editor of the *Baptist Banner* (Ronald Lora and William Henry Langton, eds., *The Conservative Press in Eighteenth- and Nineteenth-Century America* [Westport, Conn.: Greenwood, 1999], 230; Tad Evans, ed., *Macon, Georgia, Newspaper Clippings (Messenger) 1859–1865* [Savannah: Evans, 2001], 183).

† *MT*, May 11, 1861, reported that "owing to the hurry and confusion of preparing for hasty departure the Review by the Governor did not take place yesterday . . . much to the disappointment of the troops and the public."

South and in favor of fighting to *save* the *Union*! I was a strong Union man until lately but now it has got to having a stinking savor since I have seen which measures are taken in order to *save it*. They say that they will either *bring back* the seceded states or *exterminate* them by fire and sword! Can it be possible that this is a free republican country and that our States are *free* and *sovereign* and yet such a course is to be pursued with them because in conventions of their people they have decided that their safety requires that they should retake the powers that they have delegated to the Government of the U.S. and combine in a new and more congenial confederacy for mutual safety and well being. Surely a just and righteous God will not favor such oppression and outrage.—

Sunday 12. [May 12, 1861]

This is afine day, but warm. Rev Mr. Carter[,] Chaplain of the Clinch Rifles preached us a good sermon today upon the universal duty of the Christians living for the glory of God and the advancement of his cause. *Dick* was not at Church and Miss Gould our *air* singer has gone back to the North, and Mrs Parsons got very wrathy because Rufus took Mary around to that side to fill her place which Mrs P. thought she was competent to do herself!* Mrs. P. is a big ugly creature always getting in a muss about something.—Martha and I went to Camp Oglethorpe at 4½ this aft' and heard Mr. Wills "War Sermon" repeated from the stand in the open air to the soldiers and citizens.† His text was "Cursed be he that acteth deceitfully and that holdeth back his sword from blood" tho I may not quote exactly.

Monday 13. [May 13, 1861]

My weight today in summer rig is but 123 lbs quite a light weight indeed.—Sallie rec^d a letter from Harriet today.—This morning I picked our first mess of snap beans and a few peas also more onions and lettuce. Yest we had our first Dewberries of the season, not of our own raising tho!—Garden and crops are doing finely.

Sat 18. [May 18, 1861]

I have been alone at the store today as Asa has been on a rural excursion to his Grand-Pa's a few miles in the country to fish and feast on

---

*SPR referred to SVVR's sister, Mary, and her husband, Rufus Evans.

†Martha Van Valkenburg was SVVR's sister. Rev. David Wills was pastor of First Presbyterian Church in Macon (Young, *History of Macon*, 296). During this time, Camp Oglethorpe, created in 1843 as place for Georgia Volunteer Companies in the area to parade, saw a great number of military drills attended by local spectators (*MT*, May 11, 1861; Iobst, *Civil War Macon*, 28–29).

strawberries.* We have not yet had any more fighting tho' from all accounts it will not be long before hostilities re-commence. I hope, however, still that this may be averted; it seems such utter folly thus to kill and destroy to no purpose. We now number ten stars in our New Flag and hope for *two* more at least. Kentucky, Maryland and Delaware we fear we shall not have at present at least. We had a sing tonight and prepared some hymns for the funeral service of James W Griffin a young man of our city the victim of consumption.

Sat 25. [May 25, 1861]

We were aroused at 2 oclock this morning by the Fire bells and I went up to Oliver Chappels which was just in the rear of the fire and liable to be burned, and indeed his kitchen was in flames soon after I got there and before the engines could get to work. Chappel moved out his furniture as the danger seemed imminent but the house did not burn. I returned home just as the day was dawning; 4 Oclock. This morning I met our *Club* at Mrs. Boykins to practice for our second concert which we expect to give next Friday. Schreiner gave one last night which he tried hard to pass off as *No 2* of our "Soldiers' Concerts" tho' none of our Club assisted except perhaps Mrs. Boykin played several pieces in the place of her little sister who was sick—We hear from Virginia that the Federal troops have taken possession of Alexandria so we shall probably soon hear of some serious fighting as they will not be allowed long to pollute Virginia soil. We hear that Col Ellsworth who led the N.Y. Fire Zouaves and who attempted to pull down a southern Flag at one of the hotels at Alex*a* was shot dead by Mr Jackson the landlord and he in turn was cut to pieces by the Zouaves, thus nobly giving his life in defence of our flag.† North Carolina has this week put another star in that flag, *No 11*—Oh! long may it wave.—Our Organist was not out tonight having been used up by a two hours drill in

---

* Asa E. Sherwood worked as a clerk at SPR's store.

† A native of New York, Elmer Ellsworth moved to Illinois before the Civil War and studied law under Abraham Lincoln in Springfield. After his mentor's election, Ellsworth commanded and recruited soldiers for the 44th New York Zouave Regiment and was ordered to occupy Alexandria, Virginia, just across the Potomac from the nation's capital. In a daring but perhaps foolish decision, Ellsworth decided to seize a Confederate flag flying atop a local hotel. Although he captured the flag, he was quickly shot by the hotel's manager, James William Jackson, who was then killed by Ellsworth's soldiers. Both men became immediate heroes in their respective regions (David S. Heidler and Jeanne T. Heidler, eds., *Encyclopedia of the American Civil War: A Political, Social, and Military History*, 5 vols. [Santa Barbara, Calif.: ABC-CLIO, 2000], 2:647).

the ranks of the Volunteers, Dick Branham Captain. —— Matthews is a Yankee not long out and can handle and *pedal* the Organ better than a musket! It is Vice Versa with Capt Dick.—

Sunday 26. [May 26, 1861]

Our organist has recovered from his fatigue and was on hand today as usual, which I was glad of for I don't like Branham's halting performance much. Today has been the hottest of this season quite anticipating the coming Summer. Our thermometer stood 95° at 4 oclock this afternoon in as cool a part of our hall as could be found, which is pretty fair elevation for May or July either. I selected a thermometer lately from our whole stock with the utmost care in order to get a correct one.—My [Sunday school] boys today began Vol 3 of Union Questions beginning at The Creation and they had a good lesson as usual. Our school I regret to say is suffering for want of more efficient officers but there is little prospect of getting them.

Friday 31. [May 31, 1861]

Our "Soldiers' Concert" No 2 came off tonight and we had even a better audience than at the first one and it went off quite satisfactorily.* Sister Nell went with Martha and myself; she came up from her So[uth] Car[olina] home last night at eleven oclock with her two little girls Florence and Olive and Stephen the baby.—My clerk Asa E Sherwood left me today to go into Camp with a company who are going to War soon. Asa has been with me exactly four years and has given me satisfaction very generally, he is a good young man and I am sorry to have him leave.—

Sunday 2. [June 2, 1861]

I took my first shower bath this morning of the season! We have had 5 or 6 cucumbers from our garden since my last entry.—Nell left us yesterday for Atlanta where she expects to spend the Summer.—Our Sunday School officers were all re-elected today and I was elected chorister for the school.—Rev Mr. Cabeness one of our China Missionaries preached for us this morning and was very entertaining and convincing in his argument in favor of the mission cause showing that the Anglo Saxon race now so enlightened and conceited withal was once in a state of barbarism and heathen idolatry and that the Christian missionaries who went from Greece and Rome to convert them labored for one hundred years before they succeeded!—This afternoon he addressed the children in our church and we sang three songs from the "Bell."—Our regular communion ser-

---

* MT, May 31, 1861, editorialized in favor of attendance at the concert.

vice was observed also at five o'clock.—At night Mr. Cabiness lectured upon the religion of the Chinese, stating that their worship of idols was not quite so senseless as usually supposed to be, as the intelligent portion of them do not worship the material image but the *spirit* that they suppose dwells therein. Likewise the food that is offered to idols is not so foolishly set there, as the *spirits* of the idols are supposed to eat the *spiritual part* of the food and after this is done the *people* eat the material portion thereof!

Monday 3. [June 3, 1861]

Tonight Mr Cabaniss lectured upon the products of China and stated the reason why they could not supply cotton to England and France. He says there are 900 persons to the square mile and all the available land for cotton, with the exception of a small *patch* for home purposes, is needed to *raise food* to sustain the inhabitants, and the rent of the land is six dollars per acre which would make their cotton cost so much in the start that they could not compete with our producers. They can beat us with *tea* and *silk* because the tea and the mulberry grow on poor and rugged land and *labor* is so cheap there and the culture of these articles is *easy work*. Cucumbers are freely eaten in China and accounted very wholesome and an excellent diet in sickness when such strong food as *rice* cannot be eaten.

Tuesday 4. [June 4, 1861]

Tonight Mr. C described the condition of woman in China—the marriages—customs—costumes, &c, the latter illustrated by *trotting out* Deacon Deloache and Miss Cassidy in Chinese toggery much to the amusement of the audience or rather to the spectators but the *actors* were rather sheepish in their strange garb especially the lady who was not at home in such short petticoats and no hoops! The little *shoes* she did not try to wear!

Wed 5. [June 5, 1861]

Mr Cabiness gave his last lecture tonight, being a description of the "City of Heaven" (or Canton) and various fine temples and fine natural scenery that he saw in that land. he also sang us one of their religious Chinese songs; that is, the words were Chinese but the tune quite familiar English!

Sat. 8. [June 8, 1861]

I got a letter from Mr Craig last week which I answered this week and I also wrote to George to try to impress upon him the great necessity of being prepared for a death that he might meet at almost any moment.

James' wife is very ill, *dangerously* so, the doctor says, but doctors *lie* so that there is not much trust to be put in them. A new singer joined our choir tonight, Mary Napier[,] a young and accomplished lady just from Paris with finished education and a sweet voice; she is the daughter of one of our richest female members. The "Central City Blues" of which Asa is an officer left tonight for Virginia. I have expected Asa to call all day to say Goodbye, but he did not come.*—Sallie has not been out for about a month, and I have to go alone except when Martha goes with me which is nearly always though. My wife has been so used to accompanying me that it requires a considerable exercise of the virtue of patience to stay at home alone and we have been "on the go" very often of late. However I hope her "Great Expectation" will be realized ere long!†

Tuesday 11. [June 11, 1861]

Today Eddie Van came and entered upon the duties of his office as far as he knew how. I like his looks and think he will learn readily to be of some assistance to me.‡

Wed. 12. [June 12, 1861]

I received a letter from George today by Ensign Hardie of his company.§ They are at Sewells Point and expecting to engage the enemy in battle soon. George says he and Mr Craig are "spoiling for a fight"! I hope the fight wont *spoil them* any worse when they get it. We hear of various small fights in that region with the "Hessians" as the Northern vandals are usually called now.

Thursday 13. [June 13, 1861]

This is Fast Day by proclamation of President Davis and I am now writing at the house at 8 o'clock A.M. Business will be very generally suspended today I think. Religious services in our church begin at 10 o'clock. It required considerable self denial to resist the nice rolls and cucumbers of the breakfast table, but for that very reason I thought that was the very time to fast; there is little virtue in fasting when one has no

---

* On June 9, 1861, Asa E. Sherwood joined Company H, 12th Georgia Volunteer Infantry Regiment, also known as the Central City Blues, as a corporal. He was promoted to sergeant the following April (Henderson, *Roster*, 2:223).

† Among genteel women, it was common practice to go into "confinement"— to avoid public appearances—during the last month of pregnancy.

‡ Eddie Van Valkenburg was SVVR's younger brother.

§ George W. Hardie served as ensign of Private George S. Van Valkenburg's unit until June 1861, when he joined the Home Reserves (Henderson, *Roster*, 6:782–83).

appetite. I eat very heartily now a days and enjoy excellent health. This is a time if ever when our whole people should humble themselves before God, and earnestly entreat his favor and assistance. I believe he will hear us if we feel our need to him and ask in faith and sincerity. That our cause is a just one in His sight I have not a doubt and I do not fear but that it will eventually succeed, tho' God *may* intend to chastise and humble us first on account of our sins. Our preacher gave us a good discourse from the Book of Esther particularly enlarging upon the *fast* of three days that the jews of Shushan observed at Esther's request and the glorious result of the deliverance of the Jews from the hands of their enemies. *Every store* was closed in our city and all business suspended, and the place was in appearance just as on Sunday but every body did not go to church; Many embraced this opportunity to *go a-fishing* for which we know they had apostolical precedent!—

Sunday 16. [June 16, 1861]

This day is hot and dry; we are needing rain now very much and our garden begins to dry up. The mercury stands as I write at 95° in our hall but a breeze is blowing that makes this high tempre endurable. Eddie joined my class this morning. Yesterday while I was gone to dinner he sold a $4 Gold Pen for $1.00, but we fortunately found out who the buyer was and got the balance of the price.

Wed 19. [June 19, 1861]

Irene has taken the whooping cough but only has one spell of whooping per day at present and that comes on at night soon after she gets to sleep.—Miss Marian Rose, one of our choir, died today of typhoid fever after a short illness and we are to meet to sing *her* funeral songs at 9 O'c tomorrow. The ladies of the Episcopal choir her old schoolmates will sing their Burial Chant on the occasion by the desire of the bereaved friends. We have the particulars of another fight in Virginia at "Great Bethel" in York Co in which 1100 of our troops repulsed with great slaughter over 4000 "Hessians," killing some 200 it is said with a loss of *one* man on our side.*—It is very dry and no sign of rain.

---

* The Battle of Big Bethel, Virginia (also called Great Bethel), occurred on June 10, 1861. In spite of Virginia's secession, the Federal army still controlled a small area of the state that included Fort Monroe. A force of several thousand Federal soldiers attacked a detachment of twelve hundred Confederates. The assault was badly executed. Confederates lost one soldier dead and seven wounded, while the Union suffered eighteen dead, fifty-three wounded (Herman Hattaway and Archer Jones, *How the North Won: A Military History of the Civil War* [Urbana: University of Illinois Press, 1983], 39).

Thursday 20. [June 20, 1861]

Bro Warren preached Miss Rose's funeral sermon at 9 oclock this morning to a large audience. . . . I rec^d a letter from Kate today from which I learn what I before only surmised that William and Cornelia are sympathizers with our enemies and aiders of this unrighteous war.—

Sunday 23. [June 23, 1861]

Yesterday and today have been *real hot.* . . . our garden is already ruined past remedy tho' last night we watered some things to try to save them. . . . the thermometer is now at 101° in our passage at the coolest end too. It was 98° at the store yesterday. . . .

Monday 24. [June 24, 1861]

We have had rain at last a nice shower fell this aft, not enough but very acceptable and more in reserve we trust.—Burning Fluid is getting scarce and dear and we have just gone back to first principles and made eight tallow candles by the light of one of which I am now writing. I saw two large "Shells" this evening just imported from the *sea shore* at Sewalls Point in Virginia. One is a large ten inch round shell that did not explode when fired by the Hessians and the other is a percussion shell that was fired over our camp from a Rifled Cannon four miles off and fell without exploding. These *munitions* are much more elaborate *pieces* than I had expected and must cost a good deal of money each one.—

Sunday June 30. [June 30, 1861]

No news of any very certain or definite action has reached us the past week but "rumors of wars" in abundance. It is thought that a terrible conflict is close at hand and the "Glorious Fourth" may be celebrated by a horrid fight between the "Sons of Freedom" who have so long and often united in celebrating the Day of Independence. Irene has the W. Cough pretty bad now and *Dora* too must have it although she does not whoop at all but has frequent coughing paroxysms but not nearly so bad as Rennies.—Martha has been sick abed all week until yesterday. And Eddie was sick one day and I do not feel well today. Charlie DuBose called on us Friday night and we talked about Jabez and our connection in business and Charlie thinks that we ought to wind up and have a settlement as soon as possible, at any rate—the latter.* We have never come to any

---

* By 1861, SPR and JJR had been business partners for twelve years. Periodically, especially after disagreements over business affairs, SPR wrote about wanting to separate their assets. Such appears to have been the case here. As in the past, the brothers resolved their dispute. Martha and Eddie Van Valkenburg, SVVR's unmarried siblings, appear to have resided with the Richards family in Macon during this time.

settlement since we began trade 12 years ago and it is really time we had one. I returned to Charlie the money we borrowed of him last year $750 with about $50 interest as we are not paying any money North now and don't want to have our funds lying useless on our hands and pay interest on it.—June is about gone and Sallie still *lying around*—her time is *not yet* come.

Sunday 7. [July 7, 1861]

Another week has gone and no very important War tidings that are reliable tho' we hear of various skirmishes taking place in Virginia. It was said that we should see hot work before July 4th but so far it has not been proved. "The Fourth" passed off very quietly with us, there seemed to be no enthusiasm on the usually jubilant occasion. We have had fine rains this week nearly every day one or more. Our little ones are all "under the weather[.]" Irene has a hard time with her cough and coughs out all her supper every night and Dora *whoops* now in orthodox style[.] Arthur has been ailing for several days with diarhea and now begins to cough a good deal. Our organist was absent last night and this morning and *Dick* had to play or *try to*. Our night service has been dispensed with for two months.—

Tuesday 9. [July 9, 1861]

"Long looked for" came at last! In the person of a little girl sister to Dora Rennie and Artie. We had about concluded to postpone the affair until cold weather but this don't seem to have suited Miss, so at seven P.M. she gave intimation of her coming and at nine I went in a thunder shower for Mrs Carver and at 5 minutes before eleven my little lady made her entree and announced herself immediately. This was the quickest time that Sallie ever made, *through* in four hours from the start. The baby weighed ten lbs which is half lb more than Arthur weighed. We had not decided upon a name before she came but we have called her *Alice* now.— I would have preferred a boy but as we have had two boys since Irene it was hardly to be expected we should have another now. I am thankful that it is over at last & all doing well.—Dora sees the baby dressed in the clothes that she has seen before and wants to know if God sent the baby naked all through the rain! And she is moreover curious to know why her Mama is always sick abed when God sends her a baby.—

Thursday 11. [July 11, 1861]

I did not sleep much last night on account of Miss Allie; she was hungry or ill at ease in some way and wouldn't be quiet more than half an hour at a time all night.—I rec^d a letter from Mr Craig yest[;] he seems pretty well contented but thinks he shall be ready to quit when the year of their enlistment is up.—Our old friend John H Ellis was taken away yesterday in a very sad and unexpected manner. He had just moved into the store below us this week and Tuesday night was suddenly struck down by paralysis or Apoplexy in his bed room and there was found by his negro boy next morning lying on the floor senseless and in a more distressing state. He lay unconscious all day yesterday and died at nine oclock last night and has *got back into the church* I think where no injustice can drive him out. Our church will now never have the opp[ortunit]y to make amends to him for their unjust treatment of him.—

Sat. 13. [July 13, 1861]

Cousin Mary Stone came up Thursday night en route for home via Louisville Ky.* in company with a gentleman from Americus. I have today written to Addison to send by her, and he was the only one of our Northern relatives that I felt inclined to correspond with. I also have written to father and mother informing them of Miss Alice's advent.—

Sunday 14. [July 14, 1861]

Bro Warren has been called away to the sick bed of his sister in Florida and Bro Haywood preached wh' I regretted as there were a good many of other churches at ours this morning and Haygood is not *much preach*. I wrote in several books and sent them by Mary Stone to her mother and Sarah and Hattie with one for herself. She expected to go tonight but the gent who was to escort her has declined to go at present.—

Monday 15. [July 15, 1861]

I gave Artie some quinine today as old Dr. Branham recommends it for wh' cough and he seems to have warm fever (?)in slight degree. Mary Stone is going tonight with some of our Macon folks.—

Sat. 20. [July 20, 1861]

A letter from Jabez today brings the news of the birth of a son (and heir!) to Henry and "Ellie" born on the morning of the same day that brought our little *Alice,* so that they got the start of us some hours. Their boy weighs 7½ lbs and is named "Henry William" to be called "Harry."† When *Stella* gets through (as expected shortly) Father and Mother will have just a *score* of grand children. Our *Cousin Bill* too has a son we

---

* SVVR's cousin, Mary Stone, lived in Brooklyn, New York. The Richardses visited her and her family in 1864 (see chap. 7).

† Henry Richards was SPR's youngest sibling; his wife was named Ellen.

hear. We also have reason to believe that our "Cousin Mary [Hathaway]" will shortly be in *the way* of "doing things up *Brown*"! but this is a great secret!*—Steve Whitehead came from Atlanta this aft and took tea (or coffee) with us before leaving for home at ten o'clock. Our little ones are all *barking* loudly now and I have got some medicine for them which Dick Branham says is excellent. If it proves so I will give the *Recipe* for the same. Arthur has been more lively since I gave him quinine whether owing to that or not I am unable to say.—I wrote to father today having had to delay in order to obtain his address which is now "St Helenaville, Beaufort District S.C." We are having plenty of rain now and the weather is cool and pleasant in consequence.—Sallie got up on Wednesday and is now *all about*. The little Alice is lively and good and gaining in weight.— Steve talked with Sallie while Matt and I went to singing but I returned before the singing closed leaving Mat[t] to the attentions of Mr. *Sholer* and I met Steve and went to the cars with him. Nell is still in Atlanta with her children. We hear reports of some *reverses* which our soldiers have met with in Western Virginia which is the Anti-secession part of the state. We also hear on the other hand of a victory we have obtained at "Bulls Run[.]" No *definite* news or details tho either way. Gen Beauregard is said to have replied to the remark that the name of *Bulls Run* would not sound well in history,—that it was as good as *Cow Pens*"—which left the objecter nothing more to say, of course.†

Sunday 21. [July 21, 1861]

We had a very good *sing* at school this morning; the children are improving some I think. I am introducing some tunes in the *second* S.S. Bell which are pretty. I had only one scholar today in my class, *Willie*, as Eddie has gone home on a visit and the other boys did not come.

Sat 27. [July 27, 1861]

This has been a week [of] considerable excitement and suspense but more especially of rejoicing at the great victory which God has given our soldiers over the enemy. Last Sunday the "Union Army" in full force, some

---

* The phrase "do it up brown" means to do something thoroughly and with enthusiasm and probably originated from browning meat. SPR was making a joke regarding Mary Hathaway's impending marriage to John W. Brown.

† Union soldiers under General Irvin McDowell marched out from Washington on July 16, 1861, and engaged in a skirmish with Confederate troops on July 18 near a creek known as Bull Run. Cowpens was the name of a Revolutionary War battle (Heidler and Heidler, *Encyclopedia*, 1:312).

75,000 men they say attacked our forces at Manassas Junction and a hard fight ensued lasting from early (27th)* morning until night which resulted in the total rout of the enemy and their flight to Alexandria and Washington and the capture of many prisoners and any quantity of wagons filled with munitions of war, provisions &c, and many thousand good *arms* were also obtained a thing badly needed by us.—The loss on our side is said to be about 300 killed and 1200 wounded, but very much greater on the side of the enemy.† It is supposed that it will take the Hessians several months to reorganize their army after their signal defeat. The victory is universally regarded upon our side as due to the direct interference of God for our force was not half as great in point of numbers as theirs, nor our weapons as good. The "Macon Guards" were in the thickest battle but we hear of but four killed and about 8 or 10 wounded. Last Thursday night Harriet and Mr Taylor came up from Americus with "Mollie" his son *Tom's* wife, and he and she went on to Decatur to see her husband who was about to start from there to the field of conflict. They left Harriet with us. Last night the "Amateur Club" met at Dick Branham's to practise for another Concert for the Soldier's Fund. We also met again this morning.

Sunday 28 [July 28, 1861]

Mr Taylor and *Mollie* returned from Decatur yesterday just a[s] Harriet had left for *Texas* Steam Mill. Oliver Chappel came and dined with us as his family are in Atlanta. He is troubled because several persons in Macon are trying to render him obnoxious on the charge of sympathy with the enemy; he says they are jealous of his success in business, and want to break him up.

Thursday August 1. [August 1, 1861]

We met at *ten* this morning at the Hall to have our rehearsal.—And at night the Concert came off to a pretty good house tho' not as large as our others were. The weather was hot and a false alarm of fire just at the hour

---

* SPR meant to write "(21st)."

† The first major clash of the Civil War took place on July 21, 1861, when Federal soldiers engaged Confederate forces at Manassas Junction, Virginia, the strategically important meeting point of two railroads. Confederate forces under the command of Generals P. G. T. Beauregard and Joseph E. Johnston rebuffed the Union Army, made up in large part of newly recruited volunteers. Confederates celebrated an outright victory in the fighting, which they called the Battle of Manassas to distinguish it from the skirmish a few days earlier (James M. McPherson, *Ordeal by Fire: The Civil War and Reconstruction*, 3rd ed. [Boston: McGraw Hill, 2001], 227–32).

of beginning probably prevented some from coming. The singing went off very well. I had a solo to sing; the opening part of the Chorus "Wake O Wake" in the "Operatic Boquet." The proceeds were $105—nett $87."— We gathered our first Egg-Plant today.

Friday 2. [August 2, 1861]
At Church meeting tonight there was a war of words between Dick Branham and Deacon Deloache in reference to the organ, it not being yet paid for, and Dick having failed to raise some $600 that he borrowed last year on interest the money that had been raised towards paying for the organ.

Sat 3. [August 3, 1861]
There was a Militia muster today which I ought to have attended I hear, but did not.

Sunday 4. [August 4, 1861]
Sallie went out to church this morning for the first time for several months. She came to the store yesterday and I weighed her = 125 lbs more than I weigh by 1½ lbs. "Allie" grows finely and has not yet taken the *cough*—we hope. Arthur is now the most troubled by it.—Sallie and I went to Communion this afternoon. It is pleasant to have her company again to meeting.

Wed. 7. [August 7, 1861]
Rec^d letter from father today via Atlanta with one from Jabez. Business has been much better in Atlanta than in Macon of late. Father says they are well.—Last night Sallie had one of her sick spells from cold. At meeting tonight our church resolved upon making application for admission into the "Central Association" having withdrawn from the "Rehoboth" because they are anti-(Mission) *Board* in their sentiments.† Father says William had to sympathise with the North or leave the place he occupies!—wonder what he think[s] of Bulls Run and Manassas!

Thursday 8. [August 8, 1861]
Jabe's birthday and he is *forty*! We are really becoming *old men*. In a letter just rec^d he says he is perturbed in mind by the determination of

---

* In urging attendance at this benefit concert, *MT*, Aug. 1, 1861, predicted "many beautiful gems" of music, including "Flag of the South."

† In August 1860, First Baptist Church asked for a letter of dismission from the Rehoboth Association after a disagreement regarding the direction of missionary activities. First Baptist then joined the Central Baptist Association (Batts, *History of the First Baptist Church*, 46–47).

Mary and John W. Brown to marry *next Tuesday* and the plan is for her to stay in Atlanta while he goes to Virginia to try to raise a company of soldiers there or perhaps *here* to go *there*.* Jabez is quite *put out* by his breach of promise in regard to the payment of $70 which he owes for board last winter. He was to have sent it from Pensacola out of the first months salary he received which he might very well have done it would seem as his pay as *Lieutenant* was $1000 per annum. He has now however resigned his office and returned to Atlanta to get married. I fear that Mary will have cause to regret the step she is about to take if those things are so. Jabez is not apt to suspect a person of duplicity—before there is reason for it, he is usually *too* credulous and unsuspecting.—

Sat 10. [August 10, 1861]

I borrowed a gun and at ten oclock appeared upon *parade* at "general muster" at Camp Oglethorpe in accordance with the summons of the officers of the Georgia Militia.—Seven or eight hundred persons were present with *arms* of various kinds[,] guns, rifles, muskets or pistols! And we had a pretty hot tiresome tramp for four hours in the hot sun. There was too much *marching* and too little *drilling*.—We have abundance of rain now, showers *every* day: one fell on us while on drill and gave us a considerable wetting. A full turn out of our choir was on hand tonight. The week has been a dull one both as respects business and *news*—no tidings of consequence from Virginia since the big fight at Manassas.

Sunday 11. [August 11, 1861]

Rev Van Hoose from Griffin exchanged with Bro Warren today and gave us a sermon from the words "Having loved his own he loved them unto the end." A hard shower of rain fell just as the congregation was dismissed. Jonathan Virgin and *Wm* Ellis *and his wife* were there. Rev Van Hoose preached again at night and again the folks were caught in the rain but not so hard as in the morning.†

---

* Mary Hathaway, the younger sister of JJR's first wife, had resided in his household for nearly twenty years. Her future husband, John Wesley Brown, served as second lieutenant of Company D, 1st Confederate Regiment of Infantry, Fulton County, Georgia, before resigning on July 31, 1861. He later joined Company A, 7th Georgia Cavalry, and was elected lieutenant. His military record contains this sentence: "Appears without remark as to presence or absence on roll from Oct. 1 to Dec. 31, 1864. No later record" (Henderson, *Roster* 1:35–36).

† Azor Van Hoose served as Baptist pastor at Griffin, Georgia and ministered to soldiers in the Confederate Army (*History of the Baptist Denomination in Georgia* [Atlanta: Harrison, 1881],550–52).

Monday 12. [August 12, 1861]

We have had a wet unpleasant day and tonight are sitting by *a fire*. The girls have gotten over the worst of their coughing and Arthur does not have it as hard as it was. Alice has escaped so far.—

Sunday 18. [August 18, 1861]

Still raining every day until the door and windows, drawers &c stick tight and move reluctantly with the swelling thereof! *Dick* was not at church today so I had to be the leader. This is but little trouble or care when the organist is present. Miss Landrum was at church today.

Monday 19. [August 19, 1861]

Read "Ingomar" and "Armand" today two good plays that I felt interested in from reading Mrs Mowatts Autobiography.* "Armand" is her own and *Parthenia* in "Ingomar" one of her favorite characters.—Sallie and Dora went with me to our Soldiers prayer meeting today—The first response to the tidings of the Manassas fight came to us from Europe today[.] The London Times thinks the North has a "hard nut to crack."—

Sat 24. [August 24, 1861]

I returned today from Atlanta to which place I went on Thursday to consult with Jabe upon the important question of *removal* from this place to Atlanta—all our interests, as the season is now near to rent store and houses again for another year and it is a question whether it will pay us to keep up our business here another year as our stocks are decreasing and the prospect of supply very unpromising. Another thing which I did in going was to witness the marriage of Mary E Hathaway to John Wesley Brown on Thursday night at Jabe's house so Cousin Mary is now "Mrs Brown." Her husband is a young man of good personal appearance and address and sensible I should think but Jabe and Stella are not much

---

* *Ingomar, the Barbarian*, adapted by Maria Lovell from a German play, included the character Parthenia. *Armand; or, The Peer and the Peasant*, was written by Anna Cora Mowatt Ritchie. Both plays debuted in 1851. Ritchie wrote poetry, novels, and plays during a literary career that began in the 1830s and continued to the late 1860s. During the 1840s and 1850s, partly to earn money because of the declining health and fortune of her husband, she became a stage actress. She continued to act following her husband's death but quit the theater to marry the editor of the *Richmond Enquirer*, from whom she eventually separated. In 1854, she published *Autobiography of a Stage Actress* (Edward T. James, Janet Wilson James, and Paul S. Boyer, eds., *Notable American Women, 1607–1950*, 3 vols. [Cambridge: Harvard University Press, 1971], 2:596–98).

pleased with their experience as regards him and fear that Mary will see trouble. The cause of their dissatisfaction I have partially revealed a few pages back.—I walked out with Jabe to Henry's house and lot and saw *his baby* "Harry." The baby will do pretty well but the *house* is a small affair. Nell and her children are still at Jabes. While Jabe was swinging me in a *hammock* that Mary's Soldier had put up, the head staple came out and down I fell with a squelch that for a minute knocked all the breath from my body and I couldn't speak a word; providentially I escaped serious injury. We have about decided to *remove* but the subject has sorely exercised and troubled my mind.

Sunday 25. [August 25, 1861]

As our preacher is away we went to the Pres- Church this morning and heard some young man preach. I feel regretful at the thought of leaving Macon after making it home for 13 years and so does Sallie especially as her relatives live here and in Atlanta she will probably see but little of them. But like a dutiful wife she seems willing to go if it is deemed advisable.— All our friends who have lived in Atlanta or visited there are much pleased with it and it is no doubt a more healthy and salubrious place than Macon. I have earnestly sought direction from heaven in this decision.—

Sat 31. [August 31, 1861]

This has been a week of indecision and perplexity to me. I wrote to Jabez last Monday proposing to rent here again for six months if I could, and not moving until next Spring and he replied, agreeing to the proposal; but I could not rent for less than a year and this afternoon wrote to Jabe that I had about concluded to do that (viz rent for another year) when before I mailed my letter I got another from him giving such strong reasons for *immediate* removal that I at once decided again to go—so *go it is* Oct 1.—We went to singing tonight and it made me sad to think of having to leave the church and choir and the more so because I know that the choir at least will suffer from my absence and I say it without any self conceit.—We have heard startling news today of the exploits of a fleet of War Steamers that lately sailed from Fortress Monroe to our southern states. They attacked some small (?) forts on the coast of North Carolina and succeeded in taking them, with, it is said, 7 or 8 hundred prisoners!*

---

* On Aug. 29, 1861, Union naval vessels firing on Fort Hatteras in North Carolina forced its Confederate garrison to surrender, thereby denying Confederates a possible blockade-running route, taking seven hundred prisoners, and lifting spirits in the North after the disastrous Union loss at Manassas the previous month (Heidler and Heidler, *Encyclopedia*, 2:946–48).

So we must lookout for similar attempts upon our own sea-coast ere long. Another event quite unexpected by me was the receipt of a letter by mail from Nashville, from W. C. Richards written at Albany N.Y. and sent by Express. His chief object in writing was to ask me to pay up the annual premium upon a $2000 Life Policy which he had at Columbia S.C. and which I have taken steps to do—*enemy* as he is. His letter enclosed one to father giving expression to his feelings in reference to these awful times, and while he seems to feel no diminuation of love towards his relatives and friends here he freely confesses that his sympathies and his hopes are with the despotic government that is doing their utmost to destroy us and make slaves of freemen. He asks me to write and give him a true statement of affairs here assuring us that the whole of the "loyal states" are determined to be satisfied with nothing less than the *full vindication of the honor of the stars & stripes*. Knowing as I do the resolve of the South never to live under the wave of a flag so sullied by blood and oppression as that same Stars & Stripes, I fear we have yet terrible times in store. I did not think that our brother William was such a fanatic.

Sunday 1. [September 1, 1861]
Rev W J Hard preached for us this morning from the history of the *Barren Fig Tree*. He is traveling in behalf of the sick and wounded soldiers and from his account there is much suffering and deficiency of necessary comfort and care in our army. He says "men die for the want of a cup of tea!" surely this ought not to be. Oh what a model Republic the United States is! One half the country having the advantage of the most men and the most *means* trying to destroy and subjugate the other half by cannons and ships of war, spilling the blood of their bretheren as remorselessly as tho' it were only that of savages! How utterly disregarded is that great fundamental doctrine that true Republicanism is that which secures the *consent of the governed*. And to think—that a brother of ours who professes to love the South and who knows her wrongs, can yet advocate this horrid war upon her rights and liberties and the very lives of father, mother brothers & sisters and their little ones—oh! renegade!—

Thursday 5. [September 5, 1861]
I have again been suffering from doubts and indecision in regard to moving altho' I thought I had quite decided to go last Sat night. I even made our store landlord Gabriel Roberts an offer for the store which he refused in the morning and accepted in the afternoon but by that time I had rather veered round and determined to refer the matter to Jabez for final decision, and tonight I got his answer which is in spite of all my

objections is still *come!* So *now* I am going *sure* (D.V.)* Oct. 1. Tonight Sallie and I went to hear the "Atlanta Amateurs" Concert at Ralstons Hall given for the Soldier's Aid Society's benefit. There was a crowd there and the performance was quite amusing. The music apart from the comic was decidedly mediocre and they attempted to sing the quartette "Come where my love lives dreaming" and *executed* it effectually!† I rather think *our* club did it differently quite. *Barnes* the manager and chief singer is quite a genius in his line and certainly the life and soul of the company.‡

Sat 7. [September 7, 1861]

Received a letter from David Craig from Sewell's Point today. He says he has not been sick at all but that there is a good deal of sickness in their battalion, tho' not of an alarming kind. We hear of Brantley and Spaulding Baptist Ministers from Philadelphia returning to their Southern homes driven away by the despotism of the Northern government but our traitor brother not only remains there, but sympathises with coercionists and prays for our destruction.§ I pity him for his blindness and infatuations. Our Congress has passed a law of sequestration of all Northern possessions in the South, so I suppose the $5000 that we owe will never reach the hands of those to whom we owe it which I regret for I hate to have any one come to loss through trusting us. But their own government has set the example of confiscation and of course they can expect no less

---

* *Deo volente*, Latin for "God willing."

† "Come Where My Love Lives Dreaming" is a song by Stephen Foster.

‡ The *MT*, Sept. 9, 1861, gave the Atlanta Amateurs a better review than SPR did, praising the "sterling band" and the dramatic tableaux. The concert raised four hundred dollars. Billy Barnes served as manager of the Atlanta Amateurs. Iobst, *Civil War Macon*, 89–90, records many theatrical and musical fund-raisers for Confederate soldiers held in Macon during the fall of 1861.

§ William T. Brantley Jr. and Albert T. Spalding were native-born Southerners serving congregations in Philadelphia at the beginning of the war. Both returned to the South—Brantley to Atlanta's Second Baptist Church and Spalding to a church in Selma. Brantley, born in Beaufort, S.C. and raised in Philadelphia, had already had a distinguished clerical career before accepting the call at Second Baptist. A graduate of Brown University, he served as pastor of First Baptist Church of Augusta from 1840 to 1848, taught at the University of Georgia from 1848 to 1856, and was pastor at Tabernacle Baptist Church in Philadelphia from 1856 until Dec. 1861. He remained at Second Baptist for most of the time until 1871 (*History of the Baptist Denomination*, 56–58; C. Douglas Weaver, *Second to None: A History of Second–Ponce de Leon Baptist Church* [Brentwood, Tenn.: Baptist History and Heritage Society, 2004], 20).

than that ours should retaliate.* There is henceforth a wide gulf fixed between the North and South, which it will take many long years to bridge over. Our family hitherto has been united in feeling and affection if not in bodily presence but now we are widely separated indeed and have nothing in common.—It is evident that William is not a true republican but an aristocrat and upholder of despotism and "*strong* government"—He may bid a final adieu to the South; she will have no use for those who have forsaken her in her time of need and gone over to aid and comfort her enemies.—

Sunday 8. [September 8, 1861]

Bro Warren preached a good sermon today showing the uselessness of a profession of faith without any corresponding works, he says he will not give his consent for us to go away!—Dora is seven years old tonight. She is tall enough for her age but quite slender: not very forward in her education as she can only read in simple words yet. We have not tried to teach her much as we do not care to begin schooling her until she is eight years old except to teach her to read and the first elements of writing and arithmetic perhaps, which can be done in the next year of her life. We have a letter from Harriet today, she don't know we are going away yet.—

Tuesday 10. [September 10, 1861]

It is 9 P.M. and Eddie and I are alone at the house. My wife and babies are all gone to Grandpa's to visit for a few days. It will be a dull time in this big old house while they are away.—Today was "training day" but I got off from duty.—I wrote to Mr Craig tonight, as I got a letter from him a few days ago. I forgot to state before that brother Jabe and Sister Stella have got a baby—born on the 27th ult[imo]. It is a girl and they have called it *Ethel, not Bethel* as might have been expected under the circumstances!—

Thursday 12. [September 12, 1861]

Have bought 27 boxes today to pack our books in which begins to look like going.—Traded off 10 Maps of Macon to Burke for Copy Books also. The City Fathers to whom I offered the lot (about 40) at cost did not "deem it expedient to buy them" not even in payt of *our taxes*, so they seem to think we are *good* for the taxes. Got a note from

---

* The Sequestration Act to which SPR referred made the Confederate government the legally constituted recipient of debts owed by Confederate citizens to citizens of the United States (Daniel Hamilton, "The Confederate Sequestration Act," *Civil War History* 52 [December 2006]: 373–408).

Wifey today saying that they are coming home tomorrow. Dr Green called at the store to know why I would not let the workmen proceed to shingle the house and I told him that we could not get it done when we wanted it and now we didn't want the muss and risk of it just as we are about to leave.* If the house is not rented at once it will trouble no one to shingle it and if rented those who are to benefit by it ought to have the trouble of it and not we. Dr Green tried to make a point that Mrs Green had let us have the house lower than she would have let it to any one else *because she liked us* but I gave him to understand pretty plainly that I thought she only did it because she knew we would pay and few other persons [who] would live here could be depended on. To tell the truth I have very little use for any of the Greens, I consider them a selfish lot and I wouldn't give a snap of a finger for all Mrs. G's professions of *love* and *regard*. She loves us as long as we are profitable to her and no longer. She promises to come to see us in Atlanta but I hope she wont.—

Sat. 14. [September 14, 1861]

I have been trying to *collect* our A/cs [accounts] all the week and my conclusion is that it dont pay to sell goods on credit and have to *run* and *dun* about a dozen times for a dollar or two and perhaps get nothing at last but curses. One of the *scum* of society vexed me today exceedingly and not for the first or *third* time even, refusing to settle a paltry a/c of 2.25 and finally told me to *go to the devil*! This was T. T. Wyche a Methodist Class Leader!† I used to think *his brother* the meanest man in town but I now think *Tom* can take the palm. It makes me *feel mean* to have to do with such.—

Sunday 15. [September 15, 1861]

Rev Landrum preached for us today from the text "Born, not of blood &c," upon the evidence of the new birth.—Just rec^d an order for Music from D. C. Spaulding who used to live here but were in Dubuque Iowa when we last heard from them before. He has met with reverses through *fire* but is now making a living in the grocery line and Mrs S is teaching music.

---

* Dr. James Mercer Green and his wife, Sarah Virginia Prince Green, were leading citizens of Macon. Before the war, Green was well regarded as a physician and applauded as founder of the Georgia Academy for the Blind in 1852. During the war, he ministered to Confederate wounded in Macon (Iobst, *Civil War Macon*, 107–8, 114–15).

† Thomas T. Wyche was a Macon cotton factor (Iobst, *Civil War Macon*, 13).

Wed 18. [September 18, 1861]

I met Jabez at the depot this afternoon, so now we are ready to "pitch in" on the morrow to pack up our stock, an undertaking of considerable magnitude and labor.

Sat. 21 [September 21, 1861]

We have worked hard for three days and nights and have packed forty boxes and *"shipped"* 26 to Atlanta. A very heavy rain caught us this evening as we went to work so that there was no choir meeting I guess.—Eddie left us today to return home as his father needs his help in the mill. We were sorry to have him go just now as we need his help. He is a good boy and willing and was getting better informed with regard to our trade.—

Sunday 22. [September 22, 1861]

This afternoon Jabez and I took a walk to Rose Hill Cemetery and found it comparatively quiet and without visitors, as usually on pleasant Sabbath afternoons there are a great many there. Perhaps the heavy rains of the previous night kept them away and it was quite damp and rather muddy in the darkly shaded walks.

Sunday 29. [September 29, 1861]

The Sabbath is a grateful cessation from the fatiguing labors of the preceding week: night and day we have been at work only stopping for necessary food and sleep and we have not been able to get off yet after all. We expected to get off to Atlanta yesterday but have had to put off our exodus until Tuesday. We finished packing our store goods yesterday and took our signs down and began at night to pack our piano and furniture so as to be ready to pack our *Car* on Monday, having chartered a car to carry the whole of the house and store furniture.—Jabe and I visited the Blind Institution this aft' as per invitation of the Principal Mr. W. D. Williams an old acquaintance of ours. I rec^d a letter from Asa last week from the Mountains of Western Virginia: he says he has not been ill one day since they first left home tho' many of his comrades have suffered a good deal.—Asa writes quite an interesting letter.

Monday 30. [September 30, 1861]

We have been hard at work all day packing our carload of furniture. Sister Nell and her husband and children passed through Macon tonight on there way home from Atlanta. We go up tomorrow to take their place. Our old house here is a desolate looking concern now robbed of all its furniture except just enough to sleep on tonight which we shall have to pack tomorrow morning before we go.—

TWO

October 1861 to April 1862

"MAY A MERCIFUL GOD GRANT US PEACE AND INDEPENDENCE."

Having cast his lot with the Confederacy, relocated his family, and invested his future in Atlanta, Sam Richards looked ahead with a combination of optimism and anxiety. On the last day of each year, he often stayed up late writing in his diary, combining his reflections on the past with musings about the year to come. On December 31, 1861, he wrote, "This has been a year of anxiety, suspense and excitement, and still the skies are dark and lowering and we know not what another year may bring forth." As in Macon, Atlanta's earlier support for Unionism all but evaporated in public discourse following the election of Abraham Lincoln and the fall of Fort Sumter. Richards, along with thousands of other former Unionists, caught the secessionist spirit. "Of one thing I am certain," he wrote, "*the Union* will not be restored!" Then he added, "May a merciful God grant us peace and independence."[1]

Business prospects appeared promising in Atlanta, which may have contributed to Sam's enthusiasm for Confederate nationalism. The Richards brothers owned stores at two locations. The main store, located on Whitehall Street in the heart of the city's business district, sold stationery, books, and music. A smaller operation on Decatur Street, staffed by Henry Richards, sold groceries. Despite his cautious nature, Sam admitted in January 1862 that "[b]usiness is pretty good and the profits *splendid* on what we do sell."[2]

Atlanta became a boomtown during the war. Richards and his family were part of a vast in-migration that took the city's population from around ten thousand in 1860 to nearly twenty-two thousand by the end of the war. Factories sprouted up to clothe and equip the Confederate

Army, offering jobs, some of them at attractive salaries, to both male and female workers. Atlanta's railroads, which had helped to launch the city in the 1830s, became ever more important in transporting men and materials to aid the South's military effort.[3]

Inevitably, given the importance of its railroads, Atlanta became a hospital center. When Confederate garrisons at Forts Henry and Donelson surrendered in February 1862, opening the door for the federal occupation of Nashville, wounded soldiers began arriving in Atlanta. On March 5, 1862, Sam estimated that between three and four thousand soldiers were recuperating in Atlanta. They were housed in public as well as private buildings, including the Atlanta Medical College, several hotels, and at least one church. Plans would commence in June 1862 for the construction of a hospital complex on the location of the Atlanta fairgrounds. In the interim, groups of women volunteers sought to ease the suffering of wounded soldiers. Skilled with a needle, Sallie Richards made "comforts"—rudimentary blankets or coverlets that women stitched, sometimes using their own bedspreads or other household linen.[4]

In addition to the losses in Tennessee, Confederates mourned the success of the U.S. Navy, which had begun the process of securing the southern coastline. At the November 4–5, 1861, Battle of Port Royal Sound/Hilton Head, a small Confederate flotilla failed to prevent the U.S. Navy from taking Forts Walker and Beauregard. As a result, the Union gained control of the Hilton Head/Port Royal area.

Union naval success wreaked havoc on the lives of Sam's extended family. His sister, Nell, reported that her coastal property was ransacked by Yankees, and William and Ann Richards were forced to flee their residence on St. Helena Island. Previously home to a large population of slaves owned by planters who grew Sea Island cotton, the island now became a haven for freed slaves. One Richards slave, Chloe, escaped to Yankee protection, although her daughter, Sue, remained with William and Ann. Sam Richards regarded Chloe's escape as a great loss for his parents and an exercise in stupidity for Chloe, who he believed would come to regret her decision to leave kind-hearted Christian owners in favor of an uncertain life with "abominable Yankee invaders." Chloe's views are not known, but any regret would have focused on the daughter she left behind. Throughout the wartime South, African Americans made difficult, often wrenching decisions about whether to use opportunities to escape even if it meant leaving behind members of their families.[5]

Church life was always important to Sam Richards, and Atlanta's Second Baptist Church provided a good spiritual home for the newly arrived

Richards family. As in Macon, Richards joined the choir and quickly became its leading bass vocalist. Sallie Richards anchored the alto singers. Mary West and Sidney Root provided leadership among the soprano and tenor vocalists. These four singers also comprised a quartet that performed at Baptist services and in a group of amateur singers that met periodically, calling itself the Mozart Club. Sallie Clayton, an Atlantan who wrote a memoir of life during the Civil War, recalled that Second Baptist was "noted for its lovely choir composed of Mr. and Mrs. [S.] P. Richards, Mr. and Mrs. West, and Mr. Sidney Root, the tenor. This church had no organ and the choir simply led the congregation in singing, not elaborate music, but appropriate hymns."[6] The lives of Sam and Sallie Richards became closely linked with those of West and Root during and after the war.

West had previously lived in Macon, where she sang in James Van Valkenburg's Baptist choir. When Sam visited his brother, Jabez, in Atlanta during the late 1850s, he made note of her move there. West and her husband, Thomas, who were childless, became fond of the Richards children and often socialized with the family. Thomas West owned a soda water factory on Whitehall Street.[7]

Root became one of Atlanta's richest merchants and most colorful figures during the Civil War era after he launched a daring and profitable business as blockade-runner. His background was much like that of Sam Richards. Both men were born in 1824, the fourth sons in large families of modest means. Both families supported the Whig Party, with the Georgia-based Richards family lionizing Kentucky's Henry Clay and the Root family, based in Massachusetts, cheering for that state's Daniel Webster. Root moved to Lumpkin, Georgia, in 1843 at the behest of his brother-in-law, who operated a store there. Through a combination of skill, hard work, and an advantageous marriage to the daughter of an affluent local merchant, Root became a successful businessman and the owner of several slaves.[8]

In an unpublished memoir written for his family in 1893, Root recalled that he relocated to Atlanta in 1857 because he was "fascinated with the idea of building a town." Like Jabez Richards, Root saw possibilities for making money and admired the spirit of Atlantans, whom he described as "rugged, hopeful people." Root formed a partnership with another recently arrived businessman, John N. Beach, and the two opened a dry goods store on Whitehall Street. The business prospered, and Root invested in real estate. He lived with his family on Washington Street, near Jabez Richards.[9]

Like many Southern moderates, including his friend, Sam Richards, Root moved from support for Unionism to support for secessionism. "I had been an intense Union man," welcoming Henry Clay's Compromise of 1850 "with satisfaction," Root recalled. However, "after ten years' experience of constant intimidation and aggression from the North, I concluded the two sections *could not* live in harmony and had better separate." When Atlanta formed its Minute Men in anticipation of southern secession, Root was chosen as speaker for a big rally following Lincoln's election. Because of his wealth and social standing, Root became part of the committee that escorted Jefferson Davis to his February 1861 inauguration.[10]

Root and Beach saw opportunities for making money in the nation's present circumstances. Beach departed for Liverpool, ostensibly laying the groundwork for a successful cotton-exporting business when the Confederacy achieved independence but in fact laying the groundwork for a blockade-running operation. The Confederate government eventually appointed Beach and Root as cotton agents, and they operated out of offices in Liverpool and Le Havre, France. Meanwhile, Root secured $150,000 in supplies for the Atlanta store, leaving their local operation well stocked for the coming months. A dedicated Christian, Root also served as choir director and Sunday school superintendent at Second Baptist.[11]

Signaling his decision to make Atlanta his permanent home, Sam Richards paid a thousand dollars for a lot on Washington Street early in 1862.[12] The next step would be to build a house. In making such plans, Richards hoped to bring stability to his personal life and to showcase his success as a businessman. Wartime conditions ultimately led him to defer construction of a home for many years. As in the 1850s, Sam Richards became a boarder in Jabez's home, thereby saving money and receiving housing in close proximity to the Richards store. Although the brothers regarded this as a temporary arrangement, Sam and his family remained part of Jabez's household for most of the next four years, with Sam, Sallie, and their four children sandwiched into two rooms. With two families living in such close contact and members of the extended Richards family visiting frequently, the household at times became too crowded for comfort.

By early 1862, the war had begun to affect daily life for Atlanta's civilians. Sam Richards complained of high prices for coffee, salt, and bacon and shortages of paper goods such as stationery and envelopes. Because the Union blockade made cloth hard to obtain, he bought Sallie a dress made out of homespun, a throwback to the days before machine-made goods had freed women from spinning and weaving. Sallie's view of the dress is not known, but Sam regarded the fabric as an object of such curiosity that he promptly wrote to his brother, Addison, and enclosed a sample of the cloth.¹³ Over the coming months, shortages and high prices would become less the subjects of lighthearted correspondence and more the subjects of discontent.

Notes

1. SPR diary, Dec. 31, 1861; Thomas G. Dyer, *Secret Yankees: The Union Circle in Confederate Atlanta* (Baltimore: Johns Hopkins University Press, 1999), 28–29.

2. SPR diary, Nov. 13, 1861, Jan. 9, 1862; Frank J. Byrne, *Becoming Bourgeois: Merchant Culture in the South, 1820–1865* (Lexington: University Press of Kentucky, 2006), 125.

3. James Michael Russell, *Atlanta, 1847–1890: City Building in the Old South and New* (Baton Rouge: Louisiana State University Press, 1988), 92.

4. SPR diary, Mar. 5, 1862; Jack D. Welsh, *Two Confederate Hospitals and Their Patients: Atlanta to Opelika* (Macon, Ga.: Mercer University Press, 2005), 12–13.

5. SPR diary, Nov. 16, 1861, Feb. 15, 1862; *WPA Guide to the Palmetto State* (Columbia: University of South Carolina Press, 1992), 290, 335–36; Clarence L. Mohr, *On the Threshold of Freedom: Masters and Slaves in Civil War Georgia* (Athens: University of Georgia Press, 1986), 70–75.

6. Sarah "Sallie" Conley Clayton, *Requiem for a Lost City: A Memoir of Civil War Atlanta and the Old South*, ed. Robert Scott Davis Jr. (Macon, Ga.: Mercer University Press, 1999), 36–37.

7. SPR diary, Sept. 6, 1858; V. T. Barnwell, *Barnwell's Atlanta City Directory and Strangers' Guide* [Atlanta: Intelligencer, 1867], 76, 271. No city directories were printed in Atlanta during the Civil War.

8. Sidney Root, "Memorandum of My Life," 1–4, unpublished typescript, 1893, AHC.

9. Ibid., 5, 9. Shortly before moving to Atlanta, Root planned a trip to visit another up-and-coming city, Chicago. The train that carried him from St. Louis to Chicago crashed, leaving Root with an arm broken in five places. While he convalesced in a Lexington, Kentucky, he hired railroad lawyers Leonard Swett and Abraham Lincoln to represent him in a lawsuit seeking damages. Swett handled the case, but owing to a technicality, Root never saw the one-thousand-dollar judgment the courts gave him.

10. Ibid., 6; Thomas H. Martin, *Atlanta and Its Builders: A Comprehensive History of the Gate City of the South*, 2 vols. (Atlanta: Century Memorial, 1902), 1:158–61.

11. Root suspected that New Jersey–born Beach remained a Unionist even after Georgia seceded. If so, Beach kept it to himself (Root, "Memorandum," 6–8; Frank J. Byrne, "Rebellion and Retail: A Tale of Two Merchants in Confederate Atlanta," *Georgia Historical Quarterly* 79 [Spring 1995]: 40–43).

12. "When Stone Mountain Was Called Gibraltar," *Atlanta Journal*, Nov. 16, 1924.

13. SPR diary, Nov. 3, 1861, Jan. 1, 9, 1862.

Tuesday 1. [October 1, 1861]

After running about until near ten oclock this morning to settle up some business I joined the folks at the depot and we all took our leave of Macon for an indefinite period of time. Our stock of mdse has already gone up—114 boxes and bdles.—We arrived in A. rather late owing to detention on the way from one of the wheels burning the axle. Before six o'clock we found ourselves safely housed at the hospitable mansion of J. J. Richards Esq and welcomed by his estimable wife to our new home.*—It is a relief to both mind and body to know that the removal so dreaded is accomplished and tho much yet remains to be done in the way of unpacking and fixing up, it can be done leisurely and in the way of regular business, after we get settled at our new abode. We expect to live with Jabe for several months at least and shall take our furniture there.—We received a number of expressions of regret from Macon friends at our leaving, but they didnt give me any gold headed cane as they did to Jonathan Collins when he left! Jabes baby "Ethel" don't look like her father much, but *takes* after her mother more.—We weighed the two babies and Ethel weighs 12 and Alice 14 lbs. We do not anticipate any difficulty in distinguishing our babies if they should get mixed up!—

Sat. 5. [October 5, 1861]

We have but just got "settled" in our rooms and we have had considerable turning up as we have taken out Jabes furniture and mostly replaced it by our own. Our rooms are the two original ones of the house before it was enlarged and we have put our Piano up in the largest *in the* beds' *stead* and shall do all our sleeping in the other room except a nap or so on the couch perhaps.—Our other "plunder" is stowed away *in spots* from the cellar to the garret[,] there to rest until we need it again.—We have upset Stella's arrangements considerably and caused her a good deal of trouble but she bears it all amiably. If Cousin Mary [Hathaway Brown] had been mistress here I should have been afraid to venture to intrude

---

* JJR's home was located on Washington Street between Fair and Jones Streets (*Williams' Atlanta Directory, City Guide, and Business Mirror* [Atlanta: Lynch, 1859], 130).

after our experience when we last lived together. The expense of our removal in actual cash paid out has been nearly $200.—We have dismissed John Hornady, Jabe's boy clerk as we found him out in lying and theft. Jabe has been unfortunate in his clerks all along. We have all had good appetites since we came here; mine has been unusually so.

Sunday 6. [October 6, 1861]

We all except the *old ladies* went to Sunday School this morning and returned for our wives to go to church afterwards and hear Mr. Clark preach from the text "Watch ye and pray lest ye enter into temptation[.]"* We did not go into the choir indeed we were not invited to.—

Wed. 9. [October 9, 1861]

Sallie's birthday.

Sunday 13. [October 13, 1861]

We have been employed the past week in unpacking our Macon Stock, but for the last three days Henry and I have been at Decatur St "taking stock" there preparatory to filling up with a better assortment to see if we can make it pay. The season is advancing and the weather gets cool tho' we have not seen any frost yet here.—We are receiving the Triweekly Macon Telegraph now so as to keep posted in the news of that city and vicinity.—Bro Root leader of the choir in the church here called on us this morning and asked us to join the choir and we accordingly went up and sang with them. They need an Alto voice very much having none but there are some half a dozen *base* singers such as they are. There is but one *air* singer, Mrs. West, but she is *some* considerable, but appears to think that she is enough alone and continues to drive away all other air singers by her *airs*. So at least Jabe says and Stella quit the choir upon that account. Mr Root complimented us by saying that they had better singing than they had had for some time.—It was Communion season and we partook of the emblems. I like the Macon way better of having a separate service for that sacred ordinance. I made an attempt to organize a class at S. School today but did not make much progress.—

---

* Formerly an attorney, John T. Clarke was ordained a minister in 1858 and the following year answered the call to pastor at Second Baptist, located at the northwest corner of Mitchell and Washington Streets, across from City Hall (*Williams' Atlanta Directory*, 22, 63; *History of the Baptist Denomination in Georgia* [Atlanta: Harrison, 1881], 128).

Sat 19. [October 19, 1861]

We have made but little progress in opening our stock from Macon, at least apparently, as we have been doing the fancy goods which take a great deal of time. Our stock at Decatur St amounts to $1900 perhaps $20 more not yet included. I was quite surprized this evening at the appearance of David Craig just from Norfolk, having given up Soldiering because he was needed as a *pattern-maker* by the Schofields' in Macon and they procured his discharge.* He and his brother and wife were at our choir singing tonight at the Church. I could not sing to my satisfaction as I had a bad cold with which I have been troubled for several days.—

Sunday 20. [October 20, 1861]

I had four larger boys in my class this morning but could not do much for want of question books. These boys are all larger and older than my Macon class but they are far behind them in knowledge of the Scriptures.—I forgot to say that last Sunday afternoon Jabe and I took a walk out to "Aunt Lipham's" who lives one mile from the Depot just outside the corporate limits of the city.† We picked and eat some of her raspberries and I carried home a cabbage leaf full. The old lady looks about the same to me that I remember her over 20 years ago in Washington Geo. Church at night—Bro Root seems to think that we can sing anything in the Music Book right off without practice.

Sat 26. [October 26, 1861]

This has been a dull week and today especially has been so only *three dollars* at Whitehall Store.—*Henry* has sold nearly twice that in dull

---

* David Craig was discharged from military duty "by reason of his labor being required in other important Government work, Oct. 10, 1861" (Lillian Henderson, ed., *Roster of Confederate Soldiers of Georgia, 1861–1865*, 6 vols. [Hapeville, Ga.: Longino and Porter, 1959], 6:798). Schofield's Foundry, founded in 1852 by John Schofield as a producer of equipment that ginned cotton and pressed it into bales, expanded into making a variety of different machinery. In a seventy-fifth anniversary tribute to the company published in *MT*, June 1, 1927, David Craig was listed among two long-term employees of the company who were "highly esteemed by their employers and the people of Macon."

† Frances Lipham was an old family friend of the Richardses. Before the war, she resided in Washington, Georgia, where SPR visited her when book-peddling trips brought him to the area. She later moved to Atlanta, where she was a founding member of Second Baptist Church (S. E. Dellinger, *History of Second–Ponce de Leon Church and Its Antecedents* [Atlanta: Poindexter, 1871], 2–3).

D. Street. It has rained all day so that we had no singing tonight at the church. We have news of a severe fight at Leesburg in Virginia in wh' our side were finally victorious and repulsed the enemy, in much superior force, with great slaughter driving them back into the Potomac River and drowning numbers.* We also hear of their being routed and chased for 20 miles at Chickamicomico or "Chicka mi comique" as it has been called in derision of the panic and flight of the Yankees and cowardly *Indiana* men. In returning from the chase our men were slowly marching through the sand upon a narrow island on the N.C. coast when a U.S. Steamer appeared and *shelled* them for several hours until night covered them from view yet wonderful to tell, not one man was killed except one who died from exhaustion! Our folks took 70 or more prisoners it is said. And yet—the Northern papers claim it as a *glorious victory* on their part in which *hundreds* of our soldiers were killed by their shells and shot!—

Sunday 27. [October 27, 1861]

This afternoon being bright and pleasant we all walked out to Henry's little place about half a mile further out of town than we live. The *three babies* had a confab.

Wed 30. [October 30, 1861]

Sallie and I went to meeting tonight and put our church letters in and rec^d the hand of fellowship from all the members present, a custom I dont approve of in general. Stella was there and we wonderd that she didn't *shake hands* forgetting that she was a "Methodis" but she is not a very strong one and *may* be brought around by the force of Circumstances.

Sat. Nov. 2. [November 2, 1861]

We have had bad weather for two days, yesterday it rained all day a cold rain and today has been cold and cloudy, but no rain. We have not yet got our Macon goods all open as out door matters occupy the greater part of Jabe's attention and I cant do much alone and wait on customers too. We have rec^d *Writs of Garnishment* upon all our debts and property

---

* The Battle of Ball's Bluff or Leesburg, Virginia, took place on Oct. 21, 1861, across the Potomac River and a short distance from Washington, D.C. Confederate forces drove U.S. soldiers to the steep cliff at Ball's Bluff. Inexperienced soldiers attempted to retreat, but seven hundred were captured and two hundred were wounded or killed as they attempted to climb down the bluff or drowned trying to swim across the river. The Union casualties included Colonel Edward D. Baker, a close friend of President Lincoln (James M. McPherson, *Ordeal by Fire: The Civil War and Reconstruction*, 3rd ed. [Boston: McGraw Hill, 2001], 236).

owned by the North. I suppose our Govt did only right in this Sequestration Act but I very much regret its personal application to ourselves as a good many goods were sold us by reason of the full confidence the parties had in our intention and ability to pay, and I believe that many of them are our friends and well wishers. Of Course we shall have to treat our brother William as we do other "Alien enemies" and what I most regret in his case is that he *is* an alien enemy[.] Our *taxes* will be quite considerable this year, probably *three* times the usual amount and we have to pay taxes on a large stock of *books* that seldom sell nowadays.

Sunday 3. [November 3, 1861]

Bright and cool today and our eyes rejoice to see the sun again. I again essayed to teach my class at S.S. but had only two boys and they behaved so rudely and insolently that I gave them a parting salute and got up and left. After my attentive and respectful class in Macon I was not prepared to put up with the impertinence of these hop-o-de-hoys. If I could have a class that would behave and try to learn, however dull, I would be patient and persevering, but shall not go any more at present.—Our little Alice is well and sweet. We weighed and measured her a few days ago and she weighed 14½ lbs and was 24½ inches long. Arthur is a fat sturdy boy but still coughs badly and has a very sore nose which he picks and aggravates continually.—Dora and Irene are well and great romps.—Provisions are getting dear especially Coffee, Salt, and bacon—Coffee 50¢ lb—Salt $10 per sack—bacon 25¢ lb. Paper & Envelopes are *up* too, the former $5 to $7 per Rm and the latter $7 to $10 per. If we had our whole stock in these articles our fortune would be made, but alas! our supply is getting small.—Jabe and I are considering the chances of doing something in the *grocery* line at D St. instead of keeping a Bookstore there. Charley Mustin has made a good deal of money speculating in Salt &c as he still holds nearly a thousand sacks of it which he bought at old prices. But possibly he may hold them *too* long and lose it all. *Ken* Mustin is drinking himself to the dogs again, fast.

Sat 9. [November 9, 1861]

We have been considerably stirred up this week by the news of an attack by the Yankee "Armada" upon our defences at Beaufort Harbour So Car and the more so because they have proved too strong for us and have taken our batteries and routed our forces and gained possession of Hilton Head Island a large island lying just over the channel opposite to St Helena where father lives. I hope he has got away from there ere this. I fear we are going to see hard times down there and should not be surprized to hear that the enemy were advancing upon Savannah. Last Tuesday was Election Day for President and Vice President—Davis and Stephens were the only candidates.* Today at Church meeting Bro Clark tendered his resignation there being much dissatisfaction in the church. A call meeting next Wed' night is to decide whether to accept or not. Mr Clark has reason to be dissatisfied with the tardiness of the church in paying him. We have been to two meetings this week and take steps toward a Concert for the Soldiers. Tuesday night we went to Mr Roots and last night to Mr McDaniels where Mrs West boards. We have not made much progress however. We cant sing such Music as we did in Macon anyhow.

Sunday 10. [November 10, 1861]

Cloudy and foggy is the order of the day. I got a letter from Addison last week in reply to mine of July; it has been only about ten weeks coming and dont contain much. He says my letter was entirely satisfactory to them. He also says that Kate Rogers was still in Charleston at that time so she may be there now. I cannot tell by what means his letter came beyond Norfolk as it has that postmark over a *U.S. 3 cent Stamp.*—His new address "Clinton Hall Astor Place." Little "Allie" is growing finely and getting fat and saucy. She has got better of a cough which has troubled her for some eight weeks. We feared it might prove to be Whooping Cough and *it may* have been a slight attack of it but if so she did not *whoop* and was but little troubled by it.

Wed' 13. [November 13, 1861]

We have had very pleasant weather for ten days past with the exception of last Sat' & Sunday and it must be the "Indian Summer" we think. At all events it is nearly as warm as Summer. We have decided to go *into* Groceries at Decatur Stret and have already bought some to begin with and employed Old Mr. Grubb at one dollar per diem to help Henry. A called Conference tonight resulted in the acceptance of the pastor's resignation, none of his friends having anything to say. We met on Monday night at Mr Craigs to practise for the proposed Soldier's Concert.—

Sat 16. [November 16, 1861]

It has seemed like *Monday* all this day in consequence of yesterday having been Fast Day appointed by the President and observed by us by

---

* On Nov. 6, 1861, Jefferson Davis and Alexander Stephens were elected to six-year terms as Confederate president and vice president, respectively; they had held those positions "provisionally" since February (E. B. Long, *The Civil War Day by Day: An Almanac* [Garden City, N.Y.: Doubleday, 1971], 135).

closing our stores and going to church, at least.* The churches on this side of the town all agreed to meet at the Presbyterian house of worship and we therefore went there and heard some very slow singing aided by an Organ and a long but good sermon from a Methodist minister. Tonight we rec^d another letter from Amelia telling us that Father and Mother had arrived there in safety bringing their little negro *Sue*, her Mother *Chloe* having chosen to try her chance for freedom by deserting to the Yankees! poor fool! she will have time to regret it. Amelia says hundreds of the negroes have run away on the Island thereabouts and gone to the Yankees. Mother will probably come up here soon. I know it will grieve her mightily to have to leave her house and property in the hands of those abominable Yankee invaders; and to think of having lost *Chloe*.—Our usual choir practise was held tonight and on last Thursday night we met again at Mr. Roots to sing for our Soldier's Concert. People from Savannah report that the people are breathing more freely now and that they dont think that the enemy could take the city if they should attempt to at least not until they had taken Fort Pulaski.—

Sunday 17. [November 17, 1861]
The weather is cooler today and more seasonable than for sometime past. Rev Jesse Wood preached for us this morning from the text ["]The love of Christ constraineth us"†—Jabe and Stella went to Methodist Chapel and they report a *crowd* out there and I thought the occasion opposite to the quotation of the verse "Broad is the road that leads to death" at which Stella was very indignant in a pleasant way! At all events the Methodists are better church goers than the Baptists in almost every place. It may be that they have more regard for *works* than the Baptists and less for *Faith*, but I wish *our* folks would *show their faith by their works* more.

* Jefferson Davis declared Nov. 15, 1861, a day of "fasting[,] humiliation and prayer." He urged citizens to attend church "and to implore the blessings of Almighty God upon our arms, that He may give us victory over our enemies, preserve our homes and altars from pollution, and secure [to] us the restoration of peace and prosperity" (*ASC*, Nov. 7, 1861).

† Jesse H. Wood attended Mercer University in Penfield, pastored in a variety of locations in Georgia, and served as editor of the *Cherokee Baptist and Landmark Banner* (later known as the *Baptist Banner*), published in Rome, Georgia, beginning in 1859 but moved to Atlanta in 1860. SPR became a contributor to this publication. With the onset of war, Wood became a volunteer evangelist with the army (*History of the Baptist Denomination*, 95–99, 597–600; SPR diary, Nov. 28, 1862).

Friday 22. [November 22, 1861]

We had *singing* at our house last night but it seems likely that the *Concert* will fall through after all as our *Soprano* singers seem to want to back out.—I have tonight written to father in reply to one from him rec^d yesterday. Sallie also received a letter from Amelia.

Sat. 23. [November 23, 1861]

We gave in our "War Tax" today, which will call for about $75 more out of our small income.* Jabez had to "muster" today. As they haven't got my name on their lists yet I do not turn out. We hear that they have begun fighting at Pensacola, Fort Pickens having opened upon one of our vessels.† Sallie did not go to singing tonight as she had taken cold and had a bad sore throat and some fever.—

Sunday 24. [November 24, 1861]

Bro Clarke fulfilled his promise today and gave us a sermon in which he said very plain things to the church about their shortcomings. I expect it is his last gun as he announced that there would be no preaching tonight. I think that this church will have reason to regret having treated him as they (some of them) have, and I am afraid that we shall not get another preacher at present that I shall like as well as him.—Deacon Sam' Smith returned safely from New York last week after a tedious and difficult journey, partly by the "Underground RR." His reappearance disappointed a good many persons who thought he had run away "for good." The very night of his return the house he slept at burned down and he lost his gold watch, and guard made from his wifes hair. The fire was on Whitehall but two squares above our store.

Thursday 28. [November 28, 1861]

Our Concert was appointed to come off tonight and came off it did although the night was anything but favorable as it was dark and lowering and the streets were dirty from previous rain. The audience was quite

---

* The War Tax Act of Aug. 19, 1861, levied taxes on, among other things, slaves, city lots, and merchandise. Confederate treasury secretary Christopher Memminger had insisted on taxing merchandise, arguing that businessmen could pass along the costs to their customers, but store owners rebutted by pointing out they were hard-pressed to acquire merchandise previously obtained through Northern concerns (Douglas B. Ball, *Financial Failure and Confederate Defeat* [Urbana: University of Illinois Press, 1991], 217).

† On Nov. 22–23, 1861, Union guns at Fort Pickens and on two naval vessels bombarded Confederate installations in Pensacola, Florida. The outcome was inconclusive (Long, *Civil War Day by Day*, 142).

"select" about 50 or 60 only being present. The pieces all went off well and gave satisfaction I believe to those who listened. Another circumstance that thinned our audience was that 300 Yankee prisoners passed through the city this evening and a great many people were drawn to the depot to see them. The Singers at our Concert were Mr Root and Mr Craig, Tenors—Mrs. Craig and Sallie, Altos—Mrs West and Miss Holbrook, Sopranos—and Mr Birth and myself, Basses. Two *Irishmen* sang a Catholic duett—"Ave Regina"—at the close of Part First.—The *proceeds* of the concert were only $25.—*

Sunday 1. [December 1, 1861]

It is a beautiful day and favorable to church-going.—Rev James E. Evans of the Methodist Conference now in session here—preached in our church from the text—"Thou shalt love the Lord thy God with all thy heart &c" and gave us quite a sanctification sermon. There are about 200 Methodist preachers in town now but only *one* of them has been to our store and bought some books—yes—I did sell a Hymn Book and Discipline to another yesterday.—We rec^d letters yesterday from Hardeeville [South Carolina.] Our folks are all there and in health. Steve [Whitehead] has moved his goods partly from his exposed place to Hardeeville and is selling supplies of meat and grain to the Army there. That is better than for the Yankees to get hold of it and pay nothing.—We have had a mild and pleasant November and Winter comes in in the same style and I hope will continue in like manner for the sake of our soldiers in the field and camp, and the poor who had but little money or work.—The enemy discontinued the fight at Pensacola after two days.

Sat 7. [December 7, 1861]

This afternoon Bro Clarke who has been a lawyer assisted us in making out our *document* setting forth the various amounts in which we are indebted to "alien enemies" in the list of which we have to enumerate W. C. Richards of Providence R.I. and a number of others more unwillingly than in his case.

Sunday 8. [December 8, 1861]

Bro Clarke preached for us this morning from the text "the way of the transgressor is hard." Next Sunday he expects to preach his farewell sermon. Next Wed. night our folks are to vote for a Pastor and they think of

---

* ASC, Nov. 28, 1861, praised the "high social position and the real musical talent of the ladies and gentlemen composing this club." Quoting a Richmond newspaper, the ASC noted the transfer of six hundred Yankee prisoners from Richmond to Tuscaloosa, Alabama.

electing W*m* T. Brantley late of Philadelphia. He has just received a call to a church in New Orleans but it is thought that he would prefer to come here, but I dont think he would be content with the salary that this church can offer.—

Tuesday 10. [December 10, 1861]

Father, Mother arrived this afternoon direct from Hardeeville, S.C. and bring news of the birth of another son to Ellen and Steve and the tolerable welldoing of the mother, child[.] Bro Clarke and his wife took tea and spent the evening with us last night.

Sunday 15. [December 15, 1861]

This morning our church was filled with those who came to hear the Farewell Address of our Pastor. The 1st Baptist Church had closed their house and many of them came to hear this sermon. Also many of other denominations were out. His text was I Cor. II. 1–4. How Paul preached the Gospel and determined to know nothing among the Corinthians but Christ and him crucified.—The preacher drew a sort of parallel betwixt himself and the Apostle in that respect and also took occasion to give our church a hard rap by stating that the reason of his leaving was that they had *starved him out*! This afternoon Jabe and Stella and Sallie and I went to the cemetery. It is far behind the Macon "Rose Hill" in both natural and artificial attractions.*—Father preached tonight from the words "Behold I come quickly—hold fast that which thou hast, that no man take thy crown"—I liked the sermon very much and think others liked it tho' father says that he had no liberty of speech but was much embarrassed as usual when he preaches in a strange place.—I expect we shall have to go to keeping house again soon as it appears that Stella is tired of having such a large family to care for notwithstanding she leaves it all to servants to do. We hear from Ellen, our girl, that Jabe and S. had a blow up about these matters two or three nights ago which I think was begun by his finding fault about something or other which she had done, or failed to do.†— Perhaps we may still live in the same house but keep separate tables. This

---

* Atlanta's City Cemetery opened in 1850. In 1872, it changed its name to Oakland and became a park as well (Cathy J. Kaemmerlen, *The Historic Oakland Cemetery of Atlanta: Speaking Stones* [Charleston, S.C.: History, 2007], 15). Rose Hill was the Macon cemetery where SPR and SVVR had buried their infant son in 1859.

† Ellen was a slave rented by SPR from her owner in Macon. In December 1862, he purchased her (SPR diary, Dec. 27, 1862).

will probably be soon advisable. There has just befallen Charleston a great calamity a very extensive fire which has destroyed a large portion of the city, some 1800 by 250 yards in extent.

Tuesday 17. [December 17, 1861]
The "Mozart Club" met at our room tonight and at the close of the exercises Jabe and I sang *Snibbs* for the amusement of the company.*

Thursday 19. [December 19, 1861]
Perry Oliver, Sallie's old sweetheart, has come to town in the capacity of Showman having charge of "Blind Tom" the wonderful negro Pianist, and we went to hear him perform tonight at the City Hall. He is truly one of the *seven wonders*[,] plays the most difficult operatic music correctly and composes pieces of his own and yet is but 12 years old and little better than an idiot.†

Sat 21. [December 21, 1861]
Very gratifying news has reached us from Europe respecting the reception of the news of the arrest by the Lincolnites of our two Commissioners, Mason and Slidell while on their way to England in a British Vessel from Cuba.‡ The despatches say that the English are very indignant at

---

* "Mr. and Mrs. Snibbs: A Comic Duet" (1842) was sheet music composed by John H. Hewitt.

† Thomas Greene "Blind Tom" Wiggins, born a slave in Harris County, Georgia, was sold along with his parents and siblings to James Bethune of Columbus, Georgia, in 1850. Sightless from birth, Wiggins manifested an early talent for music and amazed his owners with his ability to play piano pieces after hearing them performed by members of the Bethune family and to play them thereafter from memory. In 1857, he began performing on the piano, first in Columbus, then in Macon, Atlanta, and Athens. For a time, Bethune contracted with Perry Oliver of Savannah to arrange bookings for Wiggins, earning large sums of money from the proceeds of Blind Tom's concerts. After the Civil War, members of the Bethune family continued to control Tom's career even though slavery had ended. Wiggins may have been what is today called an autistic savant (Geneva Handy Southall, *Blind Tom, the Black Pianist-Composer* [Lanham, Md.: Scarecrow, 1999], 1–2, 148–54). ASC, Dec. 20, 1861, called Wiggins a "prodigy" whose performances at City Hall produced "crowded" audiences.

‡ Confederate diplomats James Mason and John Slidell, bound for London and Paris, were captured by the U.S. Navy from aboard a British mail steamer, the *Trent*, on Nov. 8, 1861. While the Northern public cheered the capture, the government of Great Britain decried this action as a violation of diplomatic immunity and Britain's officially stated neutrality. Despite heavy criticism from the public,

such an outrage on their flag that their Government has demanded the immediate surrender of the Commissioners, or take the consequences! The crazy abolitioners North seem to be determined not to give up the prisoners even if they do have to fight England and France and the South all at one time. It is to be hoped that they will continue to be of this mind and consequently get well taken down in their pride and self conceit.— Business has been pretty good this week.

Sunday 22. [December 22, 1861]

The weather which has been of the finest kind of late changed last night and today we are having regular Christmas weather cold, wet and windy. Dr Crawford who preached for us this morning was listened to by a very small congregation in consequence. Dr Basil Manly Jr is to preach tonight if the weather will admit, but I fear it will be worse before it is better.* Bro. Jno T. Clark left Atlanta last Wed' for his down-country abode.

Wed. 25. [December 25, 1861]

The weather cleared up on Monday, much to our satisfaction and has been cold but fine and pleasant since then but business has only been moderately good for the season. Father rec^d a letter from Kate [Richards DuBose] enclosing a half sheet from Mary Add of Date Dec 1. saying that they were all well and that they had not heard a word from us since my letter to Add of July last and that they were very anxious to hear of our welfare. Father conducted the prayer meeting tonight at our church.

Sunday 29. [December 29, 1861]

Dr Holmes of Decatur preached for us this morning and father is to preach tonight.† Father preached for us at night from the words "Eternal Judgment," Hebrews 5 chap. I liked the discourse very much.

President Lincoln ordered the diplomats' release, thereby averting a possible military engagement with England (Howard Jones, *Union in Peril: The Crisis over British Intervention in the Civil War* [Chapel Hill: University of North Carolina Press, 1992]). On Dec. 20, 1861, *ASC* reported that "the English journals are very bitter and hostile—contending the Trent affair is intolerable."

* Basil Manly Jr. was a professor and noted Old Testament scholar at Southern Baptist Theological Seminary in Greenville, South Carolina. His father, Basil Manly Sr., was a distinguished Baptist clergyman and president of the University of Alabama. After the Civil War, the younger Manly was appointed to the presidency of Georgetown College in Kentucky (*History of the Baptist Denomination*, 345–47).

† Rev. Adam T. Holmes, a Baptist minister in Decatur, was described by fellow Decatur resident Mary A. H. Gay as showing Unionist sympathies when William T.

Monday 30 [December 30, 1861]

A fire broke out on Decatur St early this morning and destroyed a wooden store between the Trout House and Masonic Hall without burning either of those buildings.* The "Mozart Club" sang tonight at Mr Roots.

Tuesday, 31. [December 31, 1861]

We have had beautiful weather these Holidays and the year 1861 is about closing his campaign. The great things that the Yankees were going to do to us as soon as cold weather came have not yet been done; and now it appears that there is going to be a great backing out by them from the war with England and they are going to surrender Mason & Slidell and make all proper apologies to Great Britain for having taken them! Just as I expected they would, rather than fight. This has been a year of anxiety, suspense and excitement, and still the skies are dark and lowering and we know not what another year may bring forth but of one thing I am certain, that is that *the Union* will not be restored! May a merciful God grant us peace and independence.—We have rehired "Ellen" our negro girl as she is clever, and good to the children.—I have been hard at work for the past 3 months unpacking and arranging our goods and have but just about got through putting up the Macon stock as I have had it nearly all to do myself and tend store too. Our stock is pretty full yet in most things tho' Paper & Envelopes are getting low in quantity but pretty *high* in price!— The hour of the old years death is close at hand but I believe I shall not sit up to be "in at the death" but bid him farewell and go to bed.

Thursday 2. [January 2, 1862]

Little "Sue" the small darkie that father and mother brought up, whose mother ran off to the Yankees, has the *Measles* and this morning we found Arthur broken out with it, and Stella too is sick with the same complaint and could not entertain the guests that had been invited to eat a New Years dinner so they were warned not to come.—I have just rec^d a letter from *Asa* Sherwood. He has been promoted to the office of Adjutant at a Hospital for convalescent soldiers in Western Virginia.—I bought Sallie a

---

Sherman arrived with his army (*Life in Dixie during the War, 1863–1864–1865* [Atlanta: Constitution Job Office, 1892], 69–70).

* Masonic Hall and the Trout House hotel stood side by side on Decatur Street, an unpaved thoroughfare in the city's business district. Built in 1854, the four-story Trout House was Atlanta's most commodious and elegant hotel (Michael Rose, *Atlanta: A Portrait of the Civil War* [Charleston, S.C.: Arcadia, 1999], 19, 101). ASC, Dec. 31, 1861, reported that a fire of unknown origin destroyed a grocery store and caused six hundred dollars damage to Masonic Hall. Trout House was not affected.

Homespun dress yesterday for A New Years Present it cost 50¢ per yard and is neat and strong.—

Sunday 5. [January 5, 1862]

Last night was a wet and stormy one and today is a continuation of the same. Father preached for us from the text "Certainly I will be with you" which he said is God's New Years Greeting to his people—Arthur is getting better of the Measles but Stella is still in bed and Annie and Ethel the baby both have it now. Allie seems to have escaped it so far. Sallie says I must record how clever Miss Alice is for a baby not yet six months old. She sits alone and "patty cakes" when told to and eats beef and battercakes with the best of them though her teeth have not come through yet. Oh yes, and she says *da da*! Tonight it is wet and we have no service in our church[.] Jabez and the *old folks* came to our room and we had a sing for an hour or so.—

Thursday 9 [January 9, 1862]

Cold and cloudy for several days past—I wrote bro Addison yesterday to go "via Norfolk and flag of truce" and sent a sample of Sallies new homespun dress! Our servant Ellen has been sick all this week with Measles, probably; she is up again today however.—Business is pretty good and the profits *splendid* on what we do sell. If we only had our whole stock in paper and envelopes we could make a small fortune out of it.—Sallie has taken cold and is ailing tonight.—She rec[d] a letter from George yesterday at Norfolk; he is faring well and living comfortably, he says.—She had letters also lately from Martha, "Mollie" Van and "Mathilde Schwaab" of Macon.—Our hopes of war between Old Abe and England are destroyed by the prompt surrender of Mason and Slidell upon the peremptory demand of England, and the Commissioners are again en route for England where they will probably be somewhat *lionized* by the Britishers on account of the fuss they have been the cause of.—

Sunday 12. [January 12, 1862]

Last night we had our choir *sing* at our house and as Mr Root was gone to Charleston and had not returned I expected to have to lead today. But he came back this morning. Dr Wm T Brantley preached from the text "Rich in faith[.]" Our congregation was better than usual. The sermon was a good one. The weather today is warm and windy, quite spring like—

Wed 15. [January 15, 1862]

Today has been very wet, cold and disagreeable[.] Dr. Brantley has accepted the call of our Church for this year with the condition that he is not to enter upon his duties here until June 1 as he expects to spend several months in New Orleans. He will preach for us though two more sabbaths of this month. Our *Measley* folks are getting well and no new cases—as yet, Alice has not taken it. Nothing of much interest is occurring now. The Yankee Army dont seem inclined to advance. There seems to be *some* indication of the political sky clearing up ere very long— the Yankees are quarreling among themselves and the sympathies and interests of European nations are with the South and it is thought that they will soon recognize the independence of the Confederate States and come to get our Cotton.—*Then* wont the Yanks be "hoppin' mad!" I hope they will get into a quarrel with Europe and get a sound drubbing between them and the South. "Pride must have a fall" sooner or later[.]

Sat 18. [January 18, 1862]

Dr Brantley came to our house this evening to spend the Sabbath, and our choir met also in our room so that we spent quite a pleasant evening. Our new pastor seems to be a very sociable man and a true christian. Stella is laid up again with rheumatism, from cold.

Sunday 19. [January 19, 1862]

We have spent a pleasant Sabbath enjoying the privileges of the Sanctuary and the society of our minister. It is to be regretted that he cannot continue with us now.—

Sat 25. [January 25, 1862]

Today is bright and pleasant after a long *spell* of bad weather. We have bad tidings from Kentucky of the defeat of our forces under Gen Crittenden and the death of Gen Zollicoffer a noble man and gallant officer.* It is supposed to be probably the severest reverse our arms have met with in the war. We have selected a *lot* to build our house upon, just below Jabez's. The price is $1000 and I would have bought it at once but the owner has gone to New Orleans. Tonight our choir met at Mr Wests just across the street from here.

---

* In the Union slave state of Kentucky, Confederate forces led by General George B. Crittenden were defeated in efforts to engage Federal troops on the Cumberland River near Beech Grove. In the confusion caused by weather conditions and smoke, Confederate General Felix Zollicoffer was killed (David S. Heidler and Jeanne T. Heidler, eds., *Encyclopedia of the American Civil War: A Political, Social, and Military History*, 5 vols. [Santa Barbara, Calif.: ABC-CLIO, 2000], 4:2172).

Sunday 26. [January 26, 1862]

Dr Brantley has preached twice for us today and this morning the Lord's Supper was celebrated. The text tonight was "God is love."—

Sunday Feb 2. [February 2, 1862]

The weather has been bad again nearly all the week but yest' aft' it cleared off and the stars shone brightly at night but clouds obscured the sky this morning again and now at one o'clock it begins to rain. Dr Brantley preached this morning to a good congregation from the words of Paul "I know in whom I have believed &c[.]" He is staying at Mr Roots where we went last night to sing. Our Yankee enemies have lately beset Savannah having succeeded in getting some of their smaller gunboats into the river *inside* Fort Pulaski by passing through some cuts at high water which had been obstructed, but these had been removed by them or partially so.—It is still uncertain whether they can get near enough to shell the city.

Sat 8. [February 8, 1862]

The weather has been wet and unpleasant all the week again though it has not *rained* today. We hear more bad news from Kentucky; that the enemy have taken Fort Henry on the Tennessee River I think it is.[*] Nothing more from Savannah, except that the defences of "Red Bluff" Steves place have been abandoned as untenable and the vandals had sent a shell through Steve's house and stolen seven of his negroes. Nell had been told so, but was not certain that it was true about the shelling and stealing.— Our choir met at our rooms tonight. Business has been good this week, one day we sold $110 cash. Letter Paper we now sell at $15 per ream or 75¢ per quire.—good *Yankee* envelopes at 40¢ pack.—*Cotton* sells at 30 to 40¢ in New York! it is about 7¢ here but manufactured cotton goods are high even homespuns. and printing paper is three times its usual price, they say. All kinds of *foreign* goods and supplies are getting scarce and selling high. We hear that Dr Brantley has gone to New Orleans.

Sunday 9 [February 9, 1862]

Father preached this morning from the text "For ye know the grace of our Lord Jesus Christ, that tho' he was *rich* yet for your sakes he became poor, that ye through his poverty might be rich."—Sallie had an ill turn

---

[*] Confederate General Lloyd Tilghman withdrew most of his garrison from Fort Henry in an effort to fortify Fort Donelson. Possession of Fort Henry opened the Tennessee River to Federal control and cleared the way for Union domination in Nashville (Long, *Civil War Day by Day*, 166–67).

last Monday: it came on suddenly after dinner and they sent for me. She was siezed with severe pains in the stomach and chills. Hot flannels (wet) applied to the affected part relieved her and she was about again the next day.—Stella went down to dinner today for the first time since her relapse. It is quite cold tonight and there being no service in our church we all stayed at home.

Sat 15. [February 15, 1862]

We have fine clear weather for several days of this week but it is again wet and disagreeable, indeed today has been the *ugliest* day we have had this winter. *Valentines* have been very *slow* this season; we have not sold out even our limited stock. We hear today from Nell confirmation of the report that the Yankees had been at their place stealing and destroying their property. She wishes us to rent a house for them to live in this year in Atlanta. We are encouraged by good news today of the complete success of our folks at Fort Donelson on the Cumberland River in Kentucky in repulsing the enemy's attack for two successive days after hard and continued fighting. It is but a few days since we were *set down* a good deal by the startling news that the "Burnside Fleet" had captured Roanoke Island on the coast of North Carolina and taken 3000 of our men prisoners the number though has been modified to 1700.* The Yankees are said to have had five times our force in this fight. This gives the enemy access to a great portion of the N.C. coast which depended solely on Roanoke for defence.—The Government has made a requisition for 12 Regiments more from Georgia and the Governor has issued his proclamation that unless the requisite number is *Volunteered* by the 4th of March a *draft* will be resorted to to supply the deficiency!† It is thought though that this will not yet have to be resorted to, and I hope not. It is too wet for our sing tonight at Mr. Clarke's.—Our relentless and cruel enemy is raging mad to descend upon and destroy us, confis-

---

* On Feb. 7, 1862, a Union fleet began bombarding Confederates on Roanoke Island off the coast of North Carolina. Their success cleared the way for General Ambrose E. Burnside to land a force of 10,000 on the island, easily prevailing and taking 2,580 Confederate prisoners (Heidler and Heidler, *Encyclopedia*, 4:1659–61).

† On Feb. 11, 1862, Governor Joe E. Brown issued a proclamation calling on Georgians to enlist, with each volunteer to receive a bounty of fifty dollars and the right to elect his own officers. If twelve regiments had not been raised by Mar. 15, a draft might follow (*ASC*, Feb. 15, 1862).

cate our property to pay the cost of the devilish war they are waging, and drive us from our homes poor and friendless. Will the God we serve permit them to succeed in their unholy purposes?—surely not. The *Christian Index* comes to us again this week under date of Feb 11 after a suspension of several months.* I am entitled to *six months* of it from this time.—

Sunday 16. [February 16, 1862]

The rain continues and there was no service at our church this morning in consequence.—In the afternoon we met at Mr C Roots and had a sing, but it was difficult to get there through the mud. They gave us cake and wine, which we did not refuse.

Sat 22. [February 22, 1862]

This is Washington's birthday and our President and Vice are to be inaugurated today at Richmond. This has been a gloomy week indeed; the weather very dark and wet and the war news very discouraging. Our forces at Fort Donelson were compelled to surrender the fort on Sunday last after twice repulsing the foe; but their numbers were increased and became too much for us.† The first news we received was that 5000 Confederates were killed and 10,000 taken prisoners and the enemy marching on Nashville which we could not hold. How much of this is true we cannot yet tell accounts are so various and conflicting but no doubt things are bad enough. The great many lives must have been destroyed on both sides at the battle of Fort Donelson, even the Yankee accounts admit that it was dearly bought victory. Some of our citizens are very desponding and think we are done for but I guess we shall not give it up yet, but I fear we shall see hard times indeed before the war ends. This has been a good day in our trade as we have sold more than we ever did before in one day

---

* The *Christian Index*, begun in Washington, D.C., in the 1820s as a Baptist newspaper, moved its base of operations to Washington, Georgia, and then to Penfield, Georgia, where SPR lived as a young man. In 1857, the newspaper moved to Macon, and early in the Civil War, it moved again to Atlanta (Chase L. Peeples, "Christian Index," in *New Georgia Encyclopedia*, available online at http://www.georgiaencyclopedia.org [accessed 24 September 2008]).

† Fort Donelson, on the Cumberland River, fell into Union hands after General Ulysses S. Grant famously demanded its "unconditional and immediate surrender." Grant's forces killed somewhere between fifteen hundred and thirty-five hundred Confederates and took fifteen thousand prisoners. Grant's victory also enabled Union forces to take Nashville, the first Confederate state capital to fall under U.S. control (Heidler and Heidler, *Encyclopedia*, 2:728–31).

I think except bills to peddlers. $211 cash our days sales foot up. $160 of it we sold of School Books for the Georgia Military Institute at Marietta.*
If the country was at peace and property secure we should be in very good spirits with our present trade. Not having paid any Northern debts in nearly a year we have nearly $6000 in bank that we have no *immediate* use for. I expect to use $1000 of it next week to pay for our lot. We sang at Bro Clarks tonight.—

Sunday 23. [February 23, 1862]

This is a bright and pleasant morning and is delightful after the dark wet weather we have had all the year thus far with only a day or two of *shine* now and then. Rev Mr Rambaut preached for us in the morning and Jesse H. Campbell at night.† In the afternoon Sallie and I took a walk with the children out to the end of Washington St. being the street we live on and from thence we cut across to Henry's house to join father & Mother and returned home with them.

Thursday 27. [February 27, 1862]

Having free tickets I took Sallie tonight to see the performance of the "Queen Sisters" a Thespian family of Juveniles.‡ They gave us considerable fun and some good music vocal and instrumental as they had a good *band* with them. As we returned through the Car Shed we passed three boxes containing dead soldiers brought down on the Rail Road, a sad commentary upon the evil times in which we live.

Friday 28 [February 28, 1862]

Being the day appointed by the President for fasting and prayer we did not open store but had prayer meetings at the church. I walked around our new lot this morning and found it 292 paces—Jabe's lot is but 236. I think there must be nearly ¾ of an acre, being of such an irregular form it is hard to tell.—Our city is now full of sick soldiers many of the large

---

* Founded in Marietta as a private school in 1851, the Georgia Military Institute began receiving support from the state the following year. By the time the Civil War began, it had between 150 and 200 students (Barton Myers, "Georgia Military Institute," in *New Georgia Encyclopedia*).

† Rev. Thomas Rambaut was president of Cherokee Baptist College in Cassville, Georgia (D. B. Ragsdale, *Story of Georgia Baptists*, 2 vols. [Atlanta: Foote and Davies, 1932], 1:234).

‡ The Queen Sisters and Palmetto Band from Charleston, South Carolina, performed periodically in Atlanta during the war. Their act included singing, dancing, and dramatic presentations (*ADI*, July 10, 12, 1862).

hotels and public buildings being appropriated as hospitals.* Mrs West proposed that we should go and see the soldiers and we went to one of the hospitals but soon got enough of seeing such miserable beings as the sick soldiers are—dirty and ignorant as well as sick. One poor fellow died today who in coming here passed within 30 miles of his wife and prayed to be put out there that he might go home to die, but the rules of war would not permit so he had to die among strangers. Oh what dreadful misery this horrid war has produced and the end is not yet. It seems to me that this war waged by our Northern brothers (!) is the most atrocious and wickedly unnatural that ever was undertaken since the world began. We went tonight to Mr Roots to sing in "Club" capacity but did not progress much.—

Sunday 2. [March 2, 1862]

Father preached for us this morning from the text "What shall it profit &c[.]" The weather was so uncertain that but few persons were present. I went to S School today at Bro Davis' request to take charge of a class of young ladies whose teacher had left, Mr Blanchard. Their names are as follows[:] Mattie Andrews, Ella Neal and Mittie Rucker. They used no question books and the lesson for today was Gen 17 all about *Circumcision* which I could not make very interesting to a class of young ladies!— Mattie I think is the smartest and prettiest of the three but they all seem well behaved and I hope to get along better with them than I did with my first class here. Bro Davis is Superintendent Bro Smith being away again, *gone North* we suppose on business for his Insurance Companies!—

March 3. [March 3, 1862]

Another milestone on the road of my life I pass today at the mature age of thirty eight years.

Tuesday 4. [March 4, 1862]

A grand muster of all the Militia of Fulton County some 1,000 or 1200 strong took place today in order that the required number of men might be made up to fill the Governor's requisition, either by Volunteers or failing that by a *draft*. Jabez and I both turned out and were kept out until

---

* On the advice of Atlanta's mayor, the City Council voted on Feb. 21, 1862, to begin making formal measures to care for the soldiers. In June 1862, plans commenced to build a hospital complex on the location of the Atlanta fairgrounds (Welsh, *Two Confederate Hospitals*, 12–13).

about four oclock about six hours. There was no draft but the number of men required was not quite made up at the time.*

Wed 5. [March 5, 1862]

I received from Wm Solomon today the deed for my lot and gave him a check for one thousand dollars making me a *land owner* for the first time in my life. If times were not so unsettled I would proceed at once to build upon my lot. The names of Jabez and myself were published in the muster roll of the "Atlanta Leyden Artillery" a few days ago, which we regretted as we had not the slightest intention to join the Company. Some of the young men who were getting up the company proposed a plan to us whereby we might they said be exempt from draft, which plan was that we should "furnish a substitute" by equipping a man whom they would bring to us and bind ourselves to pay to him or to his family some $10 per month during the term of his service and upon the strength of this they took the liberty to publish our names as members of the Company and if we had not remonstrated with them and requested our names taken off I expect we should have been smuggled into service on yesterday. My whole nature revolts at the thought of going into this war to be cast for months or years perhaps into the company of such men as form the greater part of our army—to be ordered about by incompetent, drunken officers and to engage in scenes of blood and carnage, from which I have ever turned with loathing and horror. I have no ambition to acquire military renown and glory—and "It is not on the battlefield that I would wish to die." Yet all our times are in the hand of the supreme Ruler of events and if it should fall to my lot to enter into the service, it will be unspeakable comfort to know that He is still near me and that though "Plagues and death around me fly, 'Till He bids I cannot die; Not a single shaft can hit, 'Till the God of life sees fit."—At prayer meeting tonight but few were present; Father led the meeting. It seems now certain that Nashville is in the possession of the Yankees, which seems very strange, so much so that many people think it is a trap to lure the enemy to destruction. We hear of a *great victory* gained by Price in Missouri over the Yankees but do

---

* In addition to calling on soldiers to muster on Marietta Street above Bridge Street at nine o'clock in the morning, *ADI*, Mar. 4, 1862, contained multiple calls for new soldiers along with much-needed sacks of corn, bales of hay, and transportation wagons. In "The Big Muster," *ASC*, Mar. 6, 1862, called the gathering "the largest military muster ever held in the county" but editorialized in favor of a draft to fill the ranks with able-bodied men.

not know how true it is.*—Our City is now full of sick and convalescing soldiers some 3 or 4 thousand are said to be hear and Sallie has been going to help make "comforts" to keep them warm in the absence of blankets.—

Sat. 8. [March 8, 1862]

Yesterday was the Governor's Fast Day, but coming so soon after the President's appointment it was not so closely observed as it otherwise would have been. We had no services in our church but went to the Methodist in the morning. I was at the store most of the day with the door closed but not *fastened*. This morning (yesterday) was the coldest we have had this season as the mercury was 24° and our pitcher frozen up! This being a pleasant day Sallie brought Dora to town to visit the Dentist's Rooms to have her teeth taken out of the way of the permanent ones which are growing out crooked. Dora was very much troubled at the thought of having it done. Two lower front teeth came out without hurting her much but a third one made her cry out, but then it was over. I fear she will not have very good teeth. Our quartettete met at our room tonight to sing but Mrs West was hoarse and could not sing much so we spent two hours in talking.—Sallie wrote today to Amelia at "Woodlawn" in So Carolina near Augusta where she is upon a visit to her friend Bettie Merriweather formerly *McKie*. I paid her a visit there years ago when she was there teaching and I was *peddling* books. Bettie was then a maiden and Amie thought she would like her as a sister—now she has *four children*, and Amie and I each four; twelve human beings have thus come into our existence since then.

Sunday 9. [March 9, 1862]

Nell's birthday; and she has four children too. She has given up the idea of coming to Atlanta this spring to live fearing she should be no safer here than in Hardeeville. Two only of my class were present today Mattie and Ella. Mr Rambaut preached from the text "I would that thou wert cold or hot."—Tonight Rev Mr Dickinson Agent of the Army Bible and Tract Colportage Society gave us an interesting address in regard to the good that has been done and that may be done by supplying the soldiers with

---

* The Union gained a victory. Efforts by Confederates under command of Sterling Price, Ben McCulloch, and Earl Van Dorn to eliminate the Union Army from Missouri failed when U.S. general Samuel R. Curtis defeated them at the Battle of Pea Ridge, Arkansas, March 6–8, 1862 (Heidler and Heidler, *Encyclopedia*, 3:1466–68, 1562).

good books or tracts.* Our galleries were filled, for the first time since we have been here, with *darkies* who kept coming in and going out all the time of the discourse.—

Sat 15. [March 15, 1862]

A great Naval fight occurred last Sat & Sunday at Norfolk between our "Virginia" (the old U.S. Steamer "*Merrimac*" which had been *raised* from her watery bed in which the Yankees had sunk her about a year ago, and had been iron-clad and newly named) and the enemy's vessels. Their vessels "Congress" & "Cumberland" were soon destroyed, the latter a large vessel (360 men and 22 guns) was sunk and many lives destroyed. The "Congress" was set on fire and exploded (480 men and 50 guns) and several other vessels were injured and driven off by our iron-monster and two or three gunboats.† Last Wednesday Talley and Haynes two officers of the Leyden Artillery came into the store and insulted us by saying that they considered us *unsound* and asserting that we had been watched for some time and were considered unreliable!‡ This charge was first made by Haynes who was *miffed* by Jabe's having asked him to pay a small a/c [account] he was owing us. We told Mr Root in whose store Talley has been clerking of the ill conduct of his young man and I suppose he gave him a talking to for the young man came over and apologised for his talk, acknowledging that he had said more than he intended, being angry. I do not think such men are fit to *command* when so unable to rule his own spirit. We have been very busy in the store this week there have been so many soldiers in town. Some one of them stole my comfortable hat from

* The general superintendent of army colportage, Rev. A. E. Dickinson, was on a trip to raise the money necessary to purchase and distribute Bibles and tracts to soldiers (*ASC*, Mar. 9, 1862).

† On Mar. 8, 1862, the CSS *Virginia*, an older vessel previously known as the *Merrimack* and reoutfitted by the Confederacy with ironclad sides, attacked old-style wooden Union ships outside Hampton Roads, Virginia. The *Virginia* badly damaged or destroyed the twenty-four-gun *Cumberland* and the fifty-gun *Congress*. The following day, however, the U.S. Navy sent its own ironclad, the *Monitor*, to face its Confederate counterpart. Although neither ship destroyed the other, the *Monitor*, with its revolving turret, prevented the *Virginia* from breaking free and sailing past the Union blockade, thereby ending any serious threat of Confederate naval dominance (Long, *Civil War Day by Day*, 181–82).

‡ Lieutenant William A. Haynes Jr. and Lieutenant Algernon S. Talley served as officers in Georgia's 9th Artillery Battalion, commanded by Major Austin Leyden (Janet B. Hewett, ed., *Georgia Confederate Soldiers, 1861–1865*, 4 vols. [Wilmington, N.C.: Broadfoot, 1998], 3:149–50).

the store one night and I had to tie my head up in a white handkerchief when I went home which gave my wife a fright she supposing I had a broken head. Yesterday was Mr Roots birthday he is 36 years old he says. We sang tonight at Mr Wests.

Sunday 16. [March 16, 1862]

My girls were all three present this morning and I gave them each a "Biblical Outline" to use as a question book. Dr Holmes did not come so Father preached upon *Regeneration*. At night Sallie and I with father and Mrs West went to the first Bap' Church to hear Mr. Hornady and their new singer Mrs Jim Ells or rather Eells as it used to be.—*

Tuesday 18. [March 18, 1862]

Father started for Hardeeville at 6 o'clock this morning leaving Mother here.

Thursday 20. [March 20, 1862]

The Vernal equinox—and the rain poured down in floods nearly all day.—

Sat 22. [March 22, 1862]

The weather continues quite cold and unpleasant and a little snow has fallen today. Trade has been quite lively for two weeks and our cash sales have been about $95 per day average. We sang tonight at Mr Roots where we found Dr Brantley just come from Augusta to preach on the morrow. Mrs West acts to[o] queerly now that our sings are of but little benefit to us and give but small satisfaction. We have concluded that she is getting too old to sing and too deaf.—The Federal "Burnsides Fleet" have made a successful attack upon Newbern N.C. and taken possession of it.†

Sunday 23. [March 23, 1862]

Dr. Brantley preached this morning from the text "God be merciful to me a sinner" and in conclusion gave our people a talking to about coming out to prayer meeting. This afternoon Jabe and I went with our *women* to

---

* Mary Eliza Garmany married James N. Ells in 1861 (Ronald Lora and William Henry Langton, eds., *The Conservative Press in Eighteenth- and Nineteenth-Century America* [Westport, Conn.: Greenwood, 1999], 230; Tad Evans, ed., *Macon, Georgia, Newspaper Clippings (Messenger) 1859–1865* [Savannah: Evans, 2001], 183).

† On Mar. 14, 1862, a Union force of eleven thousand men under the command of Ambrose Burnside captured New Bern, North Carolina, after defeating Confederates numbering about four thousand (Long, *Civil War Day by Day*, 184).

escort them to the house of a poor, sick woman a member of our church they say—a deserving object of charity.—

Sunday 24. [March 24, 1862]

This is Fathers birthday and he is sixty four, and it is sad that at that age he should have to be driven from his home and church to wander about without employment or charge. And to think that his own eldest son, himself a pastor, should be living at a comfortable home and praying for the success of the atrocious vandals that have driven out his old gray headed father from his island home! Truly it seems as Charlie DuBose says that William is "Without natural affection" and lost to all the common dictates of humanity. Charlie came here to attend Court this week and brought two letters that Kate had lately rec^d from ladies in Norfolk who had just come from the City of New York and had been boarding in the same house with Add and Mary. Their names are Mary Kleine and Bessie Sheppard. They say that they wrote at the request of Add and Mary to assure us of their love and sympathy and these ladies say that they are true to the South while William is a Republican and preaches *terrific war sermons*! What a renegade he must be; I hope he will never have a chance to put his foot again upon southern soil.—

Wed 26. [March 26, 1862]

I scratched out *two teeth* in Alice's mouth this morning, her first attempt.

Sunday 30. [March 30, 1862]

Quite Spring like today and we had a pretty good congregation. Dr Brantley preached from the 20th verse of Luke 10. and I took notes of the sermon as father requests that we give him the heads of discourse occasionally and I was intending to write to him and have this aft done so. We have had two long letters from him in the last two weeks in both of which he urges us to write and as yet *no one* has acceded to his request.—or had not before I wrote. I supposed that Jabez would reply to his letter ere this as father did tell him to write but did not say anything to us.—Jabe and Stella and Mother have gone out in Mrs Liphams carriage to see her as she is ill. Sallie and I are going this afternoon to the Epis' Church with Mrs. West to hear Dr Freeman (I am not so sure he's a *Dr*)[.]*

* Andrew E. Freeman was rector of St. Philip's Episcopal Church. He organized the St. Philip Hospital Aid Society from among his congregants and turned the church into a hospital (Alex M. Hitz, *A History of the Cathedral of St. Philip* [Atlanta: Conger, 1947], 18–20).

Sunday 6. [April 6, 1862]

We have had real April weather for the past week and vegetation is considerable advanced. Fathers 3rd letter arrived yesterday and he had not rec^d one from us and reproached us for our neglect of him. I expect he got my letter however on the day he mailed his last.—My girls did'nt know their lesson very well today at least only Mattie Andrews and she was not as prompt as usual. Ella Neal is remarkably dull and stupid or appears so.—Our congregation was quite large this morning as the pastors of the two Pres Churches are absent at Presbytery. Dr Brantley preached a good sermon from the text "Thou fool, this night thy soul shall be required of thee." Dr Brantley preached at night from the text "In whom the whole family in heaven and Earth, are named" and if any of our Pres friends were there (and some were) they could have found no fault with him for want of clarity. We have had a pleasant day and blessed privileges.—

Monday 7. [April 7, 1862]

I remained at the house and gardened until dinner time for variety— This afternoon we have news of a terrible fight at Corinth, Miss and the success of our army—8 batteries and several thousand Federal prisoners taken!* The enemy in full retreat! Thank God.

Tuesday 8. [April 8, 1862]

Conflicting reports reach us this aft. One says that the foe is reinforced and our forces obliged to retreat and give up all the batteries they had captured; another dispatch from a soldier says he has been in this fight two days unhurt and our side is successful; but I *fear* we have met with disaster.—Tonight it is raining hard.

Sat 12. [April 12, 1862]

The great battle of *Shiloh* near Corinth Miss seems from all accounts to have been a great victory for the South but General A. S. Johnston was killed and his death is a great loss to us. Well for us that Beauregard was

---

* At the Battle of Shiloh, near Corinth, Mississippi, on Apr. 6, 1862, Confederate forces under the command of General Albert Sidney Johnston attacked Union forces under General Grant in the early morning hours. Grant struggled to keep his men from panicking and running, but Johnston received a fatal wound, and the Confederates were unable to unseat Union soldiers in the area called the Hornets' Nest, thereby allowing Grant time to shore up his defensive line. Succeeding Johnston in command, General P. G. T. Beauregard attempted unsuccessfully to resume the Confederate offensive. Casualties were horrendous on both sides (McPherson, *Ordeal*, 247–50; James Lee McDonough, *Shiloh—In Hell before Night* [Knoxville: University of Tennessee Press, 1977], 152–53).

there to take command.—On yesterday the intelligence came that a large force of Federals had taken possession of Huntsville Ala on the Memphis & Charleston RR thus cutting of[f] our communication until they are dislodged.* Yesterday also I went to the meeting of the Stockholders of the "Confederate Insurance Co" in which we have taken a thousand dollars worth of stock—ten shares.—Today the startling intelligence comes that Fort Pulaski at Savannah has surrendered to the foe, seven breaches having been made in the walls and most of the guns rendered useless tho' no one was killed and *only four* wounded.† It was hardly expected that this Fort could hold out long. Steve Whitehead called in on us this morning.—

Sunday 13. [April 13, 1862]
The weather is very wet and disagreeable today but as it did not rain this morning much; some of us went to church and heard Dr Brantley preach from the text "In all the ways acknowledge Him and he shall direct thy paths[.]" Mrs West and Sallie were the only females present.—Our Sunday exercises and privileges are now so pleasant and desirable that I am disappointed whenever the weather deprives us of their enjoyment.

Sat. 19. [April 19, 1862]
No event of importance seems to have transpired during this week, except the passage of the "Conscript Bill" which as far as we now learn, provides that *all* persons between the ages of 18 and 35 who are not exempt from Military duty shall be considered as in the military service and must hold themselves ready for duty when called upon.‡ So it seems that I am *too old* to be drafted for a soldier which is a source of satisfaction and relief I acknowledge for the life of a soldier never had any charms for me, and a soldier's death I do not covet.—If I may stay at home and rejoice in

---

* Huntsville, a railroad junction in northern Alabama, changed hands several times during the war, beginning with its capture by Federal forces on Apr. 11, 1862 (Heidler and Heidler, *Encyclopedia*, 2:1022).

† Fort Pulaski fell to the Union Navy after bombardment from nearby Tybee Island. One Union soldier and one Confederate died; other Confederates were wounded. Fort Pulaski's fall contributed to a tightening of the Union blockade of the Confederate coastline (Long, *Civil War Day by Day*, 198).

‡ The Confederate Congress passed an Apr. 1862 conscription bill that made all physically able white men between the ages of eighteen and thirty-five eligible for the draft, including those who had volunteered for military service in the spring of 1861 and had served one year. The law relieved from service several categories of men, including preachers, teachers, and war workers. In October, a new exemption was added: planters who owned at least twenty slaves (McPherson, *Ordeal*, 202–3).

the success of our armies I shall be thankful. I pray God that we may not have to submit to the rule of the hated Yankees again, for rather would I have *England* to take us under *her* protection and government.

Sunday 20. [April 20, 1862]

It is not very pleasant today being cool and showery and our congregation was rather small in consequence. Dr Brantley's text was Matt. 25:34 "Then shall the King say &c.["] My girls were all at school but only Mattie Andrews said a lesson. She as usual knew it well but the others seem to take no interest at all in the matter. I wish I had more of Mattie's stamp, there would be some pleasure in teaching such a class.—

Wed 23. [April 23, 1862]

I had the pleasure of greeting our Macon pastor Rev E. W. Warren this afternoon and tonight, of hearing him address us at prayer meeting. Bro John T. Clark the former pastor of this church was also present. They are on their way to the Baptist Convention in La Grange.* Yesterday afternoon Sallie and I went in company with Mrs West to the Cavalry Encampment at the Fair Ground and heard Dr Brantley preach to the soldiers in the open air, from the words "A good soldier of Jesus Christ." Mr Root was there and we did the necessary singing. Jim Eells and his wife were there and he was determined to renew our acquaintance despite our evident avoidance of him, and came up and spoke to us. I did not greet him with much cordiality.—

Sat 26. [April 26, 1862]

Telegrams from New Orleans today state that the enemy's vessels have passed Fort Jackson and are in sight of the city and great excitement reigned there in view of the approaching attack.† It seems impossible for our folks to resist with any success the attack of our foes upon the water, but they have not gained any considerable fight on terra firma during the war and before they can subdue us they must leave their gunboats and

---

* The Georgia Baptist Convention met in LaGrange in 1862, affirming its support for Confederate nationalism and emphasizing its ministry disseminating religious tracts to soldiers (James Adams Lester, *A History of the Georgia Baptist Convention, 1822–1872* [Nashville: Curley, 1972], 182–83).

† The strategically important port city of New Orleans became a Union target in 1862. The Confederate defenses—Forts Jackson and St. Philip and a modest fleet—posed no serious obstacle for David Farragut and the U.S. Navy. On Apr. 24, Union ships sailed past the two forts, and three days later, Farragut claimed the city (Heidler and Heidler, *Encyclopedia*, 3:1412–13).

fight us more equally on land.—It is quite cool today and fires conduce to comfort.—Tonight we had singing again at our house; as the leader Mr Root has gone to the Convention I had to take his place as far as to direct the proceedings.—

Sunday 27. [April 27, 1862]

Rev Mr. McDonnell who has char[g]e of the Trinity Methodist Chapel supplied our pulpit today in the absence of our pastor and preached a good sermon from the text "Let not your hearts be troubled &c" Jn. 14:1.* We sang "Mary to the Savior's tomb" for a voluntary.—Mr Root told me that Bro Blanchard wishes to take his class in S. School again, so I went this morning and delivered my valedictory reproving the bad scholars and exhorting them to do better and thanking *the good scholar* for her attention. I only regret giving up Mattie Andrews. I dont think I shall go any more until some other door of usefulness is opened there for me. Mother rec^d a letter from father last week. He is well and gets quite poetical and ardent in his expressions of love and remembrance writing an acrostic on his *lady love's* name &c—! He says it is the 46th year of their married life. It is sad that their evening of life should be so clouded over by the dark storm of war and desolation that is raging around us; that they should be driven away from their peaceful and happy island home by the ruthless invader of our rights and territory and still more and to think that their eldest son is praying in public and private for the success of that invading army! May he live to repent thereof bitterly.—

Wed. 30. [April 30, 1862]

Dr Brantley took tea at our house but as it was my night at the store I did not have the pleasure of seeing him[.] Bro Warren took tea there also on Monday evening and I got home just in time to see him before he left.— I have had the *deed* of our lot Recorded in the book, of the Sup Court of Fulton Co "Book F Page 161 Apr 18/62 by W R Venable Clerk."—It began to rain again tonight.—We have had but a small proportion of fair weather this year so far.

---

* Rev. George MacDonnell of Trinity Methodist Church played a cameo role in the Andrews Raid by giving religious reading material to those captured and held in Atlanta (Harold Lawrence, ed., *Methodist Preachers in Georgia 1783–1900* [Tignall, Ga.: Boyd, 1984], 349; Christopher H. Owen, *The Sacred Flame of Love: Methodism and Society in Nineteenth-Century Georgia* [Athens: University of Georgia Press, 1998], 104).

THREE

May 1862 to December 1862

> "WE HAVE SOLD MORE THAN IN ANY PREVIOUS MONTH. . . . BUT I DO NOT ENJOY *THE TIMES*."

By the second half of 1862, Sam Richards had begun to ride the crest of Atlanta's wartime prosperity, achieving a level of business success that he could not have imagined a few years earlier. As goods became available through the blockade, Richards sold them locally and sometimes to patrons as far away as Richmond. "I expect we have sold more than in any previous month since we have been in business," he wrote on August 30, 1862. During this period, he used his share of the profits to purchase city lots, believing that such investments would provide for his financial future. In December, he became a slave owner, paying the relatively high price of $1,225 for Ellen, the teenager whom he had rented for the past several years. Purchasing a slave meant that Sam had reached a new level of success as a businessman and a gentleman. Now nearly forty years of age, he had finally achieved the stature that Southern society bestowed on those who owned slaves. Sam was not alone in being optimistic about slavery's future. Reporting the top-dollar prices paid for slaves in two recent auctions, the *Southern Confederacy* crowed that "confidence in the 'institution' is unimpaired" by war.[1]

Atlanta's citizens grounded their confidence in industrial growth. The city teemed with activity as a variety of factories produced military equipment for the Confederacy. The Atlanta (later renamed Confederate) Rolling Mill and Winship's Machine Shop and Foundry manufactured cannons, armor plate, rails, and freight cars. The city's largest employer, with 5,464 men and women on its payroll, was the arsenal, which the Confederate government opened in March 1862 and which made percussion caps, cartridges, and artillery shells as well as harnesses, saddles, bridles, belts, and canteens. In addition, the Confederate Quartermaster's Depot employed more than 3,000 workers, most of them female, making jackets, shirts, trousers, caps, and shirts. As workers flooded into town seeking employment in manufacturing, conveniently located housing became scarce, and Jabez and Sarah took in a boarder who worked at the Spiller and Burr Pistol Factory.[2]

Several blockade-runners operated out of Atlanta, including Sam Richards's friend, Sidney Root. Operating first out of the port of Charleston and later out of Wilmington, North Carolina, after the U.S. Navy made Charleston too difficult to use, Root purchased a fleet of ships to run cotton to Liverpool and to bring back goods and military materials, some of which no doubt landed in the Richards brothers' stores. In an editorial notice, the *Daily Intelligencer* announced, "Our true Southern women will, doubtless, be ambitious to secure a dress from this successful venture of importers." Sallie Richards was one who did so, purchasing a calico dress from Root's store in July 1862. Sam Richards helped Root's son, Johnny, with his Sunday school work. Fearing that Johnny would enlist in the Confederate Army, his father later took him to England aboard one of his blockade-runners, enrolling him in an English school to study architecture. John Wellborn Root subsequently became one of Chicago's most distinguished architects.[3]

As an enthusiastic supporter of the Southern cause, Richards chronicled the growth in Confederate pride among Atlanta's citizens. He noted that few Atlantans still bothered to celebrate the Fourth of July, and he suggested that an alternative holiday should be chosen. If Confederates needed to find George Washington–like heroes, their armies supplied many of them. Richards wrote about the exploits of General Stonewall Jackson in the Shenandoah Valley and the success of Confederate forces in squashing the Union Army at the Battle of Fredericksburg. But no Confederate military figure seemed to excite Richards as much as John Hunt Morgan, the gallant cavalry hero whose raids in Kentucky during the summer of 1862 garnered considerable coverage in Atlanta's newspapers. The *Southern Confederacy* described Morgan's exploits as "the most brilliant, daring and successful warlike expedition that ever was undertaken in any country."[4]

While he now embraced Confederate nationalism unequivocally, Sam Richards did not look toward the future with complete optimism, writing, "I do not enjoy *the times*." The military situation remained mixed. Confederate success in Virginia was offset by the failure to make inroads in the Union slave state of Kentucky despite Morgan's efforts. The war's closeness became apparent to Atlantans in the spring of 1862 when Union spies were hanged in the city after a bold but ill-fated effort to hijack the locomotive *General*, its tender, and several boxcars. Richards personally felt the tragedy of war when his Macon clerk, Asa Sherwood, died of wounds at McDowell, Virginia. Richards never underestimated the ability of the U.S. government and its armies to cause destruction to the Confederate states. On September 9, 1862, he wrote, "Our people are far more united and determined to fight until death than were our forefathers of the former Revolution. It is possible that they may destroy both themselves and us and some foreign power may then step in and take the spoils but the once happy Union cannot be restored. They have killed it dead."[5]

Richards became increasingly alarmed at the prospect that the Confederacy might draft him into military service. Unlike many Southern men, he had never glorified military life. In 1844, at age twenty, he had performed militia duty, marching around with an umbrella since Jabez wielded the family's only firearm. Sam wrote a parody of the episode in his diary. In 1856, he complained about the "big fuss" a military parade created in Macon. Richards saw no conflict between his support for Confederate nationalism and his desire to avoid a military role. At age thirty-eight, he regarded himself as too old to fight and temperamentally unsuited to do so. Confederate military authorities did not agree. Once protected by age—the initial draft included men aged thirty-five and under—Richards now worried that military needs would lead to the drafting of older men. Hoping to avoid military service by working for a printer of Bibles and other religious texts, Richards took a part-time job with J. J. Toon, a fellow member of Second Baptist Church and proprietor of the Franklin Printing House on Alabama Street, between Whitehall and Pryor. Since clergy and typesetters were exempt from military service, Richards hoped that his association with Toon would provide an exemption.[6]

Despite ongoing fears about being drafted, Richards revealed moments of fun and even levity in his diary: giving his wife a special birthday gift, drinking beer with Jabez, eating Christmas dinner with his children. Sam and Sallie took advantage of Atlanta's lively cultural life by attending concerts, including those of the Queen Sisters and Palmetto Band. Appearing at the Athenaeum and charging seventy-five cents per ticket (half price for children and servants), the Queen Sisters pitched their singing, dancing, and acting routines to audiences steeped in wartime issues, using titles such as "Young Widow" and, ominously for Sam, "The Conscript."[7]

While the Richards family enjoyed the cultural amenities of city living, wartime life also strained the family. Sam Richards worried about smallpox, scarlet fever, diphtheria, whooping cough, cholera, and erysipelas. At times, as many as four branches of the Richards family lived at Jabez and Stella's Washington Street home—"quite a menagerie now," as Sam put it.[8] His family of six and their possessions were still squeezed into two rooms. Family tensions reached a boiling point during this time, exacerbated by the illness of Stella, who had begun to manifest the unmistakable signs of tuberculosis, the same disease that had killed Jabez's first wife. Resentful that so many relatives were moving in and out of her house, Stella tangled with Sam and Sallie on several occasions, ultimately leading Sam to move his family out of his brother's home and into separate quarters less conveniently located to the Richards store.

Although she had not wanted to leave her extended family in Macon, Sallie tried to make the best of her new life in Atlanta, including the ordeal of living in Jabez's crowded household. She volunteered with the Ladies' Soldiers' Relief Society, which appointed teams of women to oversee care for soldiers at ten area hospitals. Sallie's team was assigned to "alleviate in some degree the sufferings and wants to the sick" at Denny Hospital and to provide weekly reports to the society about hospital conditions.[9] Plagued by a variety of ailments including chronic dental pain, this mother of four children, the eldest just eight years old, now found time to help wounded and sick men.

In the fall of 1862, Sallie asserted her will at a pivotal moment. When baby Alice became dangerously ill, Sallie insisted on taking Alice and the other children to visit her sister, Harriet, in South Georgia. At this time of crisis, she wanted to be with Van Valkenburgs. While Sam hesitated to travel with their sick baby in the cold weather, he understood his wife's struggles with wartime conditions, household tensions, pressure to do volunteer work, and a variety of family illnesses. In this instance, he deferred to her.

Notes

1. SPR diary, May 24, 1862, Aug. 30, 1862, Oct. 25, 1862, Dec. 27, 1862; ASC, Jan. 9, 1862. Historian Walter Johnson (*Soul by Soul: Life inside the Antebellum Slave Market* [Cambridge: Harvard University Press, 1999], 81–82) has written that when Southerners moved from hiring to owning slaves, it was like "coming into their own in a society in which they were otherwise excluded from full participation."

2. SPR diary, Nov. 15, 1862; Ralph Benjamin Singer Jr., "Confederate Atlanta" (Ph.D. diss., University of Georgia, 1973), 137–43; Mary A. DeCredico, *Patriotism for Profit: Georgia's Urban Entrepreneurs and the Confederate War Effort* (Chapel Hill: University of North Carolina Press, 1990), 35–39; James Michael Russell, *Atlanta, 1847–1890: City Building in the Old South and New* (Baton Rouge: Louisiana State University Press, 1988), 103–4.

3. *ADI*, July 13, 1862; SPR diary, July 27, 1862; Thomas H. Martin, *Atlanta and Its Builders: A Comprehensive History of the Gate City of the South*, 2 vols. (Atlanta: Century Memorial, 1902), 2:697–99; Sidney Root, "Memorandum of My Life," 6–8, 14, unpublished typescript, AHC. Other blockade-runners included the Fulton County Export and Import Company and an operation run by Richard Peters and two associates (Russell, *Atlanta*, 96).

4. SPR diary, July 26, 1862, Aug. 2, 1862; *ASC*, Aug. 2, 1862; James A. Ramage, *Rebel Raider: The Life of General John Hunt Morgan* (Lexington: University Press of Kentucky, 1986), 91–106.

5. SPR diary, Aug. 30, 1862, May 16, 1862, Sept. 9, 1862; Russell S. Bonds, *Stealing the General: The Great Locomotive Chase and the First Medal of Honor* (Yardley, Pa.: Westholme, 2006).

6. SPR diary, Aug. 24, 1844, May 1, 1856; *ASC*, May 11, 1862. Toon had moved to Atlanta from Charleston and had purchased the printing and bookbinding shop from Wood and Hanleiter (*ADI*, July 11, 1862; V. T. Barnwell, *Barnwell's Atlanta City Directory and Strangers' Guide* [Atlanta: Intelligencer, 1867]). For a complete text of the conscription law, including exemptions, see *ASC*, May 11, 1862.

7. SPR diary, Oct. 9, 22, 1862, Nov. 2, 1862, Dec. 25, 1862; *ADI*, July 12, 1862, Oct. 23, 1862.

8. SPR diary, May 10, 1862. *ASC* printed lists of soldiers who died of disease in area hospitals; on May 11, 1862, for example, many died of typhoid fever.

9. *ADI*, July 10, 1862. Other hospitals under care of the Ladies' Soldiers' Relief Society included Empire Hospital, Henry Hospital, Gate City Hospital, City Hotel, Alexander Hospital, Concert Hall Hospital, Wilson's Hospital, Medical College Hospital, and Janes and Hayden Hospital. Two additional women's groups, the Ladies' Hospital Association and the St. Philip's Hospital Aid Society, volunteered to help sick soldiers (Jack D. Welsh, *Two Confederate Hospitals and Their Patients: Atlanta to Opelika* [Macon: Mercer University Press, 2005], 13).

Thursday 1 [May 1, 1862]

Not a very pleasant day—a fire has been comfortable, to me especially as I have suffered from tooth-ache all the time and what concerns me more is that it is the large tooth that my *one false* tooth is *attached* to and dependant on!—Yesterday we paid up the balance of our subscription to the "Confederate Insurance Co" making $1000 now paid in.

Sunday 4. [May 4, 1862]

It is pleasant today though somewhat cloudy and likely to rain. I did not go to school this morning as my "occupation is gone." We had a good congregation today and one company of soldiers came in a body, and Dr Brantley preached from the text Acts 10:1–2 subject—"the Christian Soldier" and the sermon good and appropriate to the times. Last night we met at the *Church* to sing.—I forgot to mention in its place that last Sunday night as there was no service in our church Sallie and I with Mr & Mrs West went to the First Presn Church to hear Dr. Wilson and *the choir.** The singing was not so good *but that we thought we could do better* ourselves and not compliment ourselves much either! We had each a ripe white strawberry from our garden today.

Monday 5. [May 5, 1862]

The first thing I did this morning was to give our girl Ellen a good whipping for the first time since we came to Atlanta, the immediate cause of which was that she again offended by using her mistress's toilet articles upon her own person for which offense I have before punished her.

Sat 10. [May 10, 1862]

Last night Sallie and I went with the Wests to the City Hall to hear bishop Elliott of the Epis Church preach.† He gave us a very nice essay upon the words "How long shall thy vain thoughts lodge within thee?" At 7 Oclock this evening Steve and Nell arrived with their children and servants and our house is quite a menagerie now of young animals.— We have *eleven* children under eight years old.—We went tonight to Bro Roots house to sing.

Sunday 11. [May 11, 1862]

Dr Brantley preached from Acts 26:9 "I verily thot that I ought to do many things contrary to the name of Jesus of Nazareth" showing from Paul's experience and words that the doctrine that "it matters little what a man believes if he is only sincere" is a false and pernicious one. We rec^d

---

* Dr. John Wilson served as pastor of First Presbyterian Church from 1859 to 1873 (Beth Dawkins Bassett, *A Church on Peachtree: First Presbyterian Church of Atlanta* [Atlanta: Book Development, 1998], 21).

† In 1841, Stephen Elliott Jr. became Georgia's first Episcopal bishop. During the war, he helped to create the Episcopal Church of the Confederate States of America, and he subsequently promoted the reconciliation of the denomination's Northern and Southern wings ("Stephen Elliott Jr.," in *New Georgia Encyclopedia*, available online at http://www.georgiaencyclopedia.org [accessed 24 September 2008]).

intelligence from Macon last week of the death of Sallie's brother William's wife, after giving birth to a daughter. They have only been married about two years.*—About four Oclock this afternoon we saw a dense black smoke rising in the direction of Whitehall St and going there found a crowd collected around two large provision stores from which the smoke was pouring in volumes.† It was some distance from our store so that we were not much alarmed upon our own account, tho' if the fire should get headway in the large buildings from which the smoke was rising a long row of old wooden stores would probably have burned and carried the fire a considerable distance. Fortunately this was not the result; the firemen got the flames under [control] without their destroying the brick buildings, though the fire raged in some back buildings for a long time but did not spread. Dr Brantley had but a small audience at night and invited the choir to sit down stairs. He took a text from the hymnbook "Jesus, I love thy charming name" and gave us an earnest and interesting talk.—After service we all went down to see the fire which was still raging furiously within the walls of an old warehouse full of Lard, Cotton, Bacon &c.

Friday 16. [May 16, 1862]

As today was appointed by Pres' Davis for Prayer for the Country all the stores were closed and we attended a union prayer meeting at the Central Pres Church. Steve and Jabe and I spent the morning before church time in looking for houses and lots for rent or sale, and discovered several for sale some of which we think of buying for an investment. Steve wants a house to leave his family in as he is going into the army. Tonight we went to hear Rev J[.] R. Graves late of Nashville preach at the 1st Bap' Church from this text or on this subject, viz; "The present crisis—our reverses, substantial ground of hope." He said that experience has shown that the whole course of our Government has been a series of mistakes and blunders since the failure to improve the occasion afforded by the defeat of the Federal army at Manassas until now and he argued that it was ordered by Providence so in order that there might be a long and bitter war and a final separation

---

* Mary Van Valkenburg was married to SVVR's brother, William, a lumberman (Eighth Census of the United States [1860], microcopy 653, Bibb County).

† A large fire began in a warehouse on Mitchell Street near Whitehall. *ASC*, May 13, 1862, estimated that cotton housed in the building was a total loss, while some stores of bacon, flour, rice, corn, and lard survived. The fire also damaged nearby buildings. *ASC* editorialized that cotton should no longer be stored within city limits. Although the fire was believed to have been accidental, one report had boys playing on the warehouse's flat roof and smoking cigars earlier in the day.

of the South from an infidel and corrupt North, lest if this separation had not been affected we should have been involved in their overthrow and ruin. But he was not allowed to finish his discourse—an alarm of Fire was given and the congregation dispersed after a short prayer and benediction. The fire was in some old buildings on the edge of town, uninhabited. We hear that our forces in Virginia have evacuated Norfolk and Yorktown and not being able to remove the "Virginia" that destroyed the Yankee vessels a short time ago, she was blown up to prevent her falling into the hands of the foe.* It seems as though the enemy will have possession of all our seaports soon.—Dr H. K. Green, surgeon in the army was in the store the other day. He is here on duty just from Virginia and gave us the sad intelligence that Asa Sherwood was killed at the fight at McDowell lately in Virginia!† Alas! alas! that one so young and good and giving promise of future usefulness should fall so early, a victim to this unholy and cruel war upon our dearest rights and liberties. And he is only one of many that have fallen and will fall. Asa was the pride of the family and the pet of his mother; What a blow will it be to her.—It was a consolation to think that he was prepared to die. I could not but shed a tear to the memory of one who was daily with me for three years and with whom I never had occasion to exchange a word in wrath, and who left me only to enter the service of his country to fight and die of her defence. Asa was an exception to young men in general as far as my experience goes.—he was steady, honest, industrious, conscientious and pious, a consistent member of the Methodist Church and good and obedient to his mother.

Sunday 18. [May 18, 1862]

Our preacher is in Augusta today with his family and the Augusta minister preaches for us—Mr. Huntington. His text was this morning in Ezekiel—"As I live, saith the Lord God, I have no pleasure in the death of the wicked &c[.]" I did not like him as well as Dr Brantley.—I have written this afternoon to Asa's Mother for particulars in relation to his death and in token of remembrance and sympathy.—Jabe brot Deacon Smith to take tea with us the old man seems to be so lonely. A rain came up just before dark so that there was no night preaching.—

* The *Virginia* was scuttled on May 11 (E. B. Long, *The Civil War Day by Day: An Almanac* [Garden City, N.Y.: Doubleday, 1971], 181–82, 210–11).

† Sergeant Asa E. Sherwood, who had served as Richards's clerk in Macon, was killed at McDowell, Virginia, on May 8, 1862 (Lillian Henderson, ed., *Roster of Confederate Soldiers of Georgia, 1861–1865*, 6 vols. [Hapeville, Ga.: Longino and Porter, 1959], 2:223).

Sat 24. [May 24, 1862]

This has been the week of *Real Estate* as Steve Jabe and myself have been engaged in walking, riding and inspecting city lots, houses &c. The result has been so far that Jabe and I have bought four lots[.] *No 1.* An *acre* unimproved on Crew Street of Col. Watkins for $500. *No 2* A six acre lot on the City *Line* Southward from A K Seago for $3500 with an unfinished house upon it.—*No 3.* a quarter acre on McDonough St, from Mr Root unimproved—$400. *No 4.* an half acre on McDonough St partly improved from Mr Starling H. Briant for $1100. This last property Steve first bought intending to finish the house and live there but before the deed was made out we made a bargain with him to take it off his hands and rent him the Seago lot which we are to finish up for him.—This is Arthur's birthday—no *yesterday* was on second thought he is four years old and a fat strapping boy too.—Last night at midnight we were awakened by an alarm of fire and Jabe and I went partly to town but could not see any sign of fire so we returned home. We learned next morning that there was a fire in the large brick block opposite our store but it was discovered by one of the sentinels upon guard and put out before much damage was done. This fire was caused by a *box of hot ashes* being placed upon the floor very carelessly.* Our Macon store came very near being destroyed in just the same way—a *box of ashes* left on the floor in the Bindery over the store. If it had been at night we should most likely have been burned out. Our City is in a measure under Martial Law now and we have all had to obtain *passes* to prevent our being taken up at night and put in limbo[.]† My pass or *permit* reads

> Confederate States of America
> Office of Provost Marshall Atlanta Ga May 23/62
> Permission is grant S P Richards to visit County and City upon honor not to Communicate in writing or verbally, anything that may prove detrimental to the Confederate States.
>
> W. H. Battey Capt & Provost Marshall

* The fire to which SPR referred was, in fact, caused by ashes being stored carelessly. An alert soldier standing guard near the Confederate quartermaster's storeroom observed and reported the fire, which caused minimal damage (*ASC*, May 24, 1862).

† Atlanta was not officially placed under martial law until August 1862. After unhappy residents appealed to Governor Joseph E. Brown and Confederate vice president Alexander Stephens, martial law was lifted after about one month (Thomas G. Dyer, *Secret Yankees: The Union Circle in Confederate Atlanta* [Baltimore: Johns Hopkins University Press, 1999], 100).

We have bought also this week 85 Reams of writing Paper at $17 per ream some $1450 worth—common paper that we used to buy for about 1.25 and 1.50 per Rm.—I don't like buying so largely at such blockade prices much.—Our baby Alice alias "Skeezix" has four more teeth just coming up in her upper gum. She was very fretful and restless all the night and in the morning I *grabbled* for teeth and found them!—Our choir met to sing at our house tonight. Mr. Ufford a singer from Griffin was with us by invitation. Mr Root says Dr B reports that we beat the Augusta choir!

Sunday 25. [May 25, 1862]

The weather has not been pleasant today a fire being needed for comfort this morning. Consequently, Dr Brantley had but a small congregation. His text was I Chron. 29:5. "And who then is willing to consecrate his service this day unto the Lord." Sallie and I took a walk this afternoon and visited all the property that we have purchased in 80 minutes. The *Briant* house we think of fixing up for our own residence until I am ready to build on my own lot. We have quite worn our welcome out here as far as Stella is concerned and Sallie wants to move. The Briant house is in a pleasant location though too far from town about 18 or 20 minutes walk nearly out to Henry's.—By the time we have spent $2000 upon it it will be a very comfortable little place. At night Dr Brantly preached to a pretty good audience from the words "Whosoever then shall call on the name of the Lord the same shall be saved."

Wed 28. [May 28, 1862]

This has been our *largest sale* day since we began business amounting to $1542. cash! We sold over $1200 to a Government officer for the Army, Paper and Stationery.—

Sat 31. [May 31, 1862]

Yesterday we sold a Piano for $600.—I rec[d] a reply to my letter to Mrs Sherwood, this week. We hear this week that Gen "Stonewall" Jackson in Virginia is routing the enemy and capturing many prisoners and stores and he may soon go over into Maryland.—[*]

---

[*] In the Shenandoah Valley Campaign, March–June 1862, Confederate forces defeated Union troops in a series of engagements in the heart of the South's breadbasket. The smaller but more maneuverable Southern force was brilliantly led by Stonewall Jackson, who quickly became the Confederacy's premier military hero (James M. McPherson, *Ordeal by Fire: The Civil War and Reconstruction*, 3rd ed. [Boston: McGraw Hill, 2001], 259–64).

Sunday 1. [June 1, 1862]

Dr Brantley preached today from the text: "The Lord reigneth, let the Earth rejoice" Ps 97:1. A rain in the afternoon prevented the childrens' singing and made our congregation at night small.—

Wed 4. [June 4, 1862]

After meeting tonight Miss Joiner joined our Ch' by relating her experience *to the pastor*, who related it to the ch. Bro Root having gone to Charleston to attend a sale I had to *tune up*.—Sallie was sick with a cold and headache and did not go.—

Sat 7. [June 7, 1862]

We have bought another lot of Moses Cole for $2500 tho' as yet it is not decided whether the purchase shall be made by *Steve* or us; at all events though *they* expect to live there for awhile instead of at our Seago place.—A man was *hung* here today; the leader of the band that stole the Engine and cars in the State R Road lately.* His name was Andrews and he was executed as a spy by military authority—poor fellow he ought to have engaged in better business.—He is stated to have acknowledged the justice of his sentence and to have said that he undertook the job in the hope of pecuniary reward. There has been severe fighting near Richmond this week and our folks have been victorious in two days fighting.† Many lives have been lost on both sides. We had a Church Conference tonight and changed the Church meetings to every *two months* instead of every month and *Communion* each Sunday after Conference instead of having it only once in three months.—A Miss Atkinson a cousin of Dr

---

* In an effort to a disrupt the rail line between Atlanta and Chattanooga, Union spy James J. Andrews recruited a small group of saboteurs in the spring of 1862. On Apr. 12, at Marietta, Georgia, the group stole the locomotive *General*, its tender, and several boxcars while its crew ate breakfast in a nearby restaurant. A ninety-mile chase ensued. Lacking fuel to continue their efforts, the conspirators abandoned the *General* close to the Tennessee border. Several of the men eluded capture, but Andrews and seven others were tried, convicted, and sentenced to hang. In reporting his execution on June 8, 1862, *ASC* suggested that a penitent Andrews claimed to have been motivated by financial gain (Bonds, *Stealing the General*, 89–260).

† At the Battle of Seven Pines, Virginia, May 31–June 1, 1862, Confederates under Joseph E. Johnson attacked two corps of Federals isolated from the rest of their army south of the Chickahominy and east of Richmond. The attack failed, Johnston was wounded, and Robert E. Lee replaced him in command (Long, *Civil War Day by Day*, 218–21).

Brantley's joined by experience. After Conference our choir went upstairs and had a sing but Mr Root having just got home, tired probably with travel was quite cross and we broke up in a sort of a huff about the "Fig Tree" Anthem, which we all want to sing and he don't like it, or pretends not to.—

Sunday 8. [June 8, 1862]

Dr B. preached from the words "Christ Jesus came into the world to save sinners" I Tim 1:15. At 5 o'clock this afternoon the Sunday School met to sing and the pastor gave them a talk. We were to have had the ordinance of Baptism administered to two young women tonight but the *pool* was not prepared, the force pump being out of order.

Tuesday 10. [June 10, 1862]

This morning we were called together to sing at the funeral of our old friend "Aunt Lipham" she died on Sunday night last while we were engaged in the sanctuary services she loved so well. Now she has gone to enjoy the higher delights of that upper sanctuary to which her faith has so long looked forward. It is about 24 years since I first knew this good old lady.

Sunday 15. [June 15, 1862]

Dr Brantley's text this morning was Matt 6:10 "Thy will be done on earth as it is in heaven[.]" At night he preached from the words "If any man be in Christ he is a new creature &c[.]" Two young women were baptized tonight and the services were all conducted "decently and in order[.]"

Sat 21. [June 21, 1862]

Steve came up Tuesday and they moved into their own house on Thursday thereby thinning out the crowd at our place considerably. Father also arrived Friday afternoon. No news of importance has reached us this week: It is probably the calm preceding a storm as it appears that both sides are concentrating their forces in Virginia around Richmond and a terrible struggle will probably ensue. Rumors of *in*tervention on the part of the European Powers are again rife but it may not amount to anything. English correspondents say that the want of Cotton is causing great distress there, and that *something must be done* speedily. The recent battle near Richmond is called The Battle of "Chickahominy" from the stream upon whose banks it was fought. Sister Kate writes that several families in Sparta have lost members in that fight. She sends a short letter from Bro Addison dated New York about May 1. assuring us of their continued love and sympathy. Singing at our house tonight.—

Sunday 22. [June 22, 1862]

Dr Brantley is absent today having gone to Augusta to bring up his family. The preacher we expected to preach for us did not come and father was pressed into service again. He preached from the words "Nothing can harm you if ye be followers of that which is good"—

Thursday 26 [June 26, 1862]

At 6 Oclock this morning Father and Mother and Steve left for So. Ca. The former to enter upon his duties as Missionary in the Association with which they are connected. Mother expects to travel with him I believe. Their parting was not a pleasant one as ill feeling had arisen between them and Stella on account of Mothers whims and ways whereby our sister-in-law had become highly offended, so much so that for several weeks past she had not been able to treat Mother with common politeness and hospitality. Indeed I am constrained to think that the *amiability* which at first seemed to be the chief characteristic of our brothers wife, has most unaccountably disappeared or changed into its opposite quality. We ourselves are only ungraciously borne with as a necessary evil and I want to get out of the house as soon as circumstances will permit. Bad health is not a sufficient plea; her predecessor was afflicted so, but it did not make *her* morose and ugly. Mother's ways are at times vexing; but it was a daughter's place to bear with them more patiently—and make allowance for age and habit.—I fear the marriage will not prove a happy one.

Sat 28. [June 28, 1862]

Today and yesterday we have had delightful showers to revive the dusty earth. The words of the Great Teacher came forcibly into my mind as the clouds poured forth their waters and the sun again shone forth:—"He maketh his Sun to rise upon the evil and upon the good, and sendeth his rain upon the just and upon the unjust."—Today we bought another lot of land or rather *two lots* about a quarter of a mile beyond the city limits. We bot of Mr Simms for $1500 about nine acres in an eligible location Southwest of the city. McPherson rec^d today a bale of rough Southern made Oat-Straw hats with broad brims and made Jabe and me a present of one each with the proviso that we should wear it to Church on the morrow which we accepted! I started Dora to writing "pothooks" this week in her first copy book.* She *reads* pretty well but has not yet made much

---

* Named for the hooks used to hang pots over a kitchen fire, *pothooks* is a method of teaching writing using the S shape.

progress in other branches of learning. We sang at Mr Wests tonight but Mr Root is away so that I shall have to *pitch* in tomorrow. Dr Brantley arrived this afternoon with his family.—

Sunday 29. [June 29, 1862]

We have news from Richmond of another great battle there and a Confederate victory "greater than that of Manassas" being the complete defeat and rout of Gen McClellans grand army!* My heart swells with gratitude to God for this mercy vouchsafed to us in our time of need; May He continue to aid us in driving back our invading foes until they shall be willing to leave us in peace to the quiet enjoyment of our rights and independence, is my fervent prayer. Dr B. preached this morning from the words "Good Master what good thing shall I do that I may have eternal life?" We sang as a Voly a new Sabbath morning Anthem "With joy we hail the sacred day &c[.]" Jabez came up and sang tenor with us in the absence of our regular tenor. We wait further tidings from Virginia with interest and hope, trusting that our success there may prove to be complete—and if so I think that the European Powers will interfere to prevent further bloodshed seeing how hopeless is the task of subjugation which the Yankees have undertaken and how bad the chance of a cotton supply if the war continues. This afternoon at Jabe's request I accompanied him in a walk to visit our "Simm's Lots["] just bought and after a hot fatiguing ramble of several hours we had to return without having been able to find the place!—At night owing to some mistake of Dr Brantley's we were *cut out* of our voluntary "Holley" which we had prepared to sing.—

Friday 4th [July 4, 1862]

The once "Glorious Fourth" has passed by very quietly this year—A Fireman's Dinner and a few faint *poppers* being all the *celebration* vouchsafed to it.—The day of "Spread Eagleism" has passed by with us and we shall probably choose some other day to commemorate than this *now* Yankee holiday. I want no further connection with such unnatural murderous foes to peace and liberty. The once loved *Union* and its Stars & Stripes are now *detestable*. God grant us a safe and sure deliverance therefrom.

---

* Richards referred to one or more of the small skirmishes that made up the Seven Days' Battles, June 25–July 1, 1862. This fighting east of Richmond represented the culmination of Union general George McClellan's disastrous Peninsula Campaign, during which he staged an amphibious landing of his immense army between the York and James Rivers and attempted to fight his way inland to take Richmond (McPherson, *Ordeal*, 266–70).

Sat 5. [July 5, 1862]

Sallie was not well tonight and I had to go to the sing at Bro Root's alone.—She and I and Nell were weighed this week and my weight was 135, 8 or 10 lbs more than usual in summer. Sallie weighed 113 and Nell only 84. My health has been very good since we came to A. and was not bad for sometime previous. We have not yet heard of any definite result of the fight at Richmond. It is reported today that the Yankees have managed to get under the shelter of their boats and are being largely reinforced, so that it is not improbable that they may again show fight and meet with some success.

Sunday 6. [July 6, 1862]

The past week has been very cool delightful weather and the prospect is good for a large corn crop. I have not suffered at all from heat this year so far. Sallie had set her heart upon going to visit Harriet this month with the children but I did not think it prudent to leave this cool and healthy region to spend July nearly 200 miles down the country and advised her to postpone her visit until cooler weather and invite Harriet to come up here which she did. Dr B's text this morning was "Watch & Pray" and his subject "The temptations of the present day[.]"

Wed 9. [July 9, 1862]

Little Alice's birthday—just one year old.—Stella left us yesterday morning to pay a visit to Rome (Geo) where her friend Noyes lives. She took Annie with her. The Macon Telegraph began to come again yesterday. We have missed it for a month.—Last night Sallie and I went to see the "Queen Sisters" who are again here and furnished us with complimentary tickets.—We concluded to sell off our Bank Bills finding that we could get 14% for it in Confederate Notes which we can use just as well. so that we realized $450 profit on our "pile."—

Friday 11. [July 11, 1862]

Our Union prayer meeting for the country was very thinly attended today at our church. It is a bad sign when the people are so careless in regard to seeking the favor and assistance of the Being who holds the destinies of the nation in his hands.

Sat 12. [July 12, 1862]

Singing at our house tonight. We have been having quite variable weather of late, but pleasant, generally. A letter from Martha tonight gives us some details of Macon life and manners. From what we can hear neither George nor James were injured in the late battles if indeed they were in them. James has been sick and his wife has gone on to Richmond to attend him. Rev Mr Rogers the Presbyterian minister preached for us this morning from the words of Jacob of old "All these things are against me[.]"* At night Rev Mr Dickinson Army Colporteur from Virginia gave us a repetition of the *talk* he made about three months ago, which though quite interesting then was rather tiresome in the repeatal.

Friday 18. [July 18, 1862]

Last night Sallie and I went with the Wests to the "Queen Sisters" for the third time since they came and heard the plays "Perfection" & "Dead Shot."—We have now heard "Swiss Cottage," "Lottery Ticket" "Loan of a Lover" and "Neighbor's Wife" also.—And have had about enough of it for a time.—Miss Laura's singing is a pleasant feature of the entertainment.—The chief drawback to enjoyment is the meanness of the Hall and the heat of it. This is Irene's birthday, she is six years old. I went to prayer meeting at Pres Church this afternoon and special prayer was offered for those ministers in Nashville who have been sent to the penitentiary there because they would not take the oath of allegiance to the Yankee despot.† Surely the God in whom they trust will speedily avenge his own elect which cry day and night unto him. We hear of some brilliant *dashes* of our cavalry in Tennessee and successes in their efforts to harass the foe. Abe Lincoln has called for 300,000 more men "to put down the rebellion[.]" This *rebellion*, as he calls it, will be the hardest nut *he* ever tried to crack. Oh! What an awful responsibility rests upon that man in that he could have prevented this wicked war and did the opposite. I would not be in his place for all the world.—We have bought 50 reams of home made letter paper this week at $12 which sells well at $18 and is pretty good paper. Our finest Cap Paper we get *two dolls* a quire for! Cotton Cards we sell at *eight dollars* a pair[.] Coffee is 1.75 per lb—Sugar 40¢—Syrup 1.75 to 2.00 gallon. Coarse Salt 25¢ per lb.—Sallie and Mrs Root are appointed a committee to visit one of the hospitals tomorrow to see if they are properly attended to.—

---

* Rev. J. L. Rogers served as pastor of Central Presbyterian Church from 1859 to 1863 (John Robert Smith, *The Church That Stayed: The Life and Times of Central Presbyterian Church in the Heart of Atlanta* [Atlanta: Atlanta Historical Society, 1979], 9–10).

† During the spring of 1862, Tennessee's military governor, Andrew Johnson, ordered the imprisonment of seven Nashville ministers, a college professor, and a state official for their refusal to take a loyalty oath (Stephen V. Ash, *When the Yankees Came: Conflict and Chaos in the Occupied South, 1861–1865* [Chapel Hill: University of North Carolina Press, 1995], 45).

Sunday 20. [July 20, 1862]

Our pastor preached this morning from the text "If God spared not his own Son &c" Romans 8:32. After morning service the Lord's Supper was observed having been postponed from last Sunday on account of the absence of the pastor.

Sat 26 [July 26, 1862]

I am alone at the store today Jabez having left at 4 A.M. for Rome to see his wife and perhaps buy a negro woman that Stella has taken a fancy to. So Ethel is left alone to the care of Jacob and Jimmy. Col John Morgan and his men are in Kentucky waking up the Yankees there and in Ohio. It is said he has taken possession of eleven towns capturing prisoners and stores.* Col Forrest took Murfreesboro in Tennessee last week with numerous prisoners among which were forty officers. It was a brilliant exploit.† We are hoping to hear of further successes in those States. The Yankees are trying hard to get up an excitement to promote enlistments of volunteers for the 300 000 troops called for by Abe Lincoln. The abolitionists are talking savagely and urging the necessity of freeing the negroes and arming them against the South. This will very likely be done by their fanatical, bloody Congress. Who could have believed that the people of the "Land of Liberty" were so cruelly vindictive, blind and mad.

Sunday 27. [July 27, 1862]

Dr Crawford of Penfield preached this morning from the text "I remembered God and was troubled."‡ Dr Brantley was present and will preach

---

* On July 4, 1862, John Hunt Morgan launched a raid through Kentucky, leading his men on a thousand-mile march in just twenty-four days. They cut Union telegraph lines and destroyed railroad ties but did not "liberate" the state from Union control (Ramage, *Rebel Raider*, 91–106). One Atlanta newspaper suggested that "the outraged people of the State hail Jack as the harbinger of a sure deliverance from the oppression of the Federals and are flocking to his standard in large numbers" (*ASC*, July 24, 1862).

† Colonel Nathan Bedford Forrest led a spectacular raid against a Union garrison at Murfreesboro, Tennessee, on July 13, 1862. Marching his men so that their numbers appeared larger than they actually were, Forrest hoodwinked the Union forces into surrendering (David S. Heidler and Jeanne T. Heidler, eds., *Encyclopedia of the American Civil War: A Political, Social, and Military History*, 5 vols. [Santa Barbara, Calif.: ABC-CLIO, 2000], 2:720).

‡ Nathaniel Macon Crawford, son of former Georgia senator and presidential candidate William H. Crawford, had a distinguished career as a Baptist clergyman. In 1858, he became president of Mercer University (*History of the Baptist Denomination in Georgia* [Atlanta: Harrison, 1881], 154–57).

tonight. Sallie bought a calico dress of Mr Root a part of the goods that ran the blockade lately in the "Memphis" at Charleston.* It cost 6.50 instead of 1.00¢ as formerly. The shoemakers here ask $12 to make a pair of common shoes; Boots $20.

Tuesday 29. [July 29 1862]
The folks returned from Rome bringing a darky woman with them for whom they gave $1000. Her name is "Sally[.]" She is the first piece of humanity that they have ever bought. I expect the *Yankees* would say that this was the worst possible investment under existing circumstances seeing that their Congress has declared the slaves of all *rebels* to be free!†—Sallie and I went tonight to Nell's to see if she needed any help or company with her poor sick baby "Cheevis" and as she was alone Sallie staid all night.

Wed 30. [July 30, 1862]
I went after Sallie early this morning and found the baby was dead. A sudden change had taken place at one o'clock and at *five* he died. Poor Nell, she thought last night that her child was better. We telegraphed Steve but he cant come.

Thursday 31. [July 31, 1862]
The baby was buried at five oclock this afternoon I could not attend the funeral. They put it by Sarah's grave. He died from teething and internal inflammation.‡—

Sat 2. [August 2, 1862]
Bro Blanchard has returned from a successful foray as one of Col John Morgans Officers into Kentucky during the past month in which they succeeded in destroying immense stores belonging to the enemy capturing a great many horses, mules, and wagons &c and taking quite a number of prisoners besides giving the people of Louisville and Cincinnati a dreadful

---

* *ADI*, July 13, 1862, advertised goods that Sidney Root and John Beach had brought through the blockade on the *Memphis*, one of the fleet of ships the two men employed in their remunerative blockade-running operation.

† Abraham Lincoln signed the Second Confiscation Act on July 17, 1862. It allowed for the seizure of property, including slaves, if the courts determined that owners were rebels. Like the First Confiscation Act (Aug. 1861), the second was poorly drafted and largely unenforced (Allen C. Guelzo, *Lincoln's Emancipation Proclamation: The End of Slavery in America* [New York: Simon and Schuster, 2004], 40–46, 70–72, 127).

‡ In the mid-nineteenth century, physicians believed teething to be a serious childhood malady (Sallie G. McMillen, *Southern Women Black and White in the Old South* [Arlington Heights, Ill.: Harlan Davidson, 1992], 72).

scare. Kentucky is in a bad fix, between two fires, and will no doubt prove to be again the "bloody ground" before this dreadful war shall cease.* This has been a busy week our cash sales amounting to $1118. We had begun to hope that Stella's visit had sweetened her temper somewhat but at supper last night she took occasion to make a speech for Sallie's benefit, about our leaving their house, that immediately dispelled the pleasant illusion. She is determined that we, like her other visitors (or boarders rather), shall leave in dudgeon and not want ever to come back.

Sunday 3. [August 3, 1862]

Dr B. preached this morning from the words "It is more blessed to give than to receive,["] and urged the necessity of liberality and beneficence as a part of Christian duty. At night he preached upon the *corn crop* from the latter part of the LXV Psalm. I liked the discourse very much and it was very appropriate to the times and seasons. Fine showers have watered the earth and there is prospect of abundance of corn for man and beast.—

Friday 8. [August 8, 1862]

Jabez's birthday—he is forty one. And I am but about 2½ years behind him in age. The weather is very hot this week. Business continues brisk as ever.

Sunday 10. [August 10, 1862]

Dr B. preached this morning from the words "For now we see through a glass, darkly" and at night "This one thing I do" showing the necessity of an earnest purpose and concentration of mind, to great advances in the christian life.—

Wed 13. [August 13, 1862]

Jabe left again for the "seven (hundred) hilled city" of Rome at four oclock this morning to buy two more *darkies* the daughter and brother of the woman he bought before.—I bought today nearly $1000 more of Playing Cards at $9.25 per dozen. At dark I closed up and went home to accompany Sallie to prayer meeting.

Sunday 17. [August 17, 1862]

We had a large congregation this morning who expected to listen to Dr Brantley but were disappointed as Rev Jesse H. Campbell held forth

* ASC, Aug. 2, 1862, described Morgan's Kentucky raid as "the most brilliant, daring and successful warlike expedition that ever was undertaken in any age or country."

instead.* At night Dr B preached and the ordinance of Baptism was administered to Bro & Sister Butts at the close of the sermon. The house was full. The text was "See, here is water, &c" but the sermon was not particularly *sectarian* in character. Last night our choir met at Mr Roots and we met there an English merchant Mr North fresh from the shores of Albion.—

Sunday 24. [August 24, 1862]
Our pastor preached today from the texts "We are the Lord's" and "Be sure your sin will find you out[.]"

Sat 30. [August 30, 1862]
The business of the month has closed. I expect we have sold more than in any previous month since we have been in business. Our cash sales have been $6000. But I do not enjoy *the times* the prospect for the future is so cheerless and uncertain. Our Congress now in session will probably amend the Conscription Act so as to include us and I see no way of getting off from service. Much as I rejoice to hear that our invading cruel foes are being destroyed, I cannot feel willing to engage in the work of slaying them.—Our baby Alice is now walking all about the house with confidence. She first ventured off alone last Tuesday week the 19th inst[ant]. She don't *talk* yet though. Jabez brought home a little negro girl name "Medora" and they seem to intend *calling* her 'Dora though they know that we don't approve of it. How would they like for us to buy a dirty little brat and call it "Annie?" Several of our citizens were arrested by the military authorities this week for supposed disloyalty or treasonable intentions; James Sturges was one!

Sunday 31. [August 31, 1862]
Dr B's text this morning was "For thy name's sake pardon my iniquity, for it is great."—

Sat 6. [September 6, 1862]
We had a prayer meeting tonight at our church, a sort of preparatory meeting to a series of exercises to promote a revival in our church. Quite a number of converts have been added to the First Church and a good many revivals are announced in various parts of our country. Last Wed.'

---

* Jesse H. Campbell, ordained a Baptist clergyman in 1830, served a variety of Georgia congregations before becoming a full-time volunteer evangelist with the army during the war (*History of the Baptist Denomination*, 96; see also SPR diary, Feb. 23, 1862).

night today was selected for fasting and prayer to implore the blessing of God upon our Zion.—We have been so busy that I could not keep the day suitably except in having no dinner sent which was not an act of much self denial. This is a time of suspense and excitement in our country: For a week fighting has been going on either in Kentucky or Virginia and our armies have defeated the foe in every contest and again today news arrives of another victory over Burnside's division and his own capture. Oh! that God may enable us so to conquer them that they may be willing to make terms of peace and end this cruel bloody war. It is supposed that in these last conflicts we have lost some 15,000 men and the enemy three or four times many! How little did I ever think that our fair and happy land would be the scene of such awful disasters.—As what we hear of the Small Pox being in neighboring counties has induced our authorities to order all to be vaccinated, Sallie sent for Dr Calhoun and had herself and Alice operated on the rest of the children having been well vaccinanated in 1860 in Macon.* We have closed our Store at dark this week, being so hard at work all day that we were tired out by night. Our sales continue good and our profits also good but yet I would willingly go back to old trade and moderate profits if we could only have peace and independence. We live now in a state of feverish excitement and disgust that *gain* cannot render bearable or desirable.—When will the people of the North return to their senses? When will the fact that is so evident to all around them force itself upon their minds; that eight millions of freemen who are resolved to *be free* cannot be subjugated by them. Our people are far more united and determined to fight until death than were our forefathers of the former Revolution. It is possible that they may destroy both themselves and us and some foreign power may then step in and take the spoils but the once happy *Union* cannot be restored; They have killed it dead.

Sunday 7. [September 7, 1862]

The text this morning was "Choose you this day whom you will serve." At night—"If the righteous scarcely be saved, where shall the ungodly and the sinner appear?" Jabez and I went to visit Nell in the afternoon. She had just heard from Steve with the Army in Virginia.—

* Atlanta experienced an outbreak of smallpox in the fall of 1862. Doctors, city officials, and local newspapers urged citizens to seek vaccination, and some residents, including the Richards family, were protected. Many of those who did not or could not heed these calls, including slaves, contracted the disease (Singer, "Confederate Atlanta," 156–57). *ASC*, Sept. 5, 1862, called for Atlantans to be vaccinated and warned that cases of the disease had been diagnosed in Coweta and Merriwether Counties. See also *ASC*, Jan. 24, 1863.

Monday 8. [September 8, 1862]

Dora is eight years old today. She has not made much advance in learning. She reads tolerably; writes very badly or not at all and ciphers o. I am afraid she will not learn at home but must go to school. She is more fond of play than either study or work. The children have all had remarkable good health since we came to Atlanta. Tonight there was a prayer meeting at our church but no other meetings were appointed to follow.—

Tues. 9. [September 9, 1862]

The telegrams of this day were to the effect that Gen Kirby Smiths army had arrived opposite Cincinnati, Ohio and demanded its surrender in four hours! From subsequent advices however we find that it was not so good tho' ere now it *may* be true.*

Sat 13. [September 13, 1862]

Jabe and Stella went to Rome again this morning taking their baby.— Last night Jabez and I sent letters of application for membership to the "Independent Fire Co No 4" as they say they are needing more men and it *may* be the means of preventing our being *conscripted*. Of two evils this is no doubt the less. Business has not been as lively this week as it was last month.—Sallies "vaccinate" has at last taken and she has a fine scab. Alice's is not so satisfactory but Dr Calhoun thinks it has *taken*. I went to the Provost office and got a new pass today. We have reliable information that our army has gone into Maryland at last and is in possession of Frederick City.†—The enemy's forces have retreated to Washington to defend their own Capitol instead of threatening ours. The tables are turned considerably from what they were a few weeks ago when they felt so sure that Richmond was theirs. God has truly been favorable unto us and blessed be his name.—A letter to Jabe from Rome tonight brings unpleasant intelligence namely that $1200 of the money he paid for the negroes he bought there proves to be *counterfeit*! From our books I find that the greater part

---

* In the fall of 1862, Confederate general Edmund Kirby Smith positioned soldiers in Kentucky with the hope that residents of this Union slave state might join the Confederate cause. Fearing that Smith would attack Cincinnati, Union general Lewis Wallace declared martial law, trenches were dug, and militia prepared to defend the city. An attack never came. General Braxton Bragg sent Smith away from Cincinnati to bolster Confederate efforts elsewhere (Heidler and Heidler, *Encyclopedia*, 1:438–39).

† On Sept. 6, 1862, having crossed the Potomac River, Confederate soldiers under the command of Stonewall Jackson occupied Frederick, Maryland, as a part of General Robert E. Lee's invasion of the Union slave state (Long, *Civil War Day by Day*, 262).

of the money that Jabez took there was obtained from Bro James the Broker in exchange for Bank Bills, so I have some hope that the loss will not fall upon us altogether. This counterfeiting trick was one that I *feared the Yankees* would play us—it is so like them. We were to have had a prayer meeting tonight but there was no *gas* and we had to retire after assembling at the church door. Our choir met at Bro Roots to practise both for Sunday and Thursday the national Thanksgiving day.

Sunday 14. [September 14, 1862]

Dr B preached this morning from the words—"That I may win Christ[.]" Our Communion was celebrated after preaching and we all *shook hands* with two ladies who had been received by letter a custom more honored in the breach than in the observance I think, for it is embarrassing both to the *shakers* and the *shakees*; at least I know it is to many and it looks foolish to go through such a senseless formality in the house of God, for it is but a *form* and a useless one it seems to me. I think it all sufficient for the pastor to give the hand in the name of the church. It may be thought that my heart is not warm enough to enter properly into the act and that no doubt is too much the case with the most of the members.—

Wed 17. [September 17, 1862]

Jabe and his wife and baby returned this afternoon but he could not bring his "boy" "Harvey" as Col Mitchell from whom he bought him would not deliver him up unless Jabe would obligate himself to refund for the bad money, which he was not willing to do unless he could make Bro James also refund, and they were not prepared to *prove* that the money was bad that Jabe paid, it having passed through several hands since Jabe paid over.— Irene is ailing with some kind of eruption that appeared upon her body yesterday and increased today accompanied by fever. We don't know what it is. At our meeting tonight several *knelt for prayer*—My own heart is cold and my devotion dull. Truly I need a "revival[.]" Tomorrow will be Thanksgiving Day and the exercises are to be *Union* ones in our church.—

Thursday 18. [September 18, 1862]

A shower fell this morning but the weather cleared before church time and a crowd assembled at our church to hear Dr Brantley. His text was "Now I may boldly say 'the Lord is my helper.'" The sermon of course was good and appropriate.—Irene still continues ailing and the eruption increases, so that we were fearful it might be Sca[r]let Fever some of the symptoms appearing to resemble that dreaded disease. Stella's physician Dr Chartars came to see her this afternoon and we took Renie in to him and were much relieved by his pronouncing it "Roseola" or Scarlet Rash. A heavy shower is now falling the hardest we have had during the late cloudy weather. I expect the *Equinoctial* is upon us at last.—

Friday 19. [September 19, 1862]

Just before daybreak this morning we were aroused by the cry of *Fire* and went towards town and found Bro Ed McDaniels dwelling in flames, Jabe and I helped man the brakes of the "Deluge No 4" and I worked so hard that I broke down and had to sit down to recover.* After breakfast I went to the houses we are finishing for some measurements and called at Nell's and learned that Sister Kate has *another boy* born on the 13th inst[ant.] Alice's "vaccinate" seems to have *taken* pretty well.

Sunday 21. [September 21, 1862]

We saw Lucius Stone at church this morning the "old lady" spied him out the minute he entered. Jabe and I went to see Henry this aft'; he has been laid up all the past week with Erysipelas resulting from *vaccination.*

Wed 24. [September 24, 1862]

We have had preaching every night this week with some little promise of good result. Rev J R Kendrick has been looked for for two nights but he has not yet come. Rev Frank Swanson preached for us on Monday night.† We hear of dreadful conflicts in Maryland in which it appears doubtful which side gained the advantage. But previously to this our folks took Harpers Ferry with over 11,000 prisoners and many arms and stores, and only lost two or three men.‡ Oh it is heart sickening to hear of such terrible fights between people who have been bretheren so long. Today we

---

* According to *ADI*, Sept. 20, 1862, a house fire that started in the kitchen of P. E. McDaniel's home on Pryor Street resulted from human error rather than arson, and the "loss to its owner is considerable."

† James Francis Swanson was pastor of Augusta's Second Baptist Church. In 1862, he resigned for health reasons and moved to Cedartown, in the northwestern part of the state (*History of the Baptist Denomination*, 515–17).

‡ The Battle of Antietam, Sept. 17, 1862, fought near Sharpsburg, Maryland, represented the culmination of Lee's invasion of Maryland. Although neither side won a clear victory in this bloody fight—the single bloodiest day of the Civil War—Lee was forced to withdraw because he was in enemy territory. Earlier that month, during the preliminary stages of the campaign, Confederate forces under Stonewall Jackson had scored a victory in an engagement at Harpers Ferry that included the surrender of thousands of Union soldiers (McPherson, *Ordeal*, 304–11; Gary G. Gallagher, ed., *The Antietam Campaign* [Chapel Hill: University of North Carolina Press, 1999]).

sold a large bill of school books to a military Professor for the University of Alabama $277 worth.—Irene seems to be getting better but her neck and joints are quite stiff and sore. Allie runs all over the yard and house now with the other children and is very knowing. Jabez wrote to Col Mitchell today declining to make good the money reputed bad and demanding his property the boy "Harvey" threatening suit if not complied with.—Bro James states that Banks will none of them take back any of the counterfeit bills that they have paid out and that those upon whom the money falls when discovered to be bad must bear the loss as in most cases it is impossible to identify the particular bills that were paid and make proof of the same.

Thursday 25. [September 25, 1862]

Rev Mr Kendrick came today and preached tonight a most excellent sermon from the words of the Saviour upon the occasion of his healing the woman that had the issue of blood twelve years—"Who touched me?" Our army is said to have gained a victory in the great fight at Sharpsburg Va on the 17th. The Yankees also *claim* a victory there, but they always do that.—

Sunday 28. [September 28, 1862]

This morning was rainy and we feared there would no service but it stopped raining about ten and we had a pretty good congregation. Mr Kendrick preached for the third time. His subject was *the "exalted Name of Jesus."* Phil 2:9.10.11.—At a prayer meeting yesterday morning Mattie Andrews—my former pupil—and Eugenia Clark joined the church by experience.—Her young sister Lottie Andrews died last week after a short illness from Diptheria a disease quite prevalent here now. Dora has been complaining since yesterday morning of a sore throat and was quite restless all last night and her mother and I did not rest well fearing that she might have taken that same dreadful disease. We gave her a common gargle of vinegar, pepper and honey this morning and it seemed to relieve her much. We have had a fire in our room this morning and it was very comfortable too.—Gen Bragg has captured about 5000 Yankees at Mumfordville in Kentucky and 23000 volunteers are said to have joined our army there and it is supposed that probably Louisville has been taken by our forces ere this.*—Oh that we may be able so to cripple the Yankee

---

* Confederate hopes of dominating Unionist Kentucky appeared bright when General Braxton Bragg accepted the surrender of Union forces in Munfordville. But plans to take Louisville failed, and the Confederate offensive in Kentucky

army before frost that they not be able to enter upon their projected plan of winter invasion by means of their gunboats, and may be constrained to end the war and let us go.—I wrote to father this afternoon as he appears to think that it is my turn to do so tho' in fact he owes me a letter. Dr Brantley preached at night.—

Monday 29. [September 29, 1862]

Mr Kendrick called at the store today and I asked him to preach again that sermon that I liked so much in Macon years ago; and at night he did so[.] His text was "Cut it down."—Hitherto the unconverted had not been invited forward but only asked to kneel at their seats but tonight they were called up and quite a number responded and we had a meeting time.

Tuesday 30. [September 30, 1862]

Mr Kendrick preached at night from the words of "Almost thou persuadest me to be a Christian[.]"

Wed Oct 1. [October 1, 1862]

This morning we had a pleasant prayer meeting Bro Gaskill leading, and appearing very much warmed up. Many went up for prayer mostly young girls. At night Bro K preached from the words "Come, for all are now ready."

Thursday 2. [October 2, 1862]

I went to an auction just below our store and bought some books and other articles. Bro Wood of the First Baptist Church preached for us at night from the words "It is done as thou hast commanded and yet there is room." I remember him as a very *green* young "Beneficiary" at Penfield over 20 years ago. Over 20 went up for prayer, and some professed to have found Jesus. Sallie and I both have complained of head ache and soreness in the bones since yesterday. Irene has recovered from her Roseola but Dora seems to have taken it though not much *rash* has appeared. Henry has been very ill this week.

Friday 3. [October 3, 1862]

Bro Hornady preached tonight both *prosy* and *noisy*—from Isaiahs invitation "No! every one that thirsteth come ye to the waters &c[.]"

---

ultimately ended in stalemate at the Battle of Perryville on Oct. 8, 1862. Although Bragg was not defeated decisively, he chose to withdraw toward Cumberland Gap to focus Confederate military forces on defending the Deep South (Kenneth W. Noe, *Perryville: The Grand Havoc of Battle* [Lexington: University Press of Kentucky, 2001], 337–43; Heidler and Heidler, *Encyclopedia*, 1:266).

Sat 4. [October 4, 1862]

Jabez went to Griffin today to have a settlement with Putnam and Stewart in regard to A/cs [accounts] collected for and lo! Putnam comes into our store today and Jabe has missed him. I was not able to be at meeting this morning which I regretted as 10 converts related their experiences and were received for Baptism. At night we sang at Mr Roots. We have had beautiful nights all the week, the moon shining and the air cool and pleasant—

Sunday 5. [October 5, 1862]

Dora was ill last night, though *about* all the previous day and not complaining. She began to cry about dark and had fever but soon went to sleep and twice woke up in a dreadful state of perturbation wild and incoherent—We took her into our bed and she then slept quietly until morning and awoke seemingly well again, going to school and church as usual. Twelve candidates were baptized this morning after a sermon by the pastor from the words "Why will ye die?" During the baptisms the choir sang "Children of Zion" and *three hymns* and the old baptismal Hallelujah doxology. Mattie Andrews and both her parents were among the candidates. Mr Kendrick preached at night to a large audience on the *Last Day*.—

Thursday 9. [October 9, 1862]

This is Sallie's birthday and she is 29 years old. I framed and hung up in our room the previous night a large picture of "An English Merry making in the olden time" as a birthday present.—I omitted to state that I sat up with Henry last Sunday night as his friends there were all in need of rest. Ellie slept with her baby upon a bed on the floor while I occupied my time and kept awake by reading a volume of Franconia Stories.* At four oclock Mrs Grubb relieved me and I went home and took a snooze until time for morning prayer meeting. Jabez returned from Griffin Sunday afternoon.—

Sunday 12. [October 12, 1862]

It is a gloomy cold wet day and Dora and her Mama are both lying on the couch sick. Dora is better than she was. She has been quite poorly all the week and we have been doctoring her for *worms* with a home made medicine. Sallie was too ill to go to church this morning, and last night was wet and we had no sing. Bro Root was gone to Charleston several

---

* *Franconia Stories*, by Jacob Abbott, are stories for children set in the White Mountains of New Hampshire.

days of last week and the singing devolved upon me. Eight more have professed conversion and five were baptized today among whom were the Pastors daughter and *old Mr Neal* who has been a "seeker" for forty years! I expect it was a *cross* indeed for him to go down into the water. I expect the old man feels happy though now. Lou Brantley was a long time in getting down the steps into the pool and it was quite a pretty picture to see her clinging in dread to her fathers arm for a minute before she gained courage to go down which she finally did. She is a nice little maiden.—I received a letter from father a day or two ago, and Sallie got one from Harriet last night giving the bad news that Mary had her baby there with whooping cough, which will interfere with Sallie's contemplated trip down there this month. Bro Kendrick preached his farewell sermon at night from the text "Lord, it is done as thou hast commanded *and yet there is room.*" The church made up a purse of over $100 for him. Dr Brantley was "called" by the church for next year at $2000 and will probably accept if he has not already done so.

Tuesday 14. [October 14, 1862]

Jabez and I shut up store to attend the Militia muster today: We were out three hours very uselessly. Rev Mr Rambaut preached at night from the text "The Spirit and the Bride say, come &c"—After dinner today Sallie walked to the Dentists' and courageously had two teeth extracted the first of which was a terribly hard job. Dr Huntington pulled *at* it half a dozen or more times with different instruments and was almost at his wits end before he succeeded in getting it out: he was afraid to use too much force for he might have broken the jaw. She afterwards had several teeth "filled" and was quite a heroine.—Stella is better of late and rides her new *old* horse "Peter" all around town.—A letter from Mr Sherwood gives me to infer that if he can get $1500 for *Ellen* he will sell.

Wed 15. [October 15, 1862]

Sallie is not as well today—Two young girls joined the church tonight by experience.—A bad cold on my lungs spoils my pipes for singing of late. Our bird "Dickey" that David Craig gave to Dora *died* today. He has not sung much for over a year and has been ailing a long time.—

Thursday 16. [October 16, 1862]

Sallie slept well last night but did not feel as strong to fulfil her appointment at the dentist's as she did on Tuesday but she did go and had a number of *fillings* put in. I sat there and read.

Friday 17. [October 17, 1862]

Five persons related experience tonight.—We have discontinued Dora's medicine as I don't think that she is or has been troubled by *Worms*, but as we may have occasion to use the medicine again I will annex receipt[.] A handful of *Garlic* cut fine and steeped in a pint of Whiskey with a teaspoonful of Gunpowder. dilute one half and pour a tablespoonful upon a teasp'full of sugar and give before breakfast every morning. *I* don't vouch for its efficacy myself.

Sat 18. [October 18, 1862]

The news from Kentucky is good. It is said that Bragg is driving Buell before him out of the state having routed him and taken several thousand prisoners.* At Corinth, Miss the other day our army under Price and Van Dorn attacked the Yankee works but had finally to retreat before reinforcements and the Yankees claim a great victory.—†

Sunday 19. [October 19, 1862]

This is a beautiful day and a large congregation assembled at our Church to witness the ordinance of Baptism. Eleven were baptized which makes twenty-eight in all. Two were only twelve years old. I sometimes wish that I had not joined the church so early in life as *eleven* years old that I might the more clearly recollect my feelings and experience in relation to the step, but I know that it is not too early an age for the soul to be converted and if converted then one is not too young to follow Christ. But it is more that I have made so little progress that causes regret than that I began so soon. Sallie and Dora both made out to go to church for the first time in nearly two weeks. Sallie has been ailing all the month and don't seem to gain strength or appetite. She weaned Alice over a week ago. Her head troubles her a good deal and she left church today before the close of the services to avoid the noise of the crowd going out. Going casually into the parlor this aft I overheard our sick hostess scoring us at the top of her voice as ungrateful intruders finding fault with our victuals and yet continuing to eat and live here. Poor critter—we will gladly go as soon

---

* SPR was incorrect. After Bragg's retreat following the Battle of Perryville, Union general Don Carlos Buell failed to press the Confederate leader aggressively, and Lincoln replaced Buell with William S. Rosecrans (Heidler and Heidler, *Encyclopedia*, 1:306–9).

† Confederate forces under Generals Sterling Price and Earl Van Dorn attacked the Union-held town of Corinth, Mississippi, on Oct. 3, 1862, but failed to take it (Heidler and Heidler, *Encyclopedia*, 1:500–501).

as we can, more for *our* sakes than for hers and not trouble her again. I have had hard thoughts of sister-in-law before, but those thoughts were mingled with some respect and regard, but *this one*—! Jabez I think does try to keep things cool and preserve the peace and I sincerely regret that he has been so unfortunate in the choice of a wife. I did think that at least he had got a companion possessed of health, amiability and education, but in all these I have been disappointed. Even her want of health is due in a great measure to her own imprudence and wilfulness.—Did not go out at night as Ellen was permitted to go and I did not want to leave the sick folks alone.—A meeting was appointed for Monday night which will close the series for the present I understand. The meeting has lasted four weeks—converts just *one per day.*

Monday 20. [October 20, 1862]

It was my turn to go home to dinner today but Jabez went instead whereat Sallie was very much disgruntled and *took on* considerably going into Stella's room and upbraiding Jabe for imposing upon her and me, and returning to her own room she went off into a fit of hysteria and if Stella and her servant had not come to her aid, she might have fared badly. Her nerves are very weak now and a very little upsets her.—Tonight I began the water treatment by pouring cold upon her head and then sponging her body all over with tepid water, as she could not bear it cold she said. The great flourish of trumpets about our successes in Kenty turn out to be premature as regards taking so many prisoners and driving the Yankees out of the state. We seem to have gained a victory at Perryville as stated but now Gen Bragg is falling back in order towards Cumberland Gap bringing with him a vast wagon train of army supplies secured in Kentucky.— Buell appears to be following him—From Northern papers we learn that the States of Pennsylvania Ohio and Indiana have given the Democrats a majority in the recent elections there which our people are glad to hear although the Democrats profess as much determination to prosecute the war vigorously as the abolitionists[.]* Yet they don't do it on the abolition principles as the others do.—

---

* In 1862, the United States held congressional and state elections for the first time since the beginning of the war. In addition to gaining thirty-two seats in Congress, the Democrats captured governorships in New Jersey and New York and state legislatures in Indiana, Illinois, and New Jersey. Nonetheless, Republicans continued to control the U.S. House, Senate, and most state legislatures (McPherson, *Ordeal*, 319–20).

Tues 21. [October 21, 1862]

Continued water treatment of my two patients by pouring on head and bath at night, water tepid.—Took Dora out of bed hot and restless and gave her a cold bath after which she slept well and was better next day. Sallie don't like cool water for bathing.—

Wed 22. [October 22, 1862]

We bought a small lot 35 × 95 feet today with a house on it for $1500— Bot of Mr Rogers. It is quite near town or the business part of it and it may eventually make a good *store.* My patient is rather better but still very feeble. I omitted the bath tonight as she appeared to have but little fever—I attended church.—My cold and cough trouble me a good deal this week.

Thursday 23. [October 23, 1862]

Jabez has bot a barrel of Lager Bier and we have been trying it today.— Gave wife a warm bath tonight, which suited her better than cold. She seems to improve and gain in appetite.—Her ailment may be *Roseola.*

Friday 24. [October 24, 1862]

A telegram today says that an order has been issued to enroll all able-bodied men between the ages of 18 and 40 which destroys my peace of mind as I am under 40 if not very *able-bodied*—I don't want to go to war if I can avoid it; for if I go I fear I should be of little service and destroy my own self—perhaps.*—I borrowed Br Roots buggy this aft and put "Old Pete" in harness and took Sallie and Dora to ride. We met Henry and Ellie also riding out for the first time. H—— looks very badly. He has had a hard time of it.—

Sat 25. [October 25, 1862]

This morning I sold a bill of toys &c to a man from Richmond, $140 worth, which cost I suppose about $35. Whoever buys of him will have to pay pretty well for *the whistle.* In the aft' I got the buggy again and we rode out as far as Mrs Lipham's old place. The choir met at our room tonight and Sanders McDaniel was there in his uniform[;] he is orderly sergeant. Mr Root is orderly also in the Atlanta Provost Guard but his duties

---

* D. C. Smith, enrolling officer for the Confederate armies in Atlanta, published notices in *ADI* indicating that those previously exempted from military service must go to City Hall and report their names and reasons for the exemptions claimed. See, for example, Oct. 26, 1862.

don't seem to interfere at all with his other business.* If I could have had such a place as his I would have volunteered too! He advises me to go into a company of Heavy Artillery that is forming for coast defence and I think I would if I was *sure* of having to go any how but I don't like to go until all other hope is lost.—A letter from Harriet tells us of the death of Mr Spaulding at Americus; and she wants Sallie to go down there right away as she thinks there will be no danger of the whoopg cough.—

Sunday 26. [October 26, 1862]
This is a cold blustering day, real wintry and a good fire is indispensable to comfort. Dr B preached to a small congregation on the necessity of of continual watchfulness. *One* of his texts was "The price of liberty is eternal vigilance" but this was not the *Bible text*. The church was cold as our winter supply of coal has not come. We have no further service today.

Wed 29. [October 29, 1862]
This afternoon, Sallie came down to the store at two o'clock for me to accompany her to the dentists'. Something over one hour's work finished up her job much to her relief and satisfaction. She felt well enough to go to prayer meeting at night. Two persons came forward and related their christian experiences and were received for baptism, a young man and young woman.

Friday 31. [October 31, 1862]
November is close at hand but October has given us this week a pretty strong idea of winter especially in the early part of this week. Vegetation has been taken down quite effectually. This afternoon I went to the usual meeting for prayer for the country; It was held in our church for the last time this year. Very few men attend but of females there was a considerable number.—Dora is still ill and Alice is quite poorly; we think her eye-teeth are troubling her. My wife is I hope convalescent, though she and I both are troubled with cough and colds. Stella seems to improve since the horse came.—

Sunday 2. [November 2, 1862]
We expected rain today but have been agreeably disappointed. Dr B. preached a sermon about the religious training of children as enjoined

---

* Sidney S. Root was a member of Company A, Georgia 2nd Reserves (Janet B. Hewett, ed., *Georgia Confederate Soldiers, 1861–1865*, 4 vols. [Wilmington, N.C.: Broadfoot, 1998], 2:715).

by the word of God.—Our Voluntary this morning was a new one from the Dulcimer "Cast thy burden on the Lord" but Mrs West thinking too much of her new bonnet took the wrong pitch and spoilt it.* After sermon the two candidates were baptized.—Sallie has written to Harriet that she will go down on Wed' next and she reckons upon my going with her but I hardly know what is best to do. If I join a company for the war I ought to stay and attend to it.—Allie is very poorly and don't eat anything at all, requiring to be held all the time.—

Wed. 5. [November 5, 1862]

We left Atlanta (I cant say *home* for we have none) this morning at eleven o'clock *seven in number* and started for Americus. Our *kind* sister-in-law has not been in once to ask after our sick child and did not even come out to tell us Goodbye although Sallie sent the children to bid *her* Goodbye and even went to her door herself to do so. I don't see why anyone should wish to make themselves so hateful I'm sure.—Our poor little baby was so ill that we did not like to take her out in the cold but Sallie felt constrained to go anyhow. We finally got off after nearly leaving our baggage, and the cars started in a rain, but we soon left the wet weather behind us and arrived safely at Macon under a clear sky. James' wife and Mrs Stark and her daughter *Estella* were awaiting us and *Mollie* took us all to her house and would not hear of my going elsewhere, so I concluded to drop old animosities and in these troublous times be friendly as possible with those who showed themselves friendly.† Mollie read us some letters from her husband who is Captain of the "Thomson Guards" Co. I. 61st Geo Regt. and they form a part of Gen "Stonewall" Jacksons Army in Virginia. The toothache prevented my getting much sleep. at night.—

Thursday 6. [November 6, 1862]

We left Mollie's at 9½ O'clock for Americus buying tickets for myself and wife—Dora and Ellen as I did in Atlanta but *George S. Dasher* the Conductor made me pay for Irene and Arthur also, the rascal. Mr Taylor met us with his new carriage at the depot at Americus and Harriet soon welcomed us at her house, where we felt somewhat at home.—The

---

* "Cast Thy Burden upon the Lord" was a hymn featuring words from Psalms 55:22 and was included in Isaac Baker Woodbury's *The Dulcimer; or, The New York Collection of Sacred Music* (Boston: Reynolds, 1850), 250.

† For the "old animosities," see SPR diary, Nov. 14, 1862.

toothache and our sick baby did not allow me much rest or sleep at night, though our room was a comfortable one.

Friday 7. [November 7, 1862]

A beautiful day—Mrs Spaulding came to see us. she looks naturally but older and sadder.—Tonight my tooth let me sleep pretty well and I gave up my place by Sallie to our baby that she might more easily attend to her wants—

Sat 8. [November 8, 1862]

Went down to the square with "Kell" [Seth Kell Taylor] and bought about $50 worth of mdse to sell again. Americus is certainly *dried up* the stores nearly all closed and most of the men gone to the war or somewhere else.—I took a ride with "Kell" in his buggy in the afternoon. As our baby got no better we thought best to call a physician and sent for Dr Hardwick at night. He said her disease was *Colera Infantum* and left Calomel powders for her with directions to redden her stomach with a cloth wet with turpentine. "Cousin Sue" or Miss Susannah Killam, Mr T's cousin came today. She is an old acquaintance of mine, I knew her about 24 years ago in Penfield. Sister Harriet is very kind and careful of the baby so that the poor little sufferer seems to know and like her as well as her mama which I think grieves her mama a little which is but natural enough.

Sunday 9. [November 9, 1862]

Sallie staid with her baby but the rest of us went to church and heard a sermon about something, or nothing, from Rev Hornady, our Atlanta man. I sat with Harriet in the "choir" and as Bro Sam Kendrick was late I had to do the *raising* and sing the Base.—They cant sing much there I found out. Allie is very ill: She can have better nursing here than in Atlanta as H. and also *Miss Sue* are kind and willing to help.

Monday 10. [November 10, 1862]

I rode out this morning with Mr Taylor to Dr Barlows a rich widower two miles from town about whom they tease "Cousin Sue" continually tho' *as yet* they are not acquainted with each other.—Baby was quite restless last night. Mrs Ryland Kendrick and her sister Mrs J. K. came to call upon Sallie today[.] *They* are older acquaintances even than Miss Sue as I knew them as schoolgirls at fathers school in Forsyth some 26 years ago! Arabella and Eliza Randle were their names then. The Dr came *twice* today. Mr Taylor left for his plantation this afternoon.

Tuesday 11. [November 11, 1862]

I went to town this afternoon to get turpentine and returned with Mr Taylor and found the baby looking very ill, so much so that we feared she would not live through the night and poor wife felt very sad at the near prospect of losing the darling. But towards night she rallied and seemed bright and our hopes revived. I got a letter from Jabez today enclosing one from father.—

Wed 12. [November 12, 1862]

Baby still looks bright tho' she had fever in the afternoon. I intended to start back today but deferred it until tomorrow on baby's account.—

Thurs 13.— [November 13, 1862]

I asked the Dr's opinion as to the childs recovery as I thought of leaving, and he said he could not give me any decided answer either way. He did not think when he first saw her that she would live till now and it was still doubtfull if she would recover. So hoping for the best yet fearing the worst I bade my wife and others adieu and took the cars for Macon fervently commending the dear ones to a merciful God.—I read as I rode "Astoria" by Wash Irving but my mind would continually wander to the troubles that beset me at this juncture and the dark future just ahead.* It was after dark when we reached Macon but I took up my baggage (a good load it was too) and trudged to Mollies as she had insisted upon my going there when I returned. I found Mrs Stark and 'Stella there and had the pleasure of seeing them home by bedtime.—.

Friday 14. [November 14, 1862]

I spent today in buying what I could find that we needed, *gold* and *steel* pens, books & c. After tea Mollie and I had a long and sociable talk before bedtime as we were alone.—Marriage and its joys and sorrows have much improved the young and giddy wilful girl that ran away with Jim and was married into holy wedlock by a drunken 'squire! Four children now call her Mother; she has lost none by death.—

Sat 15. [November 15, 1862]

I left Macon at 9½ this morning and resumed the reading of "Astoria" reaching Atlanta safely at 4 P.M. I found that Stella had gained so much strength since we left that she has taken a gent and wife to board at $100 per month. They are a *Catholic* couple named Haggerty from Richmond.

* Washington Irving's *Astoria* (1836) tells the story of John Jacob Astor's unsuccessful effort to create a fur-trading monopoly in the Northwest.

He is employed in a Pistol Factory here at the fine salary of *$500 per month*, I hear.* It is rather a fortunate thing for my comfort, I think, that they have to provide for others and I get my share.—

Sunday 16. [November 16, 1862]

I am sitting in our room "*alone*, all alone," bringing up my journal to date. The day is raw and dark and but a small congregation were out to hear Bro *Wood* the substitute of Dr B. preach this morning. I must now begin a letter to my wife according to promise; I wish I knew whether my baby is alive or not.—This aft Jabe and I went to see Nell and Henry. Tonight after church I got a letter from my wife bringing the welcome news that Alice was slowly improving since I left. I have just finished a six paged letter in reply.—

Monday 17. [November 17, 1862]

We have had a very busy day at the store. Yesterday morning while Rev Wood was preaching, I was not following him very closely, and an idea popped into my head which I could not get rid of, which was, that we should propose to Mr Seymour, a practical shoemaker and very devout churchman to go into the shoemaking business together as that trade is exempted from war and a money making one too if well conducted. Well today Seymour, who I supposed was on his bench at Mr Holley's, dropped into the store all in his Sunday's best and I found that he had just broken off from Holley and seemed to incline favorably to my proposal so at my suggestion he came to our house tonight and we talked it over and agreed upon terms and shall probably go into it forthwith unless he backs out upon further consideration.

Wed 19. [November 19, 1862]

I am afraid to go about town now or to the store as I hear that the officers are about, taking up the conscripts vigorously.— * * * * * *

Wed 26. [November 26, 1862]

A week has passed since my last entry a week of absence and I am again in our room at Atlanta with wife and children—but *not all*—we have left darling baby Alice in the burial ground at Macon.—At 11 o'clock last Wed morning I rec^d a telegram from Sallie at Macon telling me of the

---

* The Spiller and Burr Pistol Factory on Piedmont Avenue struggled to come up with a workforce and machinery capable of producing guns, which would explain Haggerty's relocation from Richmond and high salary (Singer, "Confederate Atlanta," 140–41).

babys death and asking me to meet her there, and I had scarce time to run down to the cars just as I was and get aboard, distressed and troubled. One thing however gave me comfort—I had asked Bro Root if I could not get employment with J. J. Toon & Co that would exempt me from conscription and he promised to see Mr Toon and thought likely it might be arranged.—I found my family at Mollies house with Mr Taylor and Harriet and our baby's corpse. She died Monday night between 12 & and 1 O'clock without much pain apparently. Sallie had put her to bed hoping she was getting better yet *fearing* that all was not right.—Dear baby, the gates of Paradise were then opening to receive her into the presence of the kind Saviour who said that "Of such is the kingdom of Heaven."—We buried her Thursday morning at eleven o'clock in Rose Hill Cemetery by the side of her nameless little brother. Bro Warren officiated for us.—We remained over Sunday in Macon as I wanted to hear from Jabez what Mr Toon could offer and also waited for him to send me some money as I went off with but little. We attended the Baptist Ch' morning and night and the Episcopalian with Mollie in the aft. Rev Joseph Wilson, Presbyterian minister from Augusta attending *Synod* there preached a good sermon in the morning from the text "I was alive without the law once &c[.]" I sang with the choir. Tuesday afternoon I rec^d the expected package from Jabez, in which he gave me to understand that an arrangement might be made with Mr Toon to employ me. While I was opening the package something came up in my throat and mouth and to my great astonishment and disgust I drew out of my mouth a *live worm* eight inches long and ⅙ inch in size at the middle; a species of stock that I did not dream I was raising!—We did think of going out to Mr Van's place for a few days but I thought I had better come up immediately and secure my place and Sallie wanted to come with me[.] Mr Van proposed that I should go and teach school out at his place or be his *Miller!**—Harriet went out there and returned yesterday and today we *all* bade Mollie Goodbye, we to come North and Harriett to go South.— Jabez has engaged a new clerk, for board and clothes wages, a young man of pleasant appearance 17 years old, John Brantley by name.—My wife has been quite cross today, complaining of pain in her jaws. I went to meeting tonight.

* James Van Valkenburg's suggestion of a teaching job may have been related to SPR's desire to avoid the draft, since teachers were exempt (McPherson, *Ordeal*, 202).

Thursday 27 [November 27, 1862]

I called to see Mr Toon this morning and made an agreement to enter his service, nominally and chiefly as "Proof-Reader and Mailer," but to make myself *generally* useful also.—So to begin he set me to going to the drygood stores to solicit contributions of Pasteboard Boxes to be use[d] to bind Testaments for the Army!—

Friday 28. [November 28, 1862]

This being the day for mailing the "Banner & Baptist" I was at my new place from nine until dark and then took home a lot of "proof" which occupied me until ten o'clock at night, Sallie reading "Copy" for me. By the by she denies the allegation that she was *cross* on Wed' night, so I suppose she was *not*, but I still think it was not a pleasant way of only "feeling badly."—.

Sat 29. [November 29, 1862]

I got a *half holiday* this afternoon and brought home our stove with some supplies for our contemplated house-keeping, a barrel of flour for instance @ $40 and a small sack of salt—20 lbs—$12. Coffee is $3. per lb; We shall not use much of that.—We put down our carpet also this afternoon and made our room much more cosy and comfortable. We went to Bro Roots after supper to sing and met there Rev Mr Huntington Baptist Minister from Augusta, whom Dr Brantly has sent to preach for us being himself detained by the illness of his wife and daughter in Augusta.

Sunday Nov 30. [November 30, 1862]

I liked Huntington better than on his former visit. He preached morning and night.—In the afternoon Jabe and I took a walk to see how Henry was fixed in their new abode, they having moved into the little house we have lately bought on Peters Street. Not finding them at home we went on to Mr Grubbs new house thinking to find them there but when we got there they had returned home so we took them on our way home[.] Henry, the baby, came to me willingly, for the first time, and sat on my knee some time quite contentedly. *We* have no baby now to pet and love: dear little angel Allie is gone.

Thursday Dec 4. [December 4, 1862]

This morning, having got up my stove, and also built the pantry that we brought the materials of from Macon, in our kitchen, I bought a load of wood and some groceries and meat and sent home and when I went to dinner I found we *had a home* of our own and something to eat! Our table did not groan under a superabundance of rare and costly dishes it is true, but as the wise man well says "Better is a dinner of herbs where love is than a stalled ox and hatred therewith."—Steve Whitehead is at home now for a little while hunting shoes for the army in Virg'a[.] We sent in to Stella tonight for a little milk for our coffee, but she didn't have any to spare! What a nice sister she is.

Sunday 7. [December 7, 1862]

This has been a real wintry day freezing cold Mercury at 28° this morning. Last night Johnny Root brought over his father's question book with a request for me to hear his class in S School in his abesence, and I concluded to do so although rather a formidable undertaking it being composed of six full grown intelligent young ladies and the lesson not studied by me. However I got along very well and *made out* I was quite familiar with the subject. Bro Toon, *my Boss*, opened the school. I had to be chorister also. Rev Mr Worrell preached but the church was not warmed and consequently we did not much enjoy the sermon. Sallie has been troubled for several days with toothache or pains in her jaw and head something of neuralgiac character which have prevented her from taking any comfort in our new position. We rec^d a letter from father last night and Sallie got one from Amelia containing many earnest expressions of sympathy in our grief for our little Alice.—She has kindred in heaven, "Manie" Chevis, Blanche, and Cornelia's little ones Willie, Ernest, Edith, and others.— "For of such is the kingdom of Heaven[.]"* Father has a strong idea now of going into the salt boiling trade if he can get kettles which are very scarce and high[.] Salt will bring $30 per bushel right where they make it father says and 150 gals of salt water will make *one bushel* salt.

Tuesday 9. [December 9, 1862]

Tonight Mr Henry W. Seymour came to our room and we drew up Articles of Agreement upon which terms we are going into the *shoe trade* for three years; *he* to give his time, attention, skill and labour, and we to put in $2000 as Capital Stock. We have rented the rooms above our store for the purpose. This is the anniversary of the wedding night of Sallie and myself: Just ten years ago at 8 'Oclock tonight we were united for better or worse. So far we have experienced *"the better"* and we still "hope for the best."

---

* SPR referred to the deaths of his nieces and nephews. Manie and Chevis were children of Amelia and Nell; Blanche was JJR's deceased daughter; Willie, Ernest, and Edith were the children of Will and Cornelia.

Wed 10. [December 10, 1862]

While we *were* waiting for some brother or friend to lead our meeting tonight we were all delighted to see our pastor come in, just up from Augusta having left his family convalescing, and Bro Deacon White felt felt so good that he made "the longest prayer of the season."

Sat. 13. [December 13, 1862]

This morning we ratified with Seymour our agreement he having already taken possession of the rooms above our store, where he keeps "Bach" as he calls it. He drove Jabe's rockaway to Decatur this afternoon taking Stella as passenger his purpose being to get leather or make arrangements to do so. Our choir met at our room tonight and we had a pretty good sing. Root has been away for over a week employed by the Govt in *impressing* supplies of clothing for the Army and he says he shall be again away for two weeks upon the same business.—He is acting under the authority of the *State*.—I bought a sack of sugar today at Auction, 129 lbs at 43¢ providing for the "sweets" of "Matrimony" this winter. I also gave *four dollars* for a pair of shoes for Arthur and ten dollars for 2½ yds of common homespun for my pants[.]

Sunday 14. [December 14, 1862]

I feared it would be wet today but was agreeably disappointed to find it bright, clear and warm. We had a good congregation and an excellent sermon from the text "We all do fade as a leaf." Sallie and I went over to see Nell and Steve in the afternoon.—

Sat 20. [December 20, 1862]

I have been considerably exercised this week in getting an exemption certificate from the enrolling officer[.] I was overhauled in the Printing Office several days ago by the sub-officer and went with him at his invitation to the office with a blank *certify* from Mr Toon that I was employed and my services necessary at his establishment but I did not get the signature of Lieut. Morgan a young "whip snapper" who is assistant Enrolling Officer[.] He questioned the legality of Mr Toon's claims, but said if I could get the certificate of the *Editor* of the paper published then I could get an exemption. So the next day I got Mr Jas N Ells to give me a certificate which he did willingly and again I repaired to the office but was again unsuccessful, Morgan saying that he should have to refer the case to his superior officer having been told that I had left a large bookstore suddenly when I found that the officer was after me and had accepted a nominal position at the printing Office just to escape conscription. This was partly true and partly false, but if it had been just as he said, if I had complied with the strict terms and letter of the law it was his duty, I opine, to give me an exemption. Upon reference to the new Officer, Lieut Mead, he said it was necessary for me to get the *affidavit* of the Editor or Proprietor—so I did that, and today I got the necessary document signed by him, with which I hope they will let me rest in peace for awhile at least. Last Saturday the Yankees made another "On to Richmond" at Fredericksburg in Virginia and again they were defeated in a desperate fight in which Gen T R R Cobb one of Georgias noblest sons fell mortally wounded, and a friend from Virginia tonight told me that it was feared that Capt Jas Van Valkenburgh was either killed or taken prisoner, but as a letter rec^d from Mollie Van tonight does not corroborate it we trust it is not so.* Stella took a notion to go to La Grange this morning to see the Roberts folks there, and off she did go. We were surprized lately at her asking Sallie to ride with her in her carriage, a thing she has never done before.—Tonight we had a sing at Mrs Wests—Mr Root is absent.

Sunday 21. [December 21, 1862]

Our pastor preached this morning upon the *New Birth*, taking as his text part of the third chapter of John. I have just finished writing a contribution for Jim Ells' Christmas issue under the caption of "A Glance Around" and I must write a few lines to Sister Kate in reply to a letter of sympathy from her after Alice's death.—Just as we were about to sing tonight the sexton in turning on the gas turned it all out except the choir lights and they were very dim. After awhile tho' we got lighted up and a Rev Mr Huff preached and afterward took up a collection in behalf of the Soldiers, to supply them with testaments and other good books.

Thursday 25. [December 25, 1862]

We had a fine *rooster* for Christmas dinner which tasted quite as well as turkey. Santa Claus, as usual brought the children some presents and

---

* At Fredericksburg, Virginia, on Dec. 13, 1862, Robert E. Lee's Confederate Army trounced Union forces under Ambrose Burnside. SVVR's brother, James, was captured but released in a prisoner exchange (James D. Van Valkenburg record, Compiled Military Service Records, National Archives, Microfilm 266, 561). General Thomas R. R. Cobb died of wounds received in this battle (Daniel E. Sutherland, *Fredericksburg and Chancellorsville: The Dare Mark Campaign* [Lincoln: University of Nebraska Press, 1998], 54, 58).

they had a fine time. The weather too is unusually pleasant for Christmas, neither wet nor cold.—We hear that *James* is well and returned home.

Sat 27. [December 27, 1862]

Mr Sherwood came up from Macon yesterday and staid with us last night and Jabe and I played the flute and sang for the company and we got up a "slim witch" and "hunted the keyhole" much to their amusement. The chief business of Mr S. was probably to sell to me the girl "Ellen" that we have hired from him for two years past, and for several hours this morning he and I tried to outgeneral each other in making a bargain, he demanding $1300 for her and declining to to *hire* her, and I offering to give him but $1200 and proposing to hire if he would not take the sum I offered. He had to leave at eleven o'clock and we had not traded at 10½ but I had ere this discovered signs of wavering in him and I finally bought her for $1225 being $275 less than he priced her at three months ago.* So now I had committed the unpardonable sin of the abolitionists in buying a negro. I am tired of the trouble of getting a servant every Christmas and we have found Ellen a pretty good girl and she is very willing to have us buy her. As near as we can tell she is 13 years old, healthy and ugly. The children are delighted at the thought that Ellen belongs to us now and will not go away. Dora says her name is now "Ellen Richards"—Today has been very rainy.

Sunday 28. [December 28, 1862]

I feared that this would be a very wet and unpleasant day but am quite agreeably disappointed as it is bright and pleasant. Dr B preached from the words of Pharoah to the patriarch Jacob "How old art thou[.]" Mr Root is at home again so that I am relieved of the responsibility of being chorister.

Wed 31. [December 31, 1862]

Another Year has nearly closed—; but before I moralize I will revert to facts—Jabez let "Sally" his servant go on a visit to Rome to see her friends and gave her *a pass* for his "boy["] "Harvey" her brother, whom his master has wrongfully detained until now—and today, sure enough, they both came back together taking "french leave"!† Our clerk John has also returned, and we have heard where "Old Pete," the stray horse, is. At

---

* ASC, Jan. 9, 1862, reported the price of male slaves sold in Atlanta as between $1,450 and $1,650.

† *French leave* means absent without permission.

meeting tonight our Pastor gave us an appropriate talk, reminding us of the mercies we have received and the obligations we are under to a kind Providence. This year has been a dark one indeed to many hearts, and one of great anxiety to nearly all; yet we have cause to bless God that it is so well with us as it is. The skies began to brighten and I feel assured that ere half of the new year has passed away that we shall be enabled to rejoice in the reign of peace, which may Heaven grant.

Samuel Pearce Richards, ca. 1848.
(Kenan Research Center at the Atlanta History Center)

Atlanta at around the time of the Civil War. A thriving community of ten thousand residents when Sam Richards moved there from Macon in October 1861, Atlanta became a major Confederate center for industry, transportation, and medical care, and its population more than doubled by the end of the war. (Painting by Wilbur Kurtz; Kenan Research Center at the Atlanta History Center)

Jabez Judson Richards, ca. 1848.
(Kenan Research Center at the Atlanta History Center)

Washington Street, 1860s. For much of the war, Sam Richards, his wife, and their children boarded with his brother, Jabez, and his family in a house on Washington Street not far from their church, Second Baptist (*left*), and City Hall (*right*). (Kenan Research Center at the Atlanta History Center)

Sidney Root, ca. 1880s. (From Thomas H. Martin, *Atlanta and Its Builders: A Comprehensive History of the Gate City of the South*, 2 vols. [Atlanta: Century Memorial, 1902])

Whitehall Street, 1864. A major business thoroughfare in Atlanta, Whitehall Street was home to the Richards brothers' bookstore. Like most Atlanta roads, it was not paved. (Library of Congress Prints and Photographs Division, LC-B811-3669)

Federal wagons in a convoy, part of General William T. Sherman's army, which entered Atlanta on September 2, 1864, after what Sam Richards described as "a day of terror and a night of dread." The tall building (*center*) is Franklin Printing, where Sam Richards worked part time during the war to avoid conscription. (Library of Congress Prints and Photographs Division, LC-B811-3610)

Atlanta in ruins, 1864. Much of Atlanta was destroyed by either departing Confederate soldiers or those of the Union Army. The city's impressive rail facilities, including the car shed shown here, were reduced to rubble. (Library of Congress Prints and Photographs Division, LC-B811-2715)

Sam Richards, ca. 1880s.
(Kenan Research Center at the Atlanta History Center)

Atlanta, 1947. The S. P. Richards Company (*lower right*) had its offices on Central Avenue, not far from the State Capitol (*center*). (Kenan Research Center at the Atlanta History Center)

FOUR

January 1863 to June 1863

"THE NEGROES WERE VERY GLAD TO BE BOUGHT BY US."

As the Confederacy reached its military high tide in late 1862 and early 1863, Sam Richards's cautious manner gave way to bombastic predictions about the South's glorious future. In January 1863, he disparaged Abraham Lincoln's efforts to free slaves through the Emancipation Proclamation and noted that Union military defeats meant "the world will laugh to scorn such a Proclamation." So sure was Richards of Confederate success that he wrote, "I have strong hopes that before the Spring ends this dreadful war will have virtually ended, and the *white* man be again free and not the niggers." Richards's optimism seemed to be borne out when General Robert E. Lee's army crushed the Yankees at the Battle of Chancellorsville, making a martyr of General Stonewall Jackson but seeming to bring the South one step closer to annihilating its enemy.[1]

Earning spectacular profits in both the stationery and grocery businesses, Sam looked for ways to invest his money. He put it into Confederate bonds and in a blockade-running business. With Jabez, he purchased acreage outside of Atlanta, including Pleasant Hill farm. The brothers bought additional slaves, with Sam predicting ever-higher prices for slaves when the war ended, as world demand for cotton expanded. With both a farm in the country and several slaves, he had become a landed country gentleman. Without hesitation, he announced that the three members of a family he purchased in May 1863 "were very glad to be bought by us." Potential buyers for slaves often asked bondspeople if they would like to be purchased, affecting concern for their welfare but more interested in hearing an obsequious reply. Sam evidently received one. Nevertheless, he proceeded to split up the family by assigning Caroline to help Sallie in their household and her husband, Joe, to work at the farm. The couple's three-year-old child would be placed in whichever household Richards chose.² In so doing, he made a mockery of slave owners' claims that the institution was a benign one, beneficial to slave and owner alike. Nonetheless, Richards never manifested any doubts regarding the morality of slavery. He had worked hard all his life and felt he deserved the success that had finally come to him.

Sam's optimistic outlook even led him to look favorably on his Yankee brother, Will, especially after Addison reported that Will identified with the Peace Democrats, a wing of the party that favored a negotiated end to the war with slavery intact. Addison later revised his assessment of Will, describing him as a "War" man but nonetheless insisting that he opposed the abolitionists. In a gesture of brotherly reconciliation, Sam gave his children a handsomely bound seven-volume set of Will's popular children's magazine, *Schoolfellow*, inscribed "Father's Gift to his Children, Atlanta, Ga, May 1863, Dora, Irene, Arthur."³ This gift and those words represented the pinnacle of Sam's optimism in Confederate victory and magnanimity toward a brother he had previously regarded as an enemy.

Yet signs of trouble, including unease about the future of slavery, had already intruded into Sam's rosy scenario. As the Union Navy continued to tighten its grip on the Southern coastline, an increasing number of white families moved their slaves inland to protect their investment in human property. Jabez Richards helped Nell Richards Whitehead and her soldier husband, Steve, by bringing their slaves from the vulnerable area along the coast to live at Pleasant Hill. In Atlanta, slave owners worried about what slaves knew of the military situation and what they were saying to each other. Sam Richards's diary reveals a mixture of pride in slave purchases and unease about slave behavior. He made frequent notations about slaves behaving in an "outrageously impudent" fashion and believed that Jabez was not harsh enough in his reactions to such episodes. In one instance, Sam was awakened in the night by the local watchman reporting that two of Jabez's slaves had been picked up and jailed for being out on the town after the city's nine o'clock curfew for African Americans. In Jabe's absence, Sam was asked to pay for their release. Atlanta court records during this time indicate very few prosecutions for slave legal transgressions, an indication that slaves such as Jabez's used wartime conditions to stretch the boundaries of acceptable behavior and avoided legal repercussions. Some ran away. But if slaves avoided prosecution, they still might incur the wrath of their owners. Sam's slave, Ellen, represents a good example. In May 1862, Ellen had helped herself to some of Sallie Richards's toiletries, not for the first time, and received a whipping. In February 1863, she allegedly stole a spool of thread and received a similar punishment. Perhaps emboldened by wartime conditions and the possibility that slavery might end, Ellen asserted her will despite the consequences. The situation clearly put Sam on edge. However dismissive he might be of Lincoln's Emancipation Proclamation, he and many other Southerners feared that unchecked acts of slave "impudence" coupled with wartime conditions undermined their authority and might lead to full-scale uprising.[4]

The speculative frenzy that helped make Sam feel wealthy also led to unrestrained inflation. Government controls over the economy, including the impressment of crops and livestock for use by the military, squeezed Atlanta residents. Because of a weak harvest the previous year, the Confederacy had some of its most severe food shortages of the war during the spring of 1863. The lack of key items troubled every household. Like many Southerners, Richards could not afford wheat flour and substituted flour made from rice or corn. He paid $10 for five chickens so that his family might have eggs and another $160 for an old cow so that they might have milk. Members of the Richards family were among the fortunate; unlike many of their countrymen, the Richardses always had food during the war. Underscoring the city's problems with inflation, on March 18, 1863, a small group of gun-wielding women held up a butcher on Whitehall Street, stealing $300 worth of food. The butcher had refused their demand that he lower his price for bacon from $1.10 per pound. Although the episode involved only a dozen women and they dispersed quickly when confronted by city marshal J. N. Williford, it showcased problems with food prices and urban unrest. After the incident, Williford collected $500 for distribution to these women. The Atlanta City Council also took action on March 31, allocating $1,854 out of $26,327 in total expenses for "pauper relief." The next day, the council applauded an act of local benevolence by Mayer Jacobs and Company, which donated one thousand pounds of rice for the benefit of Atlanta's neediest citizens. The *Southern Confederacy* asked citizens to "pause and reflect. Whither are we drifting?"[5]

Illness still claimed Sam's attention. "Our city is crowded with sick and wounded soldiers," he wrote on January 10, 1863, knowing that the situation was likely to get worse with the onset of spring military campaigns. The demise of twenty-four-year-old Stella Wheeler Richards from tuberculosis on February 15, 1863, served as a reminder of life's fragility, as did the death of a niece, Mamie Van Valkenburg. Coming so soon after Alice Richards's death, the tragedy only heightened Sam's worries about his surviving children. Smallpox was a cause for special concern in Atlanta. The City Council appropriated money to pay doctors who treated the disease and mandated that households afflicted by the scourge fly a red flag to warn others. In 1864, the City Council voted to build a hospital to isolate smallpox patients from other city residents.[6]

The death of Stella Richards led to another reshuffling of households. Jabez and his daughters moved to the country, leaving Sam, Sallie, and their children to rent Jabez's home on Washington Street. To maximize their income during high inflationary times, Sam and Sallie rented several rooms in the commodious house to a variety of boarders, including Mary Hathaway Brown and her young daughter, Isabel.

Richards remained nervous that Confederate military needs would lead to his being drafted. To ensure his exemption, he began writing stories and setting type for the religious weekly newspaper *Baptist Banner*, published by J. J. Toon. On March 28, 1863, the *Banner* published Sam's article, "Religion the Soldier's Best Armor," urging military men to embrace Jesus to realize a heavenly reward for military sacrifice. He wrote a variety of other stories, including a nostalgic view of childhood. In addition to the *Baptist Banner*, Toon's Franklin Printing published the *Southern Confederacy* newspaper and printed and bound books, mostly for resale by booksellers such as Richards.[7]

Although Richards continued to hope that employment by a religious publisher would keep him out of the army, he decided to take another step to assure that end. He hired a substitute, a path followed by seventy thousand others in the Confederacy by the end of the war. On March 4, 1863, he recorded in his diary, "Wishing to be at liberty to spend my time and labor in our business and not feeling secure of exemption in my present employ, I have obtained *a substitute*, one John D. Kugler of Carroll Co, a man 46 years old for whom we paid $2500.00." Substitutes made notoriously poor soldiers, and such would be the case with Kugler. Five months after Sam Richards hired him, Kugler deserted.[8]

On June 13, 1863, Richards focused on the military campaign at Vicksburg. "In war matters," he wrote, "things seem to be quite uncertain."[9] In the coming weeks, war matters moved from uncertainty to disaster for the Confederacy, and Richards's once optimistic predictions for the future were completely undermined.

Notes

1. SPR diary, Jan. 1, 25, 1863, May 9, 1863.
2. Ibid., May 2, 1863. For the practice of asking slaves if they wanted to be bought, see Walter Johnson, *Soul by Soul: Life inside the Antebellum Slave Market* (Cambridge: Harvard University Press, 1999), 174–75.
3. SPR diary, May 16, 1863, June 22, 1863. The volumes inscribed by Richards are in the Georgia State University Library in Atlanta.
4. SPR diary, Feb. 28, 1863, Apr. 5, 11, 18, 1863, May 5, 1862. For a discussion of the Atlanta slave curfew, see Thomas G. Dyer, *Secret Yankees: The Union Circle in Confederate Atlanta* (Baltimore: Johns Hopkins University Press, 1999), 159–60. Laura F. Edwards, *Scarlet Doesn't Live Here Anymore: Southern Women in the Civil War Era* (Urbana: University of Illinois Press, 2000), 115, discusses white people's fears of slave insubordination. For a discussion of the "breakdown of the urban slave system's complex web of legal and institutional restraints" in Atlanta and Savannah, see Clarence L. Mohr, *On the Threshold of Freedom: Masters and Slaves in Civil War Georgia* (Athens: University of Georgia Press, 1986), 207–8. Tera W. Hunter uses the example of Ellen as the opening to her first chapter in *To 'Joy My Freedom: Southern Black Women's Lives and Labors after the Civil War* (Cambridge: Harvard University Press, 1997), 4–5. According to Hunter, "Ellen transgressed feminine beauty rituals intended to enhance white bodies only. She laid claim to a measure of possession of her own person—and a womanly person at that." The Emancipation Proclamation freed slaves in areas of the South still in rebellion as of Jan. 1, 1863 (Allen C. Guelzo, *Lincoln's Emancipation Proclamation: The End of Slavery in America* [New York: Simon and Schuster, 2004], 207–11).
5. SPR diary, June 6, 27, 1863; ADI, Mar. 19, 1863; ASC, Mar. 20, 1863; James Michael Russell, *Atlanta, 1847–1890: City Building in the Old South and New* (Baton Rouge: Louisiana State University Press, 1988), 99–100. Regarding speculation in Atlanta, see Mary A. DeCredico, *Patriotism for Profit: Georgia's Urban Entrepreneurs and the Confederate War Effort* (Chapel Hill: University of North Carolina Press, 1990), 43. For food shortages in the Confederacy, see James M. McPherson, *Ordeal by Fire: The Civil War and Reconstruction*, 3rd ed. (Boston: McGraw Hill, 2001), 410–11; George C. Rable, *Civil Wars: Women and the Crisis of Southern Nationalism* (Urbana: University of Illinois Press, 1989), 96–102; Ralph Benjamin Singer Jr., "Confederate Atlanta" (Ph.D. diss., University of Georgia, 1973), 189–90; Atlanta City Council Minutes, vol. 4, Mar. 31, 1863, Apr. 1, 1863, AHC.
6. SPR diary, Jan. 10, 25, 27, 1863, Feb. 8, 1863; Atlanta City Council Minutes, vol. 4., Feb. 27, 1863, Mar. 6, 13, 1863, Mar. 18, 25, 1864. See also Franklin M. Garrett, *Atlanta and Environs: A Chronicle of Its People and Events*, 4 vols. (New York: Lewis Historical, 1954–87), 1:547–48.

7. SPR diary, Jan. 10, 1863; *Baptist Banner*, Mar. 28, 1863. See also Singer, "Confederate Atlanta," 93. ASC, May 11, 1862, printed the complete text of the draft law, including its exemptions, which included "journeyman printers actually employed in printing newspapers."

8. SPR diary, Mar. 4, 1863; Lillian Henderson, ed., *Roster of Confederate Soldiers of Georgia, 1861–1865*, 6 vols. [Hapeville, Ga.: Longino and Porter, 1959], 6:495–96. On the Confederate draft and the practice of substitution, see McPherson, *Ordeal*, 202–4.

9. SPR diary, June 13, 1863.

Thursday 1. [January 1, 1863]

We enter upon the new year with renewed hope that ere many months the dark tide of War will have passed away, and the blessings of Peace be again restored to us. The tidings of another great victory have come to us from Tennessee; the invading army of Gen Rosecrans, one of the enemy's most successful officers, has been hurled back with the loss of thousands of his men.*—This is the day for Abe Lincoln to issue his dreadful ukase which will set the sable sons of Africa all free and independent! In the face of the defeats which his grand armies have met with recently, the world will laugh to scorn such a Proclamation.

Sat 3. [January 3, 1863]

I have been at home all day suffering from a general aching, the result of a cold, which set in last night with a toothache and kept me tossing and grunting all the night restless and sleepless.—Towards night I felt somewhat better and went to sing at Mr Roots.

Sunday 4. [January 4, 1863]

It rained a great deal last night and until nine o'clock this morning, but then the sky began to clear and we went to church and heard a sermon from the text "The time is short &c"—Stella began yesterday to undergo the water treatment of Dr Coyle who has been quite successful here in

---

* At the battle of Stones River, Tennessee, December 31, 1862–January 2, 1863, Union soldiers under General William Rosecrans defeated Braxton Bragg's Confederates. Richards's belief in Confederate victory was probably grounded in the fact that Bragg attacked first, catching Rosecrans off guard. In renewed fighting on subsequent days, Rosecrans held his troops together and defeated the Confederates after receiving reinforcements from Nashville (Peter Cozzens, *No Better Place to Die: The Battle of Stones River* [Urbana: University of Illinois Press, 1990], 7–8, 83–85, 162–66, 199–202).

certain cases. She *feels* worse tho' today. At night Dr B preached from the text "Occupy 'till I come"; setting forth the necessity of our improving the "talents" that God has committed to our keeping, and that we shall have to render an account for them when the Lord comes.

Sat 10. [January 10, 1863]

Again, we were to[o] fast in our exultation over our conquest in Tennessee; for our Army after being victorious for awhile, had finally to give back in turn before the augmented force of the enemy and we retreated in order to [be] some place where the natural advantages of the ground were greater for defence. Our city is crowded with sick and wounded soldiers and Mr Toon *shook in his shoes* lest the authorities should see proper to take his establishment for a Hospital! Military rule is a great tyranny. I have been trying my hand at setting type and did set 15 or 20 lines finding it easier at the start than I expected[.] We bought a farm of 202 acres last Thursday for $6500[.] It is four miles from the city upon a good road, and known as the ["]Beasley Place." Jabez too has just bought another colored girl named "Sarah" in spite of Lincolns proclamation[.] Our Shoe Shop has got well under weigh with three first rate *jours* [journeymen] at work who all left *one shop* at once to work for Seymour. If the war should last sometime as it has been it will no doubt pay pretty well.

Sunday 11. [January 11, 1863]

Yesterday was wet, and promised foul weather today; but again the clouds have dispersed and the sun shines. Dr B preached this morning, about the "unspeakable Gift." It was our communion season.—

Wed. 14. [January 14, 1863]

Our "Boss," Mr Toon, went to Macon today, and I had to go into the Bindery to *saw* the backs of Testaments for the *girls* to sew, as Mr Flynn, the Binder, was sick.* Tonight, our prayer meeting was held in the basement room of our Church, but it is not a pleasant place. Before the exercises closed we were disturbed by the cry of *Fire* and upon going out found an old brick Stable burning and the wind blowing hard in the direction of Whitehall gave us some anxiety lest it should extend; but fortunately the firemen succeeded in arresting its further progress.

* Many women found employment as seamstresses in Atlanta during the Civil War. Three thousand of them did piecework, receiving relatively low wages for making individual items of clothing for the Quartermaster Department of the Army of Tennessee. Others, like the women described by SPR, sewed the binding on books (Singer, "Confederate Atlanta," 141–42, 165, 176).

Friday 16. [January 16, 1863]

I was very busy today; in the morning, in the Bindery, and in the afternoon, mailing the "Banner." I have written an *essay* on "Childhood" and set up the type, all ready for the press; about half a column. *I am a Printer!**

Sat 17. [January 17, 1863]

Mr Toon came home this afternoon.—I brought home tonight a pair of $18 Goatskin shoes that were made in our shop for my wife such as in ordinary times might sell for 2.50. Singing at Wests tonight.

Sunday 18. [January 18, 1863]

The weather has been freezingly cold for several days; and this morning our church was cold and uncomfortable. Dr Wilson, Presbyterian minister from Augusta came into the church and took a seat near the door, but Dr Brantly, espying him, pounced on him, and put him up to preach; which he did, briefly and well, from the text, "The kingdom of heaven suffereth violence &c." This is the same gentleman whom we heard preach in Macon, lately. Dr B. preached at night about Esau's birthright and his selling it for a mess of pottage.—

Wed 21. [January 21, 1863]

After meeting tonight, a church meeting was held for business; and among other things done a collection was taken to buy "Sacred Lutes" for the use of the Lecture Room.

Friday 23. [January 23, 1863]

The "Banner" was ready to mail early today so I left the *sawing* books to some of the others and set-to to mail it. I had a piece of "poetry" in this issue styled "The Banner over us," which I also *set up*. This afternoon, my *mailing* being done before dinner, Jabez went with Sallie and myself, in the rockaway, to our "plantation[.]" The road was less good than I expected being much cut up and I concluded it to be *five* instead of *four* miles out there. At this season there are few attractions there and the *house* is a mere *log cabin*, out of repair. There is a good orchard which at the proper season might be attractive.—We think that some one is *depredating* on our wood, as there is no one living there to take care of the place. We are somewhat troubled to know what to do with our "*Elephant*[.]" It was so late when we started, that we had very little time to look around, and it was after dark when we got back home.—

* SPR's "Childhood" appeared in the *Baptist Banner*, Jan. 17, 1863.

Sat 24. [January 24, 1863]

We rec^d over $100 worth of Writing Paper to-day from So. Carolina but I was not at well pleased with the lot as I expected to be from the *sample.*—Singing was at our house tonight, Mr Root being away.—

Sunday 25. [January 25, 1863]

It was warm and Spring-like today—the winter is fast passing away and *as yet* our foes have not done any of the tremendous things that they were going to do, and unless they do them quickly I hope their opportunity will have passed away forever. I have strong hopes that before the Spring ends this dreadful war will have virtually ended, and the *white man* be again free and not the niggers.—Dr B. preached this morning from the words "The Name of our Lord is a strong tower; the righteous run into it and are safe." Our singing went off very well, I think. In Mr Roots absence Jabez sang tenor for us.—There is a good deal of Small Pox and Scarlet Fever now in Atlanta. God protect us and keep us from the "pestilence that walketh in darkness" as well as "the arrow that flieth by day," and "the destruction that wasteth at noonday."—Tonight when we went to church we found it all dark and *no gas* to be had. After some delay a few candles were procured and "darkness being made visible" Dr B. preached from the text "Knock, and it shall be opened"[;] we had quite a good audience.—We made several balks in our singing owing to Mrs West's inattention and deafness.—Last night Irene woke at one o'clock with *croupy* symptoms and breathed with difficulty. We put a snuff and tallow plaster on her chest and rubbed her throat with "Bone Linament" and it eased her directly and she went off quietly to sleep.—

Monday 26. [January 26, 1863]

Our next neighbor, Crankshaw, lost their son today by Scarlet Fever after four days illness, and their little "Maggie" is taken sick of the same dreadful complaint. We feel quite anxious lest it come into our *fold.* We have hung Asafetida-bags around the children's necks as haply it may do some good.* My feelings were inexpressibly touched by what our little boy Arthur said to his Mother as she put him to bed tonight: knowing that Johnnie Crankshaw had died and hearing us talk about our children taking it, he asked "Mama, are you going to bury us where you did little Alice?" Fat, rosy, and full of frolic, he seemed to be taking it for granted

---

* Asafetida is the gum of plants in the carrot family. During this period, it was a folk medicine that was believed to have properties that protected people against disease.

that he was soon to die and be buried and it didn't seem to terrify or trouble him much. I could not sleep much tonight for some reason or other—

Tuesday 27. [January 27, 1863]

I obtained some Belladonna today from Dr Cleveland as a preventive to Scarlet Fever tho' he says it is not Scarlet Fever but a bad form of sore throat with a rash, which, he says, he has treated successfully in all cases, with Belladonna and *apis*.* Tonight we are having a regular *Snow Storm.*—We see from the Telegraph that James and Mollie [Van Valkenburg] have lost their little daughter "Mamie" that they thot so much of, as she was their only girl.—†

Wed 28. [January 28, 1863]

This morning the face of Nature was white with Snow, some two inches deep where it did not melt. Having *sawed* enough books for the Sewers this morning, I took the Banner Mail Books up to the house and wrote up in the afternoon. No meeting at night.—

Sat 31. [January 31, 1863]

We sang at Mrs Wests tonight, as Mr Root has not got back as he was expected to do. The prospect is not fair tho' for church service tomorrow, as it looks like rain.—We are brought in safety, through War and Pestilence, to the close of another month: the next will probably witness more scenes of blood and carnage, the desperate efforts of our foe.

Sunday 1. [February 1, 1863]

Sure enough, to-day came in wet and dismal. Nevertheless, we went to church through the rain and Mrs West also went and got her white stockings dirtied. Dr Sehon Methodist refugee from Nashville, preached for us from the words of Jacob "Surely, God is in this place, and I knew it not." Considering the inclement weather our congregation was pretty good. Dr Baird, a Presbyterian, is to preach tonight in our church if the weather allows. Dr Brantly is in Augusta.—The rain continued so that we had no

---

* Belladonna is a form of poison derived from the nightshade plant. Its flowers and berries yield atropine. Apis or Apis mellifica is a preparation made of mashed bee stingers or whole bees used to treat skin complaints.

† Mary F. Van Valkenburg, daughter of SVVR's brother, James, and his wife, Mary, was two or three years old in 1863. James and Mary Van Valkenburg also had three sons: Charles M., Albert C., and James E. (Eighth Census of the United States [1860], microcopy 653, Bibb County).

service at night I employed myself in the afternoon in writing a piece for the Banner on "The Sabbath" three letter pages.—

Wed 4. [February 4, 1863]

We are having Winter now in earnest; another snow storm came in Monday night after a pleasant *day* and tonight it is cold indeed. I have been at home all the afternoon writing up my Mail Books, Book *sawing* having given out for a time.—I have also been adding up our Whitehall Sales for 1862 and find the amount $45,250^{00} mostly cash only $1750 of it credit and most of that has been paid already.—Stella has sent off her Water Doctor and called in an old school practitioner again. She is very far gone we all think though she don't seem to realize it. Poor Jabez has a hard time of it with his sick wives: he has not enjoyed the married state much.

Sat 7. [February 7, 1863]

This has been a very disagreeable week as far as *weather* can render time disagreeable; snow and slush, cold and wet all the time.—Mr Root having returned, we went to his house to sing tonight.

Sunday 8. [February 8, 1863]

The snow still covers the ground except in thawed spots, and the way to and from church lay through mud and water or half-thawed snow and ice. Dr B preached from the text Psalms 1:1. "Blessed is the man &c[.]" We are daily looking for an attack by the Federals upon either Charleston or Savannah, or both. Our little fleet at the former place recently made a sortie upon the blockaders and succeeded in destroying several of their vessels and driving the rest away, so that, for a time at least, the port of Charleston was opened. Our victorious little fleet returned in triumph to the city.* This afternoon, a doctor called at our house with a little boy to take *matter* from and re-vaccinated myself and the children.† Sallie made out she could not pull her sleeve up far enough. Dr Raborg, was the man's name I have since learned.—We had a dark and dirty trudge to church at night and being but a small audience we sat down stairs to sing.—

* On Feb. 7, 1863, three blockade-runners evaded Union gunboats to arrive safely in Charleston's harbor (E. B. Long, *The Civil War Day by Day: An Almanac* [Garden City, N.Y.: Doubleday, 1971], 319).

† Because of ongoing fears of smallpox and the need to inoculate citizens, doctors in Atlanta periodically sent out medical officers to find healthy people from whom to collect vaccine material (Jack D. Welsh, *Two Confederate Hospitals and Their Patients: Atlanta to Opelika* [Macon: Mercer University Press, 2005], 31).

Monday 9. [February 9, 1863]

I went to the store after supper tonight to send off some orders that Jabe had not time to do.—

Tuesday 10. [February 10, 1863]

Cousin Mary Brown arrived at two o'clock this morning with her baby, Miss Isabel. Jabez had sent for her to come and see Stella before she dies, as she soon must. Mary looks about as of old but it seems strange to see her have *a baby*—and a fine, bouncing baby too—quite pretty. From Mary's account she is not living on the fat of the land in Augusta, Mr Brown is in the service and she has not seen him for five months.—

Wed 11. [February 11, 1863]

We have had quite a Spring day and the snow has disappeared before the genial beams and the mud has dried. I have now advanced in the Binder's trade from *sawing* to *covering*, from covering to *rounding* and rounding to *glueing*!—Tonight I had to do the singing as Mr Root is again away.

Sat 14. [February 14, 1863]

Valentines are all gone except cheap and comic. I went to Mrs Wests to sing tonight; Sallie did not go as Stella was so low that she was expected to die at any time. Our Grocery has done a good business this week having taken in over $1000.—

Sunday 15. [February 15, 1863]

Stella is yet living and Sallie did not go out this morning.—Dr B. preached from Ps 50:15. "Call upon me in the day of trouble—I will deliver thee."—The vaccinations of last Sunday don't seem as though they will any of them "take."—At 3¼ oclock this afternoon we received the sad intelligence that Stella was dead. Her spirit took its flight at that hour as nearly as they could tell, for she died so quietly that it was not known by those in the room at what moment the soul departed. Jabez is left again alone and a mourner, for whatever she was to *us*, she was kind and loving to him and he grieves for her deeply.—Mrs West came and sat up with me and Mary and Sallie. The rain fell in torrents nearly all night I wrote to father tonight at Jabe's desire, and proposed that he should come up and take charge of our farm.—

Monday 16. [February 16, 1863]

The day has been very inclement and more so during the afternoon. At four o'clock we listened to the funeral services of the departed, and attended her remains to their last resting place. She was buried by the side of Sarah—Jabe's first wife.—The following notice was put in the City papers "Died, in this City, on Sunday the 15th inst[ant] of Consumption, *Stella Wheeler Richards*, wife of J. J. Richards, aged 24 years."—It was difficult to realize that she was not *ten years* older than she was.—

Tuesday 17. [February 17, 1863]
    I did not go to the Office at all today as there was so much to be done in the store in the way of answering letters sending of orders, Bundles &c.

Wed 18. [February 18, 1863]
    Inclement weather prevented our meeting again.—

Sunday 22. [February 22, 1863]
    Last Friday was as clear and beautiful a day as could be desired but it was of short duration, and yesterday and today are again cloudy and raining at times.—Dr B. preached this morning from the words in Prov 9:12.—Our singing went very well I thought.—The choir met at our room last night, stormy as it was.—At night Dr B. preached from the words "There shall be no night there"—Neither literally or figuratively.—The voluntary we sang happened to be peculiarly apropos "Jerusalem my glorious home."—

Monday 23. [February 23, 1863]
    I trimmed 30 reams of Note Paper at the Bindery this morning for Mr/s J. J. Richards & Co.—This afternoon I did not go to the office at all making in all three days and two afternoons I have been absent.—Cash Sales in the Store last month were $6773.80, being, I think the largest months sales yet. *Some* of our profits are enormous truly; today Jabez sold a bill of Pens & Holders for $28. which cost originally about 75¢!— But as a general thing our stock sells lower in proportion than any other kind of goods. For *books* in general we only get *double* former prices.— We rec^d a letter from Father yesterday. He says he cannot go to farming at present. I bought a pound of Coffee today at 3.50 tho' it sells at $4.00—

Sat 28. [February 28, 1863]
    It has rained all day, this last day of the month. February came in rainy and has been a wet and disagreeable time all through with an occasional fair day now and then. If this had been Leap Year there would have been *five Sundays* in February. I have worked hard today at the trimming-machine with Mr Flynn.—We have bought another lot this

week, from Marshall Clark with a school-house upon it price $2500.—We bought it partly with reference to father's coming here to teach school next winter. It will make a very good and desirable dwelling-house lot, tho' being quite rolling would be expensive to improve properly.—We have had some trouble this week with our servants Jabez especially as his *crew* has proved mutinous and dishonest—"Tiny" his last and *dearest* girl has stolen, first, about $150 from him and receiving no punishment she next stole about the same amount from Dr Coyle! The money has been mostly recovered. Harvey and Sally have been outrageously impudent as well as dishonest and *Ellen* seems to have taken a spool of thread from her mistress' drawer and given it to Sally,—and I therefore had to whip her for that and other misdemeanors—

Sunday 1. [March 1, 1863]

The month has come in bright and pleasant, and it is pleasant to the eyes to behold the sun.—Dr B's discourse this morning was from the text "Fight the good fight of faith."—Mr Root being absent the singing fell to my charge—We went prepared at night to light up the church with candles as *gas* had given out; but we found the lights burning though so dimly that fearing they would go out we lighted up our *tallows*; but did not long need them as the gas revived.

Tuesday 3. [March 3, 1863]

"There's another milestone" on the road of life. I am today thirtynine years old. The years now fly fast.

Wed 4. [March 4, 1863]

I have today taken an important step, and one that I am afraid I shall repent. Wishing to be at liberty to spend my time and labor in our business and not feeling secure of exemption in my present employ, I have obtained *a substitute*, one John D. Kugler of Carroll Co, a man 46 years old for whom *we* paid 2500\frac{00}{}$[.]* I had yesterday engaged one who was 53 years old who I much preferred on account of his greater age but I was disappointed in getting him. My chief concern now is, lest Congress may extend Conscription beyond 45 years in which event I suppose I should again become liable to serve in the place of my man who would then himself be a conscript.—

---

* J. D. Kugler enlisted in Company A, 64th Regiment, Georgia Volunteer Infantry, Fulton County, Georgia, on Feb. 16, 1863. Five months later, he deserted (Henderson, *Roster*, 6:495–96).

Sat 7. [March 7, 1863]

We have had cold, wet and disagreeable weather this week. Spring has not advanced much as far as nature is concerned. Our foes are threatening our seaboard cities but delaying to attack. Gov Brown has called out the militia to go to the defence of Savannah, said militia consisting only of the *commissioned officers* who were exempted by him from conscription.*— The Lincoln Congress has passed a Conscription Bill which makes every man between the ages of 18 and 45 subject to the call of Lincoln so that they are determined at all events to continue the war, not withstanding the majority of the people are for peace.† O Lord, "how long shall these heathen rage?"—The "Banner" this week contains a poem by "S.P.R." entitled "Jesus Wept" which I concocted in the bindery while *rounding* testaments one afternoon. The scope of it is the death and raising of Lazarus.—72 lines.—The account of this event in John 11. has always been to me one of peculiar and touching interest. We sang at night at Bro Roots. Henry and his family have just returned from So. Ca. He is improved somewhat in health. I have been busy enough in the store four days—trade very good. Lead pencils sell at 1.50 apiece—Violin Strings 1.25—Playing Cards of ordinary quality 5.00 per pack. But *books* in general we only get *double* the old price which is not enough *as money is.*—

Sunday 8. [March 8, 1863]

Dr B preached this morning from the words—"Having loved his own He loved them until the end."—It was our Communion Season.—Dr B's discourse at night was a continuation of his sermon of last Sunday night, from the text, "Lord, what will thou have me to do?"

Sat 14. [March 14, 1863]

We sang at the Wests tonight, and Mr Root informed us that today he is 38 years old, just about a year my junior.—On Thursday night the "Mozart Club" met again at Mr Roots and resucitated our old times just *for fun.* Birth has taken a wife since we used to meet, and brought her with him. The rest of our club were not present.—Dr Brantley has gone to Augusta.—

---

* *ADI,* Mar. 6, 1863, reported that the force would "exceed four thousand of as good fighting men as the state contains."

† As the Confederacy had done the previous year, the Union began drafting soldiers in 1863. The Enrollment Act of Mar. 3, 1863, created a quota system by congressional district. If a district failed to make its quota through volunteers, men aged between twenty and forty-five might be drafted (McPherson, *Ordeal,* 384).

Sunday 15. [March 15, 1863]

It is cloudy today and betokens rain again soon.—Dr Crawford of Penfield preached for us this morning from the words "Testifying both to the Jews, and also to the Greeks, repentance towards God and faith towards our Lord Jesus Christ" Acts 20:21.*—It was a very good sermon. Mary [Brown] received a letter today from her husband who is in the army at Charleston. He states that he is hard-worked and fed on *corn bread* alone, at least, that was all he had for his breakfast that time, and the soldiers were much dissatisfied with their fare. It is too bad to work so hard for so poor pay and get nothing fit to eat either.

Tuesday 17. [March 17, 1863]

This afternoon I took Harvey and the necessary tools and went to the Briant house and opened a ditch to let off the water from the basement. The carpenters' work is now progressing and if we could get bricks the house might soon be habitable and comfortable. We had to work hard to get our job done before night; but we finished it and I stopped at Nell's on my way home and she treated me to a piece of a *Shad* that she had dined off of, and sent an invitation to Jabez to breakfast with her and eat another, as Steve had sent her *two* from Augusta. I took some home also.—

Wednesday 18. [March 18, 1863]

At 6 o'clock this morning Jabez proposed to me to walk out about 1½ miles to look at a *lot* of land containing ten acres north west of the city and about ¾ of a mile from the edge of it. Said lot is partly *improved* and was offered for Sale. We came upon an acquaintance who volunteered to show us the place and at the same time said all he could in disparagement of it. We were notwithstanding favorably impressed with our visit and inclined to invest $6500 in the purchase. As it was past our breakfast hour when we got back to town, I went with Jabez to Nell's and partook of her Shad No 2.—We ate with a good appetite after our long long walk, and Nell's Shad soon wasted away to a *shad-ow.*—

Sat. 21. [March 21, 1863]

We had an interview with Mr Thomas in regard to buying his lot the day we visited it but he had *raised his price* to $7000 and we declined the trade. The next day he had concluded to sell it at the first price and upon coming in to the store he found Jabez, Henry and myself with a sample of *tobacco* in our hands, discussing the question of investing our funds in that useful article instead of buying land, and he was thereby induced to lower his

---

* Nathaniel M. Crawford was president of Mercer University (D. B. Ragsdale, *Story of Georgia Baptists*, 2 vols. [Atlanta: Foote and Davies, 1932], 1:118–19).

price to $6250, and we bought it at that price; though in reality we still pay nearly the former price as the place is rented for the year and Mr Thomas retains the rent money, $250. This tho' was the case when he proposed to sell for $6500. The "Thomas Lot" will make a very pleasant Suburban Villa one of these days if properly improved.—We have just sold our "Baker St" lot of ¼ acre for $1000. Jabez bought it from Dr C. B. Parker several years ago for $375. payable in *books*.—We went over to Mrs Wests tonight to sing which makes *four nights* this week that we have sung, or *five* counting Wed' night meeting. On Tuesday night the Mozarts met at Wests and last night Bro Eli Mustin was at our house and we invited the Wests and Mr Root over to have a *sing* for his benefit. *We four are great on sings*. Business continues good and money comes in so fast that we hardly know how to dispose of it to advantage, tho' to be sure, it takes a large portion of it to buy food and clothing in these days of exorbitant prices. Flour is now $75 per barrel and *rice* 25¢ per lb though I was lucky enough today to buy a sack of rice-flour for $20, and another for Jabez. We have lived on Rice and corn for several weeks, *wheat* flour being too dear.—I like a good rice-flour bread made with buttermilk and soda quite as well as flour bread, at least for awhile. But *buttermilk* is one dollar per gallon and *rising*, and *Soda* had gone up from *ten cents* per lb to *four dollars*!

Sunday 22. [March 22, 1863]
Dr Brantley has returned and preached this morning from the text Ezekiel 9:3.4.5.6.—We sang a new "*Anthem*," as Mr Root says, this morning, "Daughter of Zion" page 340 Dulcimer New Edition. He closed his discourse by solemnly asking who of his congregation had the "*mark*" upon them that would protect them in the day of retribution.—As Col. Stone of our city is expecting to go North this week I have just finished a letter to Add. to send by him to Yankee Land. Stone is the agent of a Company of our citizens who have *formed* for the purpose of running the blockade at Charleston with Cotton and mdze. We have some idea of risking a thousand or two in it.*

* Amherst W. Stone, an Atlanta businessman, decided to leave the South in the spring of 1863. Like SPR, Stone feared being drafted into the army. Unlike SPR, Stone was a Unionist. To ensure his safe departure from the Confederacy and earn some money in the process, Stone formed the Wyly-Markham Company and planned to run cotton through the naval blockade, secretly receiving permission from Union authorities to do so. He reached New York but was imprisoned several times over the ensuing months after being erroneously accused of being a Confederate agent. For a complete discussion of Stone's blockade-running plan and his Unionism, see Dyer, *Secret Yankees*, 115–34.

Friday 27. [March 27, 1863]

This is the day appointed by the President for Fasting and Prayer and the 1st and 2nd Baptist Churches united and met at our Church this morning for prayer, and tonight they met at the 1st Church.*—Last night, the *Mozarts* met at our house to sing.—Spring has not come yet, the cold weather still prevails and vegetation is retarded.—Sallie has the desire of her heart gratified in being put in possession of a gold watch! I have bought Mary Brown's watch and chain for her for $100—but as she is not willing to part with it altogether, I have agreed that she may rebuy it when the war is over by paying me the same amount that I give her for it in addition to what it will now cost to repair it, which is $5.00. This time during which she is to have the privilege of redeeming it is limited to *five years from the close of the war*, and it is to be redeemed in gold or silver or their equivalent. Mary is going to Augusta tonight to settle her affairs there and then return to Atlanta for an indefinite period.—The number of the watch is 19388 "L. Perret Muller of Geneva," maker.—We went at night to the first Baptist Church and were charmed with the singing—O.T.L.! Mrs. James Ells, their head singer on the treble, sang in the Voluntary, "Come! ye disconsolate," so *powerfully* and peculiarly, that it reminded me of the *Calliope* that so charmed our ears in this region some time ago!—Mrs West is not perfect but she'll *do* after that.

Sunday 29. [March 29, 1863]

It was raining this morning when we awoke but held up before church time and we had a pretty good congregation. Dr B preached from the words "And He led them forth by the right way" Ps 107:7. and took occasion to show that the word of God teaches that all our steps are ordered by God and yet we are ourselves conscious that we are *free* agents,—and no man was ever yet able to explain this great mystery, and reconcile Gods sovereignty and mans free agency. My contribution "Religion and Soldiers' best Armor" appears in the "Banner" of last week but as the Editor was absent it was badly *murdered* by the printers there being no less than eight errors in it, some of them mortifying blunders.† At night the text was "Unto whom God swore in His wrath that they shall not enter into my rest *because they believed not*" and showed that *unbelief* was the chief

---

* Confederate President Jefferson Davis declared Mar. 27, 1863, a day of "fasting, humiliation, and prayer." In his official proclamation, Davis added that in the past, God "has been graciously pleased to hear our supplications, and to grant abundant exhibitions of His favor to our armies and our people" (*ADI*, Mar. 28, 1863).

† *Baptist Banner*, Mar. 28, 1863.

of sins.—We sang a Voluntary learned the previous night called "Heart, be still."—

Thursday, April 2. [April 2, 1863]

I have been suffering all day with toothache and this afternoon did not go to the store but nursed my tooth at home. Mary Brown came back from Augusta this morning at 6 o'clock and she and Sallie have been busy all day making a coat for Jabe to wear to South Carolina tomorrow morning.

Sat 4. [April 4, 1863]

So far, we have had only real March weather this month. Yesterday was so windy and dusty that it was the most disagreeable day that we have had for a good while. Jabez left yesterday morning for So. Ca. to bring mother back with him next week. I sent off my letter to Addison this week that is *if* Col Stone went as expected. Our Clerk John leaves us tonight to accept a more lucrative office as Manager of a News Paper Agency at this place.

Sunday 5. [April 5, 1863]

I was awakened this morning at 4 o'clock by a knock at the door and upon enquiring what was wanted two Watchmen informed that "Jim and Sally" had been put in the Caboose and I had to fork over one dollar to get Sally out. *Jim* I told them must take care of himself. He is to be Sally's *husband* I believe*—Dr B preached this morning from the words "Their rock is not as our Rock; themselves being the judges."—A collection for the Mission Cause was taken up after the sermon. Our choir gave over $100—$50 of which Mr Root gave. The text tonight was "And thou when thou prayest &c[.]" I liked both of today's sermons very much, and was not sleepy which rather surprised me as I have had rather broken sleep for several nights.—

Sat 11. [April 11, 1863]

The calm into which the country had settled was broken this week by the news that the attack upon Charleston had begun.† On Tuesday last the first movement was made and on Wed 8th ten *Iron clads* steamed into the harbour and the fight began. A terrific cannonading was kept up for

---

* Sally and Jim were slaves owned by JJR. Subject to the same nine o'clock curfew that pertained to all African Americans, free and enslaved, and out and about without a pass, the two were the responsibility of their out-of-town owner. His absence left the responsibility to SPR, whose reference to Jim as Sally's intended "husband" reflected the lack of legal standing for slave marriages.

† Nine U.S. ironclads attacked Fort Sumter on Apr. 7. The USS *Keokuk*, struck ninety times by Confederate fire, sank the next day (Long, *Civil War Day by Day*, 335–36).

several hours until finally the enemy's vessels withdrew several of them injured and the "Keokuk" *sunk,* which was the largest and most formidable of them with two *turrets* from which to hurl death and destruction. Since then they have not renewed the attack, but they will hardly give it up yet.—Tuesday night the *Mozarts* met at Mr Births rooms over our store and had their weekly sing. Last night we met at Mrs Wests but could not sing much as the *she* part of our choir were suffering from colds and unable to sing, especially Mrs. S.P.R.—Business seems to improve as our stock decreases. We have sold about $23,000 in the past three months of this year, and, so far, April promises still greater results.—

Sunday 12. [April 12, 1863]

I went to the office this morning and took out a letter addressed To/ Rev W. Richards which I recognized as in Addison's handwrite and took the liberty to open and peruse. It was written on the 27th ult[imo] in New York and sent via Nassau by private hand and mailed in Charleston on the 10th inst[ant]. We were very glad to hear from them for we have not heard a word since last summer.—Add says they are going about as usual except William who has returned to his old trade of *Lecturer* with some success.* He says his (Will's) *school in B* is not doing much. We are left in the dark as to *where* and *what* this school is. Wm seems to have given up his church in P[rovidence]. Perhaps Cornele is teaching in *Brooklyn* and Kate Rogers is assisting her as Add says a letter to Kate from Miss Bates of Charleston informed them that we were well. Add says William has turned back or over to the views held by the peace-Democrats or Compromise Party, which I am glad to hear.† He speaks hopefully of peace ere long, says he thinks people there are getting tired of war and beginning to wonder how they could ever have run into it so madly.—Addison seems to wish very much to hear from us and I hope has done so ere this by my letter. Dr B's text this morning was John 20:29 "Jesus saith unto him, Thomas, because thou hast seen me thou hast believed; blessed are they

---

* For a time, William Carey Richards served as professor of chemistry at Berkshire Medical College, which may explain SPR's reference to his lecturing. See Rossiter Johnson and John Howard Brown, eds., *The Twentieth Century Biographical Dictionary of Notable Americans,* 10 vols. (Boston: Biographical Society, 1904), 9:90–91.

† Peace Democrats advocated a negotiated end to the Civil War with Southern independence. Their numbers reached a peak about the time Richards wrote this entry but began to decline after the Union victories at Vicksburg and Gettysburg in July 1863.

who have not seen and yet have believed." Mary and Sallie went to Nell's with me this afternoon. Dr B preached tonight from Luke 7:34 "A Friend of publicans and sinners."

Sat 18. [April 18, 1863]

Last night the *Mozarts* met at Mr Roots to sing but only our Baptist Choir quartette were on hand. Mr Root had invited several friends to hear the singing, but they were only desirous of hearing their own voices, and paid no more attention to our music than if we had been hired musicians employed to make music to drown their voices as they gabbled. Tonight our Choir again met there for our usual singing practise. Last Thursday night according to promise I went to the Episcopal Church to sing base at Mrs Robinsons request upon the occasion of Bishop Elliotts preaching there. Although their music was not familiar to me I got along pretty well. The text of the Bishop was taken from the Psalms—*Prayer Book Version*—"I am so fast in prison that I cannot go forth." I would much rather hear one of Dr Brantleys sermons than such as this.—This afternoon Jabez returned bringing Mother and a lot of crippled and infirm negroes belonging to Steve Whitehead's household. Father remained behind awhile when he too is coming up to stay.

Sunday 19. [April 19, 1863]

The usual services in our church this morning but at night it rained and our choir sat down stairs but notwithstanding, the audience was fair.

Monday 20. [April 20, 1863]

Today we bought $6000 worth of Confederate Bonds bearing 8% interest.—*

Sat 25. [April 25, 1863]

Mr Root and Dr Brantley having both gone to the Baptist Convention at Griffin and in consequence there being no service in our church tomorrow we did not have any choir practise tonight.† We have enjoyed pleasant Spring weather this week and the woods are turning green fast.—

---

* The Confederate Congress passed a series of acts, beginning with that of Feb. 28, 1861, selling bonds to finance the war at rates of return ranging from around 4 percent to 8 percent (Douglas B. Ball, *Financial Failure and Confederate Defeat* [Urbana: University of Illinois Press, 1991], 144–48).

† At its 1863 meeting in Griffin, the Georgia Baptist Convention focused on efforts to minister to soldiers in the Confederate armies (*History of the Baptist Denomination in Georgia* [Atlanta: Harrison, 1881], 234).

Sunday 26. [April 26, 1863]

At Mr Roots request I went to School this morning to hear his class recite their lesson in Romans. I told them I had some intention to join the class myself as a scholar and they cordially invited me to do so!—We went to hear Dr Baird at the Central Pres Church. They have a new *crack* choir now that is going to take the palm for fine music, it is expected—They can at least make more noise than we can, and today sang pretty well.—In the afternoon we went to Epis. Church and I was requested to sit in the choir, which I did. At night, Sallie went with the Wests to Pres. Church again, but I did not feel inclined to go, having been out twice. My wife was so bewitched by the music that she could not think of staying away.—

Sat 2. [May 2, 1863]

Have been somewhat exercised in mind today in reference to buying a family of negroes, which we have just seen for the first time. Jabez has decided to buy a similar family viz "George"—"Clementina" his wife, and "John" their child, ages, *probably* 35. 30. & 3. tho called 30. 22. & 3! Price $5000.—As more force is needed on the farm I concluded to buy the other family, viz "Joe" "Caroline" and "Mandy"—ages *probably* 36 21 & 3 though Joe is *called* 30—I think him *at least* 35. Price $4250. a cheaper lot than the other I think.—Caroline we expect to keep for our house if she proves to be a good servant but Joe will be out on the farm.—I was very doubtful as to the advisability of investing in this property but Father and Jabez were so much in favor of it that I gave in, hoping that it may prove for the best. The negroes were very glad to be bought by us. George and Joe are stout healthy "boys" and will probably do good service on the farm *if properly managed.* This afternoon we had a hunt after "John" who while his parents were gone after their *effects* strayed off to find them and it was not until after more than an hours search that he was found out beyond the town line in the woods having cried until he could cry no more.—Caroline says "Mandy" was three years old last January[.] Father came up on Wed' last and has been out twice to the farm looking around. The season is so far advanced that I am afraid they will not be able to clear expenses this year.—Their working force will be four regular hands viz George, Joe "Clem" and Harvey with occasional help from Sally and perhaps Caroline—saying nothing of "Old Dinah," crippled "Laura" "Medy" &c—They *ought* to make things stand around.—We bought *Ellen* just at the right time; she would sell now readily for $2000 being a very "likely nigger"—say 14 years old. I must make out "descriptive lists" of my darkies and record in my journal for future reference.—It is said, and I think with truth that when we come to a successful end to this war that negroes will command very high prices as there will be so much demand for labor to raise cotton and a great many will have been taken away by the Yankees. Last night Jabe came to our room and we got into a rather warm contention about not having moved from his house, and about Stella's conduct and feelings toward us. We did not come to blows however and parted amicably. I wish we had managed to get another house a year or more ago, as it would have been better and more pleasant for all of us and we should have had better thoughts of the departed.

Sunday 3. [May 3, 1863]

A real *April day*, rain and shine alternating. Dr B preached this morning from Song of Solomon 2:12 "For lo! The winter is past &c" being a sermon on the lessons from the season. Tonight his text was II Peter 1:4. The precious promises of the Gospel[.] Arthur and Isham went off and staid all the afternoon at the car shed "to see the cars come in" and we were rather anxious about them, and when they at last got home I gave them both a switching on their sitting down part, as they had been told before not to go there.

Sat 9. [May 9, 1863]

We have had several days of quite cool weather not at all seasonable. On Thursday we sent Caroline to the farm to help in getting the seed in the ground but she came back at night sick and has been abed ever since. John, the little runaway, is also sick with Pneumonia.—The Yankees have made another attempt to get to Richmond and have again been driven back with loss. We have also sustained a loss in the left arm of Gen "Stonewall" Jackson which having been shattered in the fight was amputated below the shoulder. This is styled the Battle of Chancellorsville*—I went to the railroad the other day and saw a batch of Yankee prisoners being part of a cavalry force of 1600 men that had made a descent upon Rome last Sunday and been *surrounded* by 600 of our men under Gen

---

* At the Battle of Chancellorsville, Virginia, May 2–4, 1863, Confederate troops were victorious but suffered the loss of Stonewall Jackson, who was struck by friendly fire. Although he survived the amputation of his arm, pneumonia later set in, and he died on May 10 (Herman Hattaway and Archer Jones, *How the North Won: A Military History of the Civil War* [Urbana: University of Illinois Press, 1983], 379–82).

Forrest and captured!* Our city was quite excited last Sunday and Monday by a telegram that this force had taken Rome and would be in Atlanta soon, which proved to be the truth but they were *brought* here instead of coming of their own goodwill.—I trust that this is the only way we shall see the rascals here while the war continues.—

Sunday 10. [May 10, 1863]

We met to sing last night at Mrs Wests Mr & Mrs Craig assisting us in Mr Root's absence. Dr Baird preached for us this morning from the "Barren Figtree" text. I went to S.S. and heard Mr Roots class again. Dr Brantley told me that he had promised the young ladies whom I used to teach that I would again take charge of that class, but this morning Dr Massey was with them I believe.—Father will preach tonight.

Tues 12. [May 12, 1863]

We went tonight to Mr Craigs to sing. The sad tidings has come that Gen T. J. Jackson, the Christian hero, has been called to lay aside forever the weapons of earthly warfare both temporal and spiritual, and *go up higher*. This is gain indeed to him but a sad loss to us and to the country in her time of need. "No sound shall awake him to glory again."†

Sat 16. [May 16, 1863]

We have bought another negro "boy" this week named "Frank" for $2125[,] *26 years old* or more.—Sallie and I have concluded to rent Jabez's house and take boarders to defray the expense. We are to pay one hundred dollars a month for it!—Our little nigger "Mandy" has the *measles* we find but all of our children have had it so we don't fear for them. We have sent the little darkie John to the farm as it is not safe for him to have the measles while sick with Pneumonia.—We went to Mr Roots tonight to sing. They have this evening returned from Charleston.—Dr Brantly and family also came today from Augusta. A letter from Harriet tells us that they have been called upon to give up their son '*Gus* the favorite son who died in Virginia in the hospital of sickness. She also tells us that George,

---

* On May 3, near Rome, Georgia, 1,466 federal soldiers under Colonel Abel Streight surrendered to Nathan Bedford Forrest, who had just 600 men but who convinced the Federals that he had a much larger force. Another 200 U.S. soldiers were later captured (Jack Hurst, *Nathan Bedford Forrest: A Biography* [New York: Knopf, 1993], 123–24). Southern newspapers loved the story; see *ASC*, May 8, 1863.

† SPR is quoting from "The Grave of Bonaparte," a traditional song by an unknown author.

Sallies brother was wounded in the arm at the late battle of Chancellorsville*—Mary Brown has had a falling out with Jabe and has "left his *board*" (but retains his *bed*) and came to live with us and takes our young ones *to task* every morning, which they needed some one to do very much. Irene cannot read yet and Arthur only just has learned the alphabet. I have just given the children a set of "The Schoolfellow" in *seven* volumes green and gold muslin binding which they are very proud of, Dora especially— Dora *begins* to write tolerably well, and I hope will learn fast now she has a teacher. It is a pity I think that Annie should be taken off to the country when she ought to be studying with her aunt Mary.†—If we rent this large house we shall have a pleasant home to invite our *big sister* in Americus &c. They are coming to visit us in July next—

Sunday 17. [May 17, 1863]

I went to S.S. this morning to enter upon my duties as teacher, but Dr Massey was there and don't seem to be going to quit so I had nothing to do and did not stay long.— Dr B's subject this morning was "The Friend that sticketh closer than a brother." Tonight his text was "I will bless the Lord at all times &c[.]" Today the ordinance of the Lord's Supper was celebrated.

Tuesday 19. [May 19, 1863]

The Mozarts met tonight at Mr Roots and he broached a bottle of "Catawba" for our refreshment, but it was not very popular with the guests, and I for one like the sweet wines better.

Thursday 21. [May 21, 1863]

Henry and Ellie were blessed(?) this morning at two o'clock by the birth of a daughter whom they have named *Kate*.

Sat 23. [May 23, 1863]

Arthur's birthday—5 years old, and as I had promised him a *Slate* as soon as he knew all his letters and the *Governess* states that he has

---

* Augustus Taylor was one of seven children of Seth K. Taylor and a stepson of Harriet Van Valkenburg Taylor (William Bailey Williford, *Americus through the Years: The Story of a Georgia Town and Its People, 1832–1875* [Atlanta: Cherokee, 1975], 249).

† In the spring of 1863, SPR and SVVR moved into JJR's house and hired Mary Hathaway Brown to serve as teacher to their children. SPR expressed regret that Annie Richards, JJR's older daughter with his first wife, Sarah, was not allowed to remain in Atlanta, live with his household, and be tutored by her maternal aunt, Brown.

fulfilled the terms I gave him the slate, and a colored pencil for a birthday gift!—The War news from the West is rather gloomy, our forces in and around the gallant little city Vicksburg being closely besieged by the enemy in great force*—Pussy died this week, probably poisoned by eating rats killed by arsenic—a warning to future cats and to cats masters and mistresses who have a regard for their welfare—Pussy leaves two young kittens to mourn their irreparable loss. I have spent an hour and half each morning this week in working in *our garden* and find its culture has been sadly neglected the earth being as hard as a beaten road in many parts of it.—We have had several treats of strawberries though from it this week. Last week I gave *two dollars* in books for one quart of them!—Since the war commenced we have felt more fully our need of an iron safe to keep our money and papers in so we have bought one for $300 just four times the old price.—

Sunday 24. [May 24, 1863]

Mr Root being away again I was called upon to teach his class of ten young ladies and I had to guess at the lesson and to my chagrin guessed the one that the class had gone over so I had to essay the task unprepared and was conscious of performing it rather imperfectly. It was announced that Dr B would today deliver a discourse on the life and death of Gen Jackson the Christian Hero. As Mr Craig was sick and we were in want of a tenor Mr West brot to our house last night a[n] Englishman named Dickinson of whose singing abilities he has been talking for some time past, so that we thought ourselves fixed finely. But our satisfaction was dispelled as soon as we tried the first tune, for our crack tenor could not sing even tolerably, and lest he should spoil the singing on this day in church Mr West had to tell him that he was too unaccustomed to our musical notation and had better not sing. Jabez took his place and we got along pretty well. The Church was crowded and the discourse was a good one from the words of the great Apostle "I have fought a good fight &c"—Two quarts of green peas in shells $1.

Sat 30. [May 30, 1863]

The weather today has been showery and shiny alternately. Thursday night we had a continual and abundant rain, and this morning I was busy in the garden getting out beets and tomatoes.—The war news this week

---

* Vicksburg, Mississippi, became a military focal point of the war in the West. Union forces under General Ulysses S. Grant attempted to take the city by frontal assaults on May 19 and 22. Vicksburg held out until July 3, when the city surrendered after a long siege (Hattaway and Jones, *How the North Won*, 395).

from the West is that the enemy in force had six times assaulted the defenses of Vicksburg and as often had been repulsed with terrible slaughter and the stench of their unburied dead, was poisoning the air.—Hon C L Vallandigham of Ohio has been arrested by the Abolition Government and sentenced to exile and he has come South for refuge. Opposition to the war policy of Lincoln and freedom of speech with reference thereto were his offences.*—We went to Mrs West's tonight to sing—Mr Root is still away.—

Sunday 31. [May 31, 1863]

Mr Root got home this morning so I did not have the trouble or the pleasure of teaching his girls again.—Dr B preached this morning from the words "My Yoke is easy and my burden is light."

Monday 1. [June 1, 1863]

Today the old folks and Jabes family moved out to the farm or "Pleasant Hill" as father has named it. So we are left in sole possession of the house.—Our "boy" Frank came in with Jabez and Harvey to drive out their cows but was taken ill with *measles* I believe, and was left behind the next day as a storm portended and he feared to get wet in going out.

Sat. 6. [June 6, 1863]

We have had a great deal of rain lately, somewhat it is thought to the detriment of the wheat crop as it is about harvest time.—Vicksburg still holds out though closely invested on every side, and we hope that the enemy will not be able to take it but will be forced to raise the siege and depart. Our forces at Port Hudson below Vicksburg have signally repulsed an attack made on that strong hold this week.—Yesterday I gave ten dollars for five fowls intending to keep them to lay eggs for us.—We moved into the room that Jabez used to occupy and made a parlour of our old room—Jabez has been at the farm all the week and just came in this afternoon. I don't expect I shall see much of him this summer.

Sunday 7. [June 7, 1863]

Mr Root did not get home as expected and as usual I went to hear his class recite. Dr B preached from the words "If any man love not the Lord

---

* Clement L. Vallandigham of Ohio became the most visible and vocal Peace Democrat. After issuing warnings that treasonable speech would not be allowed, General Ambrose E. Burnside ordered Vallandigham's arrest. He was quickly tried by a military court, found guilty, and sentenced to imprisonment for the war's duration. President Lincoln changed the sentence to banishment behind Confederate lines (McPherson, *Ordeal*, 374–77).

Jesus Christ, let him be Anathema Maranatha[.]" At night we were all highly indignant at seeing Mr. Gaskill go up into the pulpit and then we understood that Dr Brantley was to preach at the First Church.—

Sat 13. [June 13, 1863]

We have had abundance of rain this week *too* much, as far as our short sight can see.—Yesterday afternoon I went with Sallie to the Episcopal Church to try to repair some defects in their Melodeon, at Mrs Robinsons request. I took it all to pieces and found it in a very bad way, similar to that of Jabe's melodeon that I repaired several years ago. The rubber cloth in the valves had melted and stuck fast, of course silencing the note. Its *lungs* are sound as one might say, but its *bronchial tubes* badly diseased, and there is no remedy but to *recover* the valves with new rubber cloth, which can hardly be obtained now. I worked at it this morning from 5 until 10 o'clock but could not do much good, but if I had new cloth I could make it as good as ever I think.—We have letters from Mary Evans and also from Martha [Van Valkenburg]. They contain the good news of their brother George's conversion. He was severely wounded in the arm and it was feared he would lose either the limb or his life, but it is now hoped that both will be saved and what is of far greater importance, we trust his soul is safe.—In war matters, things seem to be quite uncertain. The siege of Vicksburg still continues, and both sides *seem hopeful*! The fall thereof would cast a gloom over our whole confederacy, and be the cause of great rejoicing to our enemies. They would rejoice because they think it would shorten the war, but *we* know that it would only prolong it.—Business has not been as good this week as heretofore. We have had fifteen thousand bricks hauled to the Briant House. They cost $30 per— and $4 per—for hauling!

Sunday 14. [June 14, 1863]

Dr B preached this morning from the text II Cor 5:1 "For we know that if this earthly house &c[.]" Tonight he is to preach about the "rich in good works."—When we arrived at church tonight we found it all in darkness the gas being deranged in some way, and it was some minutes before its illuminating power could be induced to return.—

Sat 20. [June 20, 1863]

"The situation" at Vicksburg seems to remain the same; at least we hear of no change there. Grant the Yankee General seems to be still fortifying his position and digging trenches and mines to take the place if possible and what our forces are doing we cant learn, but hope they are not idle or careless—We have the news of a Confederate victory at Winchester Virga over the army of Milroy in which his army of 7000 was taken prisoners with a large quantity of munitions of War, stores &c—*

Sunday 21 [June 21, 1863]

Dr B took for his text this morning the words "Thy Word is truth"— Last Monday night, I omitted to state, we went to Mr Craig's to see David Craig and his wife who were here on a visit from Macon, and Tuesday night James Craig and his wife brought Mrs David Craig to our house to singing. Tomorrow we expect Mr and Mrs Huston a gentleman and lady to board with us at $150 per month, what seems to be a high price but little enough when we take into consideration the high price of provisions, rent &c. A heavy rain fell this afternoon and Sallie did not feel very well and did not go to church tonight. I was very sleepy tonight.—Dr B preached from the words "What is your life &c?" in reference to the death of a young lad who was a clerk at Root's. I wrote today to George Van V to express my joy at hearing that he had become a *Christian* soldier.

Monday 22. [June 22, 1863]

Simms set in to do the Mason work at the Briant place this morning.— Our expected boarders disappointed us having made arrangements to remain where they now are.—I got a letter from the office tonight or today rather which had a Yankee look, and it proved to be as I expected from Mary Add. They had received my last letter three days before the date of theirs which was April 24. It was a long letter and *intensely* Southern. She don't acknowledge herself a Northerner and holds the War party of the North in *utter detestation*! Pretty good for a *Providence* girl! From what she says William is a *War* man still though opposed to the Abolition administration. He says *we rebels* must be whipped and brought back into the Union! He had better come and help do it I think. Their address is still

---

* After frontal assaults failed at Vicksburg the previous month, General Ulysses S. Grant had his men dig tunnels in an attempt to use mines to blow holes in the Confederate lines. The Second Battle of Winchester, on June 14, 1863, began Robert E. Lee's campaign that ended in the Battle of Gettysburg. General Richard Ewell, who replaced Stonewall Jackson in command of the 2nd Corps, surprised and trounced Union forces under Robert Milroy in a victory that brought four thousand prisoners along with several dozen artillery pieces and hundreds of wagons (David S. Heidler and Jeanne T. Heidler, eds., *Encyclopedia of the American Civil War: A Political, Social, and Military History*, 5 vols. [Santa Barbara, Calif.: ABC-CLIO, 2000], 4:2131–32).

Clinton Hall Astor Place N.Y.C. and she says write them and enclose an envelope addressed "John Malcolm Esq Nassau, New Prov."

Sat 27. [June 27, 1863]

Jabez came in this morning and went with me to look at some cows at Mr Wells'. We bought one each. His cost $200 and mine, an old cow, but one likely to give us more milk, I got for $160. I bought 30 reams of Blue Note Paper today for $990. Our choir met at our house tonight and I read Mary Add's letter to the singers. Mr Root says tell Addison to send him—via Nassau to Joseph Atkinson of that place, one of his best pictures, and he will give him $500 in *Confed.*—We have sold out the Grocery Store to Dr Calhoun & Co who are to take possession and pay us the money next week. Vicksburg still holds out but is still closely besieged.—

Sunday 28. [June 28, 1863]

Dr B preached in the morning but at night the pulpit was filled by a Rev Tovel of Nashville who after being imprisoned there for seven months was sent South at a few hours notice quite destitute. His offence was, denouncing the murderers of an old man who was killed by Fed. soldiers in his own house, and at whose funeral he was officiating.

Tuesday 30. [June 30, 1863]

The *Mozarts* met tonight at Mrs Holbrooks house, for their usual singing.—

FIVE

July 1863 to December 1863

> "THE ABOLITIONISTS ARE DETERMINED TO
> PERSECUTE THE SOUTH TO THE BITTER END."

The optimism that Sam Richards expressed in the first half of 1863 soon disappeared, replaced by feelings of pervasive gloom. After learning that on October 17, Abraham Lincoln had called for an additional three hundred thousand volunteers to fight what Northerners called the "Rebellion," he wrote grimly, "The Abolitionists are determined to persecute the South to the bitter end."[1] Military disappointments, tensions and illnesses within his extended family, acts of "insubordination" by slaves, and new reports about the Unionism of his brother, William, left Sam Richards with little to cheer about. Along with many others in the South, he felt increasing anger toward the Confederate government, complaining about high taxes, impressment of goods, and the closure of the loopholes that kept him, along with his brother, Jabez, and others, out of military service.

Confederate losses at Vicksburg and Gettysburg preoccupied white Southerners, including Sam Richards. Richards took solace only from knowing that the Vicksburg campaign had been "dearly bought by the Yankees" in both money and lives. That fall, Confederate general John Pemberton appeared in Atlanta, the guest of Richards's friend, Sidney Root. Many Southerners regarded Pemberton as a disgrace for having surrendered Vicksburg to General Grant and speculated that this native Northerner had intentionally given up the fight. Pemberton hoped that a court of inquiry would exonerate him of the charges, but no such hearing ever took place. Root defended Pemberton. Richards suggested only that by surrendering on July 4, Pemberton received more favorable terms, since the Yankees wanted a victory on that day for symbolic purposes.[2]

The relentlessness of military campaigns saddened and depressed Richards. No doubt basing his interpretation on local newspaper reports, Richards first believed that Robert E. Lee's army had prevailed at Gettysburg in July 1863 and had taken forty thousand prisoners. Then he admitted that "further accounts seem to modify the first." The one bright spot on the military front came in September 1863, when Confederates defeated federal forces at Chickamauga, yet even this welcome news failed to cheer Richards up, for he admitted, "Every victory as well as every defeat, brings sorrow and distress to many hearts." The battle, which brought more soldiers to Atlanta's hospitals, also touched Richards in a more personal way. Occurring as it did in Northwest Georgia, the Battle of Chickamauga reminded Richards that an invading Yankee army was turning its attention toward the prime military target of Atlanta.[3]

In 1863, the Confederate government became an increasing presence in Sam Richards's life. President Jefferson Davis came to Atlanta in October to see about military and civilian affairs in a city whose threat from Northern capture had become a source of grave concern to the Confederate government. He had also come to encourage "harmonious cooperation" among his generals, a matter in which he would not succeed. Sam was surprised one day to open his door and find the president waiting outside. Davis had come to call on Margaret Sumner McLean, who rented a room from the Richardses and was a close friend of both Jefferson Davis and his wife, Varina.[4]

Richards did not give an opinion of Davis as Confederate leader but expressed considerable anger toward the Confederate government, which Richards regarded as oppressive in its efforts to centralize authority. As the war turned against the South, its citizens became increasingly resentful of taxes, impressment of goods needed by the army, and compulsory military service. Richards frequently complained about taxes, noting in one instance that he had to give the government five hundred dollars for gross sales at the store between April 24 and July 1. He also criticized the government's decision to impress "valuable horses" needed by the Army of Tennessee's cavalry, despite the fact that this action did not affect him personally. Like many of his fellow citizens, Richards seemed unwilling to acknowledge that the Confederacy needed a strong central government to create a nation. States had to forfeit some of their sovereignty, and citizens had to be willing to make personal sacrifices. Richards was happy to benefit from wartime profits but quick to raise objections when asked to contribute personally to the war.[5]

The specter of compulsory military service haunted Richards during the latter half of 1863. In the weeks following the twin losses at Gettysburg and Vicksburg, Jefferson Davis called for all able-bodied men ages eighteen to forty-five to report to conscript camps. Even the newspapers expressed confusion as to whether the president's decree applied to those who had already hired substitutes. Richards continued to look for ways to avoid the draft, attempting to shore up his connections to religious publishing by purchasing a partial interest in the *Baptist Banner*.[6]

Sam and Jabez also purchased a newspaper, the *Soldier's Friend*, from A. S. Worrell for five thousand dollars. Worrell remained the paper's corresponding editor and collecting agent. The weekly newspaper, printed above the Richards brothers' store, provided Confederate soldiers with war news, Christian inspiration, and indoctrination about continuing the fight against Yankee oppression. Jabez Richards often asked for contributions to support dissemination of the publication to the Southern armies in the field and to soldiers in hospitals, printing lists of those who did so. The April 14, 1864, issue reported $53.33 in donations from soldiers in the Army of Northern Virginia, an indication of the newspaper's appeal outside the immediate vicinity of Atlanta. Sam did not reveal his source of paper, but with a blockade-runner among his closest friends, many items unavailable to others found their way into his hands.[7]

Articles in the *Soldier's Friend* emphasized soldiers' need to be spiritually devoted and morally and mentally clean. The August 27, 1863, issue of the newspaper contained a list of "Good Resolutions" for soldiers, including keeping "my *person* and *clothes* as clean as practicable" and living "as near to, and be as much like, Christ as I can." The newspaper at times ventured into the realm of politics and military affairs, as on December 10, when it editorialized about the need for Christians to pray for the appearance of another Stonewall Jackson–like general, "a man that has indomitable *will*, inexhaustible *energy*, and ardent *trust* in God." Despite praising General Lee, the article suggested that his failure to pray adequately when planning the 1862 and 1863 invasions of the North had led to Confederate defeat. One 1863 article speculated about whether if the war ended with the abolition of slavery, it would be a sign of divine condemnation for an institution in which generations of white Southerners had believed. The unsigned article concluded that slavery's biblical sanction left no doubt as to its moral correctness and further suggested that if it were abolished, fault would lie with "*deficiencies* of the masters."[8]

As in most years, Sam Richards sat down to write in his diary on the last day of 1863. His mood was doleful, and the cold, wet weather outside did nothing to improve his spirits. Although he was grateful to have a new pair of boots that fit well and would protect him in the winter weather, they had cost him the outlandish sum of seventy-five dollars. Three days earlier, the Confederate Congress had ended any ambiguity over the practice of hiring substitutes by voting to end the practice in all cases, thereby eliminating the major loophole through which Richards had avoided service. He called it "a grand Government Swindle" and wished he were back in England with his wife and children. He concluded, "god save us from evil in the year to come."[9]

Notes

1. SPR diary, Oct. 31, 1863.

2. Ibid., July 11, 1863, Sept. 5, 1863; *ADI*, July 16, 1863; Samuel Carter III, *The Final Fortress: The Campaign for Vicksburg, 1862–1863* (New York: St. Martin's, 1980), 304–5. After his loss at Vicksburg, Pemberton resigned, but he later returned to the army as a lieutenant colonel in the artillery.

3. SPR diary, July 11, 1863, Sept. 25, 1863. *ADI*, July 9, 1863, printed a story about Gettysburg: "In Pennsylvania, the success of General Lee's army, according to the admission of the Northern press, is unprecedented.—Hooker's old army, commanded by his successor, Meade, has been completely demolished, 40,000 of them having surrendered as prisoners of war, while doubtless, many thousands of them have been wounded or slain."

4. SPR diary, Oct. 29, 1863; E. B. Long, *The Civil War Day by Day: An Almanac* (Garden City, N.Y.: Doubleday, 1971), 427; John M. Carroll, ed., *List of Staff Officers of the Confederate States Army* (Bryan, Tex.: Carroll, 1983), 111; Janet B. Hewett, ed. *Roster of Confederate Soldiers*, 16 vols. (Wilmington, N.C.: Broadfoot, 1995–96), 10:520. McLean was the daughter of Edwin V. Sumner, a major general in the U.S. Army, and the wife of Eugene E. McLean, who served as a staff officer to Confederate generals Joseph E. Johnston, Albert Sidney Johnston, and finally P. G. T. Beauregard, achieving the rank of lieutenant colonel. Margaret McLean traveled widely during the war to be with her husband, living in Montgomery, Richmond, and Atlanta, among other places. Her wartime diary was excerpted as "A Northern Woman in the Confederacy," *Harper's Weekly*, Feb. 1914. For Margaret McLean's friendship with the Davises, see Joan E. Cashin, *First Lady of the Confederacy: Varina Davis's Civil War* (Cambridge: Harvard University Press, 2006), 104–5.

5. SPR diary, Aug. 15, 29, 1863; Mary A. DeCredico, *Patriotism for Profit: Georgia's Urban Entrepreneurs and the Confederate War Effort* (Chapel Hill: University of North Carolina Press, 1990), 43. See also Bruce W. Eelman, *Entrepreneurs in the Southern Upcountry: Commercial Culture in Spartanburg, South Carolina, 1845–1880* (Athens: University of Georgia Press, 2008), 113, 127–29.

Assessing the political dynamic in the wartime South, historian George C. Rable concluded, "Most Southerners better understood the sort of government they wished to avoid than the sort they hoped to create" (*The Confederate Republic: A Revolution against Politics* [Chapel Hill: University of North Carolina Press, 1994], 38). Such was the case with Sam Richards.

6. SPR diary, Aug. 21, 1863, Sept. 5, 1863. For SPR's military service, see Janet B. Hewett, ed., *Georgia Confederate Soldiers, 1861–1865*, 4 vols. (Wilmington, N.C.: Broadfoot, 1998), 3:322; *ADI*, July 18, 1863.

7. SPR diary, Aug. 21, 1863; *Soldier's Friend*, Apr. 14, 1864; Rable, *Confederate Republic*, 133.

8. *Soldier's Friend*, Aug. 27, 1863, Dec. 10, 1863.

9. SPR diary, Dec. 31, 1863; Long, *Civil War Day by Day*, 449.

Thursday 2. [July 2, 1863]

"Calhoun, Gaines & Co" paid us today $3491. for our Grocery stock; so that is off our hands.

Sat 4. [July 4, 1863]

The "Glorious Fourth" passed off quietly enough, without a gun or a cracker as far as I could hear. Although, as some of our papers argue, we have as much right to this holiday, or more, than the Yankees, our people seem to take but little interest in it since the *Secession* of the South, being too much engaged in again achieving their independence of a tyranny more hateful far than that under which the Colonies lived before the Old Revolution. The news from Tennessee is not inspiring as they say Gen Bragg is *falling back* before a superior force of the enemy under Gen Rosencranz, As, however some of his soldiers passed through Atlanta today en route for Vicksburg, it may be only the result of a wise policy and not fear of the enemy. If they can drive out Grant and raise the siege of Vicksburg, then will be the time to turn again and attend to Rosencrans in Tenn.* We have had some real hot weather this week Our expenses for provisions this month or rather *last* month amount to $145. as much as half a years outlay before the war.—

---

* In the June–July 1863 Tullahoma Campaign, Union forces under William Rosecrans pushed Confederates led by Braxton Bragg out of Middle Tennessee all to way to Chattanooga, near the border with Georgia (David S. Heidler and Jeanne T. Heidler, eds., *Encyclopedia of the American Civil War: A Political, Social, and Military History*, 5 vols. [Santa Barbara, Calif.: ABC-CLIO, 2000], 4:1980–82).

Sunday 5. [July 5, 1863]

Dr Brantley preached this morning from the words "The hairs of your head are all numbered" his theme being the "Special Providence of God." At night just at church time a shower of rain came up and prevented people going. I went alone from our house and found but few there, but we had a discourse and a young man was baptized, as appointed.—

Sat 11. [July 11, 1863]

We have had bad news this week from Vicksburgh, that strong hold having been compelled to capitulate to the enemy on the 4th inst[ant] the brave garrison being worn out and nearly starving they say. A severe fight has also taken place at Gettysburg in Pennsylvania the first accounts of wh' represented our forces as victorious, and 40,000 prisoners taken! But further accounts seem to modify the first until I am quite uncertain whether we have gained any advantage at all. We hear also that another attack has commenced on Charleston and is now progressing, or was at last accounts. Vicksburg has been dearly bought by the Yankees. Millions of money and thousands of lives has been the price they have paid for it. I was greatly in hopes that we should be able to disappoint their expectation of getting it at all. We have paid this week the first instalment of *Interest* on A/c [account]. Alien Enemies sequestrated by our Govt $177.$\underline{00}$ for one year. We went to Wests to sing tonight. Mr Root has not come home.—

Sunday 12. [July 12, 1863]

Dr B's sermon this morning was from the text "All things work together for the good &c[.]" This was our Communion Season.—

Tues 14. [July 14, 1863]

Harvey brought the carriage in this morning to take us all out to the farm to pick blackberries! We arrived there at 9 o'clock and picked berries until *two*. After dinner we went out again for an hour and towards evening returned to the city with a bushel of berries, and, as we found out soon after, hundreds of *red bugs* in our flesh which tormented us for days. Sallie's *foot-handles* were completely spotted all over and they nearly ran her crazy! On Monday afternoon last at five o'clock we attended a Union Prayermeeting in the City Hall. This meeting has just been started at the suggestion of our church. And surely we need such a meeting in this hour of trial and time of our countrys need. Another of our strong places on the Mississippi has finally been starved out by the enemy—viz Port Hudson.*

* Confederates gave up on holding Port Hudson following Ulysses S. Grant's victory at Vicksburg.

Wed 15. [July 15, 1863]

Mr & Mrs Taylor and Martha [Van Valkenburg] came this afternoon. Martha has got to be a great big girl as tall as Harriet, and quite good looking.—There was a great turn out of the citizens this afternoon to show how large a force could be raised to repel any raid of our enemies. There is a strong probability that they will endeavor to come here this summer. We hear that Gen Lee's army has returned from Pennsylvania and recrossed the Potomac into Virginia.

Sat 18. [July 18, 1863]

This is Irene's birthday—seven years of age—Jeff Davis has called for more soldiers, all up to fortyfive have now to go to war, so that Jabez is now called upon to go or *not to go* by doing something to render him exempt but what that is to be I don't know. I don't suppose a substitute can be obtained now under eight or ten thousand dollars!

Sunday 19. [July 19, 1863]

Rev Mr Teague of La Grange preached for us today as Dr B has gone to that city to preach the Commencement Sermon for a female college there.* Mr Teague's text was this morning "To show the light of the knowledge of the glory of God in the face of Jesus Christ." Mr Root got back this morning, much to our satisfaction at five o'clock in the aft I went over to the First Church to hear an address from Rev Mr Dayton to the Sunday Schools.† Bro. Abbott came and sat by me and asked me to sing with them which I did.

Tuesday 21 [July 21, 1863]

At seven oclock this morning, Harriet, Martha, Sallie, Dora, Jabez and I, with Ellen to carry our dinner, started off to spend the day at the Stone Mountain. A ride of fifteen miles in the cars took us to "Stone Mt." Village, within a short walk of the foot of the *big rock* itself. We reached the top of the rock about nine o'clock very comfortably as the day though warm was cloudy and the ascent gradual and easy most of the way up. The *refreshment saloon* half way up is now deserted and in ruins, also the *Tower* on the tip is nothing but a pile of unsightly stones and lumber

---

* E. B. Teague pastored at LaGrange, Georgia, from 1855 to 1865, when he became president of East Alabama Female College in Tuskegee (*History of the Baptist Denomination in Georgia* [Atlanta: Harrison, 1881], 521–22).

† A. C. Dayton was president of the Baptist Sunday School Union (William Wright Barnes, *The Southern Baptist Convention 1845–1953* [Nashville: Broadman, 1954], 84–85).

"wrecks of the past."—We sat down and took a lunch at eleven oclock and then explored the mountain until *one* when we eat dinner the only drawback to the enjoyment of it being the want of *water*: some Apples and peaches, however, helped out in that respect until three oclock by which time we had descended and slaked our thirst with nice cool water at the hotel below. It took just two pailfuls to satisfy us!—After an hour's rest we asked our hostess what we should pay and she said she did'nt charge for water when people came to her house and *behaved* themselves. While waiting for the cars at the village we went into a store and bot some butter and some baskets. The cars were full and Jabe and I had to stand, some clever men getting up to give the ladies seats.—The women folks went out to the farm on Thursday and on Friday Mr Taylor insisted on returning to Macon on the way home and off they went accordingly. He is such a discontented man away from home that it is but little satisfaction to have them visit us, and Harriet is not satisfied unless he is at her apron string all the time.

Sunday 26. [July 26, 1863]
Dr B preached this morning from the text "Peace with God."—

Friday 31. [July 31, 1863]
Henry having to give up the house he is living in and not being able to find another I have agreed to rent him two rooms at our house and we have had the trouble of moving our parlor again to the other side of the house. I am thinking of joining a Cavalry Company for home defence to avoid the *draft* for the *five hundred* State Soldiers next Tuesday.

Sunday Aug. 2. [August 2, 1863]
Dr B preached this morning from the text "To him that hath (improved) shall more be given, but from him that hath not (improved) shall be taken away even that he seemeth to have[.]" The word in brackets the preacher supplied to give the meaning of the passage more clearly—At night he preached from the words "And when Daniel knew that the writing was signed &c[.]" I have been suffering for several days with a malignant boil on my third right hand finger, the second of the kind that I remember to have had.—

Monday 3. [August 3, 1863]
At five O'clock this afternoon I went to a meeting of the "Atlanta Press Guards" and was mustered into the service of the Confederate States as a soldier for six months to defend the City of Atlanta and Fulton Co. In order to gain admittance into this Company for Local Defence I had to

renew my connection with the *Banner* and have purchased a *share* for $500 and gone again to proof-reading and so forth. Our Company does not expect or wish to do much duty as one of the members remarked our object is to have as little to do as possible, but if the Yankees come it will give us work enough.—*

Tuesday 4. [August 4, 1863]

To-day the *Draft* came off and so many had *volunteered* "outside of the quota" in accordance with the estimation of Gov Brown that nearly all the men that were left subject to draft were taken to make up the county's quota. I was told by Mr Root that my name and Jabez' were on the list for draft and I went up to the City Hall just in time to get it taken off, that is my own, upon the strength of having already *mustered in*. Jabez's name I could not get off but don't yet know whether it was *called* or not as a drafted man.—The Yankees are still "pegging away" at Charleston, and as we are in for ill news now I am fearful that we shall hear of their success soon.

Sat 8. [August 8, 1863]

This is Jabez's birthday—forty years old. Yesterday I went to the City Hall and ascertained that his name was not on the list of drafted men and then I called on Rev A. S. Worrell Editor & Proprietor of the "Soldiers' Friend" and found him favorably disposed to take Jabez as a partner in his paper so I sent for him to come in at once to secure the place and so be exempt from conscription. Yesterday afternoon I attended a drill meeting of the Atlanta Press Guards and was put through the *Rudiments*. Jabez came into town and has bought a half interest in "The Soldier's Friend" for $2500, a pretty good price I think but *under the circumstances* about as good a thing as he could do I expect, and he will probably be able to do more good to the Army and Country in that way than by going as a Soldier.—I paid J. N. Ells today $500 for a share in the "Banner" not a very profitable investment I fear as far as making money is concerned. Our business continues pretty good and has been *very* good today, Cash Sales being over $500.—We hear certainly at last that T. W. Davis our S S Supt as was, has died at Vicksburg in the hands of the enemy.†

---

* For a list of members of the Atlanta Press Guards on which SPR's name appears, see *ADI*, May 28, 1864.

† Captain Thomas W. Davis of the 42nd Georgia died of disease at Vicksburg on July 18, 1863 (Lillian Henderson, ed., *Roster of Confederate Soldiers of Georgia, 1861–1865*, 6 vols. [Hapeville, Ga.: Longino and Porter, 1959], 4:606).

Sunday 9. [August 9, 1863]

Rev Mr Holman Secy of the Home Mission Board preached for us this morning and urged the claims of the Army upon the people that they should supply the soldiers with the bread of life.—Dr B preached at night.

Sat 15. [August 15, 1863]

There has been considerable excitement in our city this week upon the *horse* question the military powers having *pressed* nearly all the valuable horses that are in the place in order to recruit the Cavalry branch of the Army in Tennessee. Many of our citizens have been deprived of carriage horses that they had refused three or four thousand dollars for and been obliged to take only a fourth part of that amount for them. I think it is a high handed and dishonest proceeding, unworthy such a government as ours professes to be. Having no horses to lose, myself, my opinion is a disinterested one in this case. If the emergency requires that horses should be taken by force the owners ought at any rate to receive *just* compensation. Our Company of "Press Guards" have met twice this week for drill and business—

Sunday 16. [August 16, 1863]

Dr B. preached this morning the funeral sermon for Capt Davis from the text, "He being dead, yet speaketh." It is sad to think how many noble men have lost their lives during the two years that this wicked war has been waged against us by the people of the North. The blood of our brothers would seem to cry from the ground in deprecation of any reunion with their murderers. Union man as I was at the beginning of these troubles, I would now much rather be ruled over by a *king* of England or France than to be made subject to that hateful race of abolitionists who are clamoring for our blood so eagerly and unrelentingly.—My *boil* is getting well now, after over two weeks.—After service this morning the members of the church were requested to remain and the subject of uniting ourselves as a church with some *Association* was considered and after some discussion it was resolved to unite with the "Central Association." The body meets next Friday at Macon, the church there being a member thereof.[*] At night we went to church though the sky threatened a storm, and sure enough

---

[*] The Second Baptist Church's membership in the Central Association lasted from 1863 to 1869, when the congregation voted to sever its ties and rejoin the Stone Mountain Baptist Association (previously known as Rock Mountain), with which it had affiliated since its inception in 1854 (C. Douglas Weaver, *Second to None: A History of Second–Ponce de Leon Baptist Church* [Brentwood, Tenn.: Baptist History and Heritage Society, 2004], 16–17, 22, 24).

before the services closed the rain was pouring down and lightning flashed and thunder roared and we had a dirty groping home by the fitful light of the storm itself.

Friday 21. [August 21, 1863]

This is our National Fast Day and all business is suspended. In the absence of our pastor Bro Conner conducted a prayer meeting in our church this morning[.] This afternoon I helped Sallie write to Mary Add to send by a friend of Mr Roots who is going through to the North tonight. We have just been interrupted by Arthur's letting a log fall on his toe which was badly hurt thereby the nail being nearly knocked off.—Yesterday we bought out the entire interest in the "Soldiers' Friend" and Jabez got an exemption as "Editor and Publisher[.]" We paid Worrel the neat sum of $5000 for it. He was not satisfied with selling the half interest and *made out* that he could not get J. exempted on that basis, but must sell the whole so we had to take it or give up the plan which we did not want to do, as no other way offered to exempt Jabe and this may be of use to me also in case a change is made in the Substitute laws which would again bring *me* liable to service. But I fear we have "bought an Elephant" and shall be troubled to know what to do with him!

Sunday 23. [August 23, 1863]

Our pastor is away today and we have had the pleasure of listening to two discourses from Rev. Major Conner, the big Irishman. Tonight, owing to the giving out of the *alcohol* with wh' the high gas-burners are lighted, they could not be used; so the church was not as well lit up as usual. The sexton "Albert" was absent, and "Isham," his substitute, it afterward appeared, allured by the odor of strong drink, had *drunk up the alcohol*, and under its influence, went into old bro. Neal's big house during the service and robbed his bureau of clothes and valuable papers but left his *old hat* there; by means of which he was speedily found out and made to disgorge!*

Sat 29. [August 29, 1863]

Father has been in town this week for the *first* time since he went out to the farm to live. He staid with us Wed night and left next morning

---

* John Neal lived in a grand home at the corner of Washington and Mitchell Streets, across from the Second Baptist Church and close to JJR's home. When William T. Sherman's army occupied the city, the general used Neal's home as his headquarters (Franklin M. Garrett, *Atlanta and Its Environs: A Chronicle of Its People and Events*, 4 vols. [New York: Lewis Historical, 1954–87], 1:638).

for Hardeeville S.C. Today I paid the first installment of the *War Tax* being 2½% on *gross sales* from Apr 24 to July 1. 1863. and the tax was only $500. for a little over two months! The Yankees are still "pegging away" at Charleston, and from all accounts have knocked Fort Sumter pretty well to pieces though our forces still hold it, and say they intend to hold it. The Yankees have thrown a number of shells into the city, with not much effect. They have been doing the same at Chattanooga this week. The authorities here are fortifying the So.west approaches to Atlanta by throwing up a fort of five guns between the city and our farm about midway to guard against the approach of an armed force from that direction as *Grant* has promised to occupy Atlanta by the 1st of Nov.*
The weather is quite cool today and tonight blankets will be necessary for comfort.

Sunday 30. [August 30, 1863]
We had a large congregation this morning, and Dr B preached from the text "As a man soweth that shall he also reap[.]"

Sat 5. [September 5, 1863]
Nothing of much interest has occurred this week There are rumors of Yankee raids upon Atlanta and part of our citizens comprising the "Fire Battalion" have been called into Camp *at the City Hall*. Col Lee wants our Company to join this battalion, but we don't incline to do so, much.†— Lieut Gen Pemberton who commanded at Vicksburg when it was surrendered is now the guest of Bro Root awaiting the decision of a court of Inquiry in regard to that matter.—Bro Root thinks his course will be sustained by the court. By surrendering as he did on the *fourth of July* (which I wondered at his doing) he obtained terms that he could not have had if they had held out several days longer which they could have done. The Yankees very much wished to get in on the "glorious fourth" and so granted more favorable terms to accomplish that end.

---

* In early Aug. 1863, Colonel Lemuel P. Grant, chief engineer of the Department of Georgia, began efforts to fortify the city. Using slaves requisitioned from individuals in the area and paying owners one dollar per day for the use of their bondsmen, Grant and his team had, by October, constructed seventeen redoubts linked to rifle pits (Garrett, *Atlanta and Its Environs*, 1:567–68).

† SPR joined Company H, 3rd Battalion, Georgia State Guards. His captain was S. P. Bassett, first lieutenant was J. N. Ells, and second lieutenant was W. A. Refo (Janet B. Hewett, ed., *Georgia Confederate Soldiers, 1861–1865*, 4 vols. [Wilmington, N.C.: Broadfoot, 1998], 3:322).

Sunday 6. [September 6, 1863]

Dr B preached today from the texts—"Restore unto me the joys of thy salvation &c" and at night "What is that to thee? follow thou me."—

Sat 12. [September 12, 1863]

No event of much note has transpired this week that I am aware of. The Yankees have gained sole possession of Morris Island, our forces having evacuated Battery Wagner when it was impossible longer to hold it. Fort Sumter is reduced to a pile of ruins but our troops still retain possession and repelled an assault, in considerable force, of the enemy, with hand grenades and *brickbats!*[*] The war cloud is gathering black and portentous in the North western part of our state, our army having evacuated Chattanooga and the foe taken possession of it, also of Knoxville and East Tenn. Truly they seem to be closing in upon us on all sides—The war party at the North is very exultant at the prospect of speedily *subjugating the rebels.* God grant that we may not be delivered into their power.—I could not bear to hold affinity again with such cruel bloody, murdering men.—Our Company met for drill yesterday after at 5½ P.M. and we had a good drill Capt Bassett being present. He has been too unwell to attend the last two meetings previous, and things did not move off well in his absence.—We have no *arms* yet.—Our "Briant" House is at last habitable and I reported it ready on Thursday 10th inst[ant] for the tenant to move in though as yet it is not painted and don't seem likely to be at present. The premises are not yet in good order and today our Carpenter Henry Somers reports himself *conscripted* and unable to finish.—

Sunday 13. [September 13, 1863]

The weather continues dry and hot, but thanks to a kind Providence the crops of corn are safe from the effects of drought and even *our late* crop will make considerable I am told. In the matter of food God has certainly smiled upon us and so let us take hope that it is not His purpose to deliver us over to the power of our vile foes.—It makes my blood boil when I think that I have a brother who sympathizes with such a horde of thieves and murderers.—Dr B preached this morning from the text "Who is a God like unto thee, that pardoneth iniquity?" It was our Communion season—and this reminds me that yesterday was our Church Meeting and

---

[*] On the night of Sept. 6, 1863, Confederates evacuated Battery Wagner and Battery Gregg on Morris Island near Charleston, South Carolina. Union bombardment had harassed both installations since July. Fort Sumter and the city of Charleston remained in Confederate hands (Long, *Civil War Day by Day*, 405).

the question of *Renting the Pews* was considered but so much opposition was made by old Bro Clarke, Root and a few others that we were fain to let it remain as it is, those of us who favored the renting.*—The text at night was "Be troubled, ye careless ones." Rev A. S. Worrel came to tea last night as we have to board him and I have consented to take him for the present. He is to sleep at our store.—

Sat 19. [September 19, 1863]

We have had our usual *storm* this week, but it has been a *dry* one, and the dust has been very disagreeable. The weather has turned quite cool too, for a few days past, and tonight we have a fire, necessary to comfort. Our city has been crowded with soldiers this week in transitu from Virginia to our Northwestern frontier to confront the army of Rosecranz and it now appears that he, in his turn, is retreating and Gen Bragg pursuing and courting a battle. Hope seems to have again sprung up that we shall yet drive out the foe from Georgia, and perhaps Tennessee. Reports are rife too of a fleet of iron clad warvessels having sailed from England to operate against our foes, vessels built ostensibly for the "Emperor of China" or *some* other party but in reality for the Confederate Government[.] There are indications also of troubles arising between the Yankees and the French, growing out of the designs of the latter upon Mexico. In Charleston, matters seem to remain in status quo.—Mr Worrel has been away three days this week to bring his wife from Alabama. Father came back this afternoon. Jabez went to Covington this week and brought back our boy "Frank" who had run away to see his wife last week but did not have sense enough to keep clear of jail and was taken up and lodged and fed and whipped for several days in Covington jail.—Today our old acquaintance Wm Somerville called and paid up his account $275 which we had long ago charged to Profit & Loss A/c [account]. He is now Captain of a Texas Cavalry Company.†—We have no *sing* tonight as Mr Root and family have gone to a *show*.—

---

* Presumably John T. Clarke, former pastor of Second Baptist, and Sidney Root, a benefactor of the church, who held considerable sway with the congregation. In 1858, Second Baptist had begun the practice of renting pews (reserving pews for individuals or families willing to pay quarterly rent) to meet its budgetary needs. The practice was resumed after the war ended (Weaver, *Second to None*, 22).

† William Somerville was captain of Company K, 32nd Texas Cavalry (Hewett, *Roster of Confederate Soldiers*, 14:332).

Sunday 20. [September 20, 1863]

Dr B preached this morning from the text, "All my times are in thy hand"—Owing to the *gas* having given out there is to be no further service in our church today.

Sat. 26. [September 26, 1863]

Hundreds of wounded Soldiers have been brought to our city this week, for a severe battle has been fought since last Friday and during several succeeding days, between our forces under Gen Bragg and those of the Federals under Rosencranz.* We were completely victorious *they say*, though the loss of men was very great on both sides. Rosencranz was driven back to Chattanooga where he has entrenched himself it is thought. We took some eight or ten thousand prisoners, 36 Cannon and a large quantity of small arms. The battle is called after the stream near which it was fought—"Chickamauga" or "Stream of Death"—Alas! Every victory as well as every defeat, brings sorrow and distress to many hearts. Major Connor was at our singing tonight at Mr Root's.

Sunday 27. [September 27, 1863]

Rev Mr Cuthbert of Augusta preached for us today twice. In the forenoon his text was *short* and *sweet* "Mary!" John 20:16. though he *read* it a little longer "Jesus said unto her, Mary!" He showed that there was a great deal of meaning in that one simple word thus uttered to that weeping woman. Our second service today was at four oclock in the afternoon, there being *no gas*. The text was "Nevertheless when the Son of Man cometh shall he find faith on the earth?" The preacher took occasion to show the probability that the coming of Christ will be *pre* Millenial; a theory that I think is supported by many scripture passages. I read a book when I was in Hardeeville several years ago called "The Voice of the Church" which made this view seem very clear to my mind.—†

---

* At the battle of Chickamauga, Georgia, Sept. 19–20, 1863, Confederate forces under Braxton Bragg decisively defeated Union forces under William Rosecrans. The arrival of soldiers from General James Longstreet's First Corps helped to turn the tide (Peter Cozzens, *This Terrible Sound: The Battle of Chickamauga* [Urbana: University of Illinois Press, 1992], 299–301, 517–21). Bragg's failure to pursue the Federal army in the battle's aftermath earned him criticism and later replacement in command. *ADI*, Sept. 24, 1863, announced, "Our victory is grand and complete" but noted "heavy losses on both sides."

† Daniel T. Taylor, *The Voice of the Church* (1855).

Wed 30. [September 30, 1863]

George Van V arrived this afternoon to make a visit of several days that we have expected for sometime[.] He was badly wounded in the left arm at the second fight at Fredericksburgh and has now but little use of the arm as the elbow is grown stiff and the double bones of the fore arm have grown to each other. He will not probably have any further fighting to do, on this account. The partial loss of a left arm is a great loss for a young man but it might have been much worse.—[*]

Sat 3. [October 3, 1863]

Today is bright and pleasant after a day and night of storm and rain. A violent storm beat upon us last night and supplied us with abundance of the much needed rain which has been withheld for over six weeks past. Mr Root has gone up to the battlefield of Chickamauga to help the wounded and has not yet returned so that we had a lame choir at practice tonight.

Sunday 4. [October 4, 1863]

Dr Brantley preached for us this morning from the words "Today shal't thou be with me in Paradise." We sang a new anthem or rather "Sentence" as a Voluntary, "Cast thy burden on the Lord."—At the second service Bro Root made his appearance in our midst.

Friday 9. [October 9, 1863]

This being my wife's birthday I gave her a little book as a love-token called "The Season" not *Thomson's*, considering it a *seasonable* gift. She is thirty years old, my dear wife, and in the *summer* of her life. May a kind Providence grant that the Winter of life may find us still side by side as we "totter down the hill." Mary's baby 'Bel is quite ill from teething and we are all anxious about her.—She seems affected in a similar way to our little Alice.—Sister Nell has moved to Augusta; and she has shown so little regard for us while here that I am not at all sorry she has gone away.—

---

[*] SVVR's brother, George, in his early twenties, was a private in the 2nd Battalion, Georgia Volunteer Infantry, also known as the Macon Volunteers. He was wounded at the Battle of Chancellorsville (near Fredericksburg, Virginia, site of a famous battle in Dec. 1862, hence SPR's reference to this fighting as the Second Battle of Fredericksburg) on May 2, 1863. His military records indicate that he later became part of the Medical Department at Montgomery, Alabama (Henderson, *Roster*, 6:794).

Sat 10. [October 10, 1863]

George left us this morning and went back to Macon to see his sweetheart, I suppose.—Tonight we went to Mr Roots to sing and found there Mrs Grinnell an English lady who has come to our country as a "Florence Nightingale" and has made herself very useful in the hospitals near the battlefields. She is an educated lady and a very entertaining talker indeed and we all enjoyed her society for an hour or two very much, singing to fill up the pauses.—Mr Grinnell is an officer in the Confed. Service*—Little 'Bel is so ill that Sallie is going to sit up part of the night with Mary and Ellie.

Sunday 11. [October 11, 1863]

Dr B. preached this morning from the text; "Strive to enter in at the strait gate[.]" We sang a new *Motett* called "One thing have I desired of the Lord" which is very good and Mrs West was familiar with, so we got it a going last night. As we returned from ch' we received the sad tidings that little baby 'Bel was dead, and so it proved. Her pure soul had gone home to the arms of that kind Shepherd who gave His life for her, to join the angel band that Allie joined before. Poor weeping mother! be comforted—"*it is well* with the child." She began to droop last Sunday. The father has not seen the baby since it was two weeks old. Dr Baird preached for us this afternoon as our pastor had gone to preach *in Camp*. The text was "Search the Scriptures" his *forte* is *telling affecting anecdotes*—I went to Dr Brantleys house tonight to engage his services to bury the baby at ten oclock tomorrow.

Monday 12. [October 12, 1863]

We took the baby's little corpse at ten this morning to its resting place near Sarah's grave. The grass was brightly green over little Chevis' grave and neat white stones mark the spot.—Very few persons were in attendance at the Union Prayer meeting this afternoon. With one or two exceptions only, the males present were Baptists tho' the meeting was held in the First Pres. Church. Bro Worrell left for the "front" this afternoon to be gone a week or so.—One of the ladies that we were going to take to board some weeks ago has again been to see Sallie and gained her consent to take

---

* Hewett, *Roster of Confederate Soldiers*, 7:34, shows several officers by that last name: Captain Edward Grinnell of Company E, Louisiana. Mil. Leed's Guards Regiment; Lieutenant John B. Grinnell, Company B, Confederate Light Artillery, Shark's Battalion; Lieutenant Robert M. Grinnell, New Company E, Louisiana Infantry, 1st Support Battalion (Wheat's); and Major Robert M. Grinnell, Heth's Division, AA, Ig.

her until her husband comes home at any rate. Her husband Col Eugene E McLean is now in Mississippi.—Mrs McLean came to our house this afternoon.—

Sat 17. [October 17, 1863]

No war news of much importance this week. The enemy is doubtless *preparing* to bombard Charleston terribly. Pres Davis has been up to the army in Tenn. and has now gone to Mississippi. We came very near having a live President in our house this week as he and Gen. Polk spent sometime trying to find out where we lived in order to visit Mrs McLean who it seems is on quite intimate terms with him and many other notabilities.* Mr Davis promised however, having failed to find her this time, to call upon her as he returned from Mississippi. She is a Northern lady and thinks New York the only place to enjoy life in. I suppose she is a reconstructionist therefore.—

Sunday 18. [October 18, 1863]

Dr B's text this morning was "I was wounded in the house of my friends."—

Sat 24. [October 24, 1863]

No change of importance in the military status of the country during the past week that I know of. The siege of Charleston draws its slow length along. It is now one hundred days old. Mr Worrell got back from "the front" last night after an absence of ten days.—Mary Brown's "Wesley" made his appearance unexpectedly on Wed night last while I was at meeting, He has a furlough of 15 days.—I have not had to *drill* for several weeks now, as our company has never been accepted by the Governor nor our officers commissioned and so we are "laying on our oars" as it were until something turns up. We have had heavy rains this week.—

---

* General Leonidas K. Polk was a much-beloved figure in the Confederacy. After graduating from West Point in 1827, he left the army to become a clergyman and served as a bishop in the Episcopal Church before the war. A planter of considerable wealth, he raised money to create the University of the South. Polk joined the Confederate Army at the outset of the war, serving under General Braxton Bragg. The two despised each other, and their feud culminated in Bragg's accusations of disobedience on Polk's part at the Battle of Chickamauga. Hoping to end the bickering, Jefferson Davis transferred Polk to head the Department of Alabama, Mississippi, and East Louisiana (Glen Robins, *The Bishop of the Old South: The Ministry and Civil War Legacy of Leonidas Polk* [Macon, Ga.: Mercer University Press, 2006], 120–22, 168–91).

Sunday 25. [October 25, 1863]

Cool and cloudy this morning. The text was "the woman who was a sinner and washed the feet of Christ with her tears." Dr B. was more animated than his wont. In the aft. he preached from the words of John— ["]I write unto you, little children, that ye sin not[.]" Jabez came in on his new $900 mule this afternoon and calling me out to the stable began to find fault with the way the lot was managed or neglected just as tho' it was not *his* place to keep it in order. I have spent hours in trying to keep up his rotten fences and houses. And when I attributed blame to his beloved servant Harvey he got so wrathy that for the first time since he left Macon eight years ago he began to threaten to "wind up and separate" as though that was any bugbear to me! I wish it were "un fait accompli."

Thursday 29. [October 29, 1863]

We had *a call* from President Davis tonight and I had a short conversation with him, that is, he asked me if Mrs McLean was in and I replied that she was! and forthwith took him up to her room with the Aid who came with him, and they staid an hour there. Mrs McLean has an extensive Military acquaintance; the President—Gen's Polk, Hindman, Buckner and others are constant friends and visitors.*

Sat 31 [October 31, 1863]

I paid our war tax today for the *quarter* ending Sep 30—$675 being 2½% on gross sales $27000.—Mr Worrel left for Forsyth on Tuesday last and has not yet returned. Mr Brown left on Thursday. The enemy opened fire again at Charleston a few days ago and has been giving Fort Sumter a terrible hail of shot and shell ever since.—The Democrats have been badly beaten in the Governors election in Ohio and Pennsylvania, Vallandigham being left high and dry.† The Abolitionists are determined to persecute the South to the bitter end. Lincoln has called for 300 000 *Volunteers* with the notification that if they are not forthcoming by Jan 5th 1864 that a draft will ensue—The British Govt have seized the two Steam Rams that were being built on the Mersey on suspicion that they

---

* Confederate generals Simon Bolivar Buckner and Thomas Carmichael Hindman fought with Braxton Bragg at Chickamauga.

† In 1863, Pennsylvania's first Republican governor, Andrew Curtin, was elected to a second term. Clement Vallandigham, in exile in Canada, had run unsuccessfully for governor of Ohio (Heidler and Heidler, *Encyclopedia*, 1:530–31; James M. McPherson, *Ordeal by Fire: The Civil War and Reconstruction*, 3rd ed. [Boston: McGraw Hill, 2001], 374–77).

were intended for Confederate war vessels.* In Tennessee Rosencrans has been superceded by Gen Grant on account of his failure to win success at Chickamauga!† Sallie got a note from her father today but he is such a tory that it is no pleasure to hear from him.—We sang at Mr Roots tonight and he treated us all to wine—Catelonian wine—I bot a leg of pork in market for $10 today 5 lbs.

Sunday 1. [November 1, 1863]

The text of our pastor this morning was "Why stand ye here all the day idle?" and he gave us a good sermon—This aft Rev Wm C Wilkes preached from the text "My little children, let us not love in word neither in tongue, but in deed and in truth" I John III:18.‡ Mary Brown rec^d a letter from Amelia last week, she has another little *girl*.

Sat 7. [November 7, 1863]

Mr Worrell returned on Tuesday evening last and yesterday morning Mrs McLean left on a *visit* to Macon in company with Col Blake her constant attendant. The night before she left, she and Sallie made a trade, whereby the latter became possessed of a fine fancy cloth cloak and Mrs McLean became the owner of a little reticule that she had set envious eyes on, and $30 to boot. She also paid Sallie $5 for a 15¢ box of "Lily White" that I gave some time ago! No War News of much moment this week.—Tonight we sang at Mrs Wests. Holbrook had my Sweet Potatoes dug yesterday and the crop is quite small, *my third* being only about 10 or 12 bushels large and small. But as they cost me nothing they are not to be lightly esteemed.

Sunday 8. [November 8, 1863]

Dr B's subject this morning was "Christ our Advocate[.]" It was our Communion season. This aft. we had a Sunday School meeting.

Sat 14. [November 14, 1863]

We have had killing frosts this week at last. Father came in and staid with us Wed night intending to leave at four (or nearly five) oclock in

---

* In September 1863, the British government seized two iron-plated steam-powered warships being built in Liverpool for the Confederate government (*NYT*, Sept. 25, 1863).

† On Oct. 17, 1863, General Ulysses S. Grant, now in command of all Union armies, relieved William Rosecrans of command of the Department of the Cumberland following his defeat at Chickamauga, replacing him with General George Thomas (Long, *Civil War Day by Day*, 423).

‡ William C. Wilkes, a graduate of Mercer University, served as president of Monroe Female College (*History of the Baptist Denomination*, 581–83).

the morning for Augusta on the way to Barnwell Asson in So Ca. But having left mother quite poorly he felt anxious about her and decided in the morning to give up the trip and return home, which he did, but took another start on Friday afternoon by the night train. I have been called upon this week to deliver up my Substitute-Papers for awhile the reason given being that they may be sent with others to Richmond for examination and approval, but I have my doubts as to their being returned as I think it probable that Congress will soon repeal the Substitute Clause and make those having subs again liable—in some way.—Singing at our house tonight—Mr Root reported that our forces had retaken Knoxville in East Tennessee*—Arthur has just got rid of a very sore mouth that has troubled him for sometime.

Sunday 15. [November 15, 1863]

We have enjoyed a pleasant Sabbath and been three times to church. Dr B preached in the morning from the text "The Kingdom of God is not meat and drink &c" and a stranger from Missi[ssippi] preached in the aft, and tonight we went to the Central Pres. Church, which has today installed their new pastor Mr Mallard, but a Rev Stacy preached tonight a long and tedious discourse. The choir sang two tunes new to us which we soon identified after reaching home. They were "Noel" and "Transport" in the Carmina†—Mrs McLean returned this aft.

Sat 21. [November 21, 1863]

No news of interest this week though many *reports* of our forces in East Tenn having retaken Knoxville, or being *just about to do so!* Henry moved into his own house on Thursday contrary to my advice and Jabez' also, as it is too far away from the store and then he might better have rented it out for $25 more than he paid me and that would have been so much clear gain.

Sunday 22. [November 22, 1863]

Mr Root is absent and having left a request for me to hear his class at S.S. I finally decided to do so though I felt but little inclination. Dr B preached from the words "Let the wicked forsake his way, &c" and our

---

* President Davis had ordered two divisions of Confederate soldiers under General James Longstreet to take Knoxville, regarding East Tennessee as vital to Southern success. Longstreet departed from Chattanooga on Nov. 4, making slow progress. He attacked Fort Sanders on Nov. 29 without success (Heidler and Heidler, *Encyclopedia*, 3:1130–33).

† Probably the Carmina Burana, a medieval collection of 228 songs/poems found in 1803 in a Bavarian monastery.

Vol was just the thing viz "I will arise and go to my father"—This aft a stranger preached for 20 minutes which was long enough of the kind. Tonight is beautiful and Sallie and I went to hear Mr Mallard the new Pres minister and heard a good sermon from the word "To-morrow[.]"*

Sat 28. [November 28, 1863]

Before breakfast on Monday last Col McLean came to *call on* his wife. He is a large, good looking man with a pleasant, deliberate manner, and obedient to his wife! We have had bad news from "the front" this week the Yankees having attacked our position at Chattanooga or Lookout Mt. and succeeded in routing a part of our army and Gen Bragg has in consequence again *retreated* to a point much nearer to us than that he was occupying. So now the enemy has undisputed possession of Chattanooga and will doubtless hold on to it.†—I did not go to the store after dinner today remaining at home to fix up the large room that Henry vacated for a gent and bride who came to take possession this evening before tea. They are Mr & Mrs Callaway and are to pay us $5 per day each and find their own fuel and lights. So we have *now* six boarders counting Mr Worrell and Mary.—Singing was here tonight. Mr Root showed us a Nov number of Leslies, Harpers & Petersons Magazines that he brought from Wilmington. They look quite like old times before this "cruel war" began. The weather is wet and doleful and the news is of the same character and

---

* Robert Quarterman Mallard had been a Presbyterian clergyman in Walthourville, Georgia, from 1856 to 1863 before being called to Central Presbyterian in Atlanta. In 1866, he moved to New Orleans, where he remained a pastor until his death in 1904. His wife, Mary Sharpe Jones Mallard, was the daughter of prominent residents of Liberty County, Georgia, Reverend Charles Colcock Jones and Mary Jones. During the 1890s, Robert Mallard published two books extolling the virtues of plantation life during slavery times (Robert Manson Myers, ed., *The Children of Pride* [New Haven: Yale University Press, 1972], 1614–15).

† The Union victory at Chattanooga in late Nov. 1863 included the loss of 15 percent of Braxton Bragg's army and 33 percent of his artillery pieces. Bragg's failings as a commander had been apparent to many in the Confederate army for some time, but friendship with Jefferson Davis had kept Bragg in command. After the battle, he resigned. Joseph E. Johnston was appointed as Bragg's replacement and told to prepare over the winter to defend the city of Atlanta from invasion. Confederates went into winter quarters in North Georgia (John Bowers, *Chickamauga and Chattanooga: The Battles That Doomed the Confederacy* [New York: HarperCollins, 1994], 235–37).

altogether I feel very blue.—Mr Root says our Bro J H James has left with his wife for Europe.—*

Sunday 29. [November 29, 1863]

Mrs Cole, a sister of Mrs Root died last Friday and Dr Brantley preached her funeral this morning as Mr Root was of the family he sat down stairs but we got Mr Craig to sing tenor for us.—The text for the aft was "I would not live always." This is a cold windy day, and we did not go out at night.

Sat. December 5. [December 5, 1863]

No news of much importance this week except that Gen Longstreet has probably abandoned the siege of Knoxville, and is endeavoring to get his army out via Virginia†—The sky is dark and lowering over our land, though bright and pleasant enough in a *natural* sense it has been of late I am less hopeful for a speedy end of the war than I was a year ago—much less. The foe encroaches upon us so holds on so constantly to whatever he does gain and seems so determined to subdue or exterminate us.

Sunday 6. [December 6, 1863]

Our pastors text this morning was "Whether we eat or drink or whatsoever we do, do all to the glory of God[.]" This aft it was "This God is our God." In the last Index "Semei" the Richmond correspondent gives some "Spirited lines" by Rev W. C. Richards of Providence that were inspired by the Fort Donelson Victory, which the author hopes is the token of the speedy downfall of *treason* and *rebellion*! I guess he thinks it is a good while coming, now.

Wed 9. [December 9, 1863]

At about two o'clock yesterday morning I heard the alarm bell ringing and upon looking out of the window discovered a fire exactly in the direction of our store. I hastily dressed and ran down to the scene of action

---

* John H. James was a banker and broker who bought and sold gold, silver, and bullion. His business was located at the corner of Whitehall and Alabama Streets (V. T. Barnwell, *Barnwell's Atlanta City Directory and Strangers' Guide* [Atlanta: Intelligencer, 1867], 75, 176). He was a member of Second Baptist Church.

† Following his unsuccessful offensive at Knoxville, James Longstreet decided against a second assault but kept up enough of a siege to force Ulysses S. Grant to divert Union soldiers from Chattanooga. The idea was to take pressure off of Confederate forces there. Longstreet ended his Tennessee campaign on Dec. 14, at which time his army went into winter quarters (Heidler and Heidler, *Encyclopedia*, 3:1130–33).

fully prepared to find our store in flames but was much relieved at finding the fire in a building on the opposite side of the street and a little above ours, and although the wind was high I did not think it would extend further. Tonight is the anniversary of our Wedding. We have been united eleven years and during that period have not been separated for any great length of time. But tonight I feel sad and gloomy at the prospect of separation ere long as Congress is now in session and will no doubt pass such laws as will make me liable to service—justly or unjustly—and I may have to go. Somebody certainly must fight but I never was a fighting boy or man and never want to be.—

Thursday 10. [December 10, 1863]

Mary Brown's birthday 30 years old—It is also a Fast Day by Gov Brown's appointment and we have been out to three services.* Morning and night at our church Dr Stiles (Presbyterian) preached. His text this morning was "When the host goeth forth to fight keep yourselves from every wicked thing." Tonight—his subject was "Sanctification" or preparation for the service of the Lord. I could not keep awake having slept but little last night.—

Sat 12. [December 12, 1863]

Last night Dr Stiles preached to the church to exhort the members to awaken to a sense of the responsibility resting on them in view of the contemplated services of the coming week. Tonight it is raining and we had no choir meeting. I have just got my boots from Seymour and tried them on. They fit snugly. They are *footed* boots and *cost me* "only $75."—

Sunday 13. [December 13, 1863]

The day is cloudy and the walking muddy, but we had a full house to hear Dr S. His text was "The redemption of the soul is precious &c[.]" Tonight it rained hard just at church time and we did not go out as the second bell did not ring.—I forgot to say that yesterday I had to whip our woman Caroline for insubordination and impudence to her mistress. I am disgusted with negroes and feel inclined to sell what I have. I wish they were all back in Africa,—or—Yankee Land. To think too that this "cruel war" should be waged for them!

* Georgia governor Joseph E. Brown declared this day of "Fasting, Humiliation and Prayer" after the ominous Federal victory at Chattanooga the previous month, admonishing the people of the state "to humble themselves before Him in whose hands rests the destinies of our country, and to pray that he may guide us safely through the storm of invasion" (*ADI*, Dec. 10, 1863).

Sat 19. [December 19, 1863]

Dr Stiles has been preaching all the week, morning and night and I have attended all the meetings except two of the morning services. There seem so far to be but little results for such earnest faithful effort. Our singing tonight was at Mr Wests.—

Sunday 20. [December 20, 1863]

I am a cripple today by reason of a painful *soft Corn* between my toes. It used to trouble me some twelve years ago but has not done so since until this year but it is now more painful than ever before[.] I managed to hobble to church and this morning heard Dr Stiles preach from the text "One God and One Mediator betwixt God and man, the Man Christ Jesus &c[.]" We had one of our turkies today for dinner which is the second one we have had I think since we were married, so that the turkey race have not got much of a grudge against us.—Arthur has been ailing for three or four days with an intermittent fever and the attack for today seems to be just coming on.—

Friday 25. [December 25, 1863]

The weather is bright and *cold*, fine for Christmas.—I went to the store as usual but Henry left at ten oclock to "take Christmas" at his dad-in-law's. I was kept quite busy until dinner time and sold over $700 worth. Tonight Mrs McLean sent us some eggnogg and a taste of pickled oysters.—I see that the *House* has passed a bill making those who have Substitutes in service, liable again to service in their own persons, a flagrant breach of faith on the part of the Government, I think—a regular cheating!—

Sunday 27. [December 27, 1863]

Yesterday and today have been wet and cold and very few were at church this morning so that we had service in the Lecture Room and Dr B preached about Paul's discourse before Felix.—Caroline and Joe left yesterday morning to visit their friends and this morning I had enough to do making fires, cutting wood, and milking the two cows.—Sallie and Mr Root swapped watch chains last week and he gave her a French Calico dress to boot, worth $72! Singing was at our house last night so that *we* did not have to go out in the wind.

Thursday 31. [December 31, 1863]

It has been a most doleful day, cold and wet, fit ending to a year of gloom and death. In less than an hour 1863 will be among the past. Mary and I have set the fire nearly out, Sallie having taken to bed as usual several hours ago. Mary is knitting, finishing off the toe of the old year! The telegram of today is not very cheering, viz that by the vote of the Senate my $2500 Substitute becomes worthless to me. This is what I call a grand Government Swindle, and it is nothing shorter. Well, when I am obliged to go to war I expect to go, and not sooner. What a blessed thing it is to live in *a free country*! I wish I was in "Old England" with my wife and little ones.—God save us from evil in the year to come.—

SIX

January 1864 to October 1864

"THE FUTURE IS VERY DARK AND UNCERTAIN."

In 1864, the war finally came to Sam Richards. He had been touched by it many times in the past, through inflation, food shortages, overcrowding, and disease in his community and through the deaths of friends in the army. But in 1864 the war's tragic consequences touched him intimately, with the death of his brother-in-law and the arrival of the Federal army literally at his Atlanta home. "The future is very dark and uncertain," Richards wrote on August 18, 1864. A few weeks later, the Yankees had captured Atlanta, his store had been looted, his slaves had claimed their freedom, and he faced the prospect of becoming a refugee.[1]

In what would prove to be the city's last large-scale civic celebration of Confederate nationalism, Atlantans came together in February to honor John Hunt Morgan, the illustrious cavalry commander whose exploits had fascinated Atlanta's newspaper-reading citizenry for two years. After a series of spectacular raids in southern Ohio and Indiana during 1862, Morgan had been captured and held in a maximum security prison in Columbus, Ohio. Fellow prisoners spent weeks digging a secret tunnel, and Morgan slipped away through it one night in November 1863, eluding capture by pretending to be a businessman on a train ride to Cincinnati, finding Confederate sympathizers to harbor him in rural Kentucky, and finally reaching safety in Virginia. For beleaguered Confederates, Morgan's story provided hope for the future. He made appearances in Richmond and Atlanta, captivating audiences in both cities. On February 6, morning newspapers in Atlanta announced Morgan's appearance in the city. A crowd of several thousand, including Sam and Sallie Richards, gathered at the train station and then accompanied Morgan, his wife, and his staff to the city's premier hotel, the Trout House. Before the assembled crowd, Mayor James Calhoun praised Morgan's "gallant" defense of his country. Morgan thanked Atlantans for their warm welcome and "retired amid the enthusiastic cheers . . . in the street below."[2]

But Morgan's appearance offered only a temporary reprieve from ominous news. One day before his visit, the *Daily Intelligencer* announced the "certainty" that Atlanta would be the military target of the Federal army's spring campaign. "The importance of Atlanta, both to the Federal and Confederate government, cannot be over-estimated," the newspaper concluded. If Atlanta were "overrun by the enemy," the Confederacy would lose the Lower South, including its railroads, which provided the only means to supply Robert E. Lee's army in Virginia with food and war materials. The newspaper called for twenty thousand more soldiers to aid the Confederate effort.[3]

Sam Richards was not one of them. On May 24, 1864, Richards finally secured a formal exemption that protected him from the Confederate draft: "*Samuel P. Richards* is hereby exempted from Military Duty, by reason of *being a printer in the office of the Soldiers Friend*. When he ceases to be employed as such, this Exemption is hereby declared Void." Although he belonged to the Atlanta Press Volunteers, a militia company consisting of editors, writers, and typographers, and took his turn patrolling Atlanta's streets to prevent lawlessness, Richards no longer had concerns about involuntary service to the Confederacy.[4]

On July 9, 1864, Sallie Richards's older brother, James Van Valkenburg, died at the Battle of Monocacy, Maryland. He had enlisted in the 61st Georgia after Fort Sumter and had risen to the rank of lieutenant colonel. The 61st had seen fierce fighting for the past two years. Van Valkenburg had been wounded at Antietam in September 1862 and captured but exchanged after the Battle of Fredericksburg three months later. At Monocacy, his unit's losses also included Colonel John Hill Lamar. Both officers were buried near the battlefield at dawn the next day, with their divisional commander, General John B. Gordon, in attendance. Wrote Richards philosophically, "It really seems as though sooner or later the sword claims all as its victims, however long it may spare."[5]

By the time Sam learned of his brother-in-law's death, nearly a month after it occurred, Richards had numerous other concerns as well. Atlanta's situation had become perilous. After defeating Confederates at Chattanooga in November 1863, the Union Army went into winter quarters, preparing for the spring campaign to take Atlanta. Beginning in May, a vast army of one hundred thousand men under the command of William T. Sherman fought its way south by defeating Confederates under Joseph E. Johnson and later John Bell Hood in a series of flank attacks. To the men in both armies, the campaign seemed like a series of small continuous skirmishes rather than distinct battles. For the citizens of Atlanta, it seemed like an endless waiting game.[6]

Daily life in the city became increasingly difficult. By March, another round of inflation and food shortages hit. In November 1861, Sam had complained that "provisions are getting dear" when coffee reached fifty cents per pound, but one year later, the price had jumped sixfold. By March 1864, with the Federal navy making blockade-running ever more difficult, coffee sold for fifteen dollars a pound. Even locally grown sweet potatoes now brought sixteen dollars per bushel. Having used up all the pages in his diary, Sam took over the volume he had given to Sallie in 1852, in which she had dutifully recorded her thoughts for several years before abandoning the effort. Now Sam used its remaining pages as an outlet for his musings. In one of his more poignant entries, he described taking his wife and children to visit the local cemetery. "The saddest sight that I have seen is the *acre* of fresh-dug graves that are filled by dead soldiers, the result of this terrible war," he wrote. "And still the work of destruction goes on."[7]

By July, after Sherman's army got past Kennesaw Mountain, slowed but not stopped by a Confederate victory there on June 27, a "complete swarm" of thousands of Atlantans began evacuating the city. Hospitals evacuated their patients, sending wounded and ill men to other locations or home to convalesce. The city's female medical volunteers moved their hospital association to Vineville, near Macon. Newspapers ceased to publish: the *Southern Confederacy* left for Macon despite admonitions to its readers that all citizens, including women and children, must "aid the cause in some way" because "Atlanta cannot be abandoned." Members of Richards's extended family departed, including Jabez Richards and his children, William and Ann Richards, and Mary Hathaway Brown.[8]

Sam and Sallie Richards decided to stay, among the estimated two to five thousand civilians out of a total population of twenty-two thousand who did not evacuate. Most of those who remained had no other option, but Sam and Sallie turned down invitations from Kate and Charlie DuBose to join them in Sparta and from Harriet Van Valkenburg Taylor, who offered her home in Americus. Sam provided few clues about his decision to remain in Atlanta except to suggest that he and Sallie "hear terrible tales" about the Yankees but "don't think they are as bad as they are said to be." Perhaps he was naive about the risk to his family's safety posed by Sherman's army. He may have wanted to protect the merchandise from his store, some of it now at his home, for Jabez had considered but rejected the possibility of moving merchandise out of Atlanta by rail. Perhaps Sam hoped to guard his investment in slaves, of whom he now had six: Ellen, Frank, and the family group of Joe and Caroline and their daughter Mandy and infant son. Sallie may not have wanted to travel, for she had given birth to the couple's sixth child, Virginia (Virnie), on April 21. Perhaps Sam wanted to demonstrate a level of personal courage (called into question by his well-known determination to evade the draft) by remaining. He may have wanted the opportunity to observe and chronicle what he knew would be momentous times.[9]

Sherman's advancing army and especially his artillery created widespread fear and even panic among Atlantans, despite appeals for calm from the city's mayor and its remaining newspaper, the *Daily Intelligencer*. Like others who remained in town, the Richardses built a bomb shelter, called a pit or gopher hole, in the cellar of their home, hiding there during the Federal bombardment of Atlanta, which began in July and was ramped up in August. Sherman had promised his superiors in Washington that he would "make the inside of Atlanta too hot to be endured. . . . [I]t will be a used-up community by the time we are done with it." Estimates indicate that between one hundred and two hundred people were wounded and twenty died during the shelling, which also caused extensive physical damage to the city. Although shells landed in their backyard and at the bookstore, the Richards family escaped harm. By this point, Atlanta had ceased to exist as a municipality. The City Council stopped holding meetings, and the court system and police force no longer functioned, leading to incidents of looting. Firemen joined by local volunteers struggled to contain fires ignited by Union bombardment. Richards took his turn as a policeman.[10]

The Yankees finally entered the city after "a day of terror and a night of dread," and looters tore through the business district, including the Richards store. Although Sam went to the store to protect what remained of its merchandise, he could not control his slaves, who "vanished into air" with the rest of the city's African American population. The acts of "impudence" about which he had complained for more than a year now became open defiance. He saw Jabe's former slave, Sally, walking around town "as independent as can be." Sam wrote ruefully in his diary, "How I wish I had the value of our city lots and negroes in gold at this juncture." Atlanta capitulated to General Sherman on the night of September 1–2, and a week later, residents learned that John Hunt Morgan, the cavalry hero who had symbolized Confederate hopes late in the war, had been killed.[11]

"It is strange to go about Atlanta now and see only Yankee uniforms," Sam wrote on September 4. With the exception of the early looting, he was at first impressed by the relative restraint shown by Sherman's forces. He soon became angry, however, when Sherman had ordered the city's entire civilian population to leave. Exceptions would be made for Unionists, but Sam's efforts to parlay his prewar Unionism into a reprieve from evacuation fell on deaf ears. Too many people in Atlanta knew his loyalties. As early as December 1861, the Richards brothers had sent a copy of Kate DuBose's song, "God Defendeth the Right," to the *Southern Confederacy*. Sam's efforts to raise money for Confederate soldiers at benefit concerts and his friendship with blockade-runner Sidney Root were well known. So was his affiliation with the *Soldier's Friend*, a newspaper designed to raise the morale of southern fighting men.[12]

Reluctant and resentful, Sam boarded a railcar for Nashville on September 22, 1864. He, Sallie, and their four children began life as refugees. The Richardses were among the more fortunate Atlantans, for they had resources enabling them to head north to escape the war. Residents without such means were sent to Macon and other points south, where many lived in abject poverty.[13] Using both savings and funds raised by selling furniture to Union soldiers, the Richardses traveled by rail first to Nashville, then to Louisville, and finally to New York City, where members of both the Richards and Van Valkenburg families resided. Sallie and Sam took personal possessions that were meaningful to them. Sallie shipped her seraphine, which she had owned since her girlhood in Macon. Sam brought his diaries, which had survived the Macon store fire in 1850 and the Federal shelling of Atlanta in 1864.

Notes

1. SPR diary, Aug. 18, 1864, Sept. 9, 1864.
2. SPR diary, Feb. 6, 1864; *ADI*, Feb. 7, 1864; James A. Ramage, *Rebel Raider: The Life of General John Hunt Morgan* (Lexington: University Press of Kentucky, 1986), 170–98. The Atlanta City Council Minutes, vol. 4, Jan. 19, 1864, Mar. 30, 1864, Apr. 8, 1864, AHC, indicate that the city had planned for his appearance and spent more than ten thousand dollars on the occasion, hailing Morgan for having "shed so much luster on the Military prowess of our Country." For another contemporary account of Morgan's visit, see Sarah "Sallie" Conley Clayton, *Requiem for a Lost City: A Memoir of Civil War Atlanta and the Old South*, ed. Robert Scott Davis Jr. (Macon, Ga.: Mercer University Press, 1999), 92–95.

3. *ADI*, Feb. 5, 1864.

4. SPR draft exemption, private collection, displayed at AHC. *ADI*, May 28, 1864, contains a story about the Atlanta Press Volunteers and includes the names of both SPR and JJR: "The representatives of the Press in this city, though exempt from military service, by both Confederate and State legislation[,] nevertheless feel impelled by a sense of duty to form themselves into an independent organization for the defense of our homes from threatened Federal invasion."

5. SPR diary, Aug. 1, 1864; James D. Van Valkenburg record, Compiled Military Service Records, National Archives, Microfilm 266, 561. The 61st Georgia lost 65 percent of its men at Monocacy, Maryland, including Colonel John Hill Lamar and Lieutenant Colonel James D. Van Valkenburg. When the 61st surrendered at Appomattox in 1865, just eighty-one men and no officers remained (Joseph H. Crute, *Units of the Confederate States Army* [Gaithersburg, Md.: Midlothian, 1987], 115). *MT* first reported the deaths of Lamar and Van Valkenburg on July 25, 1864. In a longer article about the Battle of Monocacy, Aug. 13, 1864, the newspaper reported that "Col J H Lamar and Lt Col J D Van Valkenburg were both killed instantly—struck in head." B. Franklin Cooling, *Monocacy: The Battle That Saved Washington* (Shippensburg, Pa.: White Mane, 1997), 181–82, described the battlefield burial, based on an account by a young woman who attended. Van Valkenburg's body was returned to Macon in 1866 through the auspices of his fire company, Young America no. 3, and interred at Rose Hill Cemetery. See *MT*, June 7, 1866, July 17, 1866.

6. Lee Kennett, *Marching through Georgia: The Story of Soldiers and Civilians during Sherman's Campaign* (New York: HarperCollins, 1995), 62–64.

7. SPR diary, Nov. 3, 1861, Nov. 29, 1862, Mar. 26, 1864, Apr. 22, 1864, May 15, 1864; James M. McPherson, *Ordeal by Fire: The Civil War and Reconstruction*, 3rd ed. (Boston: McGraw Hill, 2001), 464–65.

8. SPR diary, July 3, 10, 1864; Jack D. Welsh, *Two Confederate Hospitals and Their Patients: Atlanta to Opelika* (Macon, Ga.: Mercer University Press, 2005), 35–36; *MT*, July 19, 1864; *ASC*, June 9, 1864, July 5, 1864.

9. SPR diary, Apr. 22, 1864, July 10, 1864, Aug. 7, 14, 18, 27, 1864; Albert Castel, *Decision in the West: The Atlanta Campaign of 1864* (Lawrence: University Press of Kansas, 1992), 464.

10. SPR diary, July 22, 23, 1864, Aug. 1, 29, 1864; Castel, *Decision in the West*, 462; Richard M. McMurry, *Atlanta 1864: Last Chance for the Confederacy* (Lincoln: University of Nebraska Press, 2000), 164–65; Ralph Benjamin Singer Jr., "Confederate Atlanta" (PhD diss., University of Georgia, 1973), 246, 254–56; Stephen Davis, "How Many Civilians Died in Sherman's Bombardment of Atlanta?" *Atlanta History* 45, no. 4 (2003): 5–23. *ADI* continued to publish until July 10, when it moved to Macon, resuming publication on Aug. 3. The City Council held its last meeting on July 18. The previous week, it gave authority to the mayor to decide on "the proper time to have the valuable records and papers sent out of the city for safe keeping" (Atlanta City Council Minutes, vol. 4, July 11, 18, 1864).

11. SPR diary, Sept. 1, 9, 1864.

12. Ibid., Sept. 4, 21, 1864; Thomas G. Dyer, *Secret Yankees: The Union Circle in Confederate Atlanta* (Baltimore: Johns Hopkins University Press, 1999), 202–3; *ASC*, Nov. 28, 1861 (benefit concert), Dec. 25, 1861 ("God Defendeth the Right").

13. Castel, *Decision in the West*, 548–49.

Sat 2. [January 2, 1864]

So far the weather of the New Year has been bitterly cold. This morning I am told the thermometer said 8° only and it was so cold that we could hardly keep comfortable in bed. It has been too cold to do any thing but sit over the fire. I wore my newsuit of Jeans to singing tonight—my wife made it up for me this week. Mr Calloway returned last night and brought us 20 lbs of splendid butter from his mother in law. Mrs C did not come and will not again he says as he is going to leave Atlanta. Singing was at Bro Roots tonight.

Sunday 3. [January 3, 1864]

We nearly froze at church this morning, the fires being a failure. While we were at church in the aft a wonderful thing happened,—Jabe and Annie had come in to church *about 12 o'clock* and did not go in the Aft neither did *Mary* and when we returned the children astonished us by the news that Jabe and Mary had made friends and she had gone out to the farm to stay a week! "O dear me! last year I didn't like turnips, and now I do!"

Monday 4. [January 4, 1864]

The Callaways vacated their room today. On posting up our Cash A/cs [accounts] tonight I find balances as follows

    J.J.R. Dr to Cash—total—$38,646.96
    S.P.R.   "   "   " $18,566.10

There is due to Jabe, however, Clerk's board and house rent in 1863.

Sat 9. [January 9, 1864]

Jabez has been staying in town nearly all this week as Bro Worrell is not here *to edit* for him. He went out last night however and I have had to mail the "Friend" today. We have had very severe weather ever since Christmas "the coldest ever known here" they say! Singing at Mrs Wests tonight and they gave us a feast of Eggnogg, Cake and Candy! I did not enjoy it much. No army news, except that an attack upon Wilmington N.C. is apprehended soon also another upon Savannah.

Sunday 10. [January 10, 1864]

Morning Service in the Lecture Room on account of the difficulty of making the upper room comfortable. It was our Communion Season. No further service today. Tonight I have been writing some for the "Friend," some very *friendly* pieces.—

Sat 16. [January 16, 1864]

We have had miserably cold and disagreeable weather ever since Christmas and the streets have been in a wretched state this week. Today, however, has been bright and pleasant though cold. I have been helping Cohran set type this week as the paper was badly behind and is not yet printed. I set up, over a column. Jabez went to the Enrolling office to get my exemption papers fixed up as an *employee* in the Office of the "Friend" but Lieut Morgan who gave me trouble last winter, said he could not exempt me, as his orders were to *"enroll all who had put in Substitutes"* and send them to the Camp of Instruction at Decatur, and if there was any one wrongfully enrolled, it must be there made to appear and could there be rectified. So all I can do now, will be to go to Head Quarters at Decatur and see what Lieut. Harwell the Chief Enrolling Officer will do about it. If I am forced to serve just because I put in a substitute when I was already exempt without, thinking that I was thereby benefitting the country as well as myself, I shall always feel as though I was doubly cheated and injured, and cannot be expected to serve with much love and zeal a government that has acted in such a way.

Sunday 17. [January 17, 1864]

We have had a clear and pleasant day, but tonight is cloudy again and betokens rain. It was terribly muddy getting to church this morning. Dr B's texts were "Thou art my strong habitation &c" and "And Enoch walked with God[.]" Mr Root has returned. Mary came in from the farm today and brought Annie to go to school with the children. I went to hear Bro Hornady tonight as I wanted to obtain a letter of introduction of him to Lt. Harwell. I have got a certificate from Dr Brantley to certain facts.—

Wed 20. [January 20, 1864]

Yesterday, I got Bro Root to go with me to the Enrolling Office to ask Lt Morgan if he had heard from Lt Harwell in relation to my case, and we found himself there, so that we were spared the trip to Decatur. Morgan was absent and Harwell seemed willing enough to exempt me, but while I was waiting after Mr Root had left, Morgan came in and called Harwell into the next room and when they returned he began to make difficulties and finally postponed my case until today—which was not very encouraging to me. So, today, I got Bro Hornady to go with Jabez and myself to see him and to my relief he fixed it up without any trouble and gave me a printers' exemption. I tried my hand today for the first time at *distributing* type and succeeded pretty well.—Our runaway "Harvey" returned today having been off over a week. The weather has been beautiful today. Maj Comer led the meeting tonight, Dr B being away.*

Sunday 24. [January 24, 1864]

It is a delightful day, the sixth in succession. I went to S.S. and heard Mr Roots class.—We had singing at our house last night and this morning I had to lead in the school and in the choir as Mr Root is away. Dr Baird preached for us this morning.†—We heard him again at night at the "Central" Ch.

Sat 30. [January 30, 1864]

We have had a week or more of beautiful Spring-like weather, and it is difficult not to believe that Winter is over and gone—yet it cannot be so, I fear. I have sowed radishes and set out onions this week.—I have been *printing* more or less every day this week, setting up two columns of the Friend. The Senate has modified the Exemption Bill in such a way as to cut off all papers published or started since April 1862 which if it became a law will kill the "Soldier's Friend" as that paper though the oldest of its class is only about one year old.‡—Thus they keep one continually in hot water not knowing whether he must be a soldier or not.—We took the

---

* SPR may have referred to M. L. Comer, also known as W. L. Conner, who is listed as a private in the 6th Georgia Regiment, Army of Tennessee, Hancock County (Lillian Henderson, ed., *Roster of Confederate Soldiers of Georgia, 1861–1865*, 6 vols. [Hapeville, Ga.: Longino and Porter, 1959], 1:751–54).

† Rev. Baird served as interim pastor of Central Presbyterian Church between the pastorates of J. L. Rogers and Robert Q. Mallard during 1863 and filled in thereafter on occasion while also working for the Confederate government (John Robert Smith, *The Church That Stayed: The Life and Times of Central Presbyterian Church in the Heart of Atlanta* [Atlanta: Atlanta Historical Society, 1979], 35).

‡ The bill to which SPR referred, passed by the Confederate Senate on Jan. 10, 1864, limited draft exemptions among ministers, newspaper editors, and printers to those in service to their professions since Apr. 10, 1862 (ASC, Jan. 30, 1864). The bill evidently was designed to prevent people such as SPR from choosing new professions to evade the draft.

children to Mr Births Gallery the other day and had them Photographed, and tonight I brot home the largest picture which we shall frame. It is pretty true to life, especially Arthur's face and figure as he was less *conscious* of what was doing and therefore is most natural.

Sunday 31. [January 31, 1864]

I again heard Bro Roots class today. Dr Baird preached again for us this morning.—Rev Mr Mallard preached in the afternoon from the text "In my Father's house are many mansions[.]" I like him as a preacher very much.—

Sat 6. [February 6, 1864]

Gen Jno H. Morgan who has lately escaped from the Ohio Penitentiary, was received here this morning publicly by a large concourse of citizens and we all went to see him and heard him speak. We had our big calf killed tonight as it cost too much to feed him and beef is so high that we thought it best to make her feed us.—We went tonight to Mr Roots to sing.—

Sunday 7. [February 7, 1864]

Our Pastor was at his post again today, and preached this morning from the text "Who is on the Lord's side?"—Col McLean returned today.—

Sat 13. [February 13, 1864]

We have had Mr Grubb in the store with Henry, this week, giving them $40 each. Jabez and I have been getting up a *memorial* or certificate in reference to the "Soldiers' Friend" which we expect to send to Richmond through Col. Blake, who is Conscript Officer General and appointed to make a report in reference to the *material* in the country to make soldiers of. We have obtained about a dozen names of the clergy and medical officers. We find that the Friend is very well thought of in the community. "The Baptist Banner" has moved to our office, today, so that we shall have more company than heretofore[.] Planted six *Ailanthus trees* before my lot this week.—

Sunday 14. [February 14, 1864]

We have not had the bother of selling Valentines this year as we have none to sell.—Dr Brantley preached this morning from the text "Trust in the Lord and do good &c"—In the afternoon, he continued the subject from the remaining clause of the same passage, "So shall thou dwell in the land, &c[.]"

Sat 20. [February 20, 1864]

We have met with a considerable loss this week, in the *Shoe* Department. Mr Seymour had given to Henry a package of money, $2500—to lock up for *safe* keeping, and instead of locking it up, Henry had stuck it into a shelf of the open safe and said no more about it until a week afterwards when Seymour called for it—*it was gone!* Only a few days before Henry had let some one take $200 out of our drawer. What a reliable clerk he is, to be sure! So thoughtful—so careful of our interests. The latest despatches from Richmond state that the new Military Bill as agreed to by both houses makes no material change in regard to Newspapers from the old bill: if so, there is no necessity for the *Memorial* we have prepared, and so we have not sent it. The new Currency Bill is creating considerable anxiety and flutter among the holders of *Confed* [money].* We hear that the Yankees have begun their attack on Mobile.—

Sunday 21. [February 21, 1864]

I heard Roots young ladies *recite*, this morning. Dr Brantley preached in the Lecture Room from the text, "I die daily."—This aft' we went to Epis' Church and heard Bishop Elliott preach a *confirmation* sermon from the words "I see men as trees walking." General Morgan and his wife were there. Tonight, I went to Pres' Church to hear Mr Mallard but found Dr Brantley in the pulpit. We had no *second* service in our church.

Sat. 27. [February 27, 1864]

I have been assisting Ells to mail the Banner today, and it seemed rather natural to go over the old books again.—The Yankees have made demonstrations both in Missi[ssippi] and in North Georgia this week, but retreated without doing much, in fact they were *repulsed* in our State.—†

---

* In an effort to shore up its depreciating currency, the Confederate Congress passed legislation on Feb. 17, 1864, that allowed citizens to exchange currency for twenty-year bonds to be funded at 4 percent. Otherwise, currency could be exchanged for new bills at a rate of 3:2 (Douglas B. Ball, *Financial Failure and Confederate Defeat* [Urbana: University of Illinois Press, 1991], 188).

† On Feb. 23, 1864, Union soldiers in George Thomas's Army of the Cumberland engaged Joseph E. Johnston's Confederates in the Army of Tennessee near Dalton, Georgia. Fighting in Mississippi took place at New Albany from Feb. 23 to Mar. 9 (E. B. Long, *The Civil War Day by Day: An Almanac* [Garden City, N.Y.: Doubleday, 1971], 468).

Sunday 28. [February 28, 1864]

Dr B. preached this morning from the text "Train up a child &c" and Major Conner talked to the S. School in the aft. and tonight we went to hear Rev Mallard. I like Mrs Willis's singing on the Soprano in their choir better than Mrs West's, though that is not a very great compliment to Mrs Willis either.

Monday 29. [February 29, 1864]

This is the day that comes only once in four years. We have had a month of pleasant weather for the season. What will the coming month be?

Tuesday 1. [March 1, 1864]

Jabez started this morning to attend a Convention of Editors of Weekly Papers in Milledgeville tomorrow; after which he will go to Sparta to see Kate—and *some one else* perhaps—as a certain lady of that village has been named favorably for the situation of Mrs JJR no 3! Nous venons.—*

Sat 5. [March 5, 1864]

I have had all the work to do for the "Friend" this week as regards Editorial, mailing &c—Have been doing something towards gardening today.

Sunday 6. [March 6, 1864]

Dr Brantly preached this morning from the words "I am not mad." applying it to the believer in the Bible and the follower of Christ.—I forgot to chronicle my birthday; I was 40 years old the 3rd inst[ant]. Fifteen months ago I should have counted myself happy to have been that age; *now*, it is not an occasion for any special gratification.—

Sat 12. [March 12, 1864]

Jabez got back last Wed' night in a rain storm. I have been at the Office but little this week as I worked in the garden more or less and have been otherwise busy. I have put in a few peas; also radishes, turnips, onions, beets, squashes, cucumbers, corn and potatoes.—Also fixed up the raspberry and strawberry vines.—I have had the Paper to edit for two weeks.—

Sunday 13. [March 13, 1864]

We have had a beautiful day, and indeed the weather has been fine for weeks past. Dr B preached today from the texts "And the Lord turned and looked upon Peter" and "There is now no condemnation to those that are

---

* *Nous venons* is French for "We will see."

in Christ Jesus" &c—Sallie did not go to Church this afternoon. I wrote for the *Friend* at night.

Sat. 19. [March 19, 1864]

Winter has returned this week, and I fear the fruit is injured by the freezing cold; we had ice half an inch thick Wed' morning. Jabez and Father don't get along well at the farm, and the *stock* is fast diminishing in quality and quantity. It will be a losing speculation as I have always predicted. No war-news of importance. The Yankees have been foiled in a great Raid on Richmond which was intended to destroy the city and murder the President and Cabinet.* Singing was at our house tonight.—

Sunday 20. [March 20, 1864]

We are having the Spring Equinoctial today, or the beginning of it perhaps, as it has not stormed but is threatening to do so. Dr Brantley being away, Dr Baird preached for us this morning and Rev Parks of the Methodist Church is to preach this aft. I went round to call on the latter before service hour and got $30 for *The Friend* from Rev Atticus Haygood.

Tuesday 22. [March 22, 1864]

The storm culminated today in a heavy fall of snow some four inches deep! I went to the Depository's Office and invested $12,000 in the new 4% Bonds to pay taxes with, as under the late law that will probably be the amount necessary! It is a time of perplexity now with those who have Confederate Paper Money, as on the first of April it depreciates *one third* in value. We are looking now very soon for the tiding of another severe fight in North Georgia, as the avowed intention of the enemy is to march upon Atlanta this Spring.

Sat. 26. [March 26, 1864]

The McLeans came back today. Provisions are so scarce and high that I wish they would leave us. Flour is $1^{\underline{25}}$ per pound, Sugar $10, Butter $8^{\underline{00}}$, Beef $3^{\underline{50}}$, Coffee $15^{\underline{00}}$, Sweet Potatoes $16 per bushel, Syrup $20 gallon &c &c—Thursday night Jabez and I went to the Pres Church at 7 O'c to see a couple married by Dr Brantly and we had to wait an hour and a half for them. There were *ten* couple waiters.

---

* On Mar. 1-2, 1864, five hundred Union cavalry under Colonel Ulrich Dahlgren threatened the Confederate capital but were ultimately repulsed. When Dahlgren was killed on Mar. 2, materials were found on his body implying a plot to kill President Jefferson Davis. Historians have questioned the authenticity of this plot (Long, *Civil War Day by Day*, 471).

Sunday 27 [March 27, 1864]

This is a beautiful day after a cold and stormy week. Most of the fruit is killed they say by the cold. Dr Brantly preached this morning from the text "O Lord, revive thy work." Part of the singing was *execrable*. This aft the text was II Cor 2:10 "For godly sorrow &c." Mrs Luckie was baptized, and the congregation was good.

Sat 2 [April 2, 1864]

Winter still reigns and holds vegetation in bonds still. Our boarders have rented a house and are going to leave us next week.—Tonight I discovered Jupiter above the horizon at eleven o'clock and took a *squint* at him through the glass and saw his moons very distinctly.—

Sunday 3. [April 3, 1864]

Dr B's text this morning was "Only believe" this aft. Gal 5:13. "by love serve one another[.]" Mrs West and I sat down stairs today as Mr Root was absent and Sallie did not go out. I heard Roots class today.—One of the class was married last week and as they are all *marriageable*, they will all drop off fast now I guess.—

Sat 9. [April 9, 1864]

Our boarders left for their new home on Tuesday aft. They are to live in a small house on McDonough St. On Thursday the weather having moderated I remained at home in the morning to work in the garden. The weather has been very unfavorable for gardens for several weeks. Yesterday was the National Fast day and Dr Brantley preached a first rate sermon from Prov. 16:7. "When a man's ways please the Lord, he maketh even his enemies to be at peace with him."*—In the aft there was a Union Prayer Meeting at our church.

Friday 22. [April 22, 1864]

My book being nearly filled up and no more to be had, I have to restrict my notes to items of importance, among which may perhaps be included the following: At five minutes before twelve o'clock, last night Sallie gave birth to a big little girl, weighing eleven pounds. She had given signs of her coming all the afternoon, and at 9 O'clock I went for Dr O'Keefe. After eleven, Sallie had a hard time until the child was born; though on the whole every thing went on well, and so far continues so. We have not

---

* Jefferson Davis declared a day of fasting and prayer on Apr. 8, 1864. *ADI* reminded its readers of the need to appeal to the Almighty "that He may be pleased to look with favor upon our struggle for independence and to crown our arms with victory in the coming campaign."

yet quite fixed on a name but think we shall call the baby "Margaret." The Convention met today and Dr Mell preached from the text "The will of the Lord be done."* Our visitors arrived yesterday afternoon, Mr and Mrs Ichabod Davis of Americus. My beans, okra, and cucumbers planted before the cold weather was gone did not come up and must be replanted as soon as it rains—the ground is now too dry and hard. God has been blessing us with repeated successes over the enemy of late tho no decisive battle has been fought. In Louisiana our forces have defeated Banks and Steele; captured Fort Pillow in Tenn.; Plymouth in N.C. and taken large quantities of valuable supplies of all kinds.—†

Sunday 1. [May 1, 1864]

Dr Brantley was called away by the illness of his son "Theo." and Rev Jesse H. Campbell preached for us in the morning. In the aft I went over to the new episcopal Church—"St. Luke's" they call it. We have finally decided to name the baby "Virginia" and call her "Virnie" as a pet name. We first *drew lots* between "Margaret" and "Mary" and the latter was chosen but before it was put in the Bible we changed to "Virginia" and so it was entered in the Bible.—

Sat 7. [May 7, 1864]

We have just received the tidings that the long looked for battle in Virginia has begun, and so far, with success on our side tho' a number of our

---

* Patrick Mell, a Baptist clergyman of some renown, ministered to many different congregations around the state of Georgia before 1856, when he became professor first of ancient languages and then of metaphysics and ethics at the University of Georgia. He served for twenty-two years as president of the Georgia Baptist Convention (*History of the Baptist Denomination in Georgia* [Atlanta: Harrison, 1881], 381–84).

† Confederate forces under Nathan Bedford Forrest captured Fort Pillow, Tennessee, on the Mississippi River on Apr. 12, 1864. They overwhelmed the Federal garrison of nearly six hundred, about half of them African American, reportedly killing rather than taking prisoner the surrendering troops. Outraged abolitionists labeled the killing of black soldiers (who were gunned down in higher numbers than whites) a "massacre." Union general Nathaniel Banks was repulsed at Sabine's Crossroads during the Red River expedition, which had as its overall goal gaining greater dominance of Louisiana, Texas, and Arkansas (David S. Heidler and Jeanne T. Heidler, eds., *Encyclopedia of the American Civil War: A Political, Social, and Military History*, 5 vols. [Santa Barbara, Calif.: ABC-CLIO, 2000], 1:175, 2:746–47). Confederate forces led by R. F. Hoke, aided by the CSS *Albemarle*, seized Plymouth, North Carolina, along with many supplies on Apr. 20, 1864 (Long, *Civil War Day by Day*, 487).

officers have been killed; *two* by our own troops, *by mistake*; and Gen Longstreet badly wounded in the same way.* At Dalton also the enemy seem to be making a demonstration. If we are defeated in these battles, I fear the bright and cheering hopes of peace that now animate all hearts in the South, will be dissipated quickly.—Mr Brown came to see his wife last Thursday night, and tomorrow they both go to Augusta to spend the remainder of his furlough. Mary has had a neat marble stone put up on "Baby Bell's" grave, and Jabez has been beautifying the lot.

Sunday 8. [May 8, 1864]

Father and Mother came in to church today, and heard a good sermon from Dr Houston, Methodist from Nashville now in charge of Wesley Chapel here. On account of the indisposition of Dr B our Communion was postponed and I went this aft to the black folks meeting in our Lecture Room and was somewhat entertained if not edified. A young colored woman related her experience and was received for baptism.—

Sunday 15. [May 15, 1864]

Dr B's text this morning was, "living soberly in this present world." Mr Root has not yet returned. Our Communion was celebrated in the afternoon. Father and Mother came in and dined with us. After dinner Sallie and I and the children rode out to the cemetery. The saddest sight that I have seen is the *acre* of fresh-dug graves that are filled by dead soldiers, the result of this terrible war. Not a blade of grass left growing there. And still the work of destruction goes on—we hear that there is a general engagement today all along our lines at Resaca in Upper Georgia.† No definite news from Richmond for several days. We are anxiously waiting for it.

---

* At the Battle of the Wilderness, Virginia, May 5–6, 1864, the armies of Generals Robert E. Lee and Ulysses S. Grant faced in a major bloodbath. Neither side won a clear victory, and both armies suffered enormous casualties. General James Longstreet was mistakenly shot by Confederates (McPherson, *Ordeal*, 448–50; Long, *Civil War Day by Day*, 492–95).

† At the Battle of Resaca, Georgia, May 15, 1864, Union soldiers led by Joseph Hooker defeated John Bell Hood's Confederates. Concerned about being flanked with the Oostenaula River behind him, the Confederate commander, Joseph E. Johnson, withdrew at nightfall in the direction of Calhoun and Adairsville (Long, *Civil War Day by Day*, 501–2). The cemetery described by SPR was called City Cemetery until 1872, when it was renamed Oakland Cemetery. Sixty-nine hundred Civil War soldiers are buried there (Tevi Taliaferro, *Historic Oakland Cemetery* [Charleston, S.C.: Arcadia, 2001], 7).

Sunday 29. [May 29, 1864]

The past week has been one of great excitement in our city, the army having fallen back continually and refugees from Upper Georgia constantly arriving. Our forces are said to be in good condition yet and are still facing the foe about 25 miles west of Atlanta. For several days past some of our citizens have heard the report of the Artillery at *the front.* Gov Brown has called out the militia and Jabez and I have joined a company of Printers for city defence. I trust we may never be called into action, I hate the sight of a musket. May God deliver us from our blood-thirsty foes. We have had nice strawberries from our garden for two weeks nearly every day, never less than a quart each time. Our cow has just gone dry and we have no *cream.* Sallie went out to church last Sunday and today, so that our choir is in full feather again.

Friday, June 10. [June 10, 1864]

Today was appointed by our Mayor as a day of Fasting and Prayer especially for the safety of our City from invasion by the enemy.* We had a pleasant Union Meeting at our Church to pray for our Country and City. A Col Wilkes addressed us arrayed in his army garb with his pistol in his belt. He spoke quite encouragingly in reference to the military and religious condition of the Army of Tennessee, from which he has just come. Father and Mother came in to meeting and report that Caroline gave birth to a boy at one o'c this morning quite unexpectedly.

NOTICE BY SPR

Since the last writing of my wife *War* has begun and in October 1861 we removed from *Macon* to *Atlanta,* as recorded by me in a previous volume, a continuance of wh' may be found on the page opposite this. Sallie has got her hands full without keeping a diary—

Sunday 3. [July 3, 1864]

My volume having been filled up and not being able to procure another in these times of scarcity, I have accepted Sallie's offer of her only half-

---

* The Atlanta City Council had passed a resolution calling for a day of fasting, humiliation, and prayer because "the Lincoln Government has concentrated two of the largest armies ever seen on this continent, the one under the leadership of Gen'l Grant to besiege Richmond, the Seat of Government, and the other under Gen'l Sherman to invade Georgia and capture Atlanta, 'the citadel of the Confederacy' as they term it, and have left nothing, in their power, undone to accomplish that design." Atlantans were urged to pray for "strength to resist the vandal invader and crown our arms with decisive victories" (Atlanta City Council Minutes, vol. 4, June 1, 1864).

filled book. It is a bright and pleasant Sabbath morning and the church bells are pealing out their call to the sanctuary, while mingling with their peaceful sound comes the deep booming of the distant Cannon telling of War and its dreadful scenes of blood. It is said that the enemy is very desirous of taking Atlanta by the fourth of July, and a battle has been expected to come off today as the glorious Fourth is so nigh. Our army is still at Kennesaw Mountain near Marietta about 25 miles from here and several attempts of the enemy to dislodge them have been repulsed, with great loss to the enemy. *Old Abe* has been nominated for re-election by the Baltimore Convention and *Fremont* by the *other* Abolition party. The Democratic Convention that was to have met tomorrow at Chicago has been postponed until August 29th probably to see the result of the present campaign in Virg[inia]. and Georgia. It is hoped that if these great efforts prove abortive that a *peace* candidate will be nominated by that assembly. Vallandigham has returned from exile without permission!*

Dr. Brantley preached this morning from the text "Give us this day our daily bread."—This aft I went to prayer-meeting at our church. I have been to such a meeting for prayer for the country almost every day for nearly two months. It would seem as if all christians in this extremity would be both ready and anxious to seek a throne of Grace to implore God's protection from our cruel foes, but alas! how few there are who evince any such desire. It seems to be pretty certain now that our army has again *fallen back* nearer to Atlanta since two oclock this morning. I was in hopes that this would not be necessary.†

Sunday 10. [July 10, 1864]

This has been a sad day in our city, for it has been quite evident for some days past that there is a great probability of Atlanta falling into the

---

* Because of public dissatisfaction with the direction of the war, Lincoln faced challenges from within the Republican Party for the nomination in the summer of 1864. Treasury secretary Salmon P. Chase failed in his efforts to promote himself as an alternative to Lincoln, but the 1856 Republican standard-bearer, John C. Frémont, garnered support from some abolitionists. George B. McClellan, the former Union general, received the Democratic nomination in August (McPherson, *Ordeal*, 376–77, 475–76).

† The Confederate victory at Kennesaw Mountain, Georgia, on June 27, 1864, slowed but did not stop Sherman's advance toward Atlanta. Both armies spent several days following the battle caring for wounded and burying the dead, but on July 2, Johnston moved his army south as Sherman resumed his strategy of using his larger military force to fight a series of flank attacks against the Confederates. Atlantans initially believed that their city was safe, but their confidence soon disappeared (Castel, *Decision in the West*, 335–36; Long, *Civil War Day by Day*, 531).

hands of the enemy and the city has been in a complete swarm all day and for several days. All the Govt stores and Hospitals are ordered away and of course the citizens are alarmed and many have left and others are leaving.* Dr. Brantley preached for us this morning to a small congregation, and requested the members of the Church to remain after service to determine whether we would have the communion in the afternoon, which was decided affirmatively. Only about a dozen members were present at the ordinance[,] those from the immediate neighborhood, but it was quite a touching season. Dr. B was so affected that he could hardly speak. The Church gave him liberty to go when it became necessary. His family have already left for Augusta. I took the pulpit Bible and Hymn Book home with me as it seemed almost certain that it would not be again needed there for the present. Alas! these dreadful times of war! When will they be ended? If Atlanta falls, I fear it will be a long, long time. Charlie DuBose and his son Charles came today and tonight Mary Brown has decided to go to Sparta with mother and Annie and Ethel who go in "little" Charlie's care. Mary did not much want to go. Sallie and I have about decided to stay at home, Yankees or no Yankees. We hear and read terrible tales of them, but I don't think they are as bad as they are said to be. We hear of a good many who are going to remain in the city if the enemy gets possession.

Sunday 17. [July 17, 1864]

We have been again permitted to meet at the sanctuary for the worship of God. The enemy draws nearer and nearer tho' to our city. All of a sudden Gen Johnston has been *relieved* of the command of the Army and Gen Hood or "Old Pegleg" as the soldiers style him placed in command, so that there is thought to be a prospect for a fight before Atlanta is given up, as Hood is said to [be a] *fighting* man, if he *has* only one leg.† The ordinance of baptism was administered in our church this morning to two candidates, a lady and a deaf-mute young man.

---

* Atlanta's hospitals began evacuating patients on July 6, 1864. Those well enough to be sent home were granted convalescent furloughs, while sicker patients were moved to other hospitals in locations including Macon and Milledgeville (Kennett, *Marching through Georgia*, 120; Welsh, *Two Confederate Hospitals*, 35–36).

† On July 17, 1864, believing that General Joseph E. Johnston had not shown sufficient firmness in resisting Sherman's advances toward Atlanta, Jefferson Davis replaced Johnston with General John Bell Hood, who had distinguished himself as a fighting general in several of the South's illustrious victories and had lost a leg at the Battle of Chickamauga (Castel, *Decision in the West*, 360–63).

Wed. 20. [July 20, 1864]

At 10 oclock last night a fire broke out in the brick block opposite our store and destroyed McPherson's store and stock among several others.

Friday 22. [July 22, 1864]

All last night our city was in a complete hubbub with army wagons and soldiers and marauders as though the whole army was passing through. A lot of cavalry robbers broke into the stores and stole everything that they took a fancy to. They stripped our store of the paper and other stationery that we had there, and about thirty dollars in money. Today our last newspaper departed, the "Appeal" also the Postoffice, and every other establishment and individual that intended to go, as the enemy was confidently expected to take possession tonight. But about four oclock we heard heavy firing and rapid discharges of musketry to the eastward, and before dark crowds of prisoners began to come in that our forces had taken in a successful flank movement by Gen Hardee. It then began to appear likely that Gen Hood intended to hold the city if he could.*

Sat. 23. [July 23, 1864]

We have had a considerable taste of the beauties of bombardment today. The enemy have thrown a great many shells into the city and scared the women and children and *some* of the *men* pretty badly. One shell fell in the street just below our house and threw gravel in our windows, they say. This seems to me to be a very barbarous mode of carrying on war, throwing shells among women and children. The city authorities required me to do police duty, and I had to stand on guard on McDonough St from 8 to 10 and 2 till 4 this night, and carryed a musket for the *first* time in my life! My wife and children had to put their beds on the floor behind the chimney to be secure from shells which were thrown into the city all night long. No more fell near our house however, and but little damage was done anywhere.

---

* On July 21, 1864, General John Bell Hood ordered Confederate forces under General William Hardee to march south through Atlanta via Peachtree Street in the middle of the night, startling many city residents. Hardee then shifted his troops to the east, in the direction of Decatur, where they were joined by soldiers under General Patrick Cleburne and two divisions of cavalry under General Joseph Wheeler. This combined force hoped to gain access to Union supplies in Decatur. The actions of the Confederate and Union Armies led to several battles in which the Confederate side suffered heavy losses (Heidler and Heidler, *Encyclopedia*, 1:128–46).

Sunday 24. [July 24, 1864]

The foe is still outside and continues to pop shells at us. No church in the city open. Father came in the morning but left in such a double quick that I did not see him. Jabe also came in, for the first time since he left last Wednesday night. He has moved the stock and negroes to Mr. Stanley's ten miles from Atlanta not without loss and accident[.] Father is still at the farm with Old Dinah.—

Monday 1. [August 1, 1864]

Nothing of much importance has transpired during the week that we are aware of. We have had *shelling* semi-occasionally but thus far none of the deadly missiles have reached our house and we could look upon them at a safe distance with composure. For fear that they should ever reach us I have done several hard days' work preparing a "pit" in our cellar, to retreat to for shelter. One pierced the top cornice of our store and went into Beach & Roots building opposite. I have had to stand on guard every other night the past week and drill a little with the militia, but the duties have not been arduous and I will not complain so long as we have no other duty to perform. If they go to making us do *active service* at "the ditches" or "the front" I shall try to get off from it. Our garden is helping us out a great deal [in] these hard times. We have not suffered much from thieves and have given away such "truck" as we did not need. Corn, tomatoes and butter-beans are now in full feather. The enemy have made two raids below us, one upon the Macon RR which they *cut* near Jonesboro, but not badly; another upon the Central RR near Macon, and doubtless astonished the Maconites by throwing several shells across the river into their quiet city! From what we hear, however, it seems that both these parties have "come to grief" by being overhauled by our forces.* Our city is very quiet now except when the shelling is in progress. Yesterday the Lords Day not a Protestant Church was open; all the ministers have forsaken their posts except the Catholic; they had service I noticed. The Episcopal minister I think is here but the Church is under repair. I had

---

* On July 26, 1864, William T. Sherman gave permission to General George Stoneman to launch a cavalry raid. In addition to cutting a vital rail line into Atlanta at Lovejoy Station, Stoneman hoped to liberate Union prisoners of war in Macon and Andersonville. On July 30, accompanied by fifty-five hundred mounted soldiers, Stoneman reached Macon, where he faced a well-entrenched contingent of local defenders with artillery. In the disorganized process of retreating, Stoneman and several hundred of his men were captured (McMurry, *Atlanta 1864*, 157–58).

to drill at the City Hall instead of singing at the Sanctuary. On Sat' night though, our choir met at our house and sang. We have seen it stated in a Griffin paper that Col Lamar and Lt Col Van Valkenburgh of the 61st Georgia Regt were killed at the battle of Monocasy, and I fear it is true.* It is a dreadful blow to James' wife, if so, for she seems to be devoted to him, and has been hoping and fearing for so long a time. It really seems as though sooner or later the sword claims all as its victims, however long it may spare. Sherman's host still surrounds us, no, not exactly surround, but still besiege us on the North and North West trying to *come in*. Our general is trying to out-general and *Hood*-wink them, but it appears doubtful which will gain the point. It is to be hoped the contest will not be prolonged indefinitely for there is nothing much to be had to eat in Atlanta though if we keep the RR we shall not quite starve, I trust.

Sunday 7. [August 7, 1864]

We have been to church this morning, for the first time in three weeks. Rev Atticus Haygood preached to us in the Methodist Church. Our cruel foe has the grace to cease from shelling us on the Sabbath, at least he has not done so yet. Last Wednesday night the horrid missiles of destruction whizzed *past* our house and discomposed us considerably. Heretofore they had all fallen short, but now we cannot tell at what moment they may strike us. A gentleman and his little girl, ten years of age were both killed in bed by the same shell last week, and several others have lost their lives.†—Today we received letters at last from the world without, one from Harriet says that Mr Taylor has at last had to go-a-soldiering, and she confirms James' death.—Upon entering our store today I was puzzled at finding the stove tumbled down and moved forward six feet, but the rubbish around and the side of the *flue* in the wall told that a shell had "dropped in" but where it had made its entrance I could not discover until I went upstairs and then the mystery was explained. The shell had

---

* The Battle of Monocacy, Maryland, July 9, 1864, was part of a campaign by Confederate cavalry general Jubal Early to menace Washington, D.C., at a time when the Union commander, General Ulysses S. Grant, was preoccupied with the effort to take Richmond. Although Early's men won a victory at Monocacy, his efforts there and at Frederick, Maryland (where he demanded two hundred thousand dollars in exchange for not burning the city), caused a delay that proved fatal to his efforts to take the U.S. capital (Cooling, *Monocacy*, 180–83).

† On Aug. 3, 1864, J. F. Warner and his young daughter were killed by a Union artillery shell while sleeping in their home near the Atlanta gasworks (Davis, "How Many Civilians Died?" 15).

entered the roof and passing through five partitions of wood and plaster had pierced the side wall into the flue, and its force being expended it *dropped* in the flue to the store below and there exploded, doing the mischief before spoken of. I found the butt end of the shell. The diameter of which is four inches and weighs 3 ¼ lbs. The length was probably ten or twelve inches and the entire weight 16 or 20 lbs. I hope no more such visitors will enter our premises.—A letter from Eli Mustin to Jabe in thanking him for the "Friend" says he thinks it is a greatly superior paper to the "Banner."

Sunday 14. [August 14, 1864]

Another week of anxiety and suspense has passed and the fate of Atlanta is still undecided. We have had but one severe shelling on our side of town and that was on Wed. night and kept us awake from 12 Oclock until daylight. Our *humane* foes allowed us to get well to sleep before they began their work of destruction. Another shell entered our store or rather the rooms above while I was there examining the premises to see if any more had visited them. I was enveloped in the dust made by it.—On Friday I was on a militia "detail" which worked all day. There is no fun in working hard and "finding" yourself. Last night we went to Mr Roots and spent the evening but did not sing. An Army *Band* gave the party a serenade and Root invited them in to cakes and whiskey. The shells flew about all night on the other side of town, but *we* slept pretty well. I was detailed for service today, and marched off to the *shelly* side of Whitehall Street and there kept for three hours doing nothing. We then were dismissed until 4½ o'clock this afternoon, so I joined the folks on the way to Epis' Church. I have been accustomed to being the disposer of my own time at least on Sunday, and this being ordered about by others as though we were niggers is not much to my mind. O this horrid war! When will it end?

Thursday 18. [August 18, 1864]

Jabez has just left us. He came to town on Monday to pack up and send off our stock of books &c to Macon in a hired car. I got off militia duty and we packed up the books in the store drawers, boxes &c, but changed our minds about sending it off as we preferred going to Augusta if we move the stock at all and Jabez is going first to see if a store can be obtained there. It *may* be many a day before we see him again. The "Friend" has been suspended now for six weeks and it is time it was going again. I wonder if *I* shall assist in its resumption. The future is very dark and uncertain, truly a *sealed book* to our finite minds. But God reigns and the inhabitants of the earth are but as grass hoppers in his sight as far as their power and might are concerned.

Sunday 21. [August 21, 1864]

I went to Epis' Church this morning; as it was rather wet, Sallie did not go. Yesterday for the third time only the *shells* went by our homes, and a fragment fell in our back yard. A large one entered our back store-door on Friday and bursting as it passed through the floor, tore up the latter pretty badly. It is said that about twenty lives have been destroyed by these terrible missiles, since the enemy began to throw them into the city.—it is like living in the midst of a pestilence, no one can tell but he may be the next victim. The news is that the enemy have cut the railroads again, and also, we are told that our cavalry has certainly cut off Sherman's communications by destroying the Road and bridges and blowing up the *Tunnel*! We do not know what to believe.—

Sat. 27. [August 27, 1864]

The first three secular days of this week the shells rained heavily upon our city and on Wednesday set three separate houses on fire, as is supposed, and in one of these fires our two Printing Presses, stored in McDaniels warehouse, were burnt. We have never yet had them in use but may need them ere long. On Thursday the shelling ceased altogether and it was rumored that the enemy was retreating and it is now known that they have deserted their camps around the city and are going *some*where but what is their design it is hard to tell. I fear that we have not yet got rid of them finally, but that they have some other plan in view to molest and injure us.* But in the meantime we can rest in security for a while, safe from shells. We began to remove our stock of books from the store to the house this morning, but when we had brought up two loads of drawers, we concluded to stop and await further developments. I had our *pit* dug three feet deeper this week and a barricade in front of boxes filled with dirt. A letter from Harriet gives us a kind invitation to go there and live with them if we do not wish to stay in Atlanta.

Sunday 28. [August 28, 1864]

I am on duty today and it is *hard* duty too. We have been all the morning unloading cars of Army Wagons and putting them together. At two

---

* Atlantans felt a momentary sense of optimism when, on Aug. 25, William T. Sherman ordered a cessation of the bombardment that had traumatized them for weeks. Sherman had ordered his men southwest of the city to cut rail access, which was the only remaining lifeline into Atlanta (McPherson, *Ordeal*, 477–78).

o'clock I have to go on again for the rest of the day. O when shall we be free again and at liberty to spend our sabbaths at least, in a manner more consonant with our feelings and habits. A shell has entered the roof of our church and passed through the back of the seat in the choir close to Sallie's usual place, and finally lodged somewhere in the front wall without exploding. Every thing is quiet enough now, we hear no cannon or musketry.

Monday 29. [August 29, 1864]

Sallie and I walked out Marietta Street this morning to see the devastation caused by the bombardment, and truly that part of the city is badly cut up.—Joe came in today and brought Caroline and the children as Mr Stanley and Joe have quarreled. Joe was probably impertinent and Stanley struck him. I wish they were safe in my pocket in hard coin at old valuation, or near it.—

Thursday Sep. 1. [September 1, 1864]

This was a day of terror and a night of dread. About noon came the tidings of a severe fight on the Macon RR and that our forces were worsted and the city was to be evacuated at once. Then began a scramble among the inhabitants thereof some to get away—others to procure supplies of food for their families. If there had been any doubt of the fact that Atlanta was about to be given up it would have been removed when they saw the depots of Government grain and food thrown open and the contents distributed among the citizens free gratis by the sackful and the cartload. The RR cars and engines were all run up to one place in order to be fired just as the army left. Five locomotives and 85 cars, Cousin Bill told me were to be burned. Mr West told me that the militia were ordered to be on hand to go out with the army, so I thought I would resign, as I was not bound to go. About midnight Mr West came to our back gate and called to me and told me that the Battalion had gone to McDonough and that he had backed out. I then went to the Macon depot with him and secured three sacks of meal. As we went down the Ammunition Train was fired and for half an hour or more an incessant discharge was kept up that jarred the ground and broke the glass in the windows around. It was terrific to listen to and know—the object.*—Jabez had gone to Griffin this day and I feared would not get back in time to carry away the farm darkies.

* Efforts to hold the rail line at Jonesboro having failed, John Bell Hood abandoned Atlanta on Sept. 1, 1864. Departing Confederate soldiers set fire to military materials to keep them from falling into Yankee hands. According to Mary A.

Friday 2. [September 2, 1864]

About noon today the Yankees came in[;] sure enough a party of five or six came riding by our house. A committee of our citizens went out early and met *Gen Slocum* and got his word that private property should be respected, upon which the city was surrendered to them and in they came.* The Stars and Stripes were soon floating over the city. The private houses were not molested by the soldiers and I was therefore very much surprized when I went down town to see armsful and baskets full of books and wall-paper going up the street in a continuous stream from our store and when I reached the store, the scene would have required the pencil of Hogarth to portray.† Yankees, men, women, children and niggers were crowded into the store each one scrambling to get something to carry away, regardless, apparently, whether it was any thing they needed, and still more heedless of the fact that they were stealing! Such a state of utter confusion and disorder as presented itself to my eyes then, I little dreamed of two hours before when I left it all quiet and, as I thought, safe. The soldiers in their mad hunt to [obtain] tobacco had probably broken open the door and the rabble had then "pitched in" thinking it a "free fight."— At first I was so dismayed that I almost resolved to let them finish it, but finally I got them out and stood guard until after dark when I left it to its chances until morning, as I was very sleepy. The night passed quietly and at day break I went to the store again to re-pack and prepare to move the balance of the books &c to the house. But a new difficulty soon arose;

DeCredico (*Patriotism for Profit: Georgia's Urban Entrepreneurs and the Confederate War Effort* [Chapel Hill: University of North Carolina Press, 1990], 98–99), "[T]his was a severe blow, for the goods lost in the evacuation and surrender of the city represented sources of transportation and supply that were desperately needed by Confederate armies." The ammunition train explosion described by Richards could be heard for miles. What was left of Hood's army slipped away in the night, but Sherman had achieved his strategic object, taking Atlanta (Kennett, *Marching through Georgia,* 198–203).

* Atlanta mayor James Calhoun led the delegation of citizens who surrendered the city, including several well-known Unionists. In a memorandum to Brigadier General William T. Ward, Calhoun wrote, "The fortune of war has placed Atlanta in your hands. As mayor of the city I ask protection to non-combatants and private property" (Castel, *Decision in the West,* 527–28; Dyer, *Secret Yankees,* 190–91). Henry Slocum commanded the Union 20th Corps, whose soldiers were the first to enter Atlanta.

† William Hogarth was an eighteenth-century English artist whose engravings often depicted raucous scenes of urban life.

one of the mules was stolen from the stable and the hauling stopped as Joe said. I borrowed Mr Clarks one horse wagon and putting the mule that was left (a little one) before it we began to haul with the prospect of two days work before us, but with the aid of Mrs Holbrooks dray in the afternoon we managed to get away the most of the goods. A number of books were *stolen* by the Yankees during the day before our eyes and that by men who *looked* like gentlemen! Of course their looks belied their character. Several took books and *paid* for them.

Sunday 4. [September 4, 1864]

It is strange to go about Atlanta now and see only Yankee uniforms. The City Hall is Head Quarters for the Provost Guard I guess. The enemy behave themselves pretty well except in the scramble for tobacco and liquor during which every store in town nearly was broken into yesterday. We heard the Church bells ring this morning and went to the Epis Church and heard Mr Freeman preach and a Fed. Chaplain read the prayers. When I got home Joe informed me that our *mule* had come back which I was glad to hear. This afternoon three soldiers asked for dinner saying their rations had not come and they would pay for the dinner, so Sallie had some cooked for them. They belonged to Co E 2nd Mass. Vols. But the chief spokesman was a Scotchman. They think that McClellan will be the next president as he had been nominated by the Chicago Convention.[*] At Mrs Roots request I accompanied herself and Mrs West to our church this afternoon and we heard an *Abolition* preacher from Indiana preach on the "home of the blessed." Returning to our homes we heard that another big fight at Jonesboro had resulted disastrously to the Confederates, and in confirmation of this we saw 1800 "rebel prisoners" marched into town. They filled the street from the Baptist Church to Whitehall St. It was a sad sight but the Yankees *cheered* at it lustily of course.—

Friday 9. [September 9, 1864]

We have have several days of great excitement, as it was understood that "Orders" had been, or were about to be, issued to the effect that *every* body not belonging to the army must leave the city going North or South as they saw fit, except the families of those men who had left

---

[*] Although George McClellan received the 1864 Democratic presidential nomination, he lost badly to Abraham Lincoln, carrying only New Jersey, Delaware, and Kentucky. William T. Sherman's military success helped Lincoln's chances, as did Lincoln's overwhelming support among soldiers (McMurry, *Atlanta 1864*, 204–8).

the city before the Yankees came, and such *must go South*.* Mrs. Root was the first one to feel the storm as her husband has been quite a strong secessionist and large blockade-runner, two heinous crimes in the Federal Calendar. But as yet no orders have been published specifying anything and we do not know what we have to do. We have determined upon going to New York if we are sent off, as we want to get away from the war and the fighting if we can. The news is published today in the Yankee papers that Gen John H. Morgan is killed.† The Yankees have not molested us much at the house, they have generally behaved pretty well. One unpleasant feature of present circumstances is the impudent airs the negroes put on, and their indifference to the wants of their former masters. Of course they are all free, and the Yankee soldiers don't fail to assure them of that fact. Jabe's "Sally" has come out of her hole now and is as independent as can be. "George" and "Clem" are said to be in the city too. So our negro property has all vanished into air.—

(*9th*) [September 9, 1864]

Henry's baby died last night, little Katie, age 15 mos. Mr Bohnefeld the undertaker was clever enough to give him a plain coffin worth six dollars in Greenbacks, and Joe and I dug a grave under a small oak in Henry's garden, and Rev Mr Freeman the Epis Minister officiated; and so the little one has passed away from the present evil and the "evil to come." "It is well with the child."—Yesterday was Dora's birthday; she is ten years old. I wrote her a long letter upon the importance to her giving early attention to the interests of her soul. Mr Seymour agreed yesterday to let me have $75 in gold out of $250 that he was prudent enough to secure in time, so that I shall have enough to get to New York with, at any rate, I hope. How I wish I had the value of our city lots and negroes in gold at this juncture.

---

* On Sept. 5, 1864, William T. Sherman ordered the civilian evacuation of Atlanta. According to historian Albert Castel (*Decision in the West*, 549), "Other than the expulsion of the inhabitants of three guerrilla-infested Missouri counties along the Kansas border after the Lawrence, Kansas, Massacre of 1863, the depopulation of Atlanta is the harshest measure taken against civilians by Union authorities during the entire Civil War."

† Morgan, whose appearance in Atlanta on Feb. 6 had inspired an outpouring of civic enthusiasm, was shot and killed in Greeneville, Tennessee, on Sept. 4, 1864. In this Unionist area of East Tennessee, a twelve-year-old boy had tipped off the Federal army that Morgan and his men were in the area (Ramage, *Rebel Raider*, 233–38).

Wed 21. [September 21, 1864]

This was the day fixed upon by Mr and Mrs West and ourselves to start forth from our homes exiles and wanderers upon the earth with no certain dwelling-places but I found that I could not get my effects off and having been told by Mr Dill that Jabez was waiting at Rough and Ready, under the existing "Flag of Truce," to see me I determined to run down and see him.* As I had a *pass* as one of the Refugee Committee to go and return at will, I found no difficulty and had an interview of several hours with Jabez recounting our various experiences. I anticipated difficulty in procuring a pass to go North as it was said that only those who could get vouchers for their loyalty from some one of a committee of several *Union* Citizens who had been appointed by the authorities—would be allowed passes to go. As I was only acquainted with one of these men and he was not inclined to favor me, I feared I should not be able to go North except *under guard* to be set at liberty upon taking the oath at Nashville or Louisville. And as we had sold all our furniture and provisions we were but poorly fixed to go South. But, fortunately, a young officer on Gen Sherman's staff, Capt Geo. Ward Nichols, came to our house to buy some furniture and in the course of conversation with Sallie, he found out that we were related to T. Addison Richards, an old friend and companion in art—and hearing that we expected to find difficulty in getting a passport he offered to give me a note of recommendation to Col Parkhurst the Provost Marshall which he said would help me he thought, although he was not personally acquainted with Col P. but anything from that Head Quarters generally received attention. So this morning I went and presented my letter, and I think I should have got my papers without question, even without a voucher from Mr Holcombe to the effect that I had repeatedly spoken to him against Secession and had voted against it. At all events they gave me a pass to Jeffersonville, Indiana, without trouble or question. I had already procured transportation for my books and effects—*one car load*—from Col Easton, Chief Q.M.†—The *books* were my chief trouble

---

* Rough and Ready is a town south of Atlanta in Fayette County named for Zachary Taylor, who was known that by that nickname (Kenneth K. Krakow, *Georgia Place-Names: Their History and Origins*, 2nd ed. [Macon, Ga.: Winship, 1975], 197).

† Captain George Ward Nichols served on General William T. Sherman's staff, Captain William Henry Parkhurst was provost marshal, and Colonel Langdon Cheves Easton was chief quartermaster (Janet B. Hewett, ed., *The Roster of Union Soldiers, 1861–1865*, 33 vols. [Wilmington, N.C.: Broadfoot, 2000], 33:324–25, 349–50).

as being half in open drawers, I feared they would be lost and damaged before I could get them to any market. We lay us down to take our last nights rest in our home, all ready to leave it on the morrow—to return again—perhaps never.

Tuesday 27. [September 27, 1864]

We are again in a freight car in Nashville, Tenn. waiting for the locomotive to come to take us on to Louisville. On Thursday last we got our goods and chattels loaded in a car at Atlanta and ourselves too, and after a hard day's work, took a rather comfortable supper in our car. Mr West had been of service to me and did a good deal to assist us in getting off. They, too, have decided to go to New York. Mr Seymour, too, kindly assisted me. We reached Nashville early Sunday morning, often stopping for hours waiting for trains to pass us going down to the army. We had the opportunity to boil our coffee every morning and enjoyed our meals very considerably. At night we spread our mattresses on the car floor and slept pretty well, and were in hopes that we should be allowed to go straight through to Louisville without changing our quarters. The weather which had been wet and cloudy all the week previous, cleared off on Sunday and I left my family in the car and went to deliver my letter to Col Donaldson, "Senior & Supervising Q.M." which letter Capt Nichols had given me to assist us in getting transportation through Nashville.[*] Col. D. gave me a few lines to Capt Brown with which I returned to the car and then went to get "five days rations" for our family of six, furnished gratuitously by U.S., I got 6 large loaves, a shoulder of bacon, sugar, tea and salt. While I was going again to see about transportation through, an order came for our train to be unloaded and upon my return I found them taking out our goods, and Sallie in a very perturbed state of mind, I immediately went to the agent and presented Col Donaldsons note, but did not succeed in getting our car left unloaded, for in consequence of Gen. Forrest's manoeuvers upon the railroads below, the cars were all needed to transport Cavalry to meet the "rebel" forces.[†] However, I got the privilege of putting our goods inside the depot, while the Wests and others had to

---

[*] Colonel James Lowry Donaldson (Hewett, *Roster of Union Soldiers*, 33:324).

[†] In the fall of 1864, General Nathan Bedford Forrest, commanding forty-five hundred Confederate cavalry, attempted to menace Union supply lines. He had limited success at Athens, Alabama, a Union fortification on the Decatur and Nashville Railroad, before returning to Tennessee (Heidler and Heidler, *Encyclopedia*, 2:722–24).

camp outside, exposed to the weather, and I also got the promise of a car to load up again as soon as might be. We remained in the depot until Monday afternoon all among the cavalry continually clattering in and out and our condition was not very agreeable. I found out that I could not sell my books in Nashville, so I applied again to the Agent for a car and contrary to my expectation succeeded in obtaining a good clean one and in about an hour we were again loaded up and *at home* as it were. Last night our car was "switched off" and left all night perched up upon a high trestle-work 27 feet above the ground, in full view of the Capitol of Nashville! It was a lonely spot but being so high up we were safe from robbers and meddlers.—This morning we were again taken in tow and finally left in this place to spend the day. We passed the Wests this morning at the depot waiting anxiously for transportation and we shall perhaps not see them again before we reach New York. We have had half of our bacon cooked today at an adjacent house so that we are prepared for a trip of several days between this and Louisville, though it is probable that we shall not be as much delayed on this road as we have been hitherto, as the Louisville Railroad belongs to a private company and is not so much under the control of the U.S. as the roads he has *captured*.

Sunday, Oct 9. [October 9, 1864]

To begin where I left off—At 5 oclock a locomotive and train steamed up and hitched on to our car, and we were soon travelling along at a good speed towards Louisville, and much to our surprize we found that in the car next in front of us as before were our friends, the Wests, Mackays &c! The country through which we passed that night, we could not see and the next morning did not show us anything very fine, until as we got into the Kentucky mountains the scenery was more picturesque and attractive. We passed through a long *tunnel* and over several high bridges. The distance from N to L is 185 miles and we reached Louisville at 2 P.M. when our troubles again began, for we were strangers in a strange city, and what troubled us the most was our great load of books &c which has been a great source of trouble to me ever since the Yankees took our City, and *before* too. I walked over a mile to the city to see what chance there was to get a store to display my wares. The best place I could find was next door to C C Spencer's Auction store in the store of McClellan & Bro who have since shown themselves to be two clever gentlemen, inclined to assist me all they can. Returning to the depot I found our stuff still in the car and an excise or Revenue officer there who said he must have *duty* on them. So much against my will I paid $30., and then sought where I could stow my goods for the night, as it was too late to haul them to the store. Mr Smith, Government Agent at the depot kindly aided us and Mr Van Austin RR agent was kind enough to let us unload in the depot under shelter and there we stayed all night nearly devoured by mosquitoes and annoyed by rats. Mrs West and Mrs Mackay slept with Sallie on our mattress, but their good men had to watch their baggage outside and the rain poured down in such a way as would have effectually disposed of my books if they had been exposed to it. The next day I engaged 3 Covered Express Wagons and had my goods taken to the store afore mentioned. Again the rain fell fast, and but for good covered wagons, our goods would have been wetted well. The books being disposed of by 3 Oclock P.M. I then had to look up a shelter for my wife and little ones. I began to think the prospect a bad one, when I called at the house of a widow who lived near the depot upon whose door hung a "Boarding" sign, and a pleasant faced young woman opened the door in reply to my tale of exile and distress (!) She said that her mother would not turn us off she knew; so there we took up our abode. The lady's name is Mrs Spaulding, her daughter's Mrs. Cooper, and the "help" (who is at present the sole mistress of the house) is named "Kate" a great strapping woman with a grim face but a kind heart. She had just married a young man of half *her* age, perhaps, who has conferred upon her the name of Harley. We have been in Louisville now ten days of varied light and shade. The prospect of selling our books was not bright, but by dint of effort I have succeeded in disposing of $1000. worth which is pretty well. Our boarding house is a long walk from my business and the room we occupy not very pleasant, the bed being *shucks* are hard enough, and furniture scarce. A few days ago Mrs S. and her daughter moved to the country with most of the furniture and left "Kate" in sole charge. Our fare is good enough and we pay $3.00 per day that is 6.00 per week for ourselves and halfprice for the children. Louisville is a large city and there are many fine houses both public and private. Yesterday upon going into the bookstore of Mr Maxwell I was surprised to find Mr Cohron employed there as a Job Printer. The weather which was quite wet for the first week we were here is now clear and today is quite cool and the morning was frosty. I have found much sympathy among the citizens of L. for the sufferers and exiles from the South. There are many *Union* people here but not many *Lincolnites*. The present Administration is discussed and 'cussed in many a coterie of democrats here. Were it not that we are too near the war here I should like to remain in L if I could make a living.—This is Sallie's birthday, she is 31 years old. It is not a very pleasant return of the day, to be homeless and wanderers with an uncertain future before us; but God has watched over us so far and given us a measure of success, so that we need not be without hope for the future.

Sunday 16. [October 16, 1864]

We are still in Louisville and as far as private sales of my books are concerned my trade is over; but the Auctioneer, Mr C. C. Spencer, has returned, and proposes to sell the miscellaneous books at auction beginning next Thursday night, so that we shall be here *another* Sunday if that is done. Last night there was a great Union-Abolition demonstration in the shape of a torch light procession in glorification over the "Union victories in the field and at the ballot box." It seems true that Gen Forrest has retaken Rome, Geo. With 3000 negroes and many arms. It is doubted very much whether the great "victories" of Sheridan in the Shenandoah Valley are not in fact *defeats*, or at most dearly bought successes.* at all events the gold-barometer don't speak favorably as gold is selling today at 220. I bought $200 a few days ago at 202, and wish I had bought more as I have always thought that I would change greenbacks into gold if I ever got more than I wanted to use at once. I fear that they will have a hard time in Dixie for *any quantity* of men seems to be forthcoming in Yankee land—every day one or more regiments pass through this city going to *the front* to kill and be killed probably. They are fine-looking bodies of men and will doubtless fight. There are many, however, who go through force alone and who will desert when they get a chance. I am told that whole regiments are sent from here *hand-cuffed* to the South, of unwilling conscripts. The recent elections in Indiana and Ohio for State officers indicate Abolition majorities for Lincoln in the coming Presidential election, and if he is again chosen, I shall want to get out of his dominions to a land of peace and white men.† Alas! alas! for our once happy and prosperous country. God have mercy upon us.—

---

* As part of an overall strategy to use military and economic pressure to force the Confederacy into submission, General Ulysses S. Grant gave command of the newly named forty-thousand-man Army of the Shenandoah to General Philip Sheridan. At Monocacy, Maryland, on Aug. 6, 1864, Grant ordered Sheridan to defeat Confederates in the Shenandoah Valley under Early's command and to destroy farms and crops, the equivalent of what Sherman later did in rural South Georgia. In addition to laying waste to hundreds of acres, Sheridan won a series of engagements. At Cedar Creek on Oct. 9, Confederates appeared to prevail until Sheridan rallied his men, earning himself promotion to major general and acclaim among the Northern public (Heidler and Heidler, *Encyclopedia*, 4:1756–60).

† On Oct. 11, 1864, state and congressional elections in Indiana, Ohio, and Pennsylvania produced Republican gains (Long, *Civil War Day by Day*, 582).

Sunday. 23. [October 23, 1864]

Still in Louisville—one month ago yesterday we left Atlanta, and have sojourned in this strange city for twenty five days.—Our auction sales of books began on Thursday night and continued through the week with but small success, but we still propose to continue as I want to get rid of all the books I can before going to N.Y. I wrote to Addison last Sunday, and yesterday evening I received a response, not from him but from our brother William with whom we have had no correspondence for three years, and regarding him as an abettor of this cruel war upon the South, have not had very kindly or brotherly feelings towards him. He says naught of this, however, but stating that my letter had just been rec—by Addison, says we shall be warmly welcomed there as refugees from "our poor ravaged Georgia[.]" He had been away from his home in Providence five days during which interval he had heard of another son being born to him. I suppose Addison will write soon.—We hear that Gen Hood has retaken Dalton and destroyed a great deal of the railroad.* The papers here seem to think he has got his army into a tight place. Sheridan seems to be having a "good time of it" in Virginia, beating the *rebels* in every engagement. I don't expect we shall hear anything *but* victories until after the 7th of November!

(*Oct. 23*) [October 23, 1864]

Sallie went with me to Baptist Church this morning and they seated us in *Pew* 4 up by the pulpit! If we had not got seated when we did, Sallie's face would have burst into flame, I think. We had a good view of the choir though.

Sunday 30. [October 30, 1864]

We have had a letter from Addison since last Sunday and from Mary Add from which we learn that Aunt Harriet has removed from Brooklyn to 113 Hammond St N.Y. and as Mary said she would call there the following day, and Add. promised to write again we hoped to get another letter ere this, but have not.† My sales are now over and I boxed up my books yesterday. My stock of *miscellaneous* books has been reduced to

---

* On Oct. 13, 1864, John Bell Hood and the Army of Tennessee captured the Federal garrison at Dalton, Georgia, which included the 44th U.S. Colored Infantry. Some of the black soldiers were sent to Mississippi and were enslaved. Others ran away, and their re-formed unit fought against Hood's Confederates at the Battle of Nashville (Kennett, *Marching through Georgia*, 219–21).

† SVVR's aunt, Harriet L. Stone.

one large box full. I calculate that I have sold $2000 worth but cannot tell until I get the Auctioneer's account.—We expect to start to NY. on Tuesday. We went in the afternoon to "Cave Hill Cemetery" with Mrs. Spaulding. It is a beautiful place, perhaps as much so as Greenwood though not as finished. In the morning we went to church at a new Meth' Church very close at hand in Chestnut St in order to get home the earlier, but it was the Dedication and after a sermon of over an hour we had to leave just as the dedication exercises began.

SEVEN

November 1864 to August 1865

"CHRISTMAS . . . IN THE YANKEE GOTHAM!"

The final chapter in Sam Richards's Civil War chronicle began with his arrival in New York City during the fall of 1864. Grateful for his family members' safety, Richards nonetheless expressed incredulity about their fate when he confided to his diary, "Christmas Day! We little thought a year ago that we should spend this day in the Yankee Gotham![1] Life in Gotham would be a mixed blessing for the Richards family.

New York City had changed a great deal since the Richardses had visited in 1860. Connected to the South by ties of trade before the war, New York struggled to cope with wartime economic changes. With the government buying huge quantities of materials to feed, clothe, and arm its military, manufacturing took off. Half of the city's ninety thousand garment workers labored to fill government orders. Railroads boomed as rail traffic replaced that of riverboats, whose ability to navigate the Mississippi and other bodies had been disrupted by fighting. The New York Stock Market experienced healthy growth during the war, fueled by rail stocks such as the New York Central and the New York and Erie. With businessmen, laborers, and refugees from the South moving into the city in droves, affordable housing became increasingly expensive and hard to find, as Sam Richards soon discovered.[2]

For American families divided by war, the process of reconciliation was frequently awkward. Such would be the case when the Richards and Van Valkenburg clans reunited in New York City. Like most nineteenth-century Americans, Sam idealized the family as a cohesive and loving unit. Addison had earned Sam's appreciation by conveying a sense of sympathy for Southern nationalism despite living in New York and by keeping in touch with the Georgia branch of the family via letters smuggled through the lines. William, conversely, had openly supported a vigorous prosecution of the war. Sam had previously had a high regard for Will and his oratorical, literary, and scientific achievements and had been devoted to Will's wife, Cornelia, whose intellect, warmth, and family spirit Sam believed made her a model spouse. But Sam saw William's public Unionism as an act of disloyalty to family and region and a blatant disregard for the feelings of the larger group.[3]

Family reconciliation often began with gestures of reassurance and economic assistance. This was the case with William. Not long after Sam and his family arrived in New York, Will helped Sam find Christmastime employment at the bookstore run by the D. Appleton Company, which had published books by both William and Cornelia Richards. After the war ended, Will offered to help Sam begin a printing and bookselling business in Pittsfield, Massachusetts, where William had relocated. Sam may also have felt reassured by his brother's postwar attitudes toward race relations in the South. Will told his Pittsfield congregation that "outside legislation" must not define the postwar South. Instead, "these grave questions" should be entrusted to "the statesmanship and to the conscience of the Southern people."[4]

Sallie and Sam began the reconciliation process with the Van Valkenburg family as well. They were delighted to see Sallie's beloved aunt, Huldah Van Valkenburg Turrell, who journeyed from her home in Montrose, Pennsylvania, to see them in New York, although Sam did not appreciate Huldah's abolitionism and her enthusiastic comments about Confederate military defeat.[5]

Sam maintained an uneasy relationship with his new city. The year before his arrival, New York had been rent asunder by draft riots fueled by political differences, economic woes, and racial and ethnic tensions. In November 1864, a few weeks after Sam's arrival, the national election took place. City residents feared that even larger riots would occur and would disrupt if not shut down the electoral process. Six thousand federal troops were sent to guard against such a possibility. No riots broke out, and both the campaign and the polling took place without incident. Because New York was a Democratic city, thousands—including Sam— turned out to see a torchlight parade held on November 5 to drum up support for George B. McClellan. Members of ward organizations bearing flags, banners, and Chinese lanterns marched in a long procession culminating at the Fifth Avenue Hotel, where the former Union general received the cheering crowd and women waved white flags from hotel windows.

Although McClellan won by a heavy majority in the city, upstate voters gave Lincoln a majority statewide.[6]

Later in the month, Confederate sympathizers set multiple fires in hotels and other public places in apparent retaliation for the burning of Atlanta. On November 25, arsonists left carpetbags filled with combustible chemicals on beds at more than a dozen hotels. The fires were quickly extinguished and caused minimal damage, with the St. Nicholas Hotel reporting the greatest financial losses at three thousand dollars. But the fires led New York authorities to regard all Southerners in the city with new suspicion. Military authorities now required "persons from the insurgent States" to register with the authorities within twenty-four hours of arriving in the city. The *New York Times* accused Southern refugees of driving up rents, inflating food prices, and causing fluctuations in the gold market. Sam Richards erroneously suggested that U.S. government agents had set the fires, writing on November 27, "Some say that the whole affair was *got up* by the U.S. Govt in order to cast odium upon the Rebels, who are supposed to be the perpetrators of the crime, and to give them an excuse to hold a tighter rein over the Copperhead City."[7]

As a Southern refugee in New York, Richards proceeded cautiously. The family attended a variety of churches, seeking religious fulfillment while avoiding prowar sermons and denunciations of Southerners from the pulpit. "I don't like bloody religion much," Sam wrote after sitting through a sermon in which the minister had used a diagram to illustrate military positions. In February 1865, he expressed a longing for his old congregation at Second Baptist in Atlanta, noting, "We cant feel at home in this land of aggressive and fierce war sentiment." He chose not to register with military authorities, despite the risk that he would be arrested for noncompliance, because he feared that he might be drafted into the Union Army if he registered. Although enrollment officers eventually tracked him down, he was never called to military service, perhaps because an enrolling officer misspelled Sam's name.[8]

For several weeks following his arrival in New York, Sam Richards projected a naive optimism about Confederate military victory. Ignoring the significance of Lincoln's decisive reelection victory and reading newspapers selectively, he chose to see positive developments, only to be disappointed when reality set in. At first he suggested that John Bell Hood and the Army of Tennessee were winning against the Yankees near Nashville, only to learn that Confederates had been annihilated in Middle Tennessee. After casting Sherman's March to the Sea in a positive light because the Federals had bypassed Macon and Augusta, he was forced to reassess that situation when Sherman captured Savannah. Richards finally began to acknowledge the likelihood of Confederate defeat and wrote philosophically about God's apparent will: "If it is not right in His sight for the South to be free, we ought certainly not to desire it, and I am willing to abide by His decision." But when surrender became a reality, he did not accept the war's outcome with equanimity, instead issuing a racist rant. "It grieves me to think of what the South has suffered and lost," he wrote on April 10, 1865, "... for a lot of worthless niggers which now are worse than worthless." Some of his anger was quelled by sadness over the tragedy of Lincoln's assassination, and within two months, Richards had come to see the Civil War as a national tragedy: "A feeling of regret and sadness came over my mind at the evidence that Christian men and women at the North were as sincere in the belief of the righteousness and justice of *their* cause as were the Christians of the South in their devotion to theirs. There must have been a great error somewhere—for such a dreadful strife as that of the past four years must be the penalty for great sin."[9] Richards nevertheless remained steadfast in his belief that the war was not God's punishment for slavery.

Although he considered several business prospects, including a New Jersey feed store and the Massachusetts book business suggested by his brother, Sam Richards never really wanted to make the North his permanent home. Although he expressed concern about where his family might live in Atlanta when so many of its dwellings had burned and although he was clearly nervous about paying off prewar debts to his bookstore's creditors and finding both the stock and the credit to restart the business, he wanted to go home and try again. "I feel like a stranger in a foreign clime," he wrote one Sunday in July 1865.[10] A month later, he returned to Atlanta.

Notes

1. SPR diary, Dec. 25, 1864.

2. Edward K. Spann, *Gotham at War: New York City, 1860–1865* (Wilmington, Del.: SR, 2002), 136–44.

3. Amy Murrell Taylor, *The Divided Family in Civil War America* (Chapel Hill: University of North Carolina Press, 2005), 7.

4. SPR diary, Nov. 8, 20, 1864, June 29, 1865; Taylor, *Divided Family*, 153; William C. Richards, *Thanksgiving for Peace: A Sermon Preached in the First Congregational Church at Pittsfield, Mass., on the Occasion of the National and State Thanksgiving, December 7, 1865* (New York: Sheldon, 1866), 42.

5. SPR diary, Mar. 29, 1865, Apr. 6, 1865; *NYT*, Jan. 17, 1864. After the death of her husband in the 1880s, Huldah Turrell retired to Americus, Georgia, where her three nieces lived (William Bailey Williford, *Americus through the Years: The*

Story of a Georgia Town and Its People, 1832–1875 [Atlanta: Cherokee, 1975], 448).

6. SPR diary, Nov. 8, 1864; Spann, *Gotham at War*, 172–75; *NYT*, Nov. 6, 1864.

7. SPR diary, Nov. 27, 1864; *NYT*, Nov. 26–30, 1864; *New York Herald*, Nov. 27, 1864. Spann has noted that Confederate conspirators, relatively few in number, were caught near the border with Canada (*Gotham at War*, 163). One leader, Robert Cobb Kennedy, a Confederate officer and relative of prominent Georgian Howell Cobb, was executed in Mar. 1865 (*NYT*, Mar. 26, 1865).

8. SPR diary, Dec. 11, 1864 (Sallie's fears), Nov. 27, 1864, Feb. 12, 1865 (religion), Jan. 15, 1865, Feb. 12, 1865 (draft); *NYT*, Nov. 27, 1864 (reporting on Wescott's sermon).

9. SPR diary, Dec. 4, 1864 (military events), Dec. 26, 1864 (God's will), Apr. 10, 1865 (surrender), May 28, 1865 (Christians of the North). The *New York Herald* ran many military stories excerpted from Confederate newspapers. For example, on Dec. 8, 1864, it reprinted a story from the *Savannah News* that reported, "Sherman seems to be *making no progress* in his invasion of the State."

10. SPR diary, July 16, 1865.

Tuesday 8. [November 8, 1864]

We are in the great city of New York—Just a week ago we took passage in the "Gen Buell" from Louisville for Cinncinati, which place we reached before day the next morning and took the Erie R R Cars for N.Y.—About two oclock we reached Cleveland on Lake Erie and changed cars for Buffalo. At the latter place we arrived about 12 Oclock and *missed the connection* so we had to lay over until five in the morning. We travelled through a pretty country abounding in villages and pumpkins! On the side of a rocky cut we saw a great many *icicles* though there was not much appearance of winter otherwise. At ten O'clock at night we reached Jersey-City in safety after riding 700 or 800 miles by Rail Road from Cinncinati. We crossed the river and walked up Courtlandt St. to the National Hotel where we obtained a room for the night, and retired to a good bed, thanking our Heavenly Father for the care that had protected us from the perils of the way and brought us safely to our desired haven.—The next morning was wet but I found Add and Mary and then went to Aunt Harriet's and found that she could give us a shelter for a season, until we could find a home, so that we are now there—113 Hammond St.* All the

---

* SVVR's aunt, Harriet L. Stone, was married to Roswell H. Stone, and the couple had four children, William, Mary, Sarah, and Harriet (Eighth Census of the United States [1860], microcopy 653, Brooklyn, New York, Ward 7).

family are here that we saw in 1860 and the *son* William whom we did *not* see. Mary Stone greeted me with the cordiality of a sister, and proffered a kiss.—Sarah I took a kiss from without her offer. They are both engaged to be married. Mary's lover is now a prisoner in Dixie—no other than Capt Gilbert Petit, Sallies cousin on the fathers side.* The Stones are cousins on the mother's. I found Mary & Add pleasantly situated in 83 Clinton Place and wish we could be with them. But there is no vacant room and board is too high there for exiles with no more means than we have. On Sat morning I went with Add to a Clothing Store where I shed my "butternuts" and rigged myself in an entire new suit. At night I went with Add and Mary and a Mr Johnston to see the great torchlight McClellan procession five miles long. And we stopped in at Delmonico's and ate some fine ice cream.—On Sunday Afternoon Sallie and I took a car for 43rd St and found the Wests keeping house in a small way at 223. I guess we shall have to do the same if we can get rooms. I put Sallie into a car and then walked to 117 8th Avenue and dropped in on Uncle Roberts folks. At night we went with "Uncle Roswell" to hear Dr Dowling preach from the subject "Who is the greatest Captain and Commander?"† It was not handled *politically* however, tho' the Doctor took occasion to give the South some raps as he went along. After the service I had an introduction to him and reminded him that about 35 years ago he took me up and stood me on the pump in the back yard at Hook Norton! He seemed glad to see us.—Sallie recognized Mrs. Cutting in the congregation and spoke with her.—Yesterday I went with Add into Wall Street and bot $300 in gold at 244 in the expectation that it will *go up* after the election, especially if Old Abe is re-elected which I expect will be the result of *this day's* business. This is the day upon which the man is to be chosen who shall control the destiny of this nation.—

Sunday 20. [November 20, 1864]

We are now keeping house in rooms up three flights of stairs on West 36th St No 209. We have taken the rooms furnished for one month at

---

* Gilbert Pettit was captain of Company F, 120th New York Infantry (Janet B. Hewett, ed. *The Roster of Union Soldiers, 1861–1865*, 33 vols. [Wilmington, N.C.: Broadfoot, 1997–2000], 10:265).

† John Dowling, English by birth, came to the United States and was ordained a Baptist minister in 1832. He served different New York congregations including Gothic Masonic Hall, Broadway Baptist Church, Bereau Baptist Church on Bedford Street, and South Baptist Church. He was the author of many religious treatises (*National Cyclopedia of American Biography*, 63 vols. [New York: White, 1904], 9:216).

$25. They are too small for us but as rooms are scarce we could not do better and wanted to get away from Aunt Harriets altho' they were all very kind because their friends whose room we occupied had come back and to give them back their room we had to turn William out of his. We came up here last Tuesday aft since when we have had company nearly every day or night. Abe Lincoln was elected by a large majority, so we shall probably see plenty more fighting, tho' it is rumored that liberal propositions of peace, on the basis of reunion of course, have been sent from Washn to Richmond. This or some other news probably, has knocked gold down from 260 to 209! I went down to Wall St yest to buy some at the latter rate, but it had been up again to 225 and was again falling so I waited. W.C.R. came to see us on the evening of Election Day and on Wed next I went with him to call on the booksellers and look out for a place. Will seems to have modified his ultra War Views considerably and is now opposed to the Lincoln Administration. I have been half sick for several days and for awhile was somewhat afraid that I had taken the *Varioloid* from sleeping in the bed at Aunt H's that Mr Haxton had occupied and he had that disease when he left there, ten days, before we went there!* Our baby "Virnie" has been very troublesome, crying all the time unless her mother is holding her. I went to Mr Smillies house to let them know that we had arrived and Mary Smillie *let on* about the South and the war in regular Abolition style, which I thought was a breach of courtesy and good manners.† I went today twice to the "Bloomingdale Baptist Church" of which Mr. Wescott is pastor, but is not in the city today, a Mr Baldwin preached for him.‡ The choir sings very well mostly familiar tunes to me. After service I met Sin Smith who sings in the choir and he invited me to go up and sit with them, but I don't think I shall go upon *his* invitation.— Tomorrow I enter upon my duties at the Appletons' where I have engaged until Jan 1 at the rate of $1000 per annum.—§

* Varioloid is a mild case of smallpox found in someone who has been vaccinated against or who has previously had the disease.

† James Smillie was married to SVVR's aunt, Catherine Smillie, and the couple had five children, William M., Mary E., Martha, Catherine, and Charles (Eighth Census of the United States [1860], microcopy 653, New York, New York, Ward 22).

‡ Isaac Wescott served as pastor of New York's Laight Street Baptist Church from 1851 to 1855 and subsequently became pastor at the city's Plymouth Baptist Church.

§ The D. Appleton Company began in 1825 when Daniel Appleton moved his general store from Massachusetts to New York. Six years later, he began printing

Sunday 27. [November 27, 1864]

I have been kept close all the past week at my new place of business except on Thursday which was the regular "Thanksgiving Day" at the North. We are getting somewhat accustomed to our new mode of life, doing pretty well. I did not go to preaching on Thanksgiving Day as I knew the theme would be "The Rebellion" and I have heard enough of that sort of thing. This morning I heard Dr Wescott preach upon The Resurrection but he did not advance any New ideas. He closed his prayer by invoking success upon the efforts of our soldiers and *adversity upon our enemies.*[*] The religion of the North, generally, is one of war and bloodshed. I hear that Rev Dr Scott preaches just across the street from Mr Wescotts church. He is a Pres' minister who was sent away from New Orleans by Butler, and does not preach war and Abolition and I think I shall go there.[†] I don't like bloody religion much. I took the children to Aunt Harriets this aft and I then went to see Add[.]

(*Sunday 27*) [November 27, 1864]

There was an attempt on Friday night last apparently to burn the city, as some eight or ten of their largest Hotels were fired about the same time. Fortunately not one of these incendiary fires did any great damage. Some say that the whole affair was *got up* by the U.S. Govt in order to cast odium upon the Rebels, who are supposed to be the perpetrators of the crime, and to give them an excuse to hold a tighter rein over the Copperhead City. Sallie's "Uncle Aaron" called on her today during my absence.

---

books, initially focusing on American editions of English titles. The Appleton retail bookstore at 346 Broadway was an immense and elegant space decorated inside with Corinthian columns and painted with frescoes. It burned in 1867 (Grant Overton, *Portrait of a Publisher and the First Hundred Years of the House of Appleton, 1825–1925* [New York: Appleton, 1925], 27–29, 40–41, 53–54).

* In his sermon, Wescott advocated "prosecuting the war to resist the assaults of the rebels. They commenced it, we simply resist." Wescott showed a "diagram" to illustrate the current military situation and emphasized Northerners' willingness to prosecute the war to its fullest (*NYT*, Nov. 27, 1864).

† William Scott served as pastor of First Presbyterian Church in New Orleans before and during the early part of the Civil War. A strong supporter of Southern nationalism, he left New Orleans after the Federal capture of the city and its occupation by Union soldiers commanded by General Benjamin Butler. Scott traveled first to England and later to New York City. From 1863 to 1870, he served as pastor of Forty-second Street Church, where many of his parishioners shared his political outlook (Dumas Malone, ed., *Dictionary of American Biography* [New York: Scribner's, 1936], 16:503–4).

He seems very friendly and told her that if she was ever in trouble to let him know it and he would be glad to aid her. The Smillies have been here also and were very kind.—

Sunday 4. [December 4, 1864]

The season is advancing and yet we have seen no wintry weather yet; indeed it has been oppressively warm at times of late, and I guess we shall have to go back to Atlanta for cold weather, for last year we had real cold, freezing weather there in Nov.—I am getting more *at home* in my new place but it is so large a house and the books are not classified in such a way as to facilitate a speedy acquaintance with their whereabouts—Then, moreover, prices have changed so much since the war and the books are very few of them marked, which makes it a difficult matter to get at the price and in many instances none of the clerks know except Mr Parrs the head clerk and he is such a dogmatical, pragmatical chap, that I don't much like going to him often. Bro Will has been there twice this week, having run down from Norwalk, Conn., where he is lecturing. The late attempt to fire the city has given the military authorities an excuse for again ordering the Southerners to go up to Gen Peck's Hd. Qrs. and be registered and most of our friends here advise me to go up, but I have not yet made up my mind to do so, and don't feel much inclined to do it.[*] I much prefer to *keep dark* and pursue the quiet tenure of my way without being ticketed for draft or any other military operation. Addison is decidedly opposed to my doing so and William after advising with Add was of opinion that perhaps it would be as well to delay awhile. I *ride* to and from my place of business in cars that stop very near the store, at Canal St. on Broadway. It takes me about half an hour to get there and I have to start from home at 7½ Oclock and the store is closed at 6 P.M., though about Christmas it will be later—probably nine or ten o'clock before I get home.—We hear from the Republican journals of *great victories* gained by Gen Thomas in Tenn. over Hood near Nashville, but as it is admitted that the Fed troops *retired from the ground* after the fight it *looks* more like a *rebel* success after all! Then too we are told that Gen Sherman is advancing upon his conquering tour through Georgia, but as he seems to have *gone by* Macon and Augusta and to be pushing as hard as he can

---

[*] General John J. Peck commanded the Department of the East, in charge of New York and the Canadian border (*The Union Army: A History of Military Affairs in the Loyal States, 1861–1865*, 9 vols. [1908; reprint, Wilmington, N.C.: Broadfoot, 1998], 8:195).

towards the coast, that it may after all only turn out to be a *grand retreat!**
Atlanta is without doubt again in Confederate hands, what is left of it.—
I fear our houses there will be of but little value to us in future and our
piano and furniture is probably "gone up the spout" ere this.—The *Bulls*
and *Bears* of Wall St don't seem to think much of the reported successes
of the Feds as gold continues to advance being now 232.—This morning,
my wife having got her new cloak (all finished except the button-holes!)
went to church with me leaving Dora in charge with the baby. We went to
hear Dr Weston corner of 31st St and Madison Av. where I heard brother
Will preach in 1860, in the lecture room the main building being then in
course of building.† The Smillies go there and invited us to attend. We met
them there today and were introduced to Dr W after the service. They say
that he does not preach any war or politics and he did not today, merely
praying for the success of "our armies in the field." This aft I took Dora
and Irene down to Mary Add's rooms.—Dora was ill on Friday, having
fever all day and at night. From what we have spent so far I find that our
weekly expenses for provisions are $10 about. My present salary will not
afford us much *clothing* therefore.

Sunday 11. [December 11, 1864]
When we arose yesterday morning we beheld the ground and the roofs
covered with a mantle of white snow, (It is pretty *black* in the streets
now,) the first of the season that lay on the ground at all. It continued to
fall fast until it was some six inches deep. I did not hear the 8th avenue
cars running so I went over to Broadway, the second street from us east,
and took a Stage which carried me to D. Appleton & Co's door safely and
comfortably for 10¢. After I got inside I did not regard the weather any
more until I went home at night. Friday night I was detained at the store
until 9½ O'clock unexpectedly and my wife was alarmed fearing that I
had met with some mishap and been *arrested* perhaps as a Hotel Burner!
When I got home at 10 Oclock I found Mr & Mrs West and brother Add
all there waiting to see if I would turn up. It was the anniversary of our

---

* Although SPR was correct that William T. Sherman had bypassed Macon and Augusta, the suggestion that Federal troops had ceded ground in Tennessee was wrong. In fact, General John Bell Hood had suffered a loss at Franklin, Tennessee, on Nov. 30 (James M. McPherson, *Ordeal by Fire: The Civil War and Reconstruction*, 3rd ed. [Boston: McGraw Hill, 2001], 500–503).

† William Griggs Weston, a graduate of Brown University and Newton Theological Seminary, served as pastor of New York's Oliver Street Church from 1859 to 1868 (*National Cyclopedia*, 12:143–44).

wedding-night, Dec. 9th. We have been married twelve years.—Sherman has been dragging his slow length along right through Georgia, burning and devastating as he went, but seems to have avoided Augusta and Macon and to be getting along towards Savannah or Beaufort perhaps. It bids fair to be a rather inglorious finale to his triumphant entry into Atlanta. The Herald of the *8th* inst contains a letter pub*d* in the *Appeal* giving a list of houses burned in Atlanta before the Yankees left it. *Our* house is not in the list, but Holbrook's, Inman's Lansdale's and Knox's are mentioned. It also states that there is not a house standing on Whitehall from Mitchell St to Wesley Chapel on Peachtree, so that nearly all the business part of the city is in ashes.*—This morning Sallie and I went to the "Ebenezer Baptist Church," a small plain brick building close by, as the weather was bad and the streets sloppy and slippery. The preacher pleased me in his prayer by depricating the continuance of the war and asking for peace. His discourse was rambling, "he played on a harp of a thousand strings" almost and tried to be like "a new sharp threshing instrument having teeth[.]" I think it must be a sort of Hardshell Church.—

Sunday 18. [December 18, 1864]

We have been quite busy at the store the past week but have not yet kept open after six oclock though the clerks have staid until a later hour once or twice in order to get the store fixed up for the next day. I exercised my architectural faculty in building a tower of literature formed of boxes of Juvenile books—by way of ornament to our Juvenile Department which I have been put in charge of. The military news of the week is that Sherman has reached Savannah or near that place and demanded the surrender of the city, and having taken Fort [blank] is in direct communication with the naval force on the sea coast. At Nashville our papers here say that Hood has met with several severe repulses since he sat down to the siege of that city, and at last accounts he was trying to make good his retreat!†

---

* On Dec. 8, 1864, the *New York Herald* reprinted an article from the *Memphis Appeal*, Nov. 20, 1864, written by Z. A. Rice, who provided a firsthand account of conditions in Atlanta. According to this story, only 675 of the city's 20,000 residents remained, nearly 600 of them women and 15–20 African Americans). Rice noted the destruction of "foundries, railroad shops, government works and mills" torched by Sherman's departing army and identified neighborhoods and homes that had burned.

† Union troops reached the outskirts of Savannah on Dec. 10, 1864, at which point William T. Sherman ordered his men to capture Fort McAllister, south of the city. Their success enabled Sherman to establish communications via the navy

Sallie and I went out in the snow and slush this morning to Dr Scotts Church in 42nd St and heard him preach. He was sent away from New Orleans by Butler because he sympathized too strongly with the South. We saw several U.S. Flags floating from private mansions as we walked up the street. It is a pity that this should have come to be a sure sign that the inmates are Abolitionists. Light sleighs are jingling along the streets today but if this mild weather continues there will soon be an end of the sleighing.—I went down 8th Avenue with Dora and Irene this afternoon as far as Greenwich Av. where I left them to find their way to Aunt Harriets and went myself to Add's room. I found him alone, his wife having gone out to Grace Ch. but she returned before I left. I went from thence to Mr Stone's and took the children home in a car as the walking is none of the nicest.—We are reading "Life of 'Cousin Alice'" a new book just published by the Appletons. It is the Memoirs of Emily Bradley written by Cornelia.* I used to play with her when we were children in Hudson.

Sunday 25. [December 25, 1864]

Christmas Day! We little thought a year ago that we should spend this day in the Yankee Gotham! The past week has been a busy one and for several days the work at the store has been almost too much though the chief difficulty with myself was that standing on my feet for over twelve hours consequtively in *new boots* made my feet ache exceedingly. I have not reached home until about ten O'clock almost every night in the past week. Bro William has been in the city for several days but left yesterday giving me the "Life of Cousin Alice" for Sallie and three books for the children. This morning Sallie and I went to hear Mr Westcott in 42nd St and this afternoon we took "Virnie" and went to see the Wests to see a letter that she has rec[d] from Mr Root. He writes from Nassau and says

---

with Washington. Fearing capture, the Confederate Army departed the city on Dec. 21, and news of Sherman's latest triumph reached the Northern public during succeeding days (McPherson, *Ordeal*, 500; *New York Herald*, Dec. 26, 1864).

* Cornelia Holroyd Bradley Richards, *Cousin Alice: A Memoir of Alice B. Haven* (New York: Appleton, 1865). Cornelia was SPR's sister-in-law; Emily Bradley Neal was Cornelia's sister. Using the name "Cousin Alice," Emily wrote stories for children. Under the name "Miss Manners," Cornelia wrote etiquette and advice books and columns. The sisters published in William Carey Richards's children's periodical, *Schoolfellow*, and Emily contributed frequently to *Godey's Lady's Book*, a magazine published by her friend, Louis Godey. Cornelia's memoir, written as though penned by Alice, told a story of Christian forbearance in the face of adversity and became one of Cornelia's best-selling volumes.

he has left his wife and children at Cuthbert Geo except Johnny who has gone to school in England.* He himself is on his travels for three months when he expects to return to Georgia. (perhaps?) He seems to be as much of a *Rebel* as ever. I don't think he will get back to Dixie in so short a time unless things change for the better there soon.—He gives a very glowing description of the tropical beauties of Nassau. Mrs West treated us to nuts, candies and raisins. Mr West is again out of employment. It does not appear to be an easy thing to make a living in this city.

Monday 26. [December 26, 1864]

Yesterday being the Sabbath, today is very generally observed as a holiday. Our store is closed so I am at liberty; but as it is *wet* we cannot much enjoy the opportunity. We intended to go to the Park and see the *skating*. Last night I took the little girls to Aunt Harriet's at her request, to go to a S. School Exhibition at Dr. Dowling's church. The house was filled by 7 O'clock and the children began the entertainment by singing a song. They sang well and that part of the exercises was quite a success. But the speaking part did not suit me so well. There was too much Lincoln-War talk to be palatable. All the Baptist Churches seem to be alike in that respect; their gospel is one of war and bloodshed, not that of "peace and goodwill toward men[.]" The evening papers reported the capture of Savannah with 25,000 bales of cotton and large supplies of guns &c, but Hardee and his army had made their escape.†—Verily it would seem true as Napoleon is reported to have said that "Providence is on the side of the heaviest battalions." But "the Judge of the whole earth will do right" and

---

* The Union assault on and eventual capture of Fort Fisher (Dec. 1864–Jan. 1865) ended the port of Wilmington as a center for blockade-running and the wartime career of Sidney Root. Root claimed that he and his partner, John Beach, had co-owned "if I remember correctly, from 19 to 21 ocean steamers" and estimated the partnership's wartime losses at "something over $1,700,000 in greenbacks. This will be partially explained by the loss of over 2,000,000 bales of cotton which, at the close of the war, was worth $1,000,000 in gold. In Atlanta we lost, in the conflagration of Atlanta, thirteen buildings, ten of which were among the best brick buildings in Atlanta" (Sidney Root, "Memorandum of My Life," 14, 18–19, unpublished typescript, 1893, AHC).

† On Dec. 21, 1864, William T. Sherman sent a telegram to President Abraham Lincoln: "I beg to present you, as a Christmas gift, the city of Savannah, with 150 guns and plenty of ammunition, and also about 25,000 bales of cotton." This telegram was widely reprinted. General William Hardee had been in charge of the Confederate defense of the city but evacuated his soldiers shortly before Sherman's arrival (*NYT*, Dec. 24, 1864).

if it is not right in His sight for the South to be free, we ought certainly not to desire it, and I am willing to abide by His decision.—Many who seem to be good pious people give the war their cordial approval apparently forgetful of or indifferent to the misery that is thus unjustly brot upon thousands of their fellow beings.—

Sunday 1. [January 1, 1865]

Another year is now among the bygones, an eventful year and long to be remembered by a good many of us as a year of trouble and apprehension and perplexity. How little did I suppose at the opening of 1864 that when it should close I and mine would be sojourners in the land of the enemy and the invader so many hundred miles from our Southern home! It is sad to think of the homes made desolate and property destroyed during the march of the Northern Vandals through our once happy and prosperous state. Truly our Southern land is undergoing a baptism of blood and fire. God only knows when or how it is to be accomplished. Humanly speaking it does seem almost impossible that she will obtain the independence for which she is striving, and if the cause is not a just and righteous one in the sight of God, there is no hope, but if He approves, all the armies the North can raise will be insufficient to prevent it.—We have not had as much to do at the store as we had the week before Christmas and we have had a good deal of bad weather[.] Another snowstorm set in yesterday morning before light and lasted nearly all day but today the sun has come out clear and bright and tho' cold it has been a pleasant day. God grant that it may prove to have been an omen for good to our war cursed land. I fear that my "occupation is gone" as when I asked Mr John Appleton if I should come back any more, he said that he did not think their business would justify them in employing me longer though he said they were *sorry to part* with me. But as he said he supposed I would be there on Tuesday, I shall go as usual and stay until they tell me to quit.* It is said that a great many persons will be thrown out of employ at this time on account of the slackness of trade.—This morning Sallie and I went to a fine new Epis Church corner of Madison Av. and 35th St and heard the rector preach from Mal 1.11 "From the rising of the sun &c" it was a good Missionary sermon and we did not hear a tirade about the war and the *rebellion* and our noble soldiers and the barbarous, inhuman savages of the South, which form the basis of most of the sermons in our Baptist pulpits. As churches are so abundant I think I shall visit around and not "put up" at any one at

---

* John Appleton was one of Daniel Appleton's four sons, all of whom worked in the family publishing house and bookstore (*National Cyclopedia*, 2:509–10).

present. We have been to six different churches already.—This afternoon the children trudged down to Aunt Harriets with a handkerchief for Mary from Sallie as a slight return for her kindness in making her cloak, and I sent also a book apiece for Aunt H. and Sarah, that we brought with us from Atlanta. I would have gone to see Cousin Sallie but I did not know the address, so I took a walk to Uncle Roberts' to find it out. I found only the old folks at home but had quite a chat with Aunt, and she regaled me with some real old style English mince pie, plum pudding and a glass of port wine of California vintage.—Tonight I am left to keep house and take care of the baby while wife and Dora have gone to church.—

Sunday 8. [January 8, 1865]

Today is bright and cold enough but we have had a good deal of bad weather during the past week. Sallie and I went down to 16th St Baptist Church and heard Rev Mr Michals preach and Mr Elder play on the organ. The latter is a blind musician whom my wife knew 15 years ago, and who used to give her music lessons. We introduced ourselves to him and walked up the Avenue with him after church. This Church was the one Sallie used to go to when she lived in York before. This aft I went to call on Sallie Sherwood whom I have not seen since she was a little girl some 16 years ago but I think I should have recognized her. She is a nice little woman now and the mother of two children. Tonight I went to see Add and Mary and took a whiskey toddy and fruit cake with them. Last Monday was a holiday in place of New Year's Day[.] I bought Arthur a sleigh as he seemed to wish for one so much. In the afternoon I rode over to Brooklyn to call on the Bradleys, but only found Mrs. Rogers at home. Kate Rogers is at Cambridge Mass and Kitty Neely has gone to see her.

Sunday 15. [January 15, 1865]

Two evils have fallen upon me since my last entry. An enrolling officer has called at our rooms and put me down for the draft in February and I do not know how to proceed, whether to try to get my name taken off or to let it go and take the chances. From what Sallie says I guess that they have got me down as *Richings*. Just think of my being a *Yankee Soldier*, to whom the sight of a blue coat is as bad as a blue pill reminding me of scenes of distress and trouble that I would fain forget.* I don't *much* expect ever to go a-soldiering in Yankee company. I didn't come away from the South for *that* purpose at all events. If I were *forced* to fight I should

---

* Blue mass in either pill or syrup form was a common remedy for a variety of ailments, including parasites, constipation, and dental pain.

much rather kill a Yankee than a *rebel*, so-called, but being a man of peace, I have no desire to do either.—The other evil, and the greater one perhaps, is that I was informed last night by a polite note from Mr John Appleton that their present business would not warrant their keeping me any longer; so I am *at large* with but slim prospect of any employment. I received for my services at Appletons $152.77—I was pleasantly situated there, though closely confined, and as they had let me continue two weeks of the New Year I was in hopes that I should be retained longer.— We went to call on the Smillies the other night but only the girls were at home.—This morning we went to hear Dr Weston in Madison Av., and he preached a good sermon from the text "And Orpah kissed her mother-in-law, but Ruth clave unto her." The singing there is good in an artistical and musical sense but whether it is devotional as it might be is questionable, though I was touched by it, today, in one hymn to tears.—A S.S. Meeting was given out by the pastor for this afternoon at which there was to be talking and singing by the children and I took all the young ones and went up in the gallery and the church soon filled up with people but there were but few children and it proved to be a regular service of some other church I think who are awaiting the finishing of their own edifice. A preacher whom I did not know gave us an elaborate lecture on "*Eve, our first Mother.*" I guess the S.S. Exercises must have been held in the S.S. Room behind the church, so we missed our mark. I have since been told that this preacher was Dr Armitage.*—The S.S. Exercises as I supposed were held in the other part of the edifice.

February. Sunday 12. [February 12, 1865]

It is four weeks since my last entry—during which period I have suffered more physical pain than I ever did before to my knowledge in the same length of time. Before I left the Appletons for several days I was troubled by a pain in my right fore finger which I thought was one of the bad boils I have had at various times, but for several days I did not apply any remedy but let it take its course. On Monday Jan 16th I went down to Add's studio with Sallie to let her see his pictures.—When we returned home we learned that another man had been there *enrolling* me for the anticipated draft! They may as well save themselves the trouble for they wont get me to help do their murdering. For ten days and nights after this I had no rest with my finger which proved to be a *bone felon* a thing which

---

* Thomas Armitage served for many decades as pastor of Fifth Avenue Baptist Church and was a founder of the American Bible Union (*National Cyclopedia*, 9:199).

I always have dreaded, but never before was visited with.* I kept poulticing my finger with flaxseed but it seemed as though it would never come to a focus and break. Dr Ball to whom Sallie had twice taken Virginia to be vaccinated, came three times to our room, as it failed *to take* the first time. He put matter in twice more and the second application succeeded. The Doctor advised me to have my finger *cut*, but as I had born the pain so long and thought it must soon break I declined, and Mr West having told me of a Dutch woman who had a great reputation for treating such complaints I went to her. That same day the pent up matter began to ooze out, and the pain was somewhat modified, tho' it was some time yet ere I could *lie down* or sleep in any other than a sitting posture. I have been going to the Dutch Lager Beer woman ever since until today I dressed my finger myself and don't think I shall trouble Mrs. Franze Vogt any more as I am tired of sitting there half an hour at a time listening to their eternal Dutch jabber and watching the sauer kraut boil! I am inclined to think that if I had doctored myself instead of going to her I should have gone quite as well; tho' it might not have been so. The finger is rather stiff in the joints but I hope will come out right tho' perhaps a little deformed. I feared I might lose the use of it. I hope and pray that I may never again have a *felon* finger—I am now writing without its aid, as it is not yet fit for use. Miss Serena Cornish came to see us a few days ago looking as *young* and blooming as of old!—The air has been laden with rumours of *peace* for a month past and "Peace Commissioners" have gone to and from the cities of Washington and Richmond, and the last one was composed of such men as really betokened the probability that something might come of it. Alex H. Stephens, Vice Pres. Confed States and two other men of note came into the Yankee lines and had a Conference at Fortress Monroe with Abe Lincoln and his Prime Vizier Seward. But alas! nothing came of it, and it appears that all Mr Lincoln could offer the *rebels* was a liberal forbearance in the execution of the laws against which they had offended if they would lay down their arms and submit to his authority.† The Richmond papers are very indignant at the insult, as they call it. Yesterday I

* A bone felon is an inflammation of the soft tissue of the fingers.

† In the waning months of the war, several efforts at a negotiated peace produced no results. The negotiations to which SPR referred took place on Feb. 3, 1865, at Hampton Roads, Virginia. Abraham Lincoln and his secretary of state, William H. Seward, met with Confederate commissioners, including Alexander Stephens. With his recent reelection and Union military success, Lincoln demanded emancipation of the slaves in addition to reunification of the states, and the Confederates refused (McPherson, *Ordeal*, 506–7).

went down town and called at the bookstores for the first time in four weeks. My chief purpose tho' was to get $150 from bank to buy furniture with as we have rented rooms at 630 Sixth Avenue and expect to move there on Wed' next. We have there six rooms on the first floor over a first class *Meat Market* store at $25 per month and the *Wests* will have two of the rooms for $10. It is a tenement house with all the requirements for house keeping on each floor.

(*Sunday 12*) [February 12, 1865]

It has been snowing all day for the 50th time more or less this winter. We have not been to church today. Two weeks ago we went to Dr Spring's (Pres) Church on Fifth Ave and heard the old gentleman preach.* We went there in 1860 and heard Dr Hoge who was the colleague of Dr Spring at that time. It is 98 years since this church was founded. Alas! for the pleasant services and our plain church at Atlanta and the pleasant social choir reunions that we shall probably never enjoy there again. We cant feel at home in this land of aggressive and fierce war sentiment. Our little "Virnie" gets on famously. She is only nine months old and can almost walk alone and oh! joy, yesterday *a tooth* was discovered and no mistake!—Cousin Mary Stone came yesterday and took the girls to the Park to see the skating. This has been a fine season for the skaters, and we have been intending to go and see the fun but have not yet been able. Our friend E. M. Edwardy of Atlanta called on me at Appletons in January and said he should sail for Savannah the next day where he hoped to meet his family. Alas, for human hopes! I saw his name in the list of passengers who sank in the ill fated "Melville" and all lost but two or three.†

Sunday 19. [February 19, 1865]

We are in our new quarters having moved from our *high* position in 36th Street to a first floor over a store in Sixth Avenue No 630. We came here on Wed last in a snow storm. There are six rooms on the floor and Mr & Mrs West are to occupy two of them at the rent of $10 per month

---

* Gardiner Spring served for sixty-three years as minister at Brick Presbyterian Church on Beekman Street in New York. He helped found the American Bible and Home Missionary Societies (*National Cyclopedia*, 5:409).

† The steamship *Melville* sank in a storm off the coast of South Carolina, with only four of eighty-one passengers surviving. The ship was bound for Hilton Head. SPR's friend, E. M. Edwardy, was among those listed as dead in *NYT*, Jan. 13, 1865.

which will reduce our rent to $15. But I find that I have told all this before.—Our room is not as readily warmed as our other one and in very cold weather we might suffer some from that cause but it is more agreeable to live in a separate room from that in which the cooking is done. But my sore finger is not yet in a useful condition so I will not write more.

Sunday 26. [February 26, 1865]

It is 8½ P.M., and I am alone in our parlor having just put the baby to bed. Sallie and the girls have gone to evening service. Virginia is ten months old and has *two teeth* and *walks alone*! This morning we went to the Broadway Tabernacle and listened to a discourse from Dr Thompson, "half and half" it may be called half religious and the rest glorification of the Yankee successes in dispoiling their Southern *bretheren* of their rights and their homes.*—We have not yet had an opportunity to go to the Park and it is likely now that we shall be too late to see any good skating[.] Mr West has been sick in bed ever since they moved, and I have had considerable physic [medicine] to get for him. Add and Mary came to see us the other evening as he has felt better for some days. Yesterday, Sallie and I walked to Aunt Harriet's calling on Aunt Sarah as we went down. This aft' William Stone came up and stayed several hours. He is employed in a "Feed Store" in Hoboken and thinks the owner could be induced to sell out cheaply and wants me to buy as he thinks that it would pay very well. I am entertaining the proposition, and he is going to inquire further into the matter, and report. Such a business as that if it did not pay or if we did not wish to continue it could be very quickly disposed of without much loss. I must be doing something and it don't seem good policy to be keeping money idle and myself too. We find our present rooms much more comfortable and convenient than the *loft* we lately occupied. Our Seraphine arrived the other day from Louisville in bad *condition* if as the grammars say "*Case* means Condition &c" for the Express has nearly used up the *case* of it; but fortunately the *action* is still unimpaired.—Mr West rec^d a letter from Mr Root from Liverpool this week.—Continued success appears to attend the Yankee arms, for Charleston, Columbia and Wilmington have all been given up to them and Sherman seems to march

---

* Joseph Parrish Thompson, a Yale graduate, was a Congregational minister. In 1845, he was appointed pastor of Broadway Tabernacle Church, and he subsequently became one of the most influential clergymen in New York City. Before the war, he was an abolitionist (Malone, *Dictionary of American Biography*, 18:464–65).

whenever he pleases without let or hindrance. I should like very much to hear how our folks in Dixie are getting on.*

Wed. March 1. [March 1, 1865]

I walked to Hoboken in the afternoon stopping an hour at Aunt Harriets on the way thither. I was an hour getting to 220 Washington St where where I found Will Stone not over busy in selling *feed*. He reports that the proprietor asks $1000 for the teams and furniture of the concern, which is just *double* what they are really worth, and I don't feel inclined to pay $500 for the "good will" of such a business as that now is. It might be *made* a good deal better, I suppose.

Thursday 2. [March 2, 1865]

I went to see Add and Mary in the afternoon and it began to storm while I sat with Mary at her room. After sitting with Add awhile at the studio I took a Broadway Car home. These cars are very convenient to take in stormy weather.

Friday 3. [March 3, 1865]

I arrived at the age of forty one today, but as no one thought enough of it to give me anything I will not waste words about it myself.

Sunday 5. [March 5, 1865]

Yesterday was to have been signalized as a great public jubilee over Abe Lincoln's *coronation* and the great Union victories—but it was postponed on account of bad weather and is to come off tomorrow instead.† It is a very pleasant day or *has been* for it is now night. Sallie and Mrs West and myself went to Dr Westons church this morning and he preached from the text "Behold, I stand at the door and knock &c[.]" I believe I like his preaching as well as any I have heard in the city. Tonight, Dora and I went to "Zion Church" (Epis) Cor. Madison Ave and 38th St, and of all the *hifalutin* singing this was the tiptop! It sounded considerably more like an Italian Opera than the service of the House of God. Mrs West came to our

---

* After laying waste to Georgia, William T. Sherman's army marched through South Carolina. The capital city of Columbia burned as a consequence of the efforts of Sherman's men, departing Confederates, or liberated slaves (Charles Royster, *The Destructive War: William Tecumseh Sherman, Stonewall Jackson, and the Americans* [New York: Knopf, 1991]).

† Despite rainy weather and considerable mud in Washington, D.C., Abraham Lincoln was inaugurated for a second term on Mar. 4, 1865. By the time the president gave his address, the weather had become "bright and beautiful" (*NYT,* Mar. 5, 1865).

room this afternoon and we had a sing at the old Seraphine, until we were stopped by the arrival of Sarah Stone and her lover. Yesterday we had a visit from Israel Putnam of Griffin Geo[.] He has been at Fort Lafayette for a year charged with being a rebel "blockade runner" and giving aid and comfort to the rebels! He is now under bonds, and his case is to be tried shortly.

Thursday 9. [March 9, 1865]

Yesterday, Mr West and I took a jaunt to Newark to see Oliver Chappel. A ride of ten miles on the New Jersey RR and we were soon at the shop where Oliver holds forth in the Soda Water business, but, unfortunately, he himself had gone to New York, and we did not see him, however, we saw his wife.—I have today, written to brother Jabe to send by flag of truce, under cover to Col. Jno. E. Mulford Com of Exch' Fortress Monroe. Also, I have written to Rev. S. Landrum at Savannah to make enquiries. This is Nell's birthday; I wonder how they are getting along.

Sunday 12. [March 12, 1865]

Yesterday I took Dora and Irene to Add's room to let them see the pictures. This morning we went to Dr Westons church, and were not so well pleased as at previous attendance, for he introduced an illustration in the course of his sermon which too plainly showed his war and nigger sentiments. Tonight Mr and Mrs West came in and we had a *grand concert* of Sacred Music!

Tuesday 14. [March 14, 1865]

Last night Sallie and I went down to Aunt Harriets as I wanted to see if Will Stone had done anything about the *feed* trade. He told me that another party had bought out the store.—Tonight, Mary Stone and her *betrothed* Gilbert Pettit, my wifes cousin came to see us. He is just released from nine months confinement in a southern "pen" where he don't appear to have starved or become at all "emaciated." For Mary's sake I treated him civilly—otherwise I should not have shown much regard to a man who *volunteered* to go and fight the South.—I went to Sheldon's Bookstore today and found the gent in at last, and also met there Jackson Deloache of Macon and Mr Putnam. Deloache ran the blockade in January via Memphis, leaving his wife in Macon. I wonder how bro' Warren got along without the *deacon* and what they all thought of his running away!—*

---

* Ebenezer F. Warren of Macon's First Baptist Church was the Richards family pastor before the Civil War.

Thursday 16. [March 16, 1865]

This morning I went to Hoboken with Wm Stone to look at a vacant store that was once used as a *feed store* and which we *talk of* renting for that purpose again. We calculate that it will require about $1000 cash capital to start on. I have but $650 in currency left and I don't want to sell my *gold* at its present low rate as it has fallen to 170 contrary to my expectation entirely. Of course, it would have been much better if I had kept the *greenbacks*, instead of exchanging them for gold.—

Friday 17. [March 17, 1865]

The *Draft* has been progressing in this city for two days past and I looked over the paper this morning with some perturbation to see if *my* name was among the list of *drafted*. The nearest approach to it was "S. Richardson," and as the paper says that the draft is made from the *old* enrollment, I suppose I am not *in*.

Sat 18. [March 18, 1865]

I forgot to chronicle that yesterday being "Saint Patrick's Day" the Irish turned out in force to celebrate it, and a procession about *two hours long* went by on 34th Street gay with green flags and golden harps, and fine banners of the different Father Mathew Temperance Societies—some on wagons drawn by twelve horses and about twenty brass bands to enliven the pageant.* It was quite a fine sight. I did not know that there were so many Irishmen in New York. This afternoon I took the children down to see Van Menageri, this being the last day of its stay.† "Tippo Saib" the "Performing Elephant" behaved himself very well. There were six Lions and about as many Leopards, and a great variety of other beasts and birds. The *Panther* had his foot bitten off, which was the sad consequence of having bad neighbors—the "Brazilian Tiger" next door to him not relishing the advances he made had snapped off his extended paw!

Sunday 19. [March 19, 1865]

It has been a beautiful Spring day—and Sallie and I went to "St Stephen's Church" (Roman Catholic) as we had been told that the Music

---

* *NYT*, Mar. 18, 1865, estimated the city's St. Patrick's Day parade as between five and six miles long and including fifteen thousand people and ten Father Mathew temperance societies.

† Van Amburgh and Company charged twenty-five cents to see its "Menagerie and Great Moral Exhibition." Billed as a "Colossal Collection of Living and Wild Animals," it featured elephants named Hannibal and Tippoo Saib, an "intellectual ape" named Signor Victor, and variety of "untamed lions" (*NYT*, Mar. 18, 1865).

there was good. We were required to pay *ten cents* each to go into this *show* but as I had never seen one of the kind it was *worth the money*! Such mummeries looked supremely ridiculous in the eyes of us *heretics*. The music was quite good *of its kind*.

Wed. 22. [March 22, 1865]

At ten o'clock this morning, Mrs. West went with myself and the children to Barnum's Museum and *spent the day* there.* Sallie and Dora and I went there in 1860. There is nothing especially new there now, if we except the "three-legged wonder" a comical figure that came upon the stage and treated us to a dance on its three legs. Whether it was a *live* humbug or a *dead* one we could not tell!—The play of "William Tell" was pretty well performed.†

Sunday 26. [March 26, 1865]

We walked down to 14th St this morning to Dr Hawk's Church (Epis). He is a *Secessionist*, they say. This aft. Mr West brought Mr Frank Austin the organist at Dr Wescotts Church to our room to sing with us. He sings tenor and we had a quartette choir, and he professed to be much edified with the music and pressed us all to go to their church tonight and sing with them. There has been quite a panic in Wall St last week gold having gone as low as 147 at one time though it got up to 155 again last night. I am sorry to see it going down so, though I think it will go up again somewhat yet.‡ The *end* of the war is hardly so near as is generally supposed.—Dora and I went at night with the Wests to Dr Wescotts and Mr West and I went to the choir and sang with them. After the sermon two ladies were baptized and

---

* P. T. Barnum's museum had been a staple of New York's entertainment district for many years, an "enormous, heterogeneous collection [that] found a coherence of sorts through its promotion of entrepreneurialism, Christianity, domesticity and temperance. The strategy proved tremendously popular among respectable families" (Bluford Adams, *E Pluribus Barnum: The Great Showman and the Making of U.S. Popular Culture* [Minneapolis: University of Minnesota Press, 1997], xiv). Barnum's museum was a target of the Confederate conspirators who tried to burn the city in Nov. 1864.

† *William Tell* (1804), a play by Friedrich Schiller, tells the story of the folk hero and marksman by that name and of the Swiss people's efforts to obtain independence from the Hapsburg Empire.

‡ *NYT*, Mar. 25, 1865, discussed fluctuations in the gold market and suggested that prices were dropping because of the "absence of later military news [and] the failure last evening of one of the heaviest of the pro-Southern Gold firms in the Room, involving the abrupt settlement of a very large amount of contracts."

as the choir seats were directly over the pulpit and pool we looked right down upon the ordinance as it was administered. The choir at the church is the most conspicuous object in view, not excepting the preacher.

Tuesday 28. [March 28, 1865]

I went down town today and called at the bookstores but did not find any employment, though as the Appletons have just lost two of their *packing* clerks I possibly could get in there if I applied now. The chief objection is the wages are too little in that department, and the work pretty hard. And if I go in there it will be a bad chance to secure anything better. I went to the office of the *News* to see a list of the *drafted* men but was not lucky enough to find my own among the names. The "S. Richardson" before mentioned I found lived at 189 West 33rd St. He is very welcome to the honor I am sure.—

Wed 29. [March 29, 1865]

We were today favored by a visit from the Hon Wm Turrell, Speaker of the Pennsylvania House of Rep., and his wife, our *Aunt Huldah* of blessed memory! She was quite affectionate and I could not refuse her proffered kiss.—They did not talk any *war*.

Thursday 30 [March 30, 1865]

Mr West and I went to the choir meeting at Dr Wescott's church at night, but the woman folks (ours) did not go out on account of the wet weather. The equinox Storm seems to have come upon us now. We received pressing invitations to go on next Sabbath to sing with them.

Friday 31. [March 31, 1865]

It has stormed all day again, but, nevertheless, I took the cars this aft and rode three miles to the market and brot home a newbasket full of supplies about 20% less than the articles cost about here. I called at Uncle Roswel Stone's Store, 205 West St. He says Will can't get the Feed Store in Hoboken at a rent that will suit us.—Our Monthly Expenditures seem to average about $75 now, on Rent & Provisions about $60 and the balance more or less for Furniture, Clothing &c, not including of course the outlay in first setting up our establishment.—I do not suppose there are many people who live on as small a sum as that, who pretend to live in any comfort.—I fear we shall have to leave our present abode next month as our landlord thinks of living here himself. This moving about is a great bore. I have been at a good deal of trouble to make ourselves comfortable here and just as we get accustomed to the place and feel at home a little, off we must pack to another strange place.—

Sunday 2. [April 2, 1865]

We went to Mad' Ave Bap' Church this morning to hear Dr Weston. Two young men were baptized.—

Monday 3. [April 3, 1865]

The news of the evacuation of Richmond and Petersburg came yesterday but *we* did not hear it until today. The Yankees are all jubilant as can be and talk about the war being now over. Gen Lee's army has gone towards the West with a small and dispirited army of only twenty thousand men so say the Lincoln papers here, but the Daily "News" makes out a more favorable case of it for the Confederates.* Things look very dark and hopeless for our people truly, and humanly considered, there seems no chance of success; and yet I can not believe that the unjust and bloody programme of the North will be permitted to be carried out to completion by a righteous God. I long to see the dreadful war ended but not by the defeat and subjugation of the South by the Abolition hordes of Yankee land. The more I think about this war the more *atrocious* it seems to me to be on the part of the North. At the same time I feel and see more plainly how mistaken was the course adopted by the South in seceding as they did one by one, and thus tempting their enemies to endeavor to force them to go back.—The blood of thousands of her sons seems now to cry out against reunion.—

Thursday 6. [April 6, 1865]

I received on Tuesday an answer to my letter to Bro Landrum at Savannah. He says his charge there consists now of a few old men and many women and children all "poor as poverty."—Miss Cornish and Mrs. Turrell called on us Tuesday night. The latter is such a black Abolitionist that I don't care much to see her. It is just such fanatics as she that brought all this desolation and misery upon our country. Mary Smillie is just such

---

* Beginning in the spring of 1864, Union and Confederate forces had faced each other near Petersburg, Virginia, directly south of Richmond. The morning after Ulysses S. Grant's Federal army defeated Robert E. Lee's Confederates at Five Forks on Apr. 1, 1865, Lee was forced to send word to President Jefferson Davis that the army could no longer protect the Confederate capital. Davis fled along with his family and some members of his cabinet. Lee's army moved to the west with the ultimate goal of linking up with the meager forces of Joseph E. Johnston (who replaced John Bell Hood commanding what was left of the Army of Tennessee) in North Carolina (David S. Heidler and Jeanne T. Heidler, eds., *Encyclopedia of the American Civil War: A Political, Social, and Military History*, 5 vols. [Santa Barbara, Calif.: ABC-CLIO, 2000], 1:68).

another only more of a *squirt*—a black, loud-mouthed Abolitionist, I wish she could be *drafted* and made to fight!—Aunt Huldah was glorying in the news that Lincoln was occupying Pres Davis' house in Richmond and I *riled* her somewhat by remarking that *he* was not the only Yankee that was in a place that did not belong to him.*—Last night Aunt Harriet and Cousin Mary came up.—Mary Add was here on Tuesday and seemed quite cast down at the late News from the War. Gold fell to 145 on Monday but has got up again to 154. If Lee and Johnston are able to make their new position strong, I look for gold to go up to 200 again ere long. Having nothing much to do now a days, I have been keeping school for a week, to keep the children from forgetting all they ever learned, if they do no more. I have this week read the "Pilgrim's Progress" again.—†

Sunday 9. [April 9, 1865]

We went this morning to an Epis Church, corner 5th Av and 35th St. It was different from any other church that we have been to in being without any side windows, and lighted entirely from the top. It is "Palm Sunday" I learned from the discourse. In the aft' Mrs West came in and sang with us awhile.—At night, we, that is, Dora and myself and the Wests, went to "the Broadway Tabernacle" to hear Dr Thompson discourse on the late victories and "How to treat the Conquered," and especially to hear the singing, which was to include among other grand things the "Hallelujah Chorus" of Handel.—We went early and just succeeded in getting crowded seats in the gallery. The large church was crammed with people.—The main point of the discourse was that the war on this side was not successful until the President and Congress propitiated the favor of God by passing the late Abolition laws, and that being done, immediately the great victories were gained and the "wicked conspiracy" was overthrown! He thinks the leaders of the rebellion should not be touched in person or liberty, but that their *pride of caste* should be humbled and their power to do harm taken away by confiscating their estates and disfranchising them. The majority of the Southern people, in consideration

---

* Abraham Lincoln, who had been consulting with Ulysses S. Grant at the general's City Point headquarters, made his way to the recently surrendered Confederate capital on Apr. 4, 1865. Lincoln visited the Davis home, which had been made the headquarters of General Godfrey Weitzel, the ranking Union commander, who had entered the city the previous day (Heidler and Heidler, *Encyclopedia*, 4:1646–47).

† *The Pilgrim's Progress* (1678), by John Bunyan, is an allegory telling the story of the Christian's journey to heaven.

of their ignorance and credulity in being misled by the leaders of the rebellion, he thinks should be forgiven and received again to the benefits and blessings of the Union. The Revd Speaker made several important statements as *facts* that were wholly false, tho' in charity I will suppose that he thought they were true. One fling of contempt at the *Government* of the Confederate States was applauded by stamping of feet in the *Beecher* Church style.* The singing was good and worth going to hear.—

Monday 10 [April 10, 1865]

The first thing that met my eye this morning in looking over the "News" was this startling heading: "Surrender of Gen. Rob. E. Lee and all his army!" It appears that to prevent further bloodshed with but small hope of success, Gen Lee did yesterday agree to surrender his army to Grant, the latter allowing them the honors of war!† So now there seems to be nothing more for the South to do but make the best terms they can and give up the unequal contest, begun in too much haste and fought with such dreadful loss for four long years.—It grieves me to think of what the South has suffered and lost, *for what*? For a lot of worthless niggers, which now are worse than worthless.—

[April 15, 1865]

Startling news was published in the papers this morning, (Sat. 15) viz that Abraham Lincoln had been shot last night at the theatre in Washington by an assassin and also Secretary Seward was assaulted while lying sick in bed and his face and throat severely cut. The perpetrators of these crimes had made their escape but strong circumstantial evidence seemed to prove that the murderer of the President was one John Wilkes Booth, an actor.‡ Apart from the horror of this deed I fear it will prove to be the

---

* Rev. Henry Ward Beecher presided over Plymouth Church in Brooklyn, one of the nation's largest churches. He was known for his rich speaking voice and emotional style (Halford Ross Ryan, *Henry Ward Beecher: Peripatetic Preacher* [New York: Greenwood, 1990]).

† With desertions rampant and his undernourished soldiers unable to deter Ulysses S. Grant's onslaught, Robert E. Lee decided to surrender. When the two commanders met at the McLean house in Appomattox Court House on Apr. 9, Grant offered lenient terms: Lee's entire army would be paroled, and men would surrender their guns, but officers would be allowed to keep their sidearms and horses, which were their personal property (*NYT*, Apr. 10, 1865).

‡ On Apr. 14, 1865, while attending a play at Ford's Theater, Lincoln was shot in the back of the head by John Wilkes Booth, a prominent actor and Confederate sympathizer. Lincoln lingered through the night, dying the following morning.

worst thing for the South that could have been done at this juncture—for this excitable northern mind which had begun to turn towards the conquered South with feelings of mercy and forgiveness, is now enraged against the entire land of "rebellion" whose people they charge with instigating and abetting this horrid deed. I have no great love for Abraham Lincoln regarding him as I must as the cause of all the bloodshed and misery that has deluged our land, but I abhor such crimes as assassination. Secession and "Rebellion" are here regarded as the fruitful parents of such crimes—I look upon them as the progeny of the fiend "Abolition."—A dark pall seems to be cast over this city lately so jubilant, and both "loyalists" and "traitors" are sad.—

Sunday 16. [April 16, 1865]
We went to Dr Westons Church this morning and heard a eulogy on the dead president and several things things that I did not think came with a good grace from a gospel preacher.—He said also (and I accepted the alternatives) that either the South had been guilty of a most heinous crime in rebelling and seceding, *or, the people of the North had sinned terribly in their course* towards them in this war.—The latter has always seemed to me to be the true theory.—I *may* be wrong though.

Sat 22. [April 22, 1865]
We began over a week ago to hunt for another suite of rooms as we shall be obliged to move from our present comfortable abode in May. We have been nearly all over this upper part of the city and into many "Apartments" until we were sick of the business and well nigh in despair of finding any to suit us. Several places that would have done for us alone we lost, in delaying to try to find such as would do for the Wests also. At last we yesterday rented a first floor in a brown stone front house 862 Sixth Av. between 48 & 49th Strts. Rent—$27 per month. They are not such as

---

Lincoln's assassination was part of a conspiracy to kill prominent members of the executive branch. While Booth was at Ford's Theater, his fellow conspirator, Lewis Powell, burst into the home of Secretary of State William H. Seward and slashed him with a knife. Injured recently in a carriage accident, Seward was wearing a jaw brace that ultimately saved his life. Another conspirator, George Atzerodt, was supposed to kill Vice President Andrew Johnson but never attempted to do so. Booth and Powell initially escaped, but Booth was later surrounded and killed by federal marshals, while Powell was executed along with other conspirators on July 7 (Thomas Goodrich, *The Darkest Dawn: Lincoln, Booth, and the Great American Tragedy* [Bloomington: Indiana University Press, 2005], 92–98, 109, 168, 171–72, 261).

we want though, and will not be comfortable after our present convenient quarters.—We shall probably want to exchange them for more eligible ones when we can.—Yesterday, "Virginia" was one year old and has just got her sixth tooth. She don't talk any except to say "*I shan't*" and is very mischievous and wilful. She is a strong, sturdy baby and generally taken to be of the male *gender*.

Sunday 23. [April 23, 1865]

We went to Dr Burlingham's Church (Baptist) in 25th St at Miss Cornish's invitation, but we shall not probably go there again soon as the preacher did not please us. Instead of Christ, he preached Lincoln and seemed to think one about as good as the other.—

Tuesday 25. [April 25, 1865]

The grand Funeral Pageant of the murdered President passed near our abode this afternoon and we went to 34th St and stood for three hours in a crowd to see it pass by. The coffin was carried in a splendid car, constructed here for the occasion and drawn by 16 gray horses each led by a negro groom in mourning garb. We left as soon as the car passed us but the procession was *two hours* longer still.—Honour and respect to departed rulers is all right and proper but on the present occasion things are carried "ad nauseam"—preachers instead of a crucified Saviour, spend all their eloquence to set forth the unequalled worth of the late President, and make him out almost divine. As a set off to such adulation I was much struck by the reply of our Irish Washerwoman to a friend of hers who argued that Abraham Lincoln was like Christ and died as a Martyr on Good Friday. The rejoinder was "And Jesus Christ was not shot at a shindy!"* Though I do not think it an evidence that Lincoln was not a good man nor a Christian, that he was at the theatre even on Good Friday.—What I *do* think though, *is* that he might have prevented this awful war and saved thousands of human lives, *and did not*. I am sorry that he was killed, but would to God that he had never been born.—And yet if *he* had not been

---

* Some Americans, including SPR's washerwoman, believed Abraham Lincoln had made a moral error in attending the theater on Good Friday. According to *NYT*, Apr. 26, 1865, the funeral procession carrying Lincoln's body traveled through city streets while a vast number of people stood in "reverent silence." According to Harry S. Stout, "Throughout the North and in 'Union' pulpits in the South, the messianic praises of Lincoln rang like the peals of the mourning bells. Many lauded his Christlike character" (*Upon the Altar of the Nation: A Moral History of the American Civil War* [New York: Viking, 2006], 453).

their instrument, the haters of the South would have selected some other, equally fatal to the cause of peace and Union.—

Monday 1. [May 1, 1865]

I have often heard of May Day in New York and *imagined* the bustle and confusion that was said to prevail at that *moving* time; but I little expected to *experience* the same so soon. But so it is, and we have today changed our abode from 630 Sixth Avenue to 862 of the same Avenue and the first floor (over a store) of the same number. The Wests are still with us. It has been a wet and disagreeable day and a good deal of household stuff has had more washing today than was beneficial, and ours suffered in that respect. We are now just below 49th Street only ten streets from Central Park, within easy walking distance. Mr West and I walked to the Park yesterday afternoon and found it a very pretty place as a resort from the dusty city—green lawns sprinkled with flowers, and refreshing fountains to cool the air with their sparkling spray. The natural advantages of the place have been greatly added to by careful and costly labor.* But in strolling through such places of beauty and pleasure I think of our Southern Land desolated and destroyed by the same hands that have wrought all these beauties and of the thousands who have been driven from dear homes of beauty and delight by the ruthless invader.—We hear that Gen Johnston has surrendered his army to Gen Sherman upon the same terms that were granted to Gen Lee.†—So it would seem that the war is about over and after four years of war and desolation, what has the South gained? The result has proved what I all along thought, that it was folly to run the risk of incurring a war without first counting the cost, when, I had no doubt, the end for which the majority have been fighting might have been attained without *secession* or if that *had to be*, it ought to have been a concerted thing with all the states whose interests were threatened.—But I confess myself surprised at the result, because I have had so much faith in the *justice* of the Southern cause and so strong

---

* See T. Addison Richards, *Guide to Central Park* (New York: Miller, 1869); Mary Levin Koch, "The Romance of American Landscape: The Art of Thomas Addison Richards," *Georgia Museum of Art Bulletin* 8 (Winter 1983): 16.

† Joseph E. Johnston's Army of Tennessee could not long resist the overwhelming numbers in William T. Sherman's army, and following Robert E. Lee's surrender, Johnston sought surrender terms. Johnston and Sherman met at Durham Station, North Carolina, with the formal surrender occurring on Apr. 26 (William C. Davis, *An Honorable Defeat: The Last Days of the Confederate Government* [New York: Harcourt, 2001], 183–200).

a sense of the injustice of the North, that I expected the manifestation of the Almighty in behalf of an oppressed and injured people.—As I have always said however, if our cause was not a good one I would not expect or wish it to prosper.—

Sunday 7. [May 7, 1865]

We have become somewhat settled in our new abode though we miss various comforts that we had in our other rooms.—I think though that the *air* of these rooms is purer and healthier than that of those we left. I went with the children to Dr Wescotts Church this morning and *for once* heard a sermon that had not one word about *rebellion* or *Lincoln* in it and it was really refreshing. "Recognition of Friends in Heaven" was the theme. The weather for the past week has not been very pleasant in the house, being rather chilly and yet not cold enough for fire—for *poor folks*. The thermometer has stood at 60° most of the time.—If I had employment I should be much better satisfied, as it is, I am weary and impatient. Yet, in the prospect of being able to return to the South ere long I don't feel much like engaging in trade here.—But I am afraid that a *Yankeeized* South will not be a very pleasant place to live in.

Sunday 14. [May 14, 1865]

Wife having got her new bonnet was of course ready enough to go to church this morning, so we went to 42nd St and heard Dr Wescott preach on the "Final Destiny of the Impenitent"—The news of this morning is not such as *I* call good. Jefferson Davis and family with several other officials have been captured at Irwinsville in Irwin Co Georgia, and they are on the way to Washington under a strong guard. He is in all probability on the way to the gallows, as the present Administration seems disposed to deal harshly with the chief men of the South. The worst feature of the case is their evident intention to fix the odium of complicity in the murder of Lincoln upon Mr. Davis and to put him to death as a felon. I cannot believe that he had anything at all to do with that vile affair. If Davis is hung I think there will be another large drop of bitterness added to the hatred which the despotic course of the North has engendered in the minds of the Southern people generally, during this dreadful war.*—This afternoon at

---

* Captured by federal forces at Irwinville, Georgia, as he tried to flee south, Davis was eventually incarcerated at Fort Monroe, Virginia. Hysteria over the Lincoln assassination led many Northerners to suspect that Davis had a role in the U.S. president's martyrdom. The Confederate leader was never prosecuted and was released after two years, with no evidence having surfaced that he plotted to kill Lincoln (Davis, *Honorable Defeat*, 286–312, 349–53, 396).

two O'clock I went with the children to Dr Armitage's Church (Baptist) Cor of 5th Av. & 46th St to start them to Sunday School having had an invitation to do so last week from a gentleman who saw Irene in the street and came to our room to ask us to send them. Upon reaching the place, however, we found the house shut up and so had our trouble for nothing. So as we could not go to School, I thought I would take the children to the *Park* and did so, though I do not approve of such a way of spending the Sabbath as a general thing.—We returned home pretty tired with a three hours stroll.—Add and Mary came up at night to pay us a parting visit as they expect to leave for Providence on Tuesday on their Summer tour of several months. They brought a letter for me which had been mailed in this city but *looked* like a *foreigner* and proved to be from J.J.R. bearing date April 9. Augusta Geo. He had just rec^d mine of March 9 sent by flag of truce. His letter contained various items of interest, chief of which were that he was *married* for the third time, the fortunate lady being Miss Lou. Soullard of Sparta! The wedding came off I judge Dec 20th last. This event was not wholly unexpected by us as we knew ere we left the South that *something* was going on in that quarter. Henry, it seems, went back to Atlanta in December and is living in Jabe's house which was uninjured, and he is keeping store in the "Peters St" house which is the *only* one of our joint houses left standing, either in the city or on the farm!—But from what J. states, I think our Piano &c must be safe, as he speaks of getting his furniture and don't say that any was missing except his R. Chair, Music Stand and Vases.—So he must have had a list of the items that were stored in the Church.—*Gold* he says was *3 score & ten*. He does not mention Mary Brown. They all seem to have been well and doing pretty well *at that time*. It was just after the fall of Richmond, but before the surrender of Lee and murder of Lincoln. *Now*, I fear that they are not very flush of available funds, as *Confed* [money] must be almost or quite worthless, and I fear they had not *realized* any amount in *gold* or *greenbacks*—though *Steve* [Whitehead] *may* have taken care of himself in that way.—Jabe spoke as though he was going back to Atlanta, in time to make a garden.—I must write to him again at once.—To hear from home makes me want to be getting back there badly.—J. is still pubg the "Friend" and speaks of having just got out *No 26*. I guess his "occupation is gone" *now*.

Tuesday 16 [May 16, 1865]

I rode down town this aft' to see Add and Mary off for Providence at five Oclock in the St[eame]r "Plymouth Rock." While waiting with them, brother Will came to the boat. He is on his way to St. Louis Mo. to attend

Anniversaries there, a distance of 1300 miles by rail.—I wrote to him at Pittsfield yesterday. I went with him after Add and Mary were off, to "The World" office and made some inquiry as to whether they could give me any employment.* Mr Marble the Editor was not there and Mr Bangs did not think there was any opening.—My *felonious* finger does not get well as I hoped it would. It is *shorter* by more than 1/8 inch and the ball of the first joint is hard and tingles at being touched so that it is of very little use to me in most cases but fortunately I can use it in writing nearly as well as ever as the affected part is not on that side that in writing rests upon the pen. It would be of no use to me tho in *setting type*. I think tho' that with a little practice the *middle* finger would do nearly as well.—

Sat 20. [May 20, 1865]

I have passed the time this week in reading aloud to my wife Charles Reade's novel "Very Hard Cash."† It is a pretty good story, the moral thereof being to show the utter inefficiency of the English laws in reference to the *Mad-Houses* of that land. The hero of the story becomes the victim of unscrupelous relatives, and is decoyed away on the 'eve of his marriage, and kept a long time an unwilling prisoner in several of these institutions, notwithstanding all his efforts to obtain justice and liberty.—I am very tired of the kind of life that I am now leading, especially as it *don't pay*. I see some "City Bookstore" wants a clerk "who is not afraid of work," but the salary is only six dollars per week for the first six months, so *that* wont do for me! *Work* in New York *don't pay*.—

Sunday 21. [May 21, 1865]

It is a rainy morning so that we have not been tempted out to church. The Wests came in to our room and we sang some in the afternoon, but we felt more like hanging our harps on the willow, I believe.

Wed 24. [May 24, 1865]

I went down town yesterday and bot some summer clothes a very unpleasant business when I am limited in means. If the articles are costly I cannot afford them and if they are cheap they do not suit me—hence

---

* The *New York World* was a Democratic newspaper that had been suspended for a brief period in 1864 for having published a false presidential proclamation (Heidler and Heidler, *Encyclopedia*, 3:1421).

† As SPR suggested, *Hard Cash* (1863), by English novelist Charles Reade, focused on the abuse of mentally ill patients in private asylums (Dominic Head, ed., *The Cambridge Guide to Literature in English*, 3rd ed. [New York: Cambridge University Press, 2006], 922).

the trouble—chiefly.—This aft. it was so pleasant that the "girls"—Mrs. West and Sallie—with me for escort—took a walk to Central Park. The place is delightful or *would* be if it were not for the remembrance that we are here as strangers in a strange land—and that the people who have been beautifying this place so for four years have all that time been doing all they could to desolate our home and our land and that they have succeeded so well.—I confess I felt envious and wicked as the gay carriages of 5th Avenue whirled by filled with the careless ones who have known *none* of the dreadful ills and sorrows of this war. I have today been reading "Beatrice" the last novel of Julia Kavagnah, that Mr. Pars was good enough to lend me.* Our good "*Brother* Shelton" declined to lend me a book. I am too poor to buy. Of course I do not allow the new books I read to *look* any the *less fresh* for my reading them, so I am benefitted and nobody injured.—

Thursday 25. [May 25, 1865]
Our baby begins to speak a few words tho' I believe *two* are about all that she has yet in her spoken vocabulary. She calls "Arkar" (Arthur) quite forcibly and she says "Pap-pap-pa—" Oh yes she says "I shall" and "I shant" very apropos indeed, and with a tone and accent that makes amends for any imperfection in the utterance of the words themselves.— She is a wilful little piece, a real *young rebel*, and almost hardened to punishment. Her Ma says she grows prettier every day; of course.—We were startled the other day by hearing that one of the little girls above us was ill of *Scarlet Fever*. May our merciful Heavenly Father shield us from this dreadful disease.—

Sat 27 [May 27, 1865]
We finished our book "Beatrice" today.—It is a pretty good story though evidently founded on "Very Hard Cash" which it very much resembles in its incidents. I made a list of 48 errors in the typography thereof. One of them makes the heroine's teacher open to her mind the volumes of *classic love*—instead of *classic lore*!—

Sunday 28. [May 28, 1865]
Another rainy sunday.—I went alone to an Epis Church on 48th St close by, this morning. I brought home a "Parish Visitor" that I found in the pew I sat in and have been reading in it some account of the "Christian

---

* Julia Kavanagh was the author of *Beatrice* (New York: Appleton, 1865) and numerous other novels centered on female characters (Head, *Cambridge Guide to Literature in English*, 593).

Commission" an association formed to alleviate the sufferings, bodily and spiritual, of the Soldiers of the Union Army.* A feeling of regret and sadness came over my mind at the evidence that Christian men and women at the North were as sincere in the belief of the righteousness and justice of *their* cause as were the Christians of the South in their devotion to theirs. There must have been a great error somewhere—for such a dreadful strife as that of the past four years must be the penalty for great sin. Can it be possible that the purpose of God in permitting this war was to put an end to slavery (black slavery?) No doubt many will think so, as that seems to have been one result. *I* can readily think that the time may have come when *He* sees that the *curse* may pass away, but at the same time I believe that *hitherto* that state of things has been sanctioned and sustained by the same divine authority that first instituted it. I do not believe that the war was the punishment for the *sin* of slavery.

Thursday June 1. [June 1, 1865]

This is a National Fast day in memory of Abraham Lincoln. Having heard enough about him in the pulpit of late we did not go to church, nor did we *fast*. Of the latter form of devotion I guess there was little practiced today, anywhere.—I have written to Jabez this week and sent by Mr. Jas Ball who sails on Saturday for Savannah.—

Friday 2. [June 2, 1865]

I have been down town every day this week, except Sunday and yesterday, principally to call at the Office of the American News Co, 121 Nassau St, to see if I could not obtain employment, as they adv[ertise]d for an experienced Bookseller. But they keep putting me off, as they want one more accustomed to City trade. I have called upon several of our old friends with whom we used to trade, and most of whom we owe money to. They all seemed glad to see me, and talked very friendlily. I talked a good while with Mr Zogbaum, who has lived at the South.

Sat 3. [June 3, 1865]

There was Music today at the Park for the first time this Spring and we walked up there with the Wests at four Oclock to hear the Concert.

---

* The U.S. Christian Commission, founded in 1861, was an outgrowth of the Young Men's Christian Association. Its mission was to provide spiritual care to Union soldiers, and it did so with an evangelical flair. The Christian Commission also provided medical and nutritional aid to soldiers (McPherson, *Ordeal*, 419–21).

There were a great many people there, as the grass was made "Common" for the day it was very pleasant. We stayed until six o'clock and heard 13 pieces of Music, without charge!—I have just finished reading aloud "The Clever Woman of the Family" by Miss Yonge, pubd by Appleton.* Badly printed; I found over one hundred errors in it.—

Sunday 4. [June 4, 1865]

It is very warm today, though only so in our front room.—We went to Dr Wescotts Church this morning.—Mr Braumuller of Atlanta is now in Mr West's room. He says he is told that provisions are cheaper there than *here* but I doubt it very much.

Thursday 8 [June 8, 1865]

Brother William came up this afternoon, and I almost missed seeing him, having just been a moment too late in catching a car to go down to city. He made an attempt yest., he says, to find us by means of a direction he got from Tom Bradley who told him we lived between 36th & 40th St. Today tho he found our address at Sheldon's, with whom I left it last week.—William says he came into possession of quite a lot of Father's old journals and MS.S. that were captured at St Helena; among them some of William's Anti-Secession letters written to Father previous to the war and being returned to Providence were the means of clearing him from the charge of being a secessionist, wh, he says, was being made against him.—At all events he went pretty far the *other* way from all accounts. I shall go to the city tomorrow morning to meet Wm and exchange my two books at Appletons for some others. We yesterday finished "Fairy Fingers" a novel by Mrs. Ritchie just pubd.†—I am inducting Dora into the mysteries of *Interest* now in the course of Mathematical study that she is pursuing. She puts me quite out of patience at times by her dulness in taking into her head any new idea in reference to Fractions, and especially Decimal Fractions.—Irene has reached Compound Numbers; and Arthur has just entered *Division*. They all seem to be *dull* enough.—Sallie's Aunt Catherine, Mrs Smillie, came to see us yest' aft' which was quite an event, as she was almost the first visitor we have had since we moved last.—

---

* Charlotte Yonge, author of 160 books, including *The Clever Woman of the Family* (New York: Appleton, 1865), had a career lasting fifty years and specialized in volumes that focused on family life (Head, *Cambridge Guide to Literature in English*, 1235).

† Anna Cora Mowatt Ritchie, *Fairy Fingers* (New York: Carleton, 1865).

Another *female relative* (old) paid her a visit too, yesterday, for the first time since our baby was born! Although she did not much care to see her, Sallie will be quite discomposed now if she does not come every month in future.—I am very anxious to hear again from Jabez, to know how things progress there. I see but little chance of getting any employment here, and therefore want to get back South as soon as may be.

Friday 9. [June 9, 1865]

I went to town this morning and met Will at Appleton's and went with him to the Harpers' and was introduced to *four* of the abominable *Abolitionists.*—I met a Col Matthews, just from Atlanta, who confirms the statement that provisions were cheap there, but says that *money* is very scarce—I remained down town until six O'clock to see Will off for Pittsfield in the fine boat "St Johns" the largest and finest steamboat that I have yet seen. We visited Washington Market and Will bot a *peck* of Strawberries (more or less) and a lot of pine-apples to carry home, and he made us a present of a basket full for our tea.—I reached home about 6½ O'clock and found the women folks mightily tickled about some thing which they were not going to tell me; but Mrs West could not refrain from *hints*. She said "Tune your harps anew" and so I supposed that Mr Root had turned up; and so it was. He came up again at night and we had a *sing*—the choir of the 2nd Bap Church of Atlanta—as of old! Root has been to England, France and Spain—Bermuda—Nassau—Havanna &c, since he left Atlanta. Professes to be as strong a *rebel* as ever though a *subjected* one.—*

Sat 10. [June 10, 1865]

Began to read "Romola" by Miss Evans today.† Mr Root came at 7 O'clock according to promise and took our *girls* to "Winter Garden" to see the play "Camille," and they did not get back until nearly midnight.‡ I

---

* Sidney Root made New York his home for the next thirteen years, finally returning to Atlanta when he retired and engaging in a variety of philanthropic endeavors (Frank J. Byrne, "Rebellion and Retail: A Tale of Two Merchants in Confederate Atlanta," *Georgia Historical Quarterly* 79 [Spring 1995]: 54–55).

† *Romola* (1863) is a novel by George Eliot, a pseudonym for Mary Ann Evans (Cathy N. Davidson and Linda Wagner-Martin, eds., *The Oxford Companion to Women's Writing in the United States* [New York: Oxford University Press, 1995], 289).

‡ Alexandre Dumas's play, *Camille* (1852), was being performed at New York's Winter Garden Theater.

think they ought to be *dealt with* for such behaviour—I shd much rather see a good performance of Shakespeare's Plays[.]

Sunday 11 [June 11, 1865]
This morning we went to a fine new Presn Church on 42nd St and heard a good plain discourse. At night, Dora and I went to a Dutch Refd Church on 46th St.—In the choir at the Church we attended this morning we saw an old gray headed man, who we were told afterwards was Thos Hastings the Author and compiler of various singing books.*—Gov Brown of Georgia was in N.Y. last week and although a prisoner on parole—bought $80 worth of books at Appletons.—So he can't be feeling *very* badly.—†

Thursday 15. [June 15, 1865]
I took Sallie and Mrs West to the "National Academy of Design" this aft.—I thought Addison's pictures there were about as good as any of them—though I liked a large painting (life size) of Constant Mayer's called "North & South" (No 1 on the list) more than any other I believe.‡ The subject was a wounded Yankee private soldier lying senseless on a rock and a "rebel" also wounded, trying to render him assistance.—When we got back home we found Elbridge Smith with his wife and child just going up to our rooms.—

Sat 17 [June 17, 1865]
Yesterday I wrote to Addison in reply to a letter from him received on Wednesday. He sends us pictures of himself and Mary both striking likenesses. I shall have to get an Album to put our pictures in I suppose. I am glad that Mary sent her likeness, for I think a good deal of our Yankee sister who being surrounded by abolitionists and war-shriekers could yet

---

* In a career lasting nearly sixty years, Thomas Hastings composed hundreds of hymns and assembled and published books of sacred music (Malone, *Dictionary of American Biography*, 4:387–88).

† Georgia's wartime governor, Joseph E. Brown, was imprisoned briefly after the war, became a Republican, was paroled, became chief justice of the state supreme court, rejoined the Democrats, and participated in the state's "redemption" from Republican rule. He also spent a decade in the U.S. Senate (Joseph H. Parks, *Joseph E. Brown of Georgia* [Baton Rouge: Louisiana State University Press, 1977], 350–578). Brown purchased Sidney Root's Atlanta home (Byrne, "Rebellion and Retail," 54).

‡ French-born Constant Mayer was best known as a genre painter and portraitist. He moved to the United States in 1857 and became affiliated with the National Academy of Design, as was Addison Richards, who served as its secretary beginning in 1852 (Malone, *Dictionary of American Biography*, 12:449–50).

feel the justice and truth of the South in this unfortunate struggle, and dare to maintain her cause.

Sunday 18. [June 18, 1865]

I took the children this morning to the "5th Ave Baptist Church" Cor' of 46th St and heard Dr Armitage, the Pastor, preach the Dedication Sermon from the text "The Gate of Heaven." The Church edifice is just finished and is a very neat and elegant structure. I like the interior better than any one I have seen, I think. A new feature was introduced into the service after the sermon, at least *new* to Baptist Churches—viz the reading of Scripture verses by Minister and Congregation alternately. The Programmes had the selections in them and the responses were made in a better style than I have ever yet heard them. I think it a good idea and one that ought to be acted out in our churches generally.—In the aft, Sallie and I went again to the same church and heard Dr Weston preach. I wrote to Jabez today to send by Mr Root if I can. At night I again went to the same church to see it *lit up* and to hear Mr Chown an English preacher.—

Sat 24. [June 24, 1865]

Mrs James (of Atlanta) came up this aft to go with us to the Park, to hear the Music. We walked up there by 4½ Oclock. The green grass was very beautiful and most pleasant to the feet, and as the benches were all occupied we humbled ourselves and took seats on the grass in the shade; but Mrs West was too afraid of soiling her petticoats and dress to avail herself of this primitive means of resting, and stood until some other chance should offer.—The Katy did Polka by Jullien was about the best, or at least the better appreciated of the 13 airs the band played.—We saw the visitors eating ices and drinking juleps but as no one offered to treat us we did not indulge.—Last night we finished "Too Strange not to be True," a new novel by Lady Georgiana Fullerton, the first of hers that I have read.* It is more *strange* than *true* in my opinion.—No tidings from home yet, and we are getting impatient.

Sunday 25. [June 25, 1865]

This morning we went to Grace Church having heard so much of it for years past. The music was very *artistic* but quite undevotional and the

---

* Lady Georgiana Fullerton was a prolific writer and active philanthropist and author of *Too Strange Not to Be True* (1864) (Leslie Stephen, ed., *Dictionary of National Biography*, 22 vols. [London: Oxford University Press, 1938], 7:765–66).

sermon we could not hear. The congregation was quite thin, as the *season for worship is over* with the most of the attendants of Grace Church.—

Monday 26. [June 26, 1865]

I went down town this morning to the Appletons to get some new books to read. Called also at Sheldons' to see Major Connor (of Atlanta) but he was not there. Sheldon told me that Dr Brantley was in Atlanta preaching to the Second Church again! I brot home for the *exiles* to look at ten Stereoscopic views of Atlanta taken while the Yankee Army was there. One view of Sherman's Head Qr's (Mr [John] Neals house) and the 2nd Baptist Church &c came quite near home to us.—

Thursday 29. [June 29, 1865]

Brother William came to our room in the morning and invited me to accompany him to town as he wanted to talk with me. His proposition was to start a bookstore and printing office in Pittsfield where he lives and let me have the management of it, if I did not decide to return to the South.— I should like this plan very well for some things but I am afraid it would not succeed very well. And then I feel that it would be best to resume business in the South if the condition of affairs there warrant, in reference of a settlement of our old indebtedness at the North. Then, moreover, I don't much like the idea of living in New England the nursery of all the Pandora's Box of *Isms* that afflict our land and people.—Cornelia came to New York with William to see the Misses Bates (Mary and Agnes) who have recently come on from Montgomery, Ala, with much difficulty, as it was just before the *surrender* of the South. I went at night to see them all at Mr Marble's house 117 East 30th St. Cornelia looks about the same as ever except that she has grown *stouter*, which fact I felt safe in mentioning to her, as I recollected that her last baby was but 7 or 8 months old!—The Bateses also looked very much as I saw them in Tallahassee 20 years ago! I have not seen them since I believe.*—Miss Mary Bates tho' a New England lady is strongly Southern in her feelings now, and from the tenor of her conversation I don't think Cornele had much sympathy with her. She talked to Wm as tho' she thot of course he was a Southern man in sentiment.—I asked Agnes of my old friends Kate King and Mary Seabrook. The former she did not know her whereabouts and *Mary is dead.* She mentioned to me that Mary had thought of me and the lines I wrote about her *Star.* It is 22 years since that time when I was a *sentimental*

---

* SPR visited with the Bates sisters when he toured the Southeast with William Richards in the early 1840s; see, for example, SPR diary, Aug. 21, 1843.

youth of 19 years!—Mr Marble sang and played and the evening passed quite pleasantly.—

Sunday 2. [July 2, 1865]

We went this morning to the Pres' Ch' on 42d St to hear Rev Hastings.* It is about as pleasant a ch' to go to as any we have tried. We have had some very warm weather of late.—Friday last was the hottest day of the season. Mercury stood 90° in our room and 95° down town.—We have not heard yet from Jabez. I dont see why he dont write.—Mr Gilbert of Atlanta starts home on Wed' next and I think I will write by him.

Wed 5. [July 5, 1865]

Oh! I had nearly passed over the "Glorious Fourth" without a mention, but that will never do in *this* part of the country at all events, as the people here have been unusually patriotic on the occasion. The only way in which we observed the day was by going at night to the corner of 43rd St and Broadway to see the display of Fireworks there. Today, the postman brought us a letter from Jabez, in which he says that he had just rec^d mine by Mr Root. Also that he wrote me a long letter by Express a few days before. He is entirely *cleaned out* of money except Confed' notes. He is living at Atlanta and Henry occupies the three rooms in his house that we used to have and "even so small" a family as that is not found to be pleasant so near. Annie is going to school at the rate of $25 per quarter. Pretty considerable *getting along* with not a cent of money. I don't know where we shall find a resting place if we go there unless we live in the "Peters St" *Cottage (?)* as Jabe suggests. I feel more inclined to put up a *shanty* on my own lot.—I went to the city to find his letter sent by Express, but could not hear any thing of it, much to my regret.

Friday 7. [July 7, 1865]

I went to the city yesterday to meet William but he did not come to time. I called on several of our old creditors and asked them what they would do in regard to old A/cs [accounts] if we make a new start now, and they all seemed willing to make things as easy as they could.—Today, Mary Add made her appearance quite unexpectedly. Add was sent for to attend to some business at the Nat. Academy, and Mary said I could see

---

* Thomas Hastings served for twenty-five years as pastor of West Presbyterian Church on Forty-second Street. He later served as president of Union Theological Seminary (*National Cyclopedia*, 7:317).

him by going there at two O'clock, which I did. She brot the missing letter from Jabez which had been sent to Add's care and was forwarded to Providence. This aft' I wrote a long letter to Jabez to send by mail, also I wrote to Savannah and Louisville to get some information as to freights and transportation.

Sat 8. [July 8, 1865]

Addison called to see us about noon today, and although dinner was partly on the table before us, I was so careless as to let him go away without asking him to stay and eat with us, and I cant get over it.

Sunday 9. [July 9, 1865]

We went this morning to Dr Armitage's Church and heard that gentleman discourse from the text found in "that good old gospel mine" the eighth chap of Romans, viz "The Spirit beareth witness with our spirit." At night I was quite struck with an idea that popped into my head that I would buy a *Photog'* Apparatus and get some insight into the operation of it, and set up a *Gallery* in Atlanta in connection with our bookstore.—

Monday, 10. [July 10, 1865]

Made enquirires about the Photog' business and was quite taken down by night, and about concluded to defer the project for the present. Perhaps we may go in with some one who knows how—Mr Dill perhaps, if he is in Atlanta.*

Wed 12. [July 12, 1865]

Was in town yesterday fishing for *Credit* among the *Stationery* Houses but did not have much success. We shall have to work in a small way if we make a start. Today I shall not go down town not feeling very well, so I have written to Jabez to send by the Wests who go tomorrow the RR route. I have also applied to Washington for free transportation, but have not much hope of getting it. I represented myself as having been a law abiding, quiet Southern citizen whose intention is to return home and discharge the duties of a loyal citizen of the United States. That *is* my intention—for whatever my feelings may be, it is of no use holding out in opposition to the Govt under wh' we must perforce live. It may be all for

---

* C. W. Dill and John Maier owned a photo gallery on Whitehall Street in Atlanta (V. T. Barnwell, *Barnwell's Atlanta City Directory and Strangers' Guide* [Atlanta: Intelligencer, 1867], 163).

the best that the result has been what it has. It *appears* to be the will of God in relation to us, and if so it must be good.

Thursday 13. [July 13, 1865]

I went to town today and saw the destruction of Barnum's most popular "humbug" the *Museum*. This great resort of the people of New York and its visitors was burned to the ground at noon today, making the largest fire, I think, that I have ever seen.* It is said that the great transparencies of Jeffn Davis &c "in Petticoats" that were hung out over the front of the building gave the flames such an impetus, that they could not be controlled. That comes then of making fun of the unfortunate.†
No human lives were lost but many of the poor *dumb brutes* must have perished in the flames. I have never before seen the "Steamers" pouring water on a fire, but today there were two or three dozen, puffing away at a rapid rate. The fire spread to several adjacent buildings, but was got under [control] before many hours; but Mr Barnum's "Waxwork Show" is among the things that *were* [burned]. This afternoon the Wests left for *home*. I *kissed* Mrs. West in the morning. Sallie says she cried at leaving.—

Sat 15. [July 15, 1865]

I have been all the week calling on those we owe to get their views in regard to our old debts. They all *talk* very friendlyly and don't think of troubling us, but I should feel safer if I could get them bound up in black and white, though I think that the word of most of them will do to depend on.—I got another letter from Jabez yesterday and he has thought better of it and invites us to come to his house until we can make other

---

* P. T. Barnum's museum was destroyed by fire on July 13, 1865. The fire began in the engine room, and before long the building was a total loss. Although many animals perished, neither visitors nor museum workers died. The size of the blaze and the presence of escaping animals on city streets created quite a spectacle. After the fire, Barnum formed a partnership with Isaac Van Amburgh, whose animal attraction SPR had visited. The Barnum and Van Amburgh Museum and Menagerie became a major tourist site (Andrea Stulman Dennett, *Weird and Wonderful: The Dime Museum in America* [New York: New York University Press, 1997], 37–38).

† As Jefferson Davis was attempting to elude capture at the end of he war, he slipped away from a family group, throwing a raincoat over his shoulders. The ruse failed, and Davis was apprehended. The raincoat was his wife's, and the Northern press at times exaggerated the story, depicting Davis wearing full female dress, including petticoats (Davis, *Honorable Defeat*, 302–4, 351–53).

arrangements. Mrs West said *she* would do the best she could for us if we had nowhere to go. I wish we were there—but dread the journey.—

Sunday 16. [July 16, 1865]

We went today to Dr Scotts' Pres' Ch'. I have had but little enjoyment of the sanctuary since we came to this land. I feel like a stranger in a foreign clime, and cannot somehow feel that the religion of this people is mine. I don't feel very *Ruth*ish towards them.

Sunday 23. [July 23, 1865]

I have not passed a very pleasant week feeling uncertain how to act in reference to buying goods to take to Atlanta, and not knowing how best to ship them. I have succeeded in getting most of our creditors to sign an agreement to give us three years time to pay our old debts in and some of them will extend further credit to give us a lift. Mr Eberhard Faber's Agent, Mr Hodgskin, kindly offered me $500 worth from his stock of Stationery, on consignment; which was what encouraged me to go ahead and order some goods. Last Wed' night we were somewhat surprized to greet our wife's father just from Macon. He brot me two daily Papers pub'd in Atlanta which was an evident token that they are going ahead again, and a letter from Jabez rec^d since Mr V. came says that the place has the stir and bustle of its former life again, to a degree. So I am anxious to get back and be doing again.—This morning we went to hear Dr Wescott preach from the text "The way of the transgressor is hard." I was rather disappointed that he did not lug in Jeff' Davis and the Assassination Conspirators, but he did not.—This aft' I have written to Jabez and to W.C.R. telling them of our anticipated departure.—

Sat 29. [July 29, 1865]

This week has been one of considerable perplexity to me as I was unable to get any definite information in regard to shipping goods to Atlanta. I had about concluded to send, and *go*, via Savannah, when on Thursday I met Schreiner from that place and he gave such a discouraging view of that route that I changed my mind and ship by Louisville care "Merchants Despatch."—We have received letters both from William and Cornelia in reply to mine announcing our speedy departure.—We have also rec^d a letter from Harriet at Americus. She is very desirous that we should go back South to live.—Today having about finished my business in the city, I have been at home making cases to pack such articles as we want to carry back to Dixie, viz: our old Seeraphine, our bureau and so forth. I wish now that we had left the Seraphine with the Piano in the church at Atlanta, tho' then it seemed quite a "forlorn hope."—Mr Chaffee—a friend of the Wests—has rented these rooms, so that we shall not be obliged to get out for a few days, as he does not expect to move in just at present.—

Sunday 30. [July 30, 1865]

We heard Dr Armitage preach this morning, wh' I guess will finish up our Yankee church-going for a good while to come.—A recent letter from Jabez gives quite an encouraging a/c [account] of life in Atlanta. He says that almost as busy a crowd fill its ruined streets as in the days of its greenest prosperity! A newspaper a/c [account] also gives a very encouraging view of its future prospects. I begin to feel myself not so *very poor* after all.

August, Thursday 10.— [August 10, 1865]

We are once more at Atlanta! Altho' we cannot say with the MacGregor "My foot is on my native *heath*"*—we *can* say our feet are in our accustomed dust.—We arrived safely last evening at seven o'clock and found Jabe awaiting us at the *depot*, I was going to say—but alas! that is no more. The ruthless hand of Sherman's vandal host has left nothing of that but the debris of its materials.—But I will go back in my account to New York, and give a short history of our route and journey hither. Monday, Tues' and Wed' were spent by us in packing up and sending off our goods and baggage, and late on Wed' evening we left our now empty rooms and went to spend the night at Aunt Harriet's at their request.—I bot our tickets via Albany over the NY Central RR expecting to go to Albany by the Hudson river RR, but finding that the tickets were just as good by the Steamboat, we left N.Y. in the "Dean Richmond" at six P.M., Thursday August 3. The moon was a week old and the evening sail would have been very pleasant but for a rain storm that came up just as the boat was getting under weigh and continued far into the night, so that we saw but little of the scenery on the river.—

Friday 4. [August 4, 1865]

We landed at Albany at six in the morning, and a walk of six blocks along "Broadway" took us to the RR depot where we had to stay until nearly nine o'clock before the train for Niagara Falls started[.] "Waterfall" being just in season and Niagara being only 22 miles out of our direct route, and this being probably the last chance we should have to view its wonders, we determined to go there. We should have arrived at

* SPR is quoting *Rob Roy* (1817), by Sir Walter Scott.

the place at 9 P.M. but for a *collision* which occurred between our train and a single locomotive which some drunken employee of the road had left upon the track. No damage resulted except to the engines and several of the foremost freight cars, but if our speed had been what it was a few minutes before it would not have resulted so harmlessly, I think. As it was, it abridged our nights sleep as we did not reach Niagara until midnight. We got beds at the "Niagara House" and were soon fast asleep.—The next day we took a carriage and all together proceeded to view the sights. Crossing over the rapids of the American fall on a bridge we drove to "Luna Island" and alighted to walk to the immediate verge of the precipice where we could dip our hand into the water as it made its leap into the caldron below. We next visited the British fall and went up into the tower out in the midst of the torrent. The Stereoscopic Views of the Falls that I had seen had given me a fair conception of the reality, so that I was not surprized nor disappointed. I regret now tho', that while we were there we had not staid all the day and seen all that was to be seen there. But I was afraid that if we delayed we should have to lie over on Sunday, wh' however much I might like to do under other circumstances, we did not want to do then as it cost too much with our crowd. But after all, we found that when we reached Indianapolis on Sunday morning we should have to remain there a whole day as no Sunday trains were permitted to leave that city! We put up therefore at the Mason ("Sherman") House near the depot, about as dirty a place as one usually finds in a hotel of any pretension to decency. Monday morning, I had to hunt up my baggage and get it re-checked for Louisville, at which city I proposed to spend a day, if our friend Mrs Spaulding was still there. We reached L. early in the afternoon, but Mrs S. had moved away, so I decided to go on to Nashville and not stop in L. at night.—The ride to Nashville was a rapid one, and we got over to the Chattanooga depot in good season to buy our tickets over the U.S. M.RRds to Atlanta. On the route to Nash*e* from Louis*e* we passed through *two tunnels*. At Nashville we had to pay 2.50 for transfer to the Chattanooga depot, but we got off in time, and by this time we had become used to *extra* expense, so as to take it rather philosophically. We had a hot dry ride to Chat*a* the U.S.M.R.Rd officials being interested in the *lemonade* trade did not give us any water in the cars.—We arrived at Chat*a* at night and found that we could not leave until morning so we had to submit to be swindled by Mrs Bishop of the Crutchfield House, who charged us six dollars for two straw beds and breakfast for Sallie and myself.—We were up bright and early and after more *extras* in getting off our baggage we got off upon the last stage of our journey. Our ride today was a slow one through a desolated land. Every village and station we stopped at presented an array of ruined walls and chimneys standing useless and solitary with no signs of returning life about them. Marietta, ever so pretty and prosperous is now a desolate ruins thanks to that destroying vandal W. T. Sherman.—At seven O'clock we reached Atlanta glad to find ourselves safe in life and limb at the end of our long and dangerous journey.—We went to Jabe's house and saw our new sister "Lou" and there also found father and mother and Henry's family.—Our quarters now are in the upper room from the window of which just one year ago I used to watch the shells as they came hurtling and whizzing towards us.—This afternoon Jabe and I walked to town and a dirty, dusty ruin it is, but still, busy life is resuming its sway over its desolate streets and any number of stores of all kinds are springing up as if by magic in every part of the burnt district, and enormous *rents* are asked and obtained for very indifferent store-houses.—I guess we shall have to start in the "Peters St" house wh' is rather too much retired tho' for a store.—

Friday 11. [August 11, 1865]

We spent the morning in "prospecting" for a store but without much success. This aft, Jabe proposed to me to accompany him and Lou to singing at the Meth' Church, and I did so, and after we had sung as long as was desirable we were regaled on peaches and grapes. The Meth' Church seems to be taking the lead at this time in religious affairs. Young Atticus Haygood is the pastor.

Sunday 13. [August 13, 1865]

We have had very hot weather since our arrival here. Mercury up to 92° every aft' in our hall. Last night *our choir* met at Bro Roots and we had a sing as of old.—This morning Sallie and I went to hear Rev Mallard preach. His text was—"The love of Christ which passeth knowledge."—

Sunday 20 [August 20, 1865]

We went this morning to Meth' Ch' with Jabe and Lou and heard "Atticus" preach. In the aft' at four oclock we went to our church to witness the baptism of seven young persons by Mr Hornady.

Thursday 24. [August 24, 1865]

I have been a bachelor for three days. My wife and children left last Tuesday morning for Macon and Americus. I did not like to have them go, but we have no place to live in and I expect they can very well spare such a crowd at J's. "Virnie" was not well for several days before they left having a very sore mouth. She is beginning to talk now considerably.—On

Monday last Jabe and I took the "Amnesty Oath" or as some say "D'am nasty oath" and became once more good loyal citizens of the U.S. and began business again by opening store in the "Peters St" House which we have been fixing up for the purpose for the past week. Today, trade has been quite good—cash sales $130. We have calls for many books that we have not yet got, but we are too far out of the way of trade. I have moved my lodgings to the store to guard it.—I suppose Sallie and the babies are in Americus[.] now I should like to hear from them but as there is no mail to Americus I fear I shall not hear soon. A letter came yest' from H[arriet] to S[allie] urging her to go to see her at once and stating that it is quite healthy there now and the weather not so very hot, so I am better satisfied.

Afterword

After the war the Richards family prospered. In 1866, Sam Richards began construction on a modest stone house on the Washington Street lot that he had purchased four years earlier. The family later built a three-story home, surrounded by flower beds and fruit trees, on the same property. Over the next ten years, Sam and Sallie Richards added four more children to their family: George (born 1866), Russell (1868), Walter (1873), and Katherine (1876). Eight of the Richards children lived to adulthood.[1] The Richardses resumed their membership in Second Baptist Church, with Sam serving as its clerk for thirty-six years, teaching Sunday school, and directing the choir. Sallie played the organ.[2]

Jabez and Sam Richards reopened their book and stationery store, and by 1866, a local agent of the commercial reporting firm R. G. Dun concluded that their business had survived the war "without sustaining much loss [and with] considerable means left." By capitalizing on their established reputation and ties to Northern firms and by advertising effectively, the business became a New South success story, reaching an estimated value of between forty and fifty thousand dollars by 1879.[3]

In 1884, Sam ended his business partnership with Jabez, which had lasted more than three decades, and the brothers divided their assets. Sam continued to prosper, while Jabez struggled. When he died in 1906, his death garnered only the briefest notice in local newspapers; at Sam's death four years later, in contrast, newspapers extensively chronicled his life and acclaimed him as a "pioneer citizen of Atlanta."[4]

Sam insisted on the dissolution of the firm for several reasons. For the first fifteen years of their business relationship, Jabez had taken the lead. He was older, had more retail experience, and probably had more capital to invest in the business. Sam sometimes chafed at Jabez's domineering manner and periodically threatened to leave the partnership. During the Civil War, their roles reversed. Following the death of his second wife, Jabez left Atlanta to live in the country, and Sam emerged as the dominant partner. While both brothers invested unwisely in Confederate bonds and slaves, all of which became valueless in 1865, Jabez was more deeply involved. Sam alluded to Jabez's money problems in his May 14, 1865, diary entry and on several other occasions.[5]

The Richards siblings, once a close-knit family, became somewhat less so in the 1860s and 1870s. William and Addison had left the South decades earlier, and the rift between William and his Confederate siblings never completely healed. Their parents, who in many ways held the family together, died in the early 1870s. The youngest sibling, Henry, who had been a loyal if not always a competent clerk for Jabez and Sam over the years, died in 1875.[6] Sam shifted his focus to his children rather than his siblings. At the time of his split with Jabez, Sam's eldest son, Arthur, had reached adulthood. Sam hoped to run a book business with his four sons, perhaps in emulation of his former employer, Daniel Appleton, whose New York bookstore and publishing house had prospered.

After the Civil War, Sam expressed concern about Jabez's indebtedness as well as sympathy for his personal travails. Jabez was unlucky in his family life. He married and was widowed five times, with four of his wives and several of his children succumbing to tuberculosis. Only two of his nine children survived him. Although the tensions in the brothers' relationship were undeniable, Sam never lost affection for his older brother, and members of Sam's family frequently visited back and forth with Jabez's brood, who lived at Golden Gate Farm southwest of the city. Despite his complaints about Jabez's financial situation, Sam was prepared to help support his brother.[7]

Although Sam Richards never amassed the kind of wealth that characterized the Appletons, his business did well. He remained in control of the company until 1894, when, following Arthur's death the preceding year, Sam turned the company over to his surviving sons, George, Russell, and Walter. In 1906, the younger Richardses closed their retail business and become a wholesaler of paper products. The S. P. Richards Company continued as a family business until 1975, when it was purchased by Genuine Parts. Today the S. P. Richards Company is Atlanta's oldest business in continuous operation, billing itself as "one of North America's leading business products wholesalers," with forty-four distribution centers in the United States and Canada.[8]

Year after year, Sam Richards penned entries in his diary, but his postwar writing lacks the richness of detail and the lengthy personal reflections that characterize his earlier writing. Preoccupied by the demands of his business and family, Richards had less time for journal writing and was more likely to chronicle than to comment. Like virtually all Southern white men, he supported the Democratic Party, at least nominally, and occasionally wrote about attending political speeches, including those by Robert Toombs and Howell Cobb on behalf of the unsuccessful Democratic presidential candidate, Horatio Seymour, in 1868. He heard Alexander Stephens speak one more time, calling him "the little *great man*." He also heard William Jennings Bryan in 1904 but characterized the size of the crowd rather than the nature of the speech. He occasionally recorded his opinions, as when he condemned as "nefarious" Radical Republicans' unsuccessful effort to remove President Andrew Johnson from office by impeachment. His outlook on the appropriate place of women and African Americans changed little if at all. When the Women's Christian Temperance Union met in Atlanta in 1890, he briefly noted his disapproval of women speaking in public. After Atlanta had suffered a devastating race riot in 1906, he, like most of Georgia's whites, blamed black men for having instigated it by supposedly assaulting four white women. Richards rarely reflected on the past in any depth. A visit to the city by General William T. Sherman in 1879 garnered this benign if sarcastic response: "Gen Sherman has just honored our city by a visit to see how nicely we have builded it up after his burning it."[9]

More often than not, Sam wrote about his wife and children. His four daughters married, and grandchildren enlivened Sam's later years. When Irene's husband died suddenly in 1885, she and her children moved into Sam and Sallie's spacious home. The couple made periodic visits to see their daughter, Virginia, and her husband, who resided in Detroit. In 1893, they traveled to Chicago to see the World's Columbian Exhibition. Sam's diary entries increasingly focused on family members' illnesses and deaths. All of his siblings except Amelia preceded him in death, and he dutifully recorded their passings along with those of their spouses, members of Sallie's family, close friends, and church members. Arthur Richards's death was a terrible blow to Sam, but Sallie's death in 1906 nearly crushed him. Although she had always been more susceptible to illnesses than he, she was nonetheless almost a decade younger, and the suddenness of her demise left him stunned and heartbroken. "My pen almost refuses to write the dreadful words," he recorded in his diary. "Sarah, my dear wife, *died* at one oclock this morning. The cause like a bolt from a clear sky." They had been married for fifty-four years. Sam's last diary entry came on October 19, 1909. Although a special sermon had been given at Second Baptist Church, "I was not well enough to go to my regret." He died six months later, on April 18, 1910, at age eighty-six.[10]

When he began the diary in 1842, Sam wrote that he believed keeping a journal would give him pleasure and improve his writing. Although he clearly wrote for himself over the next sixty-seven years, his diary stands as an invaluable aid in understanding the rapidly changing and often tumultuous times in which he lived.

Notes

1. The Richards family Bible, box 2, Samuel P. Richards Papers, AHC, lists births, deaths, and marriages. Ella Mae Thornton knew SPR when he was an old man and she was a child living in the neighborhood. She was a playmate of one of Richards's granddaughters. For her reminiscences of the original stone house and the later one, including its landscaping, see "Mr. S. P. Richards," *Atlanta Historical Society Bulletin*, Dec. 1937, 73–79.

2. Unidentified clipping, Irene Richards lesson book, box 4, folder 5, Richards Papers; SPR obituary, *Atlanta Constitution*, Apr. 19, 1910.

3. Frank J. Byrne, "Rebellion and Retail: A Tale of Two Merchants in Confederate Atlanta," *Georgia Historical Quarterly* 79 (Spring 1995): 51–53. For discussions of Atlanta's return to commercial success, see Mary A. DeCredico, *Patriotism for Profit: Georgia's Urban Entrepreneurs and the Confederate War Effort* (Chapel Hill: University of North Carolina Press, 1990), 130–54; Don H. Doyle, *New Men, New Cities, New South: Atlanta, Nashville, Charleston, Mobile, 1860–1910* (Chapel Hill: University of North Carolina Press, 1990).

4. SPR diary, Aug. 21, 1884; JJR obituary, *Atlanta Journal*, Nov. 10, 1906; SPR obituaries, *Atlanta Journal*, Apr. 19, 1910, *Atlanta Constitution*, Apr. 19, 1910. For a discussion of the dissolution, see Byrne, "Rebellion and Retail," 53.

5. SPR diary, May 14, 1865; see also June 30, 1861.

6. Ellen Richards Whitehead became the first of the siblings to die, on Apr. 6, 1866; see also July 16, 1871 (William Richards); Mar. 15, 1872 (Ann Richards); Mar. 7, 1875 (Henry Richards).

7. SPR diary, Nov. 11, 1906, May 17, 1888, June 29, 1898; Thornton, "Mr. S. P. Richards," 78. The two surviving daughters were Annie, Jabez's daughter with his first wife, Sarah Hathaway Richards, and Metta, the product of his final marriage, to Julia Holmes Richards (Pioneer Citizens' Society of Atlanta, *Pioneer Citizens' History of Atlanta, 1833–1902* [Atlanta: Byrd, 1902], 385–86).

8. SPR diary, Dec. 4, 1894; *Atlanta Pioneers*, undated brochure, AHC; "History of the S. P. Richards Company," *Christian Index*, May 15, 1919, which gives the company address as 90, 92, and 94 Central Ave. For current information about the company, see http://www.sprichards.com/home/index.php (accessed Nov. 19, 2008).

9. SPR diary, July 4, 1868 (Toombs and Cobb), May 31, 1868 (impeachment), Oct. 8, 1868 (Stephens), Jan. 31, 1879 (Sherman), Dec. 2, 1890 (Women's

Christian Temperance Union), Dec. 18, 1904 (Bryan), Sept. 23, 1906 (race riot).

10. Ibid., Aug. 31, 1885, Sept. 13, 1885 (Irene), Sept. 16, 1888 (Virginia), July 18, 1893 (Chicago), Jan. 30, 1893 (Arthur), Mar. 26, 1906 (Sallie), Oct. 19, 1909 (last entry); "When Stone Mountain Was Called Gibraltar," *Atlanta Journal*, Nov. 16, 1924.

Appendix

Richards/Van Valkenburg Family Tree

William Richards (c. 1796–1871)
m. Ann Gardner (c. 1794–1872)

1. William Carey "Will" (1818–92)
   m. Cornelia Holroyd Bradley "Cornele"
2. Thomas Addison "Add" (1820–1900)
   m. Mary "Mary Add"
3. Jabez Judson "Jabe" (1821–1906)
   m. 5 marriages [see below]
4. *Samuel Pearce* (1824–1910) m. ▫
5. Katherine Ann "Kate" (1826–1906)
   m. Charles DuBose
6. Ellen Jane "Nell" (1829–66)
   m. Stephen Whitehead
7. Amelia S. "Amie" "Mollie" (1831–1910)
   m. Henry R. Williams
8. Henry H. (1833–75)
   m. Ellen

Wives of Jabez Richards
1. Sarah Hathaway
2. Stella Wheeler
3. Louisa Soullard
4. Martelia Griffin Elliott
5. Julia Holmes

James Van Valkenburg (1804–65)
m. Mary Church (1810–51)

1. James Dunbar (1829–64)
   m. Mary Morgan
2. Harriet Louise (1831–98)
   m. Seth K. Taylor
3. *Sarah Frances "Sallie"* (1833–1906)
4. William
   m. Mary
5. Mary
   m. Rufus Evans
6. George
7. Martha
   m. David K. Brinson
8. Eddie
9. Charles

2nd m. Mary Bradley
3 daughters and 1 son by 2nd marriage

1. Dora (1854–1937)
2. Irene "Renie" (1856–1949)
3. William Arthur "Arthur" (1858–93)
4. Infant son born and died 1859
5. Alice "Allie" (1861–62)
6. Virginia "Virnie" (1864–1936)
7. George Addison (1866–1943)
8. Russell Edward (1868–1950)
9. Walter Marion (1873–1930)
10. Katherine (1876–1963)

Index

abolitionism: in Atlanta, 235; in New York City, 251, 255, 269–70, 280; in SPR and SVVR's families, 19, 23, 42, 245, 250, 268–69
African Americans, 97. *See also* slaves
American Party, 22
Andrews, Garnett, 22–23
Andrews Raid, 103, 114
Antietam, battle of, 127–28
Appleton family: publishing house of, 245, 279; SPR's employment at bookstore of, 250–55, 257, 259
Armitage, Thomas, 259, 282, 285, 288
Athenaeum, 106
Atlanta, Ga.: bombardment of, 228–33; City Council actions in, 155–56, 212, 213n2, 214n10, 225n; Confederate nationalism in, 82–83, 105, 209–10, 218, 219, 236n; cultural life in, 85, 93, 106–7, 118; destruction of, 233–36, 254, 290; disease in, 55, 108n8, 124; evacuation of, 211, 226–27, 235–43; fires in, 82, 87, 110, 111, 112, 127, 159, 205–6, 228, 232; founding of, 5; growth of, 70–71; hospitals in, 71, 93–94, 96, 108n, 159, 227; industry in, 104–5, 139; inflation in, 155, 160, 165, 169, 178–79, 206, 211, 221; looting in, 228, 234–35; martial law in, 112; military musters in, 94–95, 102; prayer meetings in, 188, 199; riots in, 155, 295; shortages in, 73–74, 79, 87, 90, 119, 121, 141, 155, 160, 169, 211, 221; surrender of, 233–35; Unionism in, 70
Atlanta Amateurs, 66

Atlanta campaign: beginning of, 210; bombardment during, 228–33; city fortifies for, 194; civilian deaths in, 212; end of, 233–35; evacuation during, 226–27; fear and panic created by, 212; looting in, 228
Atlanta Daily Intelligencer: Atlanta campaign and, 210, 214n10; editorials of, 105, 110n, 124n, 127n, 145n, 167n
Atlanta Medical College, 71
Atlanta Rolling Mill, 104
Atlanta Southern Confederacy, editorials of, 104, 105, 120n, 121n, 124n, 155, 176n, 211, 213

Ball's Bluff, battle of, 78
Baptist Banner, 39n, 49n, 231; SPR helps with, 141, 156, 159, 160, 162, 163, 167, 170, 219; SPR purchases an interest in, 191, 218
Baptist Church, 5, 254; Georgia conventions of, 102, 173; in Macon, 11, 15, 17; in New York City, 249–50, 253–59, 263–64, 266–68, 271, 274–75, 279, 282, 285, 288; in Penfield, 4; slavery and, 19. See also *Baptist Banner*; Brantley, William T., Jr.; First Baptist Church (Atlanta); First Baptist Church (Macon); Second Baptist Church
Barnum, P. T., 266, 286
Beach, John N.: blockade running of, 73, 74n11; business of, 72
Beauregard, P. G. T., 46, 59, 100–101
Beecher, Henry Ward, 270
Beech Grove, battle of, 89
Berrien, John Macpherson, 21

301

Big Bethel, battle of, 55
Blind Tom (Thomas Greene Wiggins), 85
blockade-running, 264. *See also* Beach, John N.; Root, Sidney
Booth, John Wilkes, 270
Bragg, Braxton: in Kentucky, 128–29, 132–33; in Tennessee, 187, 197, 204
Branham, Joel R. "Dick": background of, 38n; Baptist Church and, 39, 50, 57, 60–61, 63; military career of, 52; secessionism of, 38, 48–49
Brantley, William T., Jr.: background of, 66, 84; commemorates Stonewall Jackson, 178; evacuation from Atlanta of, 227; funeral preached by, 205; returns to Atlanta after war, 283; salary of, 131; sermons of, 99–102, 109–10, 113–15, 117–18, 120–23, 126, 129, 131, 135–36, 145–46, 159–61, 165–67, 169–73, 175–82, 189–90, 192, 195, 202–3, 207, 218, 220–22, 227; visits SPR, 103
Brown, John Wesley: marriage of, 62–64; military career of, 62n, 164, 168, 200; visits wife, 224
Brown, Joseph E.: declares days of fasting and prayer, 38, 96, 206; election of, 22; military and, 49, 91, 94, 167, 225; visits New York City, 281
Brown, Mary Hathaway, 75–76, 170, 200, 202, 275; child of, 156, 164, 197, 199, 224; correspondence of, 35, 168, 202; evacuation from Atlanta of, 211, 227; marriage of, 59, 62–64; teaches Richards children, 177
—relationship of: with JJR, 9, 18, 62n, 215–16; with SPR and SVVR, 164, 171, 173, 207–8
Bryan, William Jennings, 295
Buchanan, James, 22, 41n
Buckner, Simon B., 201
Buell, Don Carlos, 132–33
Burnside, Ambrose E., 91, 98, 124, 144n
Butler, Benjamin, 51, 255

Calhoun, James: surrenders Atlanta, 234n; welcomes John Hunt Morgan, 210, 212

Campbell, Jesse, 93, 122–23
Central Presbyterian Church, 110, 119, 174, 203–4, 217
Chancellorsville, battle of, 153, 175–76
Chappell, Oliver, 51, 60, 264
Chattanooga, battle of, 204, 206n, 210
Chickamauga, battle of, 184, 197, 201–2
Christian Commission, 277–78
Christian Index, 92
Christmas celebrations: in Atlanta, 144–45, 207; in Macon, 40; in New York City, 255; in Penfield, 7
City Cemetery, 84, 224
Clarke, John T.: background of, 76; gives legal advice to SPR, 83; pew rental controversy and, 195–96; resignation of, 80, 82; sermons of, 83–84, 102
Clay, Henry, 20, 72, 73
Cobb, Howell, 22, 39n, 295
Cobb, Thomas R. R., 39, 144
Confederate Arsenal, 104–5
Confederate Rolling Mill, 104
Confederate States of America: Atlanta arsenal of, 104; conscription policies of, 91, 101, 123, 125, 134, 156, 166, 184, 189, 190, 202, 206–8, 217–19; downfall of, 273; financial policies of, 43, 66–67, 78–79, 82, 173, 184, 188, 219, 221; impressments in, 192; politics in, 43, 187n5; Quartermaster's Depot of, 104
conscription: in Confederacy, 91, 101, 123, 125, 134, 156, 158n7, 166, 184, 189, 190, 202, 206–8, 216–19; in Union, 167, 246, 252, 258–59, 265
counterfeiting, 125–28
Craig, David, 131, 181; employment of, 35, 77; military career of, 47–48, 53–54, 57–58, 66–67
Crawford, Nathaniel M., 120, 168
Crittenden, George B., 89

Dalton, Ga., 224, 242
Davis, Jefferson: alleged attempt on life of, 221; capture and incarceration of, 274, 286–87; Confederate surrender and, 268–69; conscription policies of, 185, 189; declares days of fasting and

prayer, 32–33, 54, 80–81, 93, 110, 170; election of, 43, 80; inauguration of, 73, 92; military policies of, 227; visits SPR's home, 184, 200, 201
Davis, Thomas W., 191–92
Davis, Varina, 184
Dayton, A. C., 189
Democratic Party: election of 1860 and, 29; election of 1862 and, 133; election of 1863 and, 201; election of 1864 and, 245–46; Peace or Copperhead, 172, 179
Denny Hospital, 107
Dickens, Charles, 38
Dickenson, A. T., 96–97, 119
Dill, C. W., 285
diphtheria, 128
Donelson, Fort, 91–92, 205
Douglas, Stephen A., 29, 35–36
Dowling, John, 249, 256
draft. *See* conscription
drunkenness, 40, 79, 193
DuBose, Charles "Charlie" (husband of Katherine Richards DuBose), 16, 40, 211; advises SPR about business 56–57; legal and political career of, 31, 34n8, 42; visits SPR, 99, 227
DuBose, Katherine Ann Richards "Kate" (sister), 16, 99, 211, 220; birth of, 4; children of, 127; Confederate nationalism of, 31, 213; correspondence of, 86, 115, 144; marriage of, 10; musical interests of, 7; teaching career of, 8; writings of, 5, 7, 31, 213

Edwardy, E. M., 261
elections: of 1856, 22; of 1860, 23, 29, 35–36; of 1862, 133; of 1864, 241, 245–46, 249–50
Ellen (slave of SPR): illness of, 88; purchased by SPR, 104, 131, 145, 174; rented by SPR, 84, 87; whipped by SPR, 109, 155, 166; work of, 84, 133, 136, 189
Elliott, Stephen, Jr., 109, 173, 219
Ells, James N.: background of, 49; *Baptist Banner* and, 98n, 102, 143–44, 191, 219
Ells, Mary Eliza Garmany, 98, 102, 170

Ellsworth, Elmer, 51
Emancipation Proclamation, 153, 158
Evans, Mary Van Valkenburg (SVVR's sister), 20, 50, 180
Evans, Rufus (SVVR's brother-in-law), 50

fasting and prayer days, 32–33; in Confederacy, 38, 54–55, 80–81, 93–94, 96, 124, 170, 193, 206, 222, 225; in Union, 33, 278
Fillmore, Millard, 21, 22, 27n51
fire: in Atlanta, 82, 87, 110, 111, 112, 127, 205–6, 228; in Charleston, 85; in Macon, 48, 51; in New York City, 246; at SPR's Atlanta store, 18; at SPR's Macon store, 12, 112
First Baptist Church (Atlanta), 39n, 110, 129, 170, 189
First Baptist Church (Macon), 38, 39, 46–47; Central Baptist Association and, 61; missionary activities of, 52–53; organ of, 45–46, 61. *See also* Warren, Ebenezer W.
First Presbyterian Church (Atlanta), 109
Forrest, Nathan Bedford, 120, 175–76, 223, 238, 241
Fredericksburg, battle of, 105, 144
Freeman, Andrew E., 99, 236
Frémont, John C., 22, 226

Gay, Mary, 3
Georgia, politics in, 21–23, 29
Georgia Female College, 46
Georgia Military Institute, 93
Gettysburg, battle of, 183–84, 186n3, 188
Gordon, John B., 210
Grant, Lemuel, 194n
Grant, Ulysses S., 224n, 230n; Atlanta campaign and, 194, 202; Confederate surrender and, 270; Vicksburg campaign and, 180–81, 187
Green, James Mercer, 68

Hardee, William, 228, 256
Hastings, Thomas, 281, 284
Hathaway, Elizabeth "Libbie," 9, 14
Hathaway, Mary. *See* Brown, Mary Hathaway

Index 303

Hathaway, Sarah. *See* Richards, Sarah Hathaway
Haven, Alice B., 255
Haygood, Atticus: background of, 45n; contributes to *Soldier's Friend*, 221; sermons of, 45, 58, 230, 290
Henry, Fort, 90
Hill, Ben, 22
Hindman, Thomas, 201
Holmes, Adam T., 86–87, 98
Hood, John Bell: Atlanta campaign and, 211, 224n, 227–28, 230, 242; in Tennessee, 246, 252, 254
Hornady, H. C., 290; *Baptist Banner* and, 39n; First Baptist Church (Atlanta) and, 39; sermons of, 98, 129, 137, 216–17
hospitals: in Atlanta, 71, 93–94, 96, 106, 107, 108n9, 156, 159; evacuation of, 211, 227

Jackson, Fort, 102
Jackson, Henry R., 36
Jackson, Thomas J.: death of, 176, 178; military career of, 105, 113, 125n, 153, 175; portrayal of, in *Soldier's Friend*, 185
Johnson, Andrew, 295
Johnson, Hershel, 22
Johnston, Albert Sidney, 100
Johnston, Joseph: Atlanta campaign and, 211, 219n, 224n, 227; Confederate surrender and, 269, 273

Kendrick, J. R., 127–30, 137
Kennesaw Mountain, battle of, 211, 226
Know-Nothing Party, 22
Knoxville, battle of, 202–3, 205

Ladies' Soldiers' Relief Society, 107, 108n9
Lamar, John Hill, 210, 230
Landrum, Sylvanus, 13, 15, 68, 264, 268
law of sequestration, 66–67, 78–79
Lee, Robert E., 125n, 144n, 153, 181n, 210, 224n; Confederate surrender and, 268–70; Gettysburg campaign and, 184, 186n3, 189; portrayal of, in *Soldier's Friend*, 185

Lincoln, Abraham: assassination and commemoration of, 270–72, 278; conscription policies of, 167, 201; declares days of fasting and prayer, 33; election of, 36; Emancipation Proclamation of, 153, 158; foreign policy of, 85–86, 88; inaugurations of, 44, 263; military policies of, 47, 119–20, 260; reelection of, 226, 241, 249–50; SPR's views of, 23, 29, 36, 119, 272–73; visits Richmond, 269
Lipham, Frances, 77n, 99, 115, 134
Longstreet, James, 224

Macon, Ga.: Belgian Fair in, 40, 43; Civil War and, 30, 47, 49–50, 77, 229; cultural life in, 10–11; election of 1860 and, 29, 35–36; industry in, 11, 15; politics in, 20, 22; prewar population of, 10; secession crisis in, 37–38. *See also* First Baptist Church (Macon)
Mallard, Robert Quarterman, 203–4, 219–20, 290
Manassas, first battle of, 59–60, 63
Manly, Basil, Jr., 86
March to the Sea, 246–47, 252–54
Mason, James, 85–88
Masonic Hall, 87
Mayer Jacobs and Company, 155
McClellan, George B., 117; election of 1864 and, 235, 245–46
McConnell, George, 103
McLean, Eugene E., 186n4, 204, 218
McLean, Margaret Sumner: stays in SPR's home, 184, 186n4, 199–201, 203, 207; visited by Jefferson Davis, 201
measles, 87–89, 176, 179
medical treatments, 20, 91, 96, 133–34, 161, 162, 258–59, 260; for cholera, 137; for diphtheria, 128; for scarlet fever, 161–62; for tuberculosis, 18, 158–59, 163, 186; for whooping cough, 58–59; for worms, 130–32
Mell, Patrick, 223
Mercer University, 4, 9, 11
Merrimack and *Monitor*, battle between, 97, 111

Mexican-American War, 8
Minute Men: in Atlanta, 36–37; in Macon, 36, 38, 42
Monitor and *Merrimack*, battle between, 97, 111
Monocacy, battle of, 210, 214n5, 230
Morgan, John Hunt: Atlanta appearance of, 209, 218, 219; death of, 212–13, 236; incarceration of, 209; military career of, 105–6, 120, 121; newspaper reports about, 105, 120n, 121n
mourning practices, 9, 13, 165, 199, 236
mumps, 48

National Academy of Design, 8, 281, 284
Neal, John, 193, 283
New Bern, battle of, 98
New Orleans, battle of, 102–3
New York City: cultural life in, 255, 265–66, 273, 278–79, 280–82; draft riots in, 245; election of 1864 in, 245–46; financial markets in, 249–50, 253, 265–66, 269; fires in, 246, 248n7, 251, 286; Lincoln funeral procession in, 272; wartime transformation of, 244
Nisbet, Eugenius, 21, 29, 38, 41n

Oakland Cemetery (City Cemetery), 84, 224
Oliver, Perry, 85

Panic of 1837, 10
Panic of 1857, 18
Pea Ridge, battle of, 95–96
Peck, John J., 252
Pemberton, John, 183, 194
Penfield, Ga., 4, 8, 10, 11
Perryville, battle of, 128, 133
Petersburg, battle of, 268
Pickens, Fort, 82
Poe, Washington, 38
Polk, Leonidas K., 200, 201
Port Hudson, battle of, 179, 188
Port Royal Sound/Hilton Head, battle of, 71, 79–80
Presbyterian Church, First (Atlanta), 109

Price, Sterling, 95–96, 132
Pulaski, Fort, 81, 90, 101

Queen Sisters and Palmetto Band, 93, 106, 118, 119

Rambaut, Thomas, 93, 131
religion. *See* Baptist Church; fasting and prayer days
Republican Party: election of 1860 and, 23, 29; election of 1864 and, 226, 245–46, 250; Reconstruction and, 295
Resaca, battle of, 224
Richards, Alice "Allie" (daughter), 63, 89; birthday of, 118; birth of, 57–58; death of, 139–42, 144, 156, 161; growth of, 59, 61, 75, 79, 88, 99, 113, 123, 128, 132–38; illnesses of, 80, 107, 135, 136; inoculation of, 124–25, 127
Richards, Amelia S. *See* Williams, Amelia S. Richards "Amie"/"Mollie"
Richards, Ann (mother), 3, 58, 99; in Atlanta, 81, 84, 116, 173, 224, 290; Confederate nationalism of, 31; correspondence of, 58; death of, 294, 296n6; evacuation from Atlanta of, 211, 227; slaves of, 71, 87
Richards, Annie (daughter of JJR), 18, 33, 88, 118; education of, 177, 216, 284; evacuation from Atlanta of, 227; illness of, 88
Richards, Arthur "Artie" (son), 47, 136; birthday of, 177–78; birth of, 18; clothing of, 143; death of, 294; disciplined by SPR, 175; education of, 177–78, 279; fears of, 161–62; gifts to, 154, 177, 258; illnesses of, 40, 57, 58, 61, 63, 79, 87–88, 202, 207; in New York City, 266–69
Richards, Cornelia Holroyd Bradley "Cornele" (wife of William Carey Richards), 7, 23, 287; appearance of, 283; children of, 142; SPR's admiration for, 13, 245; teaching career of, 172; Unionism of, 56; writings of, 6, 25n33, 255
Richards, Dora (daughter), 23, 47, 79, 132, 136, 145; birthdays of, 67, 125,

Richards, Dora (*continued*)
236; birth of, 17; education of, 116–17, 125, 177, 279; gifts to, 154, 177; illnesses of, 48, 56, 57, 63, 96, 128, 129, 130, 132, 253; marriage of, 295; in New York City, 255, 258, 263–64, 266, 269; relationship of, with SPR, 40, 63, 281

Richards, Ellen "Ellie" (wife of Henry Richards), 58, 134, 177

Richards, Ellen Jane. *See* Whitehead, Ellen Jane Richards "Nell"

Richards, Ethel (daughter of JJR), 67, 75, 88, 120, 227

Richards, George (son), 293–94

Richards, Henry (brother): birth of, 4; children of, 58, 63, 141, 177, 236; death of, 294, 296n6; illnesses of, 20, 127, 129, 134, 167, 203; relationship of, with SPR, 127, 139, 141, 168, 190, 290; works for SPR, 18, 76–78, 80, 207, 218, 219, 275, 284

Richards, Irene "Renie" (daughter): birthday of, 189; birth of, 18; education of, 177, 279; gifts to, 154, 177; illnesses of, 20, 42, 47, 56, 57, 63, 126–27, 161; marriage and widowhood of, 295; in New York City, 253, 255, 264, 266

Richards, Jabez Judson "Jabe" (JJR; brother) 35, 81, 93, 98, 99, 124, 143, 171, 173, 229; assets of, 215; Athens store of, 9; Atlanta store of, 17–18, 70, 76–79, 140, 165; birthdays of, 61, 122, 166; birth of, 4; children of, 18, 26n42, 58, 67, 142n, 177, 296n7; conscription concerns of, 183, 189, 190, 193, 216–19, 225; correspondence of, 278, 284, 286–88; counterfeiting problems of, 125–28; death of, 293; evacuation from Atlanta of, 211; Griffin store of, 17, 130; later years of, 179, 221, 284–85, 291, 293–94; Macon store of, 10–12; marriages of, 9, 33, 133, 164, 275, 294; military and, 94, 95, 106, 131; musical interests of, 7, 117, 145, 161; relationship of, with SPR, 10, 56–57, 61, 63–66, 69, 85, 106–7, 110–11, 114, 123, 127, 132–34, 139, 160, 165–66, 168–69, 175, 189–90, 201, 237, 264; slaves of, 120–22, 153–54, 159, 171, 174–75, 196, 217; SPR and SVVR live with, 17, 73, 75–76, 84, 107, 290

Richards, Katherine Ann. *See* DuBose, Katherine Ann Richards "Kate"

Richards, Katherine "Kate" (daughter), 293

Richards, Louisa Soullard (JJR's third wife), 275, 290

Richards, Mary Anthony "Mary Add" (wife of Thomas Addison Richards): Confederate sympathies of, 31–32, 181–82, 281–82; correspondence of, 39, 86, 99, 242; marriage of, 23; sees SPR and SVVR in New York City, 238, 253, 258, 263, 269, 275–76, 284–85

Richards, Robert (uncle), 7

Richards, Russell (son), 293–94

Richards, Samuel Pearce "Sam" (SPR): appearance of, 13, 118; birth of, 3–4; childhood of, 4–8; clothing of, 17, 185, 206, 215, 249, 255, 276–77; courtship of SVVR by, 12–16; death of, 295; education of, 9; English heritage of, 7, 18, 258; illnesses of, 44, 108, 129, 134, 136–37, 140, 158, 192, 207, 259–60, 276; land owned by, 73, 93, 104, 110–11, 114, 116–17, 153, 165–66, 168–69; later years of, 293–96; marriage of, 16

—African Americans and: racism, 32, 42, 153, 161, 174–75, 206, 231, 236, 247, 264, 270; slavery, 18–20, 40, 104, 109, 153–55, 159, 166, 171, 174–75, 189–90, 206, 212–13, 217, 225, 233, 235–36, 270, 278

—Baptist Church and: in Atlanta, 71–72, 76, 118, 132, 192, 195, 206, 231–32, 235; childhood, 4–5; choir singing, 39, 42, 46, 51–52, 60–61, 64, 72, 80–83, 103, 113, 117, 126, 130, 163, 166, 169, 178, 199, 203, 205, 217, 266–67; in Macon, 35–36, 38–39, 42–46, 49–50, 54–55, 61; marriage to SVVR, 11–12, 15–17; in New York City, 246–47, 250, 253, 255, 258, 259, 266, 268, 271, 272, 274, 279, 282, 285, 288; Sunday School teaching, 52, 55, 59, 77, 79, 94,

306 Index

98, 100, 102–3, 142, 174, 176–77, 203, 217, 219, 222
—bookselling career of: in Atlanta, 17–18, 61, 70–73, 76–80, 83, 87–88, 90, 92–93, 104, 113, 119–20, 122–23, 127–28, 130, 134, 159, 161, 163–65, 167, 172, 178, 180, 182, 187, 191, 201, 219, 291; in Louisville, 239–43; in Macon, 10–12, 17–18, 43, 56–57, 61, 68–69; in New York City, 245, 250–55, 259
—Civil War and: Confederate nationalism, 65–67, 89, 94, 105–6, 110–11, 117, 119–20, 124, 153, 188, 192, 209–10, 268; conscription concerns, 95, 101–2, 106, 134, 139, 143, 156, 166, 183–84, 190–91, 202, 206, 210, 214n4, 216–19, 246, 252, 258–59, 265, 267; military participation, 48, 61–62, 94–95, 131, 200, 225, 228–29, 231–32; prewar Unionism, 20–23, 29, 40, 50, 213; printing career as conscription dodge, 141–43, 159–60, 162–65, 167, 170, 184, 191, 216–19; religious interpretations, 42, 47, 60, 146, 257, 268, 269, 271, 273–74; secessionism, 29–32, 36–42, 47, 49–50
—domestic life of: in Atlanta, 73–76, 87–88, 90–91, 106–107, 109, 113, 116, 121, 123–24, 130–34, 141–45, 160–61, 168–69, 175–79, 182, 184, 187–90, 199–201, 203–8, 218, 293–94; in Macon, 17–19; in New York City, 253, 255, 261–62, 264, 266–67, 271–74, 279–80
—interests of: gardening, 20, 43–45, 50, 52, 55–56, 60, 100, 109, 178, 202, 220–22, 225, 229; music, 7, 85, 93, 118–19, 145, 264, 276, 278–79; reading, 19, 38, 63, 130, 138, 255, 269, 276, 277, 279, 282
Richards, Sarah Hathaway (first wife of JJR), 165; children of, 18, 26n42; death of, 18; marriage of, 9; SPR and SVVR live with, 17
Richards, Sarah Van Valkenburg "Sallie" (SVVR; wife), 101, 213, 237; appearance of, 13, 118; attends dying relatives, 64, 121, 164, 199; birthdays of, 130, 197, 240; bombardment of Atlanta and, 227–28; clothing of, 73, 87, 121, 160, 170, 202, 207, 253; cooking abilities of, 17–18; correspondence of, 35, 39, 50, 68, 82, 88, 131, 136, 142; courtship of, by SPR, 11–16; death of, 295; dental problems of, 131, 135, 142, 171; as diarist, 1, 13–16, 211, 225; helps Confederate soldiers, 71, 96, 107, 119; illnesses of, 82, 88, 90–91, 107, 114, 118, 129, 132–34, 181, 188; later years of, 290–91, 293–96; marriage of, 16; musicianship of, 11, 23, 72, 82–83, 172, 213; in New York City, 244–45, 248–49, 253–60, 262–66, 276–77, 280–82; pregnancies of, 17, 18, 54, 57, 212, 222, 293; relationship of, with SPR, 63, 64, 66, 73, 99, 106, 109, 113, 118, 119, 121, 160, 173, 180, 224, 233, 253–57, 290; religion and, 11, 13–17, 37, 42, 45, 48, 61, 174, 238, 253–54; sewing abilities of, 17, 71, 171, 215; slavery and, 18–19, 155; wifely virtues of, 64, 141
Richards, Stella Wheeler (second wife of JJR), 76, 99, 118, 142, 144, 175; children of, 58, 67, 75; death of, 155, 164–65; illnesses of, 87–89, 107, 126, 135, 163; marriage of, 33; religious views of, 78, 81; slaves of, 120–21; SPR and SVVR live with, 75–76, 84, 106–7, 113, 116, 122, 132–33, 136, 138
Richards, Thomas Addison "Add" (brother), 237, 294; artistic career of, 6–8, 273n, 281; birth of, 3–4; Confederate sympathies of, 31–32, 244–45; correspondence of, 58, 73, 80, 86, 99, 115, 154, 172, 181–82, 242; marriage of, 23; sees SPR and SVVR in New York City, 248, 251–53, 255, 258, 263, 275–76, 284–85; writings of, 8, 273n
Richards, Virginia "Virnie" (daughter): birth of, 222–23; growth of, 261–62, 272, 277, 290–91; marriage of, 295; personality of, 250

Index 307

Richards, Walter (son), 293–94
Richards, William (father), 58, 86, 99, 137, 279; in Atlanta, 79, 81, 84, 193–94, 202–3, 221, 224, 229, 290; as Baptist clergyman, 3–5, 16, 84, 86, 88, 90, 95, 98, 116, 176; business career of, 4, 24n8, 142; Confederate nationalism of, 31, 40; correspondence of, 58, 59, 61, 82, 131, 164, 165, 172; death of, 294, 296n6; evacuation from Atlanta of, 211; slaves of, 71, 81
Richards, William Carey "Will" (brother), 7, 23, 83, 294; as Baptist clergyman, 45; birth of, 3; children of, 142n; education of, 5; lecturing career of, 5, 8, 172; proposes business partnership with SPR, 283–84; SPR's reconciliation with, 154, 242, 250, 252, 255, 275, 280, 287; Unionist views of, 31, 42, 56, 61, 65–67, 79, 99, 172, 181, 183, 195, 205, 245, 250, 279; writings of, 6–7
Rogers, J. L., 119
Rogers, Kate, 39, 56, 80, 172, 258
Root, John Wellborn, 105, 142, 256
Root, Mary, 119, 205, 235, 236
Root, Sidney: background of, 72, 74n9; blockade running of, 73, 88, 105, 114–15, 121, 130–31, 204, 256, 262–63, 280; defends John Pemberton, 183, 194; government career of, 143; later years of, 255–56, 280; military career of, 134–35; relationship of, with SPR and SVVR, 182, 207, 280–81; secessionism of, 72–73; Second Baptist Church and, 72, 76–77, 80–83, 113, 126, 130, 167, 171, 173, 177, 188, 195–96, 280, 290; visits Chickamauga battlefield, 197; visits SPR and SVVR in New York City, 280–81; mentioned, 90, 92, 97, 102, 103, 158, 161–63, 166, 189–90, 193, 202, 203, 213, 231
Rosecrans, William, 158, 187, 196, 197, 202

Savannah, Ga., 81, 90, 101, 163, 167, 215; capture of, 254, 256
scarlet fever, 126–27, 161, 162, 277

Scott, William, 251, 255, 287
Scott, Winfield, 22
secession crisis, 29, 41–42, 49
Second Baptist Church, 18, 95, 106, 159–60, 166; abolitionist preaching at, 235; African American participation at, 97, 224; baptisms at, 130–32, 135–36, 188, 222, 224, 227; bombardment of Atlanta and, 233; choir of, 72, 76; communion at, 126, 159, 167, 177, 188, 195, 216, 224, 227; conference at, 114, fasting and prayer service at, 170; fundraising of, 171; joins Central Association, 192; ministers of, 76, 80, 82–84, 88–89, 90; pew rental controversy at, 195–96; revival at, 123, 126, 132–33. See also Brantley, William T., Jr.
Sequestration Act, 66–67, 78–79
Seven Days' Battles, 117
Seven Pines, battle of, 114
Seward, William H., 260, 270
Seymour, Henry W.: assists SPR in leaving Atlanta, 236, 238; shoe shop at Richards store and, 139, 142–43, 206, 219
Seymour, Horatio, 295
Sheridan, Philip, 241–42
Sherman, William T., 1; Atlanta campaign and, 211, 212, 230, 232–34; Atlanta headquarters of, 283; in Carolinas, 262–63; destruction of Atlanta and, 288, 290; Joseph Johnston's surrender to, 273; March to the Sea and, 246–47, 252–55; postwar visit to Atlanta of, 295; staff of, 237; Stoneman's Raid and, 229
Sherwood, Asa: clerks for SPR, 18, 23, 50–51; death of, 105, 111; military career of, 52, 54, 69, 87
Shiloh, battle of, 100–101
Simms, William Gilmore, 6
slaves: Emancipation Proclamation and, 153, 158; freedom of, 236; owned by JJR, 120–23, 127–28, 145, 153, 159, 166, 171, 174, 179, 196, 212–13, 217, 236; owned by SPR, 104, 109, 131, 145, 153–54, 166, 168, 174–76, 207–8, 212–13, 225, 233, 235–36; owned by Stephen Whitehead, 173–74; owned

308 *Index*

by William Richards, 71, 87; rented by SPR, 18–20, 84, 87; wartime escapes of, 71, 81, 234. *See also* Ellen
Slidell, John, 85–88
Slocum, Henry, 234
smallpox, 124, 161, 163
Smillie, Catherine (SVVR's aunt), 250, 252–53, 279
Smillie, James (SVVR's uncle), 250, 252–53
Smillie, Mary (SVVR's cousin), 250, 268–69
Smith, Edmund Kirby, 125
Soldier's Friend: articles in, 185; praise for, 231; purchased by SPR and JJR, 185, 193; writing and editing of, 215–18, 220–21, 275
Somerville, William, 196
Southern Confederacy. See *Atlanta Southern Confederacy*, editorials of
Spalding, Albert T., 66
Spiller and Burr Pistol Factory (Atlanta), 105, 139
S. P. Richards Company: donates SPR diaries to AHC, 1; post–Civil War success of, 293; SPR turns over, to sons, 294
Spring, Gardiner, 261
Stephens, Alexander: election of, 43, 80; inauguration of, 92; negotiates to end Civil War, 260; speeches of, 21–22, 35–36, 295; SPR meets, 21; Unionism of, 21–23, 29, 35–36
Stone, Amherst W., 169, 171
Stone, Harriet L. (SVVR's aunt), 58, 242; SPR and SVVR live with, 248, 250; SPR and SVVR visit, 251, 255, 256, 258, 262–63, 269, 288
Stone, Mary (SVVR's cousin), 248n, 249, 258, 261, 264, 269; visits SPR and SVVR, 58
Stone, Roswell (SVVR's uncle), 248n, 249, 255, 267
Stone, Sarah (SVVR's cousin), 58, 248n, 249, 258, 264
Stone, William (SVVR's cousin), 248n, 249, 250; proposes business partnership with SPR, 262–65, 267

Stoneman, George, 229
Stone Mountain, Georgia, 189–90
Stones River, battle of, 158
Stowe, Harriet Beecher, 19
St. Philip's Episcopal Church, 99n
Sumter, Fort, 41, 45–47, 194–95, 201
Swanson, James F., 127

Taylor, Harriet Van Valkenburg (SVVR's sister): cares for siblings, 11, 13; correspondence of, 67, 135–36, 176, 230; death of stepson of, 176; marriage of, 30; relationship of, with SVVR, 50, 60, 107, 118, 211; visits with SPR and SVVR, 136–40, 189–90, 291
Taylor, Seth K. (husband of Harriet Van Valkenburg Taylor): Confederate nationalism of, 30; military career of, 230; relationship of, with SPR, 60; visits with SPR and SVVR, 136–40, 189–90
Teague, E. B., 189
Thackeray, William Makepeace, 11
Thomas, George, 252
Thompson, Joseph Parrish, 262
Toombs, Robert, 295
Toon, J. J., 106, 108n6; SPR employed by, 140–43, 156, 159–60
Trent affair, 85–88
Trinity Methodist Church, 103
Trout House hotel, 87, 210
tuberculosis, 51; death of Sarah Hathaway Richards by, 8, 33; death of Stella Richards by, 107, 155–56, 164–65
Turrell, Huldah Van Valkenburg (SVVR's aunt): abolitionism of, 19, 23, 245, 268–69; later years of, 247n5; marriage of, 23, 30; Unionism of, 30; visits SPR and SVVR in New York City, 267
Turrell, William, 267
typhoid fever, 55, 108n8

Uncle Tom's Cabin (Stowe), 19
Unionism: in Georgia, 20–23, 29; in Richards family, 30–32
U.S. Christian Commission, 277–78

Vallandigham, Clement L., 179, 201, 226
Van Amburgh and Company, 265, 286n
Van Dorn, Earl, 132
Van Hoose, Azor, 62
Van Valkenburg, Edward "Eddie" (SVVR's brother), 54–56, 67, 69
Van Valkenburg, George (SVVR's brother): military career of, 30, 47, 53–54, 88, 118, 197; religious conversion of, 180–81; visits SPR and SVVR, 197–98; wounding of, 176–77, 180
Van Valkenburg, Harriet. *See* Taylor, Harriet Van Valkenburg
Van Valkenburg, Huldah. *See* Turrell, Huldah Van Valkenburg
Van Valkenburg, James (SVVR's father): Baptist Church and, 11, 15; business career of, 11, 15, 69; second marriage of, 30; SPR's conscription problems and, 140; Unionism of, 30, 202; visits SPR and SVVR, 67, 287
Van Valkenburg, James Dunbar (SVVR's brother): children of, 162; death of, 210, 214n5, 230; marriage of, 15–16; military career of, 30, 118, 144–45
Van Valkenburg, Martha (SVVR's sister): correspondence of, 180; illness of, 56; SPR's relationship with, 20, 22, 50, 52, 54, 88, 118; visits SPR and SVVR, 189–90
Van Valkenburg, Mary. *See* Evans, Mary Van Valkenburg
Van Valkenburg, Mary Church (SVVR's mother), 11, 13
Van Valkenburg, Mary Morgan "Mollie" (wife of James Dunbar Van Valkenburg): children of, 156, 162; husband's death and, 230; husband's military career and, 118–19, 144; inheritance of, 26n37; marriage of, 15–16, 138; visited by SPR and SVVR, 136, 138, 140
Van Valkenburg, William (SVVR's brother), 110
Vicksburg, battle of, 156, 178–81, 183, 188, 191

Walker, Joseph, 7
Warren, Ebenezer W., 48, 49, 58, 103, 264; background of, 35n; officiates at Alice Richards's burial, 140; proslavery views of, 27n46; sermons of, 35, 37, 40–43, 46–47, 56, 67, 102
Wescott, Isaac: background of, 250; sermons of, 251, 255, 263, 266, 267, 274, 279, 287
Wesleyan College (Georgia Female College), 46
West, Mary: background of, 72; later years of, 285–86, 290; in New York City with SPR and SVVR, 237–40, 249, 253, 255, 261–62, 264, 266, 271–73, 276, 278–80; Second Baptist Church and, 72, 76, 80–83, 98, 136, 161–62, 170, 172, 174, 178, 188, 199; SPR criticizes singing of, 136, 220; mentioned, 96, 99, 101, 102, 109, 164, 202, 215
West, Thomas, 109, 174, 178; business of, 72; declines military career, 233; later years of, 285–86; in New York City with SPR and SVVR, 237–40, 249, 253, 255–56, 260–62, 264, 266, 267, 271–73, 276, 278–80
Weston, William Griggs, 253, 259, 264, 268, 282; eulogizes Lincoln, 271
Whig Party, 21
Whitehead, Ellen Jane Richards "Nell" (sister), 118, 124, 143, 264; birth of, 4; children of, 35, 52, 84, 96, 121, 142n; Confederate nationalism of, 31; death of, 296n6; property of, ransacked by Federals, 71, 90–91; relationship of, with SPR, 52, 59, 64, 69, 168, 109, 173, 197; teaching career of, 8
Whitehead, Stephen (husband of Ellen Richards Whitehead), 121, 127, 143, 168; later years of, 275; military career of, 124; property of, ransacked by Federals, 90–91; purchases property with SPR, 111; slaves of, 154, 173–74; visits SPR and SVVR, 59, 101, 109, 110; wartime activities of, 83, 142
whooping cough, 55–59, 131, 135

Wiggins, Thomas Greene, 85
Wilderness, battle of the, 223–24
Wilkes, William C., 202
Williams, Amelia S. Richards "Amie"/"Mollie" (sister): birth of, 4; children of, 17, 142n, 202; Confederate nationalism of, 31, 40; correspondence of, 82, 96, 142n; teaching career of, 8
Williford, J. N., 155
Wills, David, 50
Wilson, John, 109, 160

women: as bookbinders, 159; as medical volunteers, 71, 96, 107, 108n9, 119, 211; as rioters, 155; as seamstresses, 159n; as writers, 5–7, 25n33, 31, 213, 255
Women's Christian Temperance Union, 295
Wood, Jesse H., 81, 139
World's Columbian Exposition, 295
Worrell, A. S., 185, 191, 193, 196, 199, 200, 201, 215

Zollicoffer, Felix, 89

Index 311

www.ingramcontent.com/pod-product-compliance
Lightning Source LLC
Chambersburg PA
CBHW031723230426
43669CB00007B/217